# 30th Conference on Computational Linguistics and Speech Processing (ROCLING 2018)

Hsinchu, Taiwan
4-5 October 2018

**Editors:**

**Chi-Chun Lee**
**Jen-Tzung Chien**
**Min-Yuh Day**
**Hung-Yi Lee**
**Shih-Hung Wu**

**Cheng-Zen Yang**
**Chen-Yu Chiang**
**Richard T.-H. Tsai**
**Wen-Hsiang Lu**

ISBN: 978-1-5108-7751-1

# Proceedings of the Thirtieth Conference on Computational Linguistics and Speech Processing ROCLING XXX (2018)

## TABLE OF CONTENTS

**The 30th**

# ROCLING 2018

**October 4-5, 2018, Hsinchu, Taiwan**
Proceedings of the Thirtieth Conference on Computational
Linguistics and Speech Processing

# Proceedings of the Thirtieth Conference on Computational Linguistics and Speech Processing ROCLING XXX (2018)

**October 4-5, 2018**

**National Tsing-Hua University, Hsinchu, Taiwan**

*Sponsored by:*
Association for Computational Linguistics and Chinese Language Processing

*Co- Sponsored by:*
*Academic Sponsor*
Institute of Information Science, Academia Sinica
Research Center for Information Technology Innovation, Academia Sinica

*Industry Sponsors*
Cyberon Corporation
Most AI Biomedical Research Center
Chunghwa Telecom Laboratories
Emotibot Corporation
ASUS Corporation
Delta Electronics, Inc.
CT-Cloud Corporation

Chi-Chun (Jeremy) Lee, Cheng-Zen Yang, Jen-Tzung Chien, Chen-Yu Chiang , Min-Yuh Day, Richard T.-H. Tsai, Hung-Yi Lee, Wen-Hsiang Lu, Shih-Hung Wu (eds.)

Proceedings of the Thirtieth Conference on Computational Linguistics and Speech Processing (ROCLING XXX)
2018-10-4/2018-10-5
ACLCLP
2018-10

# Welcome Message of the ROCLING 2018

On behalf of the organization committee and program committee, it is our pleasure to welcome you to National Tsing Hua University (NTHU) in Hsinchu, Taiwan, for the 30th Conference on Computational Linguistics and Speech Processing (ROCLING), the flagship conference on computational linguistics, natural language processing, and speech processing in Taiwan. ROCLING is the annual conference of the Computational Linguistics and Chinese Language Processing (ACLCLP) which is held in autumn in different cities and universities in Taiwan. This year, we received 30 valid submissions, each of which was reviewed by at least three experts on the basis of originality, significance, technical soundness, and relevance to the conference. In total, we have 20 oral papers and 7 poster papers, which cover the areas including computational semantics, computational phonology, dialogue system, natural language generation, syntax and parsing, information retrieval, machine translation, NLP tools/applications, opinion mining and sentiment analysis, question answering, semantic processing, summarization, spoken language processing, speech synthesis/conversion, speech/speaker/language recognition, and speech enhancement. We are grateful to the contribution of the reviewers for their extraordinary efforts and valuable comments.

ROCLING 2018 also features two distinguished lectures from the renowned speakers in natural language processing as well as speech processing. Prof. Kathleen McKeown (Henry and Gertrude Rothschild Professor of Computer Science, Columbia University/Founding Director of Columbia's Data Science Institute) will lecture on "Where Natural Language Processing Meets Societal Needs", and Prof. Shinji Watanabe (Johns Hopkins University, Department of Electrical and Computer Engineering joint appointment in Center for Language and Speech Processing) will speak on "Neural End-to-End Architectures for Speech Recognition in Adverse Environments". In addition to the oral/poster paper presentations and the two distinguished lectures, ROCLING 2018 also arranges the Kaldi Tutorial program organized by Prof. Yuan-Fu Liao (National Taipei University of Technology) to respond accordingly to the increasing demand for rapid development of speech recognition technology. Finally, we thank the generous government, academic and industry sponsors and appreciate your enthusiastic participation and support. Best wishes a successful and fruitful ROCLING 2018 in Hsinchu, Taiwan.

General Chairs
Chi-Chun (Jeremy) Lee and Cheng-Zen Yang

Program Committee Chairs
Chen-Yu Chiang and Min-Yuh Day

# Organizing Committee

**Honorary Chairs**

Hong Hocheng, President, National Tsing Hua University

**Conference Co-Chairs**

Chi-Chun (Jeremy) Lee, National Tsing Hua University

Cheng-Zen Yang, Yuan Ze University

Jen-Tzung Chien, National Chiao Tung University

**Program Chairs**

Chen-Yu Chiang, National Taipei University

Min-Yuh Day, Tamkang University

**Local Arrangement & Web Chair**

Richard T.-H. Tsai, National Central University

Hung-Yi Lee, National Taiwan University

**Industry Track Chair**

Wen-Hsiang Lu, National Cheng Kung University

**Doctoral Consortium Chair**

Richard T.-H. Tsai, National Central University

**Academic Demo Track Chair**

Hung-Yi Lee, National Taiwan University

**Publication Chair**

Shih-Hung Wu, Chaoyang University of Technology

# Program Committee Members:

| Name | Organization |
| --- | --- |
| Guo-Wei Bian (邊國維) | Huafan University |
| Yung-Chun Chang (張詠淳) | Taipei Medical University |
| Tao-Hsing Chang (張道行) | National Kaohsiung University of Science and Technology |
| Yu-Yun Chang (張瑜芸) | National Taiwan University |
| Fei Chen (陳霏) | Southern University of Science and Technology |
| Cheng-Hsien Alvin Chen (陳正賢) | National Taiwan Normal University |
| Chien Chin Chen (陳建錦) | National Taiwan University |
| Kuan-Yu Chen (陳冠宇) | National Taiwan University of Science and Technology |
| Yun-Nung (Vivian) Chen (陳縕儂) | National Taiwan University |
| Tai-Shih Chi (冀泰石) | National Chiao Tung University |
| Chen-Yu CHIANG (江振宇) | National Taipei University |
| Wen-Lih Chuang (莊文立) | Sinitic Inc. |
| Min-Yuh Day (戴敏育) | Tamkang University |
| Hung-Yan Gu (古鴻炎) | National Taiwan University of Science and Technology |
| Wei-Tyng Hong (洪維廷) | Yuan Ze University |
| Shu-kai Hsieh (謝舒凱) | National Taiwan University |
| Hen-Hsen Huang (黃瀚萱) | National Taiwan University |
| Jen-Wei Huang (黃仁暐) | National Cheng Kung University |
| Yi-Chin Huang (黃奕欽) | Feng Chia University |
| Jeih-weih Hung (洪志偉) | National Chi Nan University |
| Hsin-Te Hwang (黃信德) | Academia Sinica |
| Lun-Wei Ku (古倫維) | Academia Sinica |
| Wen-Hsing Lai (賴玟杏) | National Kaohsiung First university of Science and Technology |
| Ying-Hui Lai (賴穎暉) | National Yang Ming University |
| Chi-Chun Lee (李祈均) | National Tsing Hua University |
| Hong-Yi Lee (李宏毅) | National Taiwan University |
| I-Bin Liao (廖宜斌) | Chunghwa Telecom Laboratories |
| Yuan-Fu Liao (廖元甫) | National Taipei University |
| Bor-Shen Lin (林伯慎) | National Taiwan University of Science and Technology |
| Shu-Yen Lin (林淑晏) | National Taiwan Normal University |
| Chao-Hong Liu (劉昭宏) | Dublin City University |
| Chao-Lin Liu (劉昭麟) | National Chengchi University |
| Meichun Liu (劉美君) | City University of Hong Kong |
| Wen-Hsiang Lu (盧文祥) | National Cheng Kung University |
| Chih-Hua Tai (戴志華) | National Taipei University |

Richard Tzong-Han Tsai (蔡宗翰)     National Central University

Wei-Ho Tsai (蔡偉和)     National Taipei University of Technology
Yu Tsao (曹昱)     Academia Sinica
Yuen-Hsien TSENG (曾元顯)     National Taiwan Normal University

Jia-Ching Wang (王家慶)     National Central University
Yih-Ru Wang (王逸如)     National Chiao Tung University
Jenq-Haur Wang (王正豪)     National Taipei University of Technology
Jiun-Shiung Wu (吳俊雄)     National Chung Cheng University
Shih-Hung Wu (吳世弘)     Chaoyang University of Technology
Cheng-Zen Yang (楊正仁)     Yuan Ze University
Jui-Feng Yeh (葉瑞峰)     National Chia-Yi University
Liang-Chih Yu (禹良治)     Yuan Ze University
Ming-Shing Yu (余明興)     National Chung Hsing University

(sorted by last names)

**Keynote Speaker I**

**Prof. Kathleen McKeown**

Henry and Gertrude Rothschild Professor of Computer Science, Columbia University
Founding Director of Columbia's Data Science Institute

**Topic: Where Natural Language Processing Meets Societal Needs**

### Abstract

The large amount of language available online today makes it possible to think about how to use natural language processing to help address needs faced by society. In this talk, I will describe research in our group on summarization and sentiment analysis that addresses several different challenges.  We have developed approaches that can be used to help people live and work in today's global world, providing access to information only available in low resource languages, approaches to help determine where problems lie following a disaster, and approaches to identify when the social media posts of gang-involved youth in Chicago express either aggression or loss.

### Biography

Prof. Kathleen R. McKeown is the Henry and Gertrude Rothschild Professor of Computer Science at Columbia University and is also the Founding Director of the Data Science Institute at Columbia. She served as the Director from July 2012 - June 2017. She served as Department Chair from 1998-2003 and as Vice Dean for Research for the School of Engineering and Applied Science for two years. McKeown received a Ph.D. in Computer Science from the University of Pennsylvania in 1982 and has been at Columbia since then. Her research interests include text summarization, natural language generation, multi-media explanation, question-answering and multi-lingual applications.

In 1985 she received a National Science Foundation Presidential Young Investigator Award, in 1991 she received a National Science Foundation Faculty Award for Women, in 1994 she was selected as a AAAI Fellow, in 2003 she was elected as an ACM Fellow, and in 2012 she was selected as one of the Founding Fellows of the Association for Computational Linguistics. In 2010, she received the Anita Borg Women of Vision Award in Innovation for her work on text summarization. McKeown is also quite active nationally. She has served as President, Vice President, and Secretary-Treasurer of the Association of Computational Linguistics. She has also served as a board member of the Computing Research Association and as secretary of the board.

**Keynote Speaker II**

**Prof. Shinji Watanabe**

Johns Hopkins University, Department of Electrical and Computer Engineering joint appointment in Center for Language and Speech Processing

**Topic: Neural End-to-End Architectures for Speech Recognition in Adverse Environments**

**Abstract**
Recently, the end-to-end automatic speech recognition (ASR) paradigm has attracted great research interest as an alternative to conventional hybrid paradigms with deep neural networks and hidden Markov models. Using this novel paradigm, we simplify ASR architecture by integrating such ASR components as acoustic, phonetic, and language models with a single neural network and optimize the overall components for the end-to-end ASR objective: generating a correct label sequence. This talk introduces extensions of this end-to-end architectures to tackle major problems of current ASR technologies in adverse environments including multilingual, multi-speaker, and distant-talk conditions. For multilingual issues, we fully exploit the advantage of eliminating the need for linguistic information such as pronunciation dictionaries in end-to-end ASR, and build a monolithic multilingual ASR system with a language-independent neural network architecture, which can recognize speech in 10 different languages. We also extend the end-to-end ASR system to deal with multi-speaker ASR where the system directly decodes multiple label sequences from a single speech sequence by unifying source separation and speech recognition functions in an end-to-end manner. Finally, we propose a unified architecture to encompass microphone-array signal processing such as a state-of-the-art neural beamformer within the end-to-end framework. This architecture allows speech enhancement and ASR components to be jointly optimized to improve the end-to-end

ASR objective and leads to an end-to-end framework that works well in the presence of strong background noise.


**Biography**
Shinji Watanabe is an Associate Research Professor at Johns Hopkins University, Baltimore, MD. He received his B.S. and M.S. Degrees in 1999 and 2001 at Ohba-Nakazato Laboratory, and received his PhD (Dr. Eng.) Degree in 2006 (advisor: Tetsunori Kobayashi), from Waseda University, Tokyo, Japan, in 2006. From 2001 to 2011, he was a research scientist at NTT Communication Science Laboratories, Kyoto, Japan. From January to March in 2009, he was a visiting scholar in Georgia institute of technology, Atlanta, GA. From January 2012 to June 2017, he was a Senior Principal Research Scientist at Mitsubishi Electric Research Laboratories (MERL), Cambridge, MA. His research interests include Bayesian machine learning and speech and spoken language processing. He has been published more than 150 papers in top journals and conferences, and received several awards including the best paper award from the IEICE in 2003. He served an Associate Editor of the IEEE Transactions on Audio Speech and Language Processing, and is a member of several technical committees including the IEEE Signal Processing Society Speech and Language Technical Committee.

The 2018 Conference on Computational Linguistics and Speech Processing
ROCLING 2018, pp. 1-15
©The Association for Computational Linguistics and Chinese Language Processing

# 基於數字文本相關之語者驗證系統的研究與實作

## Study and Implementation on Digit-related Speaker Verification

周宗鴻　Chung-Hung Chou
國立臺灣大學資訊工程學系
Department of Computer Science and Information Engineering
National Taiwan University
r05922085@ntu.edu.tw


張智星　Jyh-Shing Roger Jang
國立臺灣大學資訊工程學系
Department of Computer Science and Information Engineering
National Taiwan Normal University
jang@csie.ntu.edu.tw


蕭善文　Shan-Wen Hsiao
中華電信研究院
Chunghwa Telecom Laboratories, Taoyuan, Taiwan
swhsiao@cht.com.tw

## 摘要

聲紋驗證為生物辨識中一種重要的驗證方式，此種驗證方式最大的優點即是硬體需求簡單，只需要一般市面上常見的麥克風即可，因此常用於電話及手機的生物辨識。本篇論文目標為建立一套文本相關的聲紋驗證系統並包含三個部分：「動態時間扭曲語者驗證系統」利用強制對齊切開數字後藉由動態時間扭曲比較註冊時數字的梅爾倒頻譜係數與測試時數字的梅爾倒頻譜係數之差異、「語句級語者驗證系統」直接抽取註冊音檔與測試音檔的 i-vector 並使用餘弦相似度或機率線性判別分析來評分這二組 i-vector、「數字級語者驗證系統」利用強制對齊切開數字後抽取註冊音檔與測試音檔中各個數字的 i-vector 並使用餘弦相似度或機率線性判別分析來評分對應數字的 i-vector。

## Abstract

Speaker recognition is an important biometric identification method. The biggest advantage of using such method is the simple requirement of its hardware, which only consists of a microphone. Therefore, it is widely implemented in mobile phones and call centers. The purpose of this thesis is to create a text-related speaker verification system, for which we conduct three different approaches to analyze their result: dynamic time warping compares the differences between the MFCCs for digits at registration and digits at testing after applying forced alignment; sentence-level uses cosine similarity or PLDA to rate the two groups of i-vector retrieved from the audios at registration and testing respectively; digit-level uses cosine similarity or PLDA to rate each i-vector of every digit in the audios after applying forced alignment.

關鍵詞：語者驗證，強制對齊，動態時間扭曲，i-vector，機率線性判別分析

Keywords: Speaker Verification, Forced Alignment, DTW, i-vector, PLDA.


一、緒論

近年來由於智慧型手機及通訊網路的普及，過去許多無法達成的事情已經逐漸變得可行，例如：過去人們都是透過現金進行交易，但現在因為智慧型手機的普及，行動支付及網路購物已經能逐漸取代過去人們傳統的交易行為。然而也因為這些事情帶來許多新的問題，以行動支付及網路購物而言，問題即是要如何辨認使用者之身份，進而確認為本人使用而非盜用便成為現在非常重要的一個課題。

任何的系統都需要辨識、確認使用者之身份，因為如果無法確認使用者其身份導致個人資料外洩是非常嚴重的事情，例如：信用卡資料遭到盜用、家裡遭到小偷入侵、私密照片流出…等。傳統我們在辨識使用者的方法多為：鑰匙、門禁卡、密碼鎖…等，但這些方法往往都會有遺失並且遭到盜用的風險。近年來由於電腦運算能力的大幅進步，陸續開始有不少人提出利用人類生理特徵進行辨識使用者身份，使用人類生理特徵可以避免掉遺失並遭盜用的風險。目前市面上常見的利用人類生理特徵驗證方法有：指紋驗證、臉部驗證、視網膜驗證、聲紋驗證(語者驗證)…等。

本研究目標為建立一套數字文本相關的語者驗證系統並用於行動支付，因為行動支付多應用在智慧型手機且每台智慧型手機皆擁有錄音之功能，又錄製聲音為一件容易達成之事情，因此我們希望能藉由語者驗證來達成確認使用者之身份。

## 二、語者驗證簡介

語者驗證為依據說話者宣稱之身分及其語音內容判斷是否屬實，此種應用情境常用於：行動支付、門禁系統…等。另外語者驗證又可依照說話者語音之內容分為三大類，分別為：本文獨立（text-independent）、本文相關（text-relative）、本文相依（text-dependent）。本文獨立為語音內容可以為任意的，而本文相關為語音內容必須在某些範圍內，例如：僅能是數字或者顏色…等，而本文相依則為完全限定語音之內容，例如僅能是 Hey, Siri、OK, Google 等遭限制之語音內容。

在語音訊號處理中特徵通常我們會使用梅爾頻率倒譜係數（Mel-scale Frequency Cepstral Coefficients, MFCC）[1]，而語者驗證中除 End-to-End[2]外也多半是先抽取 MFCC 後再進行其它處理，其相關方法有：動態時間扭曲（Dynamic Time Warping, DTW）[3]、高斯混合模型（Gaussian Mixture Model, GMM）[4]、通用背景模型（Universal Background Model, UBM）[5]、聯合因子分析（Joint factor Analysis, JFA）[6]、i-vector[7]。另外值得一提的是，i-vector 在訓練總體變異矩陣時會受到不同通道的干擾，因此一般會使用線性判別分析（Linear Discriminant Analysis, LDA）[8]進行信道補償以及使用機率線性判別分析（Probability Linear Discriminant Analysis, PLDA）[9, 10]進行評分。

## 三、語料配置及評估標準

（一）語料介紹

本研究之來源語料分為兩大類，第一類為我們在台大資工系張智星教授在課堂上所搜集的錄音，第二類為交大電機系王逸如教授提供給我們的錄音，以下我們將對這兩類語料進行說明。

1. 台大張智星教授之語料

本語料共有 191 位語者，其中男生共有 160 位、女生共有 31 位，室內錄音共有 172 位、室外錄音共有 19 位。每 1 位語者皆有 10 組錄音，每組錄音之內容皆為 0 至 9 的排列組合（長度為 10），錄音裝置皆透過實驗室開發之 Android APP 進行錄音，取樣頻率為單聲道 44.1 KHz，音質為 16bit。此外我們有針對所有的音檔經由人工標記出 0 至 9 在該音檔發音開始的時間以及發音結束的時間，其標記所採用之程式為 Audacity。

2. 交大王逸如教授之語料

本語料共有 100 位語者，其中男生共有 50 位、女生共有 50 位，皆為室內錄音。每 1 位
語者皆有 10 組錄音，每組錄音之內容皆為長度 4–12 的隨機數字，錄音裝置為麥克風，
取樣頻率為單聲道 16KHz，音質為 16bit。此外該語料包含標記檔對應到每個音檔中各
個數字發音開始與結束的時間。

（二）資料配置

我們將第三章第一節之二組語料拆成訓練資料與測試資料。訓練資料部分會依照原性別
比例從台大語料中取 41 位語者（其中男生 34 位、女生 7 位）、交大語料中之所有語者
（其中男生 50 位、女生 50 位），測試資料部分取剩餘之台大語料（其中男生 126 位、
女生 24 位）。

訓練資料會全部用於訓練模型，而測試資料會分為語者正確（接受）及語者錯誤（拒絕）
這二種情況。現在我們假設註冊音檔使用二組音檔，則接受之筆數會共有 150 位語者 *
每一位語者有剩餘 10－2（8）組音檔可用於驗證，所以接受筆數共有 1200 筆；而拒絕
之筆數會共有 150 位語者 * 149 位非正確語者 * 每一位語者有剩餘 10－2（8）組音檔
可用於驗證，所以拒絕筆數共有 178800 筆。其正確錯誤比為 1200:178800 = 1:149。

（三）評估標準

語者驗證的錯誤可以分成錯誤接受（False Acceptance）及錯誤拒絕（False Rejection）二
類。錯誤接受為聲音片段並非為其宣稱之語者但系統誤判為是其宣稱之語者，我們稱之
為錯誤接受，而錯誤拒絕為聲音片段為其宣稱之語者但系統誤判為不是其宣稱之語者，
我們稱之為錯誤拒絕。

我們希望能夠從全部的測試中找一個門檻值，使得錯誤接受比例（False Acceptance Rate,
FAR）等於錯誤拒絕比例（False Rejection rate, FRR），該比例我們稱之為相同錯誤比例
(Equal Error Rate, EER)，而 EER 即為我們用來評估系統的標準。另外一提的是，雖然
一般來說 EER 即能夠反應系統的效能，但當系統要實際上線時仍需要依照應用情境對
門檻值進行抽換。舉例來說當用於高安全性的系統時，我們更在乎的會是 FAR 而非 EER，
從上述中即會發現會因為情境的不同而對於 FAR 及 FRR 有不同的要求，而這部分則可
以經過錯誤權衡圖觀察後選擇適合的門檻值。

## 四、實驗與分析

所有的實驗採用之作業系統為 Ubuntu 16.04、處理器為 Intel i7 8700、記憶體為 DDR 2400 16GB 4 條、程式語言為 Python3.6，語者驗證工具箱採用 SPEAR [11]，預設使用人工標記之結果。

### （一）動態時間扭曲語者驗證

我們依照第三章第二節的資料配置對於所有測試利用動態時間扭曲比較聲音之間的距離。其對一筆測試之詳細作法，我們先使用人工標記（強制對齊）精準地切出各個數字之片段，再使用動態時間扭曲計算註冊與測試對應數字間的距離，而這些數字之距離加總即為這筆測試之距離。由於可能有多個註冊音檔之情況，因此我們分別可以使用平均距離或是最短距離作為最終距離。反覆對於所有測試做完後，我們可以得到非常多的距離，再利用這些距離我們即可計算 EER，圖一即為本系統之流程圖。

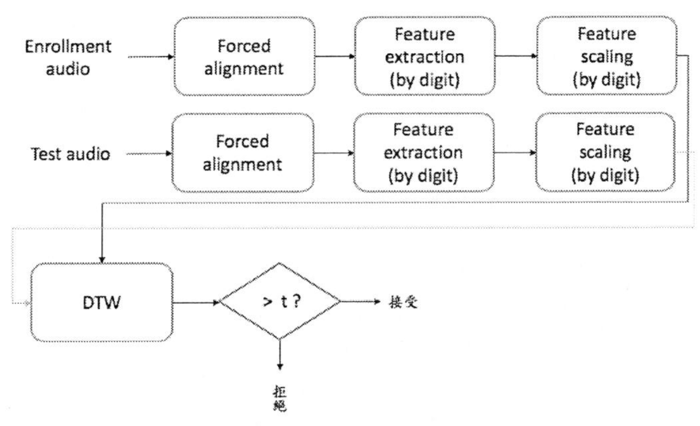


圖一、動態時間扭曲流程圖

圖二為我們使用 feature scaling 時註冊音檔數對於動態時間扭曲之比較直條圖，我們可以發現使用平均距離的 EER 並不會因為註冊音檔數的增加而有明顯的穩定下降，但使用最短距離則有明顯的穩定下降之趨勢。經過分析發現這種現象是因為「平均」用於距離並不公平，舉例來說：小明在早上時錄音註冊，在中午時又進行錄音註冊，晚上進行最後的錄音註冊，因此我們有小明的三個註冊音檔。而現在有一個小明的聲音要驗證，則該聲音會與小明的三個註冊音檔進行 DTW 算出距離，如果該聲音是在早上錄製則肯定會跟小明在早上註冊的聲音最像，但會跟中午、晚上的聲音則較不像，如果我們在這邊使用平均距離則會被中午吃飯及晚上刷牙所影響，但使用最小距離則不會受到影響。

這說明了為什麼使用平均距離錯誤率比較不會穩定下降的原因。

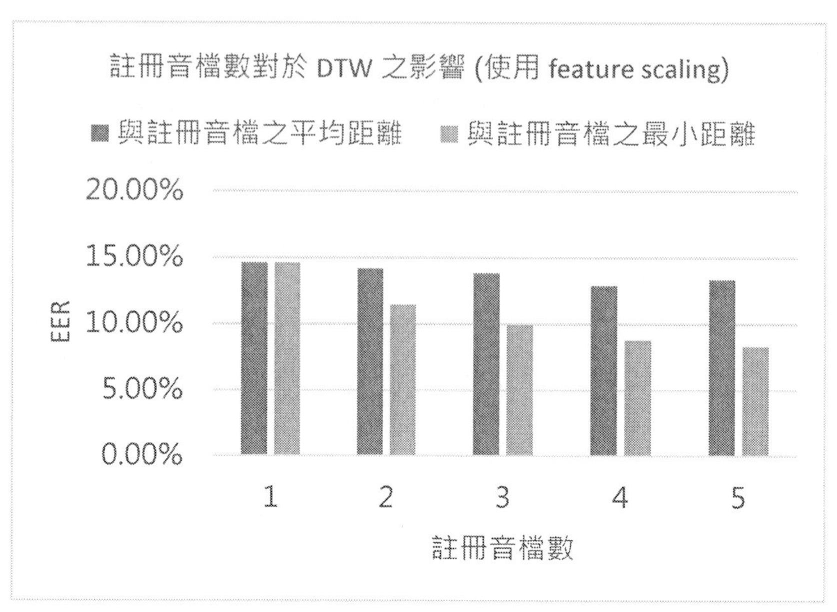



圖二、使用 feature scaling 時註冊音檔數對於動態時間扭曲之比較

此外可以觀察到動態時間扭曲應用於語者驗證上效果非常的不理想，這與我們過去的認知大不相同，經過一些分析及猜測後發現可能是進行 feature scaling 所造成的，這樣猜測的原因在於 feature scaling 會導致每一維中的 MFCC 距離影響變相同，但語者及數字特性可能主要包含於 MFCC 中的某些特定維度進而導致區分語者的能力下降，圖三即為我們為了驗證猜測所進行實驗之結果，可以發現 EER 確實有大幅降低。

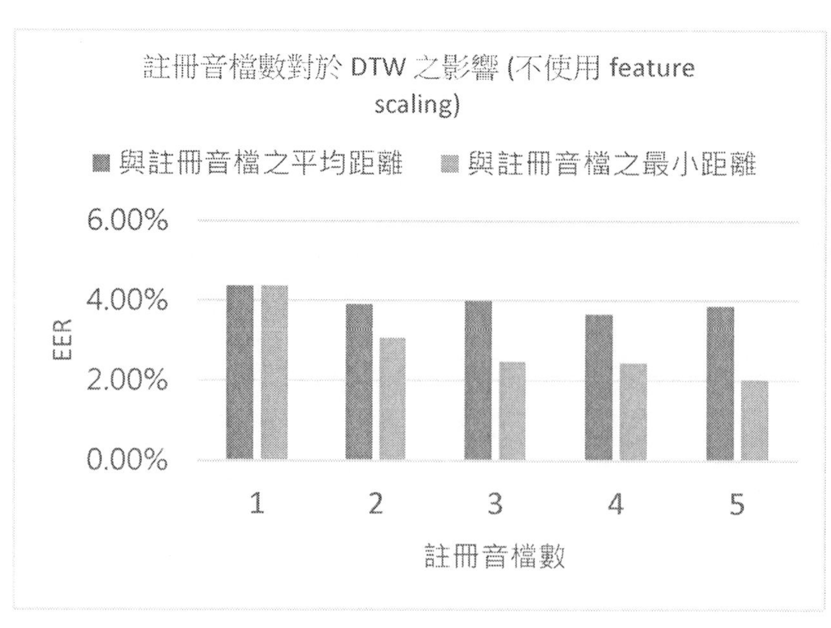

圖三、不使用 feature scaling 時註冊音檔數對於動態時間扭曲之比較

（二）語句級語者驗證

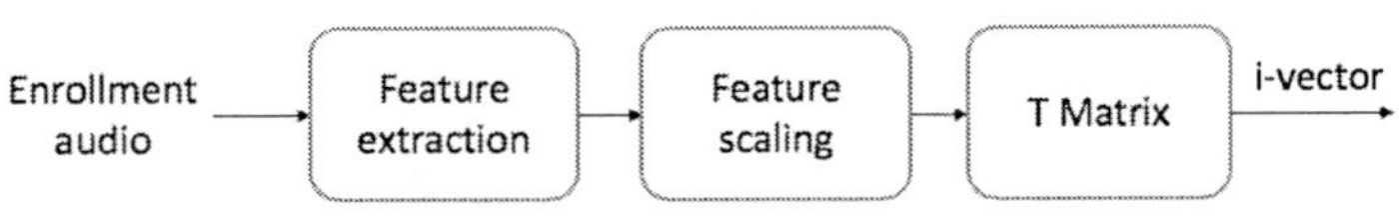


圖四、語句級註冊流程圖

圖四為語句級註冊流程圖，輸入為一位語者的 n 個音檔，抽出音檔的 MFCC 後對 MFCC 進行倒頻譜平均值與變異數正規化，最後將這些經過倒頻譜平均值與變異數正規化後的 MFCC 丟進全變異空間模型後我們即可得到該代表語者之 i-vector。

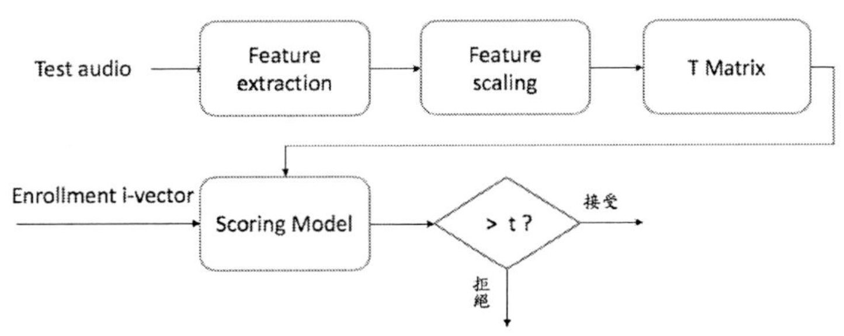


圖五、語句級測試流程圖

圖五為語句級測試流程圖，輸入為一個測試的音檔以及該測試音檔宣稱屬於語者的 i-vector，抽出測試音檔的 MFCC 並對 MFCC 進行倒頻譜平均值與變異數正規化，並將這些經過倒頻譜平均值與變異數正規化後的 MFCC 丟進全變異空間模型後我們即可得到該測試音檔之 i-vector。最終我們將測試音檔之 i-vector 以及宣稱屬於語者的 i-vector 利用評分模型即可輸出分數，反覆對於所有測試做完後，我們即可計算 EER 作為評量標準。

實驗設定部分，我們特徵參數使用 39 維的 MFCC，抽取 MFCC 使用的窗大小為 1024、重疊大小為 512，通用背景模型部分我們的高斯混合模型使用 128 個高斯分佈最多迭代 25 次，初始化使用 k-平均演算法最多迭代 25 次、i-vector 部分我們最多迭代 10 次，餘弦相似度部分我們不對 i-vector 做後處理，直接使用得到之 i-vector 進行計算。機率線

性判別分析部分，我們會先對 i-vector 使用語者之標籤做 LDA 降到 50 維，而機率線性
判別分析的語者空間以及通道空間之矩陣維度皆設定為 50 維，最多迭代 50 次

圖六為我們依照上述實驗設定所跑出來的實驗結果，我們可以發現在我們的資料上評分
方式使用餘弦相似度在 i-vector 維度較低的時候表現都比使用機率線性判別分析來得差，
但是隨著 i-vector 維度上升，餘弦相似度之表現反而比機率線性判別分析來得好。對於
這個現象之看法是：由於我們的資料僅有數字且語者數目為幾百人，因此使用機率線性
判別分析在較高維度的 i-vector 時反而有可能造成過度擬合的情形，最後亦可以發現餘
弦相似度及機率線性判別分析都在 i-vector 維度 300 時有最佳的表現。

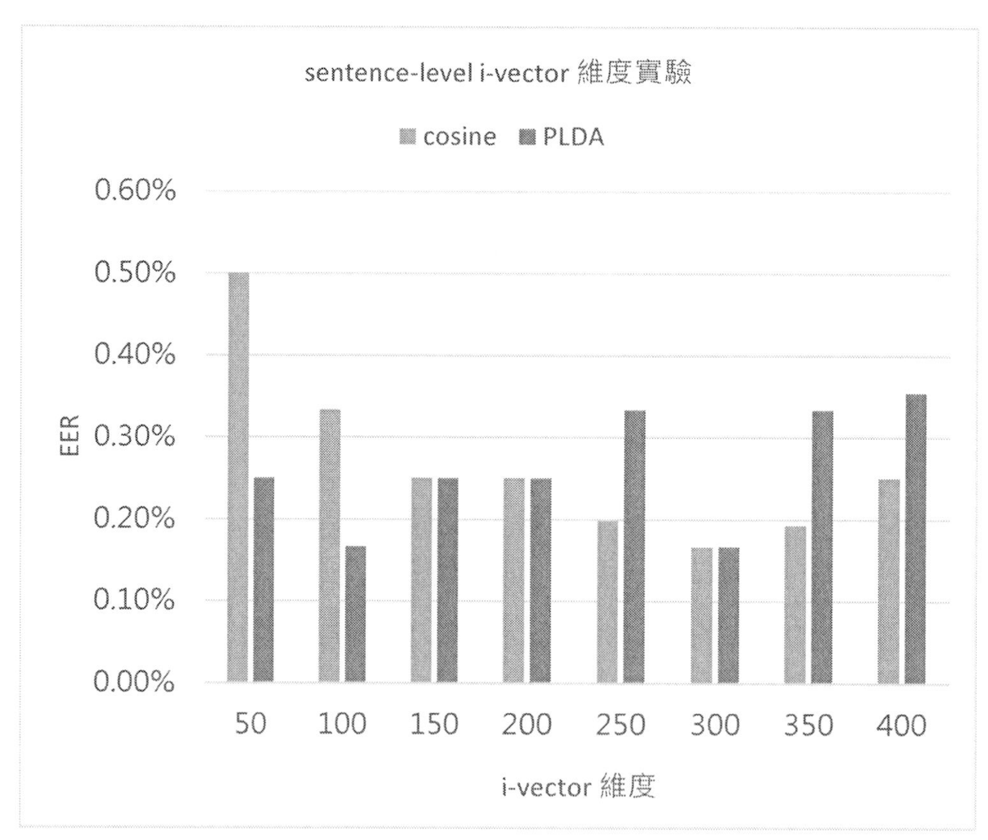


圖六、語句級使用不同評分模型以及不同 i-vector 維度之比較

（三）數字級語者驗證

數字級語者驗證之註冊流程及測試流程多半與語句級語者驗證系統相同，最大差異在於
數字級語者驗證系統會將一段序列如：1029384756 拆成 1、0、2、9、3、8、4、7、5、
6 後，再將個別數字當成「語句」送入語句級註冊（其流程圖如圖四）。以上述例子而

言，數字級語者驗證在註冊時即可得到 10 組代表語者的 i-vector（分別為 1、0、2、9、
3、8、4、7、5、6 的 i-vector），測試時將註冊時得到之 10 組代表語者的 i-vector 與切好
的數字一一對應送入語句級測試（其流程圖如圖五）即可得到 10 組分數，最後再將這
些分數進行組合即可形成最終之分數，下面為我們的二種組合方法。

1. 使用平均分數

$$score = \sum_{i=0}^{9} digit\ i's\ score\ * \frac{1}{10}$$

2. 使用加權分數

$$score = \frac{frames\ of\ dgiti\ i}{\sum_{i=0}^{9} frames\ of\ digit\ i} * digit\ i's\ score$$

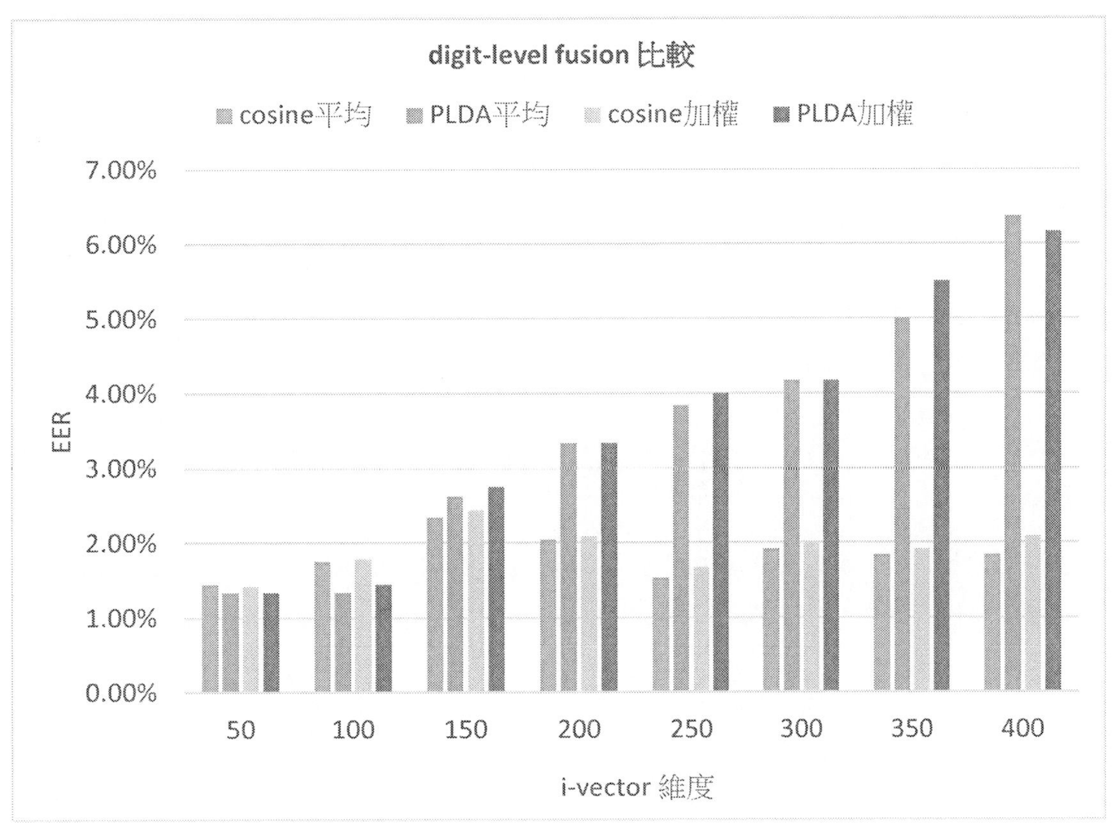


圖七、數字級使用不同評分模型、不同 i-vector 維度、不同分數組合之比較

圖七為數字級使用不同評分模型、不同 i-vector 維度、不同分數組合之比較直條圖，我
們可以從圖中發現使用平均分數以及加權分數對於錯誤率並不會有太大的影響。此外可
以發現 PLDA 隨著維度上升而整體錯誤率也有明顯上升的趨勢，我們認為其原因相同

於語句級。最後亦可以發現整體最好的表現大概落在 PLDA 使用平均時，其錯誤率落在 1.33%。

（四）錯誤分析

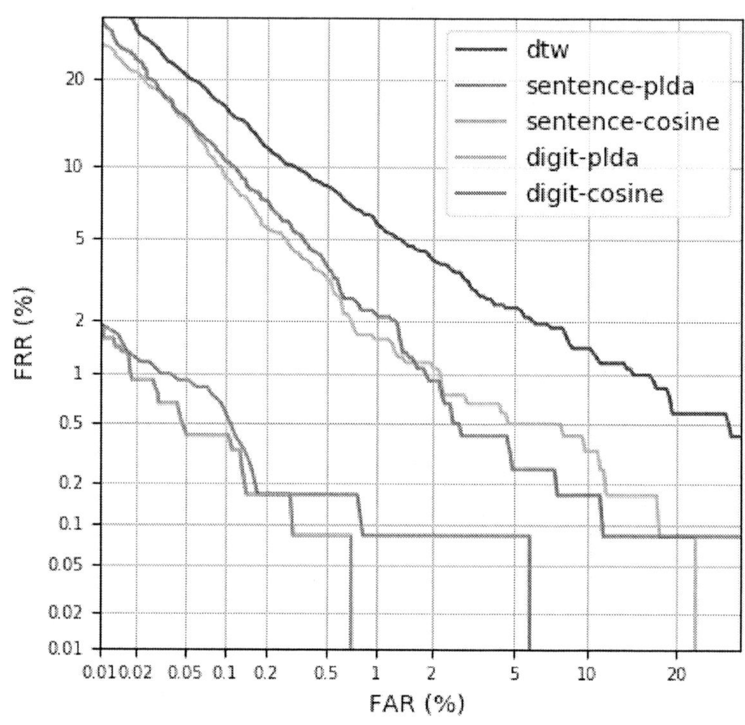


圖八、錯誤權衡圖

圖八為錯誤權衡圖，從圖中我們可以發現語句級語者驗證系統最佳，數字級語者驗證系統次佳，動態時間扭曲語者驗證系統最差。動態時間扭曲為最差的原因我們可以很直觀的猜到是因為 MFCC 中包含著雜訊、音量...等特徵，然而這些特徵並非語者的特徵，因此當我們使用動態時間扭曲進行比較距離時會受到這些特徵所影響，進而影響整體的錯誤率。然而數字級語者驗證系統效果較差並不直觀，因為數字級語者驗證系統採用的方式是文本相依的方式，直觀上我們會認為此種方式效果應該較佳，但實際上卻並非如此。因此下面我們將探討數字級語者驗證系統較差的可能原因。

首先我們檢查使用單獨數字的錯誤率，如圖九所示。我們可以發現增加註冊音檔數時每個數字的錯誤率都有明顯下降，但每個數字的錯誤率差異非常明顯，錯誤率最高的前四條線依序為：digit5、digit2、digit1、digit8。我們對於有這種現象的猜測是每個數字的發音特質不同造成，原因是我們在人工標記音檔時發現有些數字聽起來非常像是雜音，此外亦有些數字再連續唸起來時會被省略部分音或者唸過快的現象，經過觀察發現這些數字多半只有母音，若同時包含母音及子音則比較不會有此種現象。

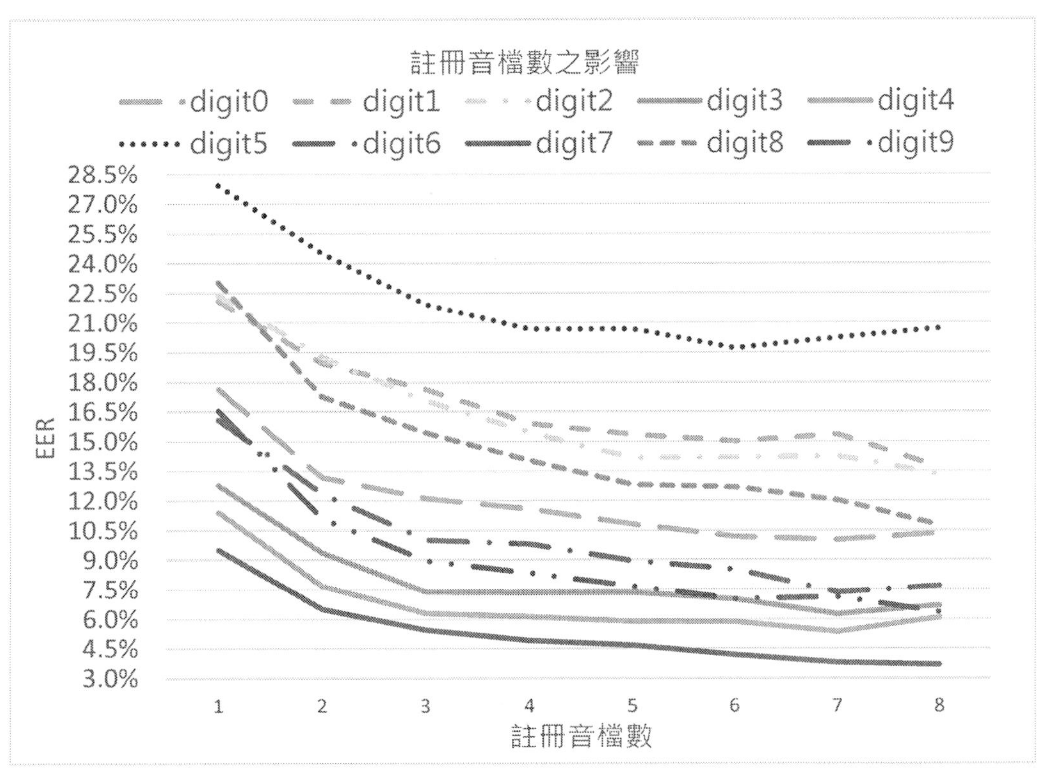


圖九、單獨數字使用 50 維 i-vector 於不同註冊音檔數之錯誤率趨勢圖

為了驗證每個數字錯誤率差異很大是否如我們猜測，我們觀察數字 0 到 9 在 Audacity 的訊號圖，確實發現到錯誤較高的數字發音較為簡單，而錯誤率較低的數字發音則較有變化。此外我們亦對註冊音檔數與錯誤率的關係做出座標圖如圖九所示，從座標圖中我們可以明顯發現有呈現反比之趨勢。圖十之結果由個別數字的錯誤率來觀察 EER 與音窗的個數之相關性，此間接可以證實發音的長度與難度與錯誤率成正比的關係。

從上述實驗中可以發現某些數字錯誤率確實比較高，也發現了這些錯誤率較高可能是因為發音特質以及長度造成的影響，因此我們認為很有可能是這些錯誤率較高的數字加入計算反而導致整體錯誤率上升。圖十一為我們使用 PLDA 評分模型在 50 維 i-vector 拿掉錯誤率最高的前 n 個數字之直條圖，從圖中可以發現當我們拿掉 1 個數字後錯誤略確實有些微提升，拿掉 2 個數字時錯誤率又再度回到不拿掉任何數字之錯誤率，拿掉 3 個以上數字後錯誤率開始逐漸升高。因此我們可以從實驗中推斷這 2 個錯誤率最高的數字對於錯誤率並無明顯助益，此外雖然拿掉這 2 個錯誤率最高的數字對於錯誤率無明顯提升，但卻也可以減少使用者所需花費的時間。

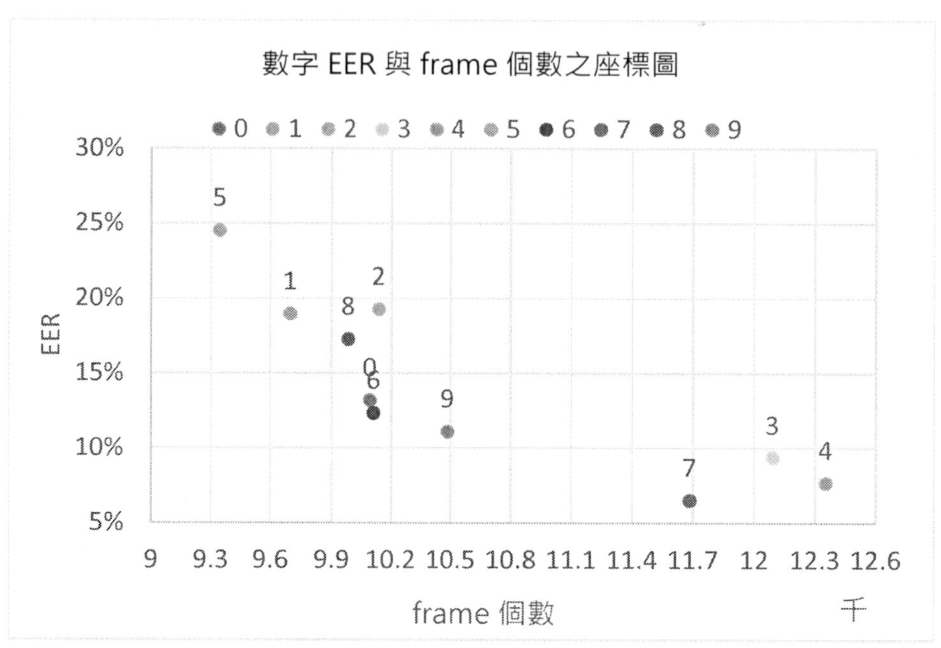


圖十、個別數字錯誤率與窗的個數之關係座標圖

由於拿掉錯誤率較高的數字後我們的錯誤率仍然比語句級高出許多，我們進而猜測連續數字發音中間的一些特徵是否有可能被移除了，舉例來說：多數人的發音時常帶著一些習慣的腔調，但因為我們要把數字強制拆開所以導致夾雜在數字中間的這些腔調也消失了。因此我們決定將語句級的音檔也進行相同作法，其做法是先抽取整句話之 MFCC 再依照數字發音時間只取數字發音時間內對應窗的 MFCC。

圖十二即為不切數字與切數字於語句級之比較直條圖，我們可以發現切數字後合併錯誤率平均落在 0.64%附近、不切數字錯誤率大致落在 0.27%附近，不切數字在任意的 i-vector 維度上表現都比切數字來得好許多，因此我們可以推斷連續數字發音中間的特徵確實包含著語者特徵。

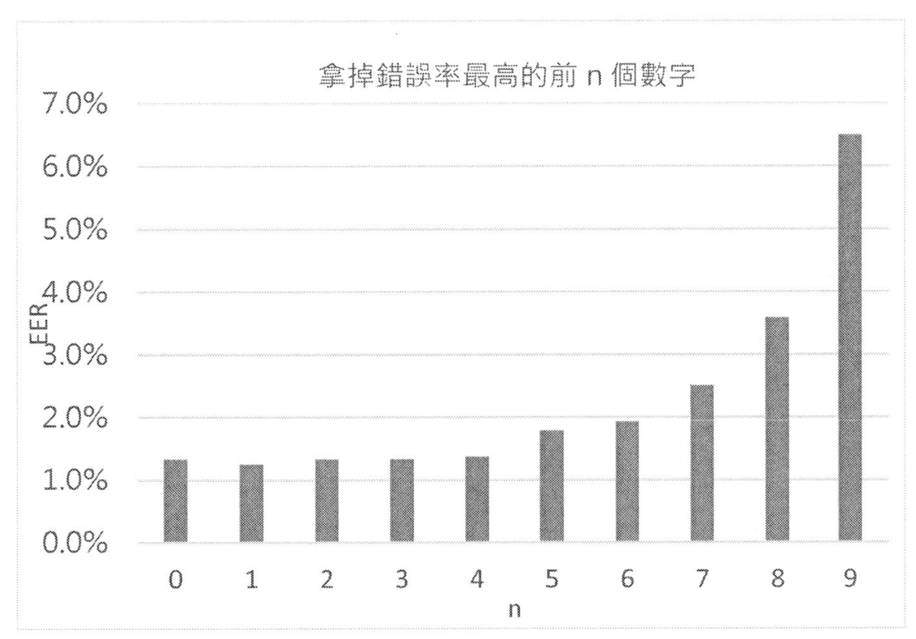


圖十一、拿掉錯誤率最高的前 n 個數字之直條圖

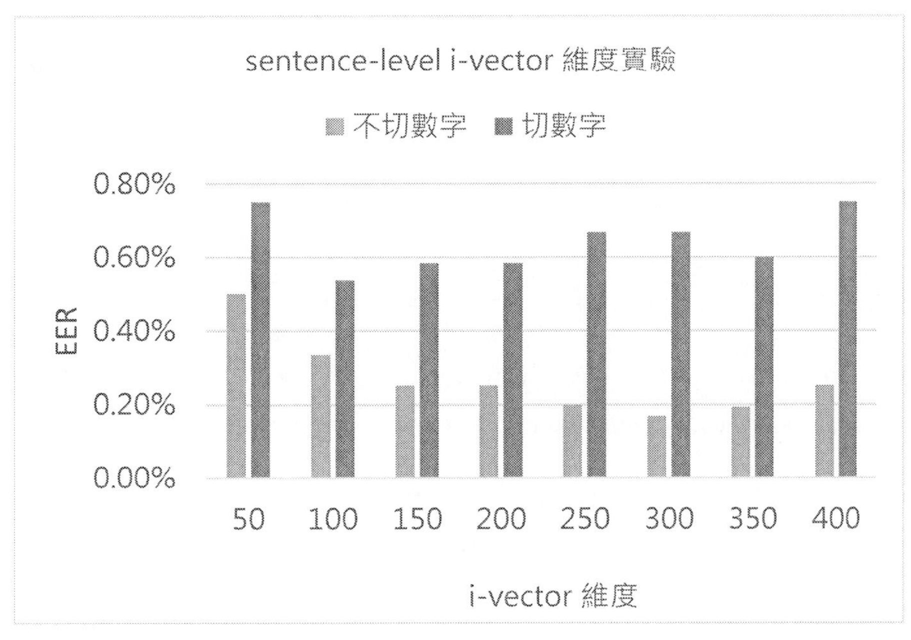


圖十二、不切數字與切數字於語句級之比較直條圖

## 五、結論

我們從實驗中得知 i-vector 的方法使用二個音檔註冊時 EER 語句級可以落在 0.2% ，而數字級 EER 落在 1.33%，但使用動態時間扭曲方法則 EER 無法低於 3%，由此可見動態時間扭曲方法之效果顯然比 i-vector 方法來得差。另外比較語句級語者驗證系統與數

字級語者驗證系統，我們發現語句級語者驗證系統效果明顯比數字級語者驗證系統來得好。此外經過近一步分析數字級語者驗證系統我們發現以下現象：

(1) 移除錯誤較高的數字對於錯誤率影響不大。

(2) 發音較長的數字比發音較短的數字用於語者驗證效果較佳。

(3) 發音較為複雜之數字的語者驗證效果也比發音簡單的數字來得好。

(4) 數字級語者驗證系統效果較差的原因之一是由於強制切開導致連續數字發音間的語者特徵消失所致。

(5) 文本內容較複雜時 i-vector 維度應該增加，文本內容較簡易時 i-vector 維度應該減少。

## 參考文獻


[1] Rabiner, Lawrence R., and Biing-Hwang Juang. Fundamentals of speech recognition. Vol. 14. Englewood Cliffs: PTR Prentice Hall, 1993..

[2] Heigold, Georg, et al. "End-to-end text-dependent speaker verification." Acoustics, Speech and Signal Processing (ICASSP), 2016 IEEE International Conference on. IEEE, 2016.

[3] Muda, Lindasalwa, Mumtaj Begam, and Irraivan Elamvazuthi. "Voice recognition algorithms using mel frequency cepstral coefficient (MFCC) and dynamic time warping (DTW) techniques." arXiv preprint arXiv:1003.4083 (2010).

[4] Reynolds, Douglas A. "Speaker identification and verification using Gaussian mixture speaker models." Speech communication 17.1-2 (1995): 91-108.

[5] Reynolds, Douglas A., Thomas F. Quatieri, and Robert B. Dunn. "Speaker verification using adapted Gaussian mixture models." Digital signal processing 10.1-3 (2000): 19-41.

[6] Kenny, Patrick, et al. "Joint factor analysis versus eigenchannels in speaker recognition." IEEE Transactions on Audio, Speech, and Language Processing 15.4 (2007): 1435-1447.

[7] Dehak, Najim, et al. "Front-end factor analysis for speaker verification." IEEE Transactions on Audio, Speech, and Language Processing 19.4 (2011): 788-798.

[8] Mika, Sebastian, et al. "Fisher discriminant analysis with kernels." Neural networks for signal processing IX, 1999. Proceedings of the 1999 IEEE signal processing society workshop.. Ieee, 1999.

[9]  Prince, Simon JD, and James H. Elder. "Probabilistic linear discriminant analysis for inferences about identity." Computer Vision, 2007. ICCV 2007. IEEE 11th International Conference on. IEEE, 2007.

[10]  Garcia-Romero, Daniel, and Carol Y. Espy-Wilson. "Analysis of i-vector length normalization in speaker recognition systems." Twelfth Annual Conference of the International Speech Communication Association. 2011

[11] Khoury, Elie, Laurent El Shafey, and Sébastien Marcel. "Spear: An open source toolbox for speaker recognition based on Bob." Acoustics, Speech and Signal Processing (ICASSP), 2014 IEEE International Conference on. IEEE, 2014.

The 2018 Conference on Computational Linguistics and Speech Processing
ROCLING 2018, pp. 16-30
©The Association for Computational Linguistics and Chinese Language Processing

# Isolated and Ensemble Audio Preprocessing Methods for Detecting Adversarial Examples against Automatic Speech Recognition

**Krishan Rajaratnam [1], Kunal Shah [2], Jugal Kalita [3]**

[1] The College, University of Chicago, Chicago, USA
[2] College of Liberal Arts and Sciences, University of Florida, Gainesville, USA
[3] Department of Computer Science, University of Colorado, Colorado Springs, USA

[1] krajaratnam@uchicago.edu, [2] kshah1997@ufl.edu, [3] jkalita@uccs.edu

## Abstract

An adversarial attack is an exploitative process in which minute alterations are made to natural inputs, causing the inputs to be misclassified by neural models. In the field of speech recognition, this has become an issue of increasing significance. Although adversarial attacks were originally introduced in computer vision, they have since infiltrated the realm of speech recognition. In 2017, a genetic attack was shown to be quite potent against the Speech Commands Model. Limited-vocabulary speech classifiers, such as the Speech Commands Model, are used in a variety of applications, particularly in telephony; as such, adversarial examples produced by this attack pose as a major security threat. This paper explores various methods of detecting these adversarial examples with combinations of audio preprocessing. One particular combined defense incorporating compressions, speech coding, filtering, and audio panning was shown to be quite effective against the attack on the Speech Commands Model, detecting audio adversarial examples with 93.5% precision and 91.2% recall.

**Keywords**: adversarial attack, speech recognition, deep learning, audio compression, speech coding

## 1. Introduction

Due to the widespread and growing use of neural networks for various tasks, it is imperative that these models be robust and secure while remaining generally usable. Although these models are quite powerful and are well-suited for a variety of tasks, they are not without their imperfections. First applied against computer vision models [1], adversarial attacks exploit the flaws of neural networks by making perceptibly insignificant changes to a source to produce adversarial examples, with the purpose of causing the neural network to misclassify the example. These attacks can be quite potent and have caused misclassification rates of above 90% in image classifiers [2]. Because of their exploitative nature, adversarial attacks can be quite difficult to defend against without sacrificing general model usability or accuracy.

The use of adversarial attacks is not restricted to the field of image recognition. Modern speech recognition has become increasingly reliant on end-to-end neural models, which are able to largely outperform traditional models that rely heavily on signal processing and hidden Markov models. These sophisticated neural models may be state-of-the art, but are also more susceptible to attack by adversarial examples. Recent work has shown that two speech recognition models, a convolutional neural network (CNN) model trained on the Speech Commands dataset [3] and Mozilla's implementation of the DeepSpeech end-to-end model [4], are vulnerable to adversarial attacks. Two separate attacks on the two models were able to generate extremely potent adversarial examples, capable of inducing a misclassification rate of up to 100%. This trend threatens the current reliability of deep learning models within the field of speech recognition. As such, there is a crucial need for defensive methods that can be employed to evade audio adversarial attacks.

## 2. Related Work

The attack against the limited-vocabulary Speech Commands model detailed by Alzantot et al. [3] shows particular relevance within the field of telephony, as it could be applied to maliciously manipulate the limited-vocabulary speech classifiers used for automated attendants. During this attack, adversarial examples created by a gradient-free genetic algorithm allow the attack to penetrate layers of non-differential preprocessing, which is commonly used in automatic speech recognition.

### 2.1 Audio Preprocessing Defenses

Recent work in computer vision has shown that preprocessing methods, such as JPEG and JPEG2000 image compression [5], resizing [6], and pixel deflection [7] are capable of defending against adversarial attacks with varying degrees of success. Preprocessing defenses have also been employed in speech recognition to mitigate adversarial examples. Yang et al. [8] achieved a high rate of success with the use of local smoothing, down sampling, and quantization in an attempt to neutralize adversarial examples produced by the attack of Alzantot et al. Quantizing with $q = 256$, Yang et al. achieved their best result of mitigating (i.e. retrieving the original label of) 63.8% of the adversarial examples. Quantization causes various amplitudes of sampled data to be rounded to the nearest integer multiple of the $q$ value; this allows adversarial perturbations with small amplitudes to become disrupted.

Work has also been done in employing audio compression, Hertz shifting, noise reduction, and low-pass filtering [9], to defend against Carlini and Wagner's attack [4] on DeepSpeech. The results of [9] suggest that the most promising preprocessing method was low-pass filtering, with which the authors were able to retrieve the original label of 90.11% of Carlini and Wagner's adversarial examples. By utilizing low-pass filtering, a selected range of higher frequencies are eliminated, preserving a lower band of frequencies in which human speech is located. If a significant portion of the of the adversarial perturbation is found within the discarded higher frequencies, the attack can be disrupted. Although this work was able to largely neutralize the threat of adversarial examples against DeepSpeech, this came at a noticeable cost to general model accuracy.

2.2 Speech Coding

Although the results of [9] imply that low-pass filtering outclasses audio compression as a preprocessing defense, this work only explored two standards of audio coding: Advanced Audio Coding (AAC) and MP3. Though those two compression standards enjoy widespread popularity, they are not necessarily adequately equipped in defending against targeted adversarial examples on speech recognition. For the purposes of teleconferencing and VoIP, speech codecs such as Speex [10] and Opus [11] are primarily used due to their ability to preserve the quality of human speech, even through imperfect conditions and lower bitrates.

In 2002, Valin [10] began the Speex project with intent on providing "a free codec for free speech." Further development allowed Speex to grow in popularity, becoming adopted by well-known, practical VoIP applications such as TeamSpeak[1] and Twinkle[2]. Speex codec is built upon the Code Excited Linear Prediction (CELP) algorithm [12], which models the vocal tract using a linear prediction model capable of minimizing differences of the uncompressed source within a "perceptually weighted domain." The minimization is achieved by applying the following weighting filter to the raw input:

$$W(z) = \frac{A(z/\gamma_1)}{A(z/\gamma_2)} \tag{1}$$

---

[1] http://teamspeak.com/en/features/overview
[2] http://www.linuxlinks.com/Twinkle/

where $A$ is a linear prediction filter with $\gamma_1$ and $\gamma_2$ managing the filter shape. This filter allows for various levels of noise at different frequencies and has proven to be useful for neutralizing adversarial perturbations whilst maintaining the quality of human speech. In addition, Speex also includes numerous features, such as voice activity detection, denoising, and support of various bandwidths. As this compression seems to resemble audio preprocessing methods proven capable of effectively mitigating adversarial examples, it seems better suited than MP3 or AAC compression for the task of defending against adversarial attacks.

The Opus codec, which is used by the highly popular proprietary VoIP application Discord[3], is a modern successor to the Speex codec [11]. By combining the CELP algorithm with SILK, a linear predictive coding algorithm developed by Skype Technologies in 2009[4], it is considered an improved and more advanced version of Speex; the application of Opus compression for defending against adversarial examples is therefore worth testing.

2.3 Ensemble Detection

Preprocessing defenses against adversarial examples can only be effective and practical if they are able to mitigate adversarial examples without greatly compromising general model accuracy. A viable form of preprocessing would disrupt the predictions of adversarial examples more than it would disrupt the predictions of benign examples. In particular, there should ideally be a small difference between the output vectors produced by passing the raw input and preprocessed input through a neural network when the input is benign, but that same difference should be much larger if the input is adversarial. This core idea can be used to apply preprocessing methods to detect adversarial examples, rather than simply mitigating or neutralizing perturbations.

Within the field of computer vision, ensembles of preprocessing methods have been used for detecting adversarial examples. Xu et al. [13] proposed the feature squeezing method for detecting adversarial examples. This method combines smaller "squeezing" methods into an ensemble, and calculates an $L_1$ score from of the maximum $L_1$ distance between any pair of output probability vectors produced by passing the raw and squeezed inputs through a deep

---

neural network (DNN). Using feature squeezing, Xu et al. were able to consistently detect over 80% of adversarial examples produced from a variety of attacks.

## 3. Methods and Evaluation

The aim of this research can be divided into two parts: using the individual methods of preprocessing independently to detect adversarial examples, and examining various methods of combining the preprocessing detectors together as ensemble detection methods. The adversarial examples are generated using the genetic attack described by Alzantot et al. against the pre-trained Speech Commands model [3].

### 3.1 Speech Commands Dataset and Model

The Speech Commands dataset was released in 2017 and contains 105,829 labeled utterances of 32 words from 2,618 speakers [14]. As a light-weight model, Speech Commands is based on a keyword-spotting convolutional network (CNN) [15] that is capable of achieving 90% classification accuracy on this dataset. For the purposes of this research, a unique subset of 30,799 labeled utterances of 10 words are used in order to maintain consistency with previous research pertaining to the adversarial examples of Alzantot, et al. From this subset, 20 adversarial examples are generated for each nontrivial source-target word pair for 1800 total examples. Each example is produced with a maximum of 500 iterations.

### 3.2 Preprocessing Defenses

A simple method for using preprocessing to detect adversarial examples is by checking to see if the prediction produced by the model changes if the input is preprocessed; if the model's prediction of the raw input does not match the prediction of the preprocessed input, it is declared adversarial. The following preprocessing methods are used in isolation for detecting adversarial examples:

- MP3 Compression,
- AAC Compression,
- Speex Compression,
- Opus Compression,
- Band-pass Filtering, and
- Audio Panning and Lengthening.

While the MP3 and AAC compressions correspond directly to preprocessing defenses in related work described in Section 2.1, the other defenses listed above have not yet been directly tested against audio adversarial examples. The band-pass filter defense builds off of the low-pass filter of [9] by combining it with a high-pass filter in order to deter additional adversarial perturbations outside of the frequency range for natural human speech. Audio panning is a form of preprocessing frequently used in audio mixing that distributes a signal across stereophonic channels, distorting channel volumes to mimic the perception of audio coming from an off-centered position. The audio panning and lengthening defense lengthens audio by 1% in addition to panning to increase the spatial distortion of adversarial perturbations in the signal.

3.3 Ensemble Detection Methods

Individual preprocessing methods as isolated defenses can successfully fend off certain adversarial attacks. However, attacks aware of the preprocessing defenses are capable of optimizing to become more robust [4]. As such, the use of any one preprocessing method alone for detecting adversarial examples would prove to be insufficient and render the model increasingly susceptible to more advanced attacks. Therefore, a combined deployment of preprocessing methods, or an ensemble, may be able to provide better security with a more complex defense.

The preprocessing detection methods described in Section 3.2 can be combined in a variety of configurations. The ensemble detection methods explored in this research are discussed below.

3.3.1 Majority Voting Ensemble

The simplest method of combining the preprocessing methods together would be by assigning each preprocessing method a vote, and declaring an audio signal as adversarial if a majority of the ensemble declares the signal adversarial. As there are six preprocessing methods that are combined into an ensemble, ties with this discrete voting scheme are possible. To err on the side of security, this procedure will declare a signal as adversarial in the event of a tie.

### 3.3.2 Learned Threshold Voting Ensemble

The majority voting ensemble declares an audio signal as adversarial if there are at least three votes in favor of it being adversarial. This threshold for deciding how many votes are needed to declare an audio signal as adversarial is arbitrary, and can adapt to different circumstances. A low threshold would result in a high recall in detecting adversarial examples, but would sacrifice precision. A high threshold would result in a lower recall in detecting adversarial examples, but would yield a higher precision. This ensemble method experiments with using various voting thresholds for detecting adversarial examples on a labeled training set, and chooses the threshold that results in the best precision and recall. To balance both precision and recall, $F_1$ scores are used for selecting the best threshold, although in practice, one could adjust the F-measure to reflect one's attitude on the relative importances of precision and recall.

### 3.3.3 $L_1$ Scoring

The previously discussed ensemble voting methods are relatively simple, as they simply examine the model's discrete prediction of the raw and preprocessed inputs for each preprocessing method. Additionally, the voting methods above are indiscriminate and treat each member of the ensemble equally. A more nuanced approach for measuring the differences in predictions between raw and preprocessed inputs is by $L_1$ scoring the different output logit vectors, similar to how Xu et al. integrated the multiple squeezing methods in their feature squeezing defense. In this method, an ideal threshold $L_1$ score is learned from training data by finding the threshold of maximum information gain, and test examples that surpass this threshold are declared adversarial. This method uses the maximum $L_1$ distance to calculate the score, implicitly assigning more importance to preprocessing methods that produce output vectors that are highly different than the output vectors produced by predicting raw signal. As such, this method would theoretically be more sensitive in detecting adversarial examples, but it may also be quite aggressive in declaring signals as adversarial at the risk of falsely declaring benign examples as adversarial.

### 3.3.4 Tree-based Classification Algorithms

The above ensemble methods discard information of the class-specific variation in the output vector for each preprocessing method, relative to the raw input. In order to preserve this information, a multi-dimensional vector can be used, with each dimension accounting for the output vector variation for that class. For the tree-based detection methods discussed in this research, a multi-dimensional vector composed of the summed absolute class-specific differences between the raw input's resultant probability vector and the preprocessed input's resultant probability vector over each method of preprocessing. In particular, the $i$th dimension of this summed absolute difference (SAD) vector $S$ is calculated as follows:

$$S_i = \sum_{p \in P} |r_i - p_i| \tag{2}$$

where $P$ corresponds to the set of output probability vectors yielded by the methods of preprocessing in the ensemble, and $r$ corresponds to the output probability vector produced by passing the raw signal through the Speech Commands model without any preprocessing.

This vector will preserve information about class-specific variation between the predictions, and will reduce the number of features of the vector inputted to the tree-based classifier down to 12 (which is the same as the number of classes). Considering the relatively small training dataset size (which is discussed in Section 3.4), having less features for tree-based classification may improve performance. However, the 84-dimensional vector formed by simply concatenating each output probability vector together would preserve the most amount of information. As such, the use of this concatenated probability (CP) vector for tree-based classification is also tested, even if the dataset isn't large enough for the classification algorithms to effectively handle that large of a vector.

Decision tree-based classification algorithms are well-suited for classifying vectors of features into discrete classes. In this research, three tree-based classification algorithms are employed for using vectors of summed absolute differences for detecting adversarial examples: random forest classification, adaptive boosting, and extreme gradient boosting. Random forest classification functions by constructing many decision trees in an attempt to stave off the possibility of over-fitting. Adaptive boosting and extreme gradient boosting are gradient boosting algorithms which function by building an ensemble of weak learners in a stage-wise fashion. Each of these tree-based algorithms are used twice in this research: once for using SAD vectors for classification and once for using CP vectors for classification. These tree-based algorithms have had quite high success in applied problems, are possibly well-suited for detecting adversarial examples.

3.4 Evaluation

The aforementioned detection methods are evaluated based on their precision and recall in detecting adversarial examples. As the simple preprocessing detection methods discussed in Section 3.2 require no training, the precision and recall measurements are calculated based off of their performances on the full set of 1,800 generated adversarial examples and 1,800 randomly selected benign examples. Many of the ensemble detection methods, however, do train and adapt based off what is seen in training data, so precision and recall measurements for these detection methods are calculated based off of their performance on a subset of only 900 adversarial examples and 900 benign examples; the 900 other adversarial and benign examples are used as a training dataset.

Within the context of defending against adversarial attacks, there seems to be an implicit tradeoff between security and general model accuracy. Although it is important to have a high recall in detecting adversarial examples for the sake of security, a low precision in detection would cause the model to decline in usability. This research takes the stance of both security and general model accuracy being equally important. To reflect this attitude, $F_1$ scores are used to combine the precision and recall measurements with equal consideration.

## 4. Results

The results of the individual preprocessing detection methods described in Section 3.2 are summarized in Table 1. Measurements indicate that all of the methods are capable of detecting adversarial examples produced by the attack with varying rates of success. The results are consistent with the findings of [9] in that MP3 compression performs adequately at best when compared with the other methods. AAC and Opus compression perform notably better, but are not able to achieve as high of a recall as Speex compression (which also yields the highest $F_1$ score).

Although the use of band-pass filtering for detecting adversarial examples is extremely precise, it yields a remarkably low recall, which suggests it is a bit too passive with its declaration of adversariality.

As many of these preprocessing methods distort audio signals in fundamentally different ways, the overall high precision (and lower recall) measurements of each of the individual preprocessing suggest that some of the ensemble methods may be more effective in detecting adversarial examples.

**Table 1:** *Precision, recall, and $F_1$ values for isolated preprocessing methods in detecting adversarial examples.*

| Preprocessing Method | Precision | Recall | $F_1$ Score |
|---|---|---|---|
| MP3 Compression | 93.7% | 70.7% | 0.806 |
| AAC Compression | 95.0% | 81.2% | 0.876 |
| Band-Pass Filtering | **97.3%** | 40.6% | 0.573 |
| Audio Panning & Lengthening | 95.8% | 82.4% | 0.886 |
| Opus Compression | 94.5% | 81.8% | 0.877 |
| Speex Compression | 93.7% | **88.5%** | **0.910** |

**Table 2:** *Precision, recall, and $F_1$ values for ensemble detection methods in detecting adversarial examples.*

| Ensemble Detection Method | Precision | Recall | $F_1$ Score |
|---|---|---|---|
| Majority Voting | **96.1%** | 88.1% | 0.919 |
| Learned Threshold Voting | 93.5% | 91.2% | **0.924** |
| $L_1$ Scoring | 76.9% | 92.4% | 0.840 |
| Random Forest Classification (SAD Vector) | 79.3% | 87.0% | 0.830 |
| Random Forest Classification (CP Vector) | 86.7% | **94.4%** | 0.904 |
| Adaptive Boosting (SAD Vector) | 83.5% | 81.8% | 0.827 |
| Adaptive Boosting (CP Vector) | 86.7% | 93.0% | 0.898 |
| Extreme Gradient Boosting (SAD Vector) | 83.0% | 84.2% | 0.836 |
| Extreme Gradient Boosting (CP Vector) | 88.3% | **94.4%** | 0.913 |

The results of the ensemble detection methods described in Section 3.3 are summarized in Table 2. The voting methods performed quite well and achieved the two highest $F_1$ scores of all the methods discussed in this paper. This may be attributed to the high precisions and low recalls of the individual preprocessing methods described in Table 1; the relatively strict voting threshold of   votes needed for an adversarial declaration capitalizes on the high precision of each of the methods and is able to increase recall. The majority voting method especially benefited from the high precisions of its constituents and yielded an extremely high precision of 96.1%. The Learned Threshold Voting method was able to learn a lower voting threshold of only two votes needed for an adversarial declaration. As such, this method was able to yield a notably higher recall than what was achieved through majority voting, but at a noticeable cost to precision. As the Learned Threshold Voting method still retained a fairly high precision, it achieved the overall highest $F_1$ score of any of the other preprocessing methods. The recall values for detecting adversarial examples using the Learned Threshold Voting method are detailed in Figure 1.

The $L_1$ Scoring method was able to achieve higher recall than either of the two voting methods, perhaps due to its aggressive nature. However, this was achieved at the cost of precision, which evidently lowered the $F_1$ score.

Although tree-based classification algorithms can be quite powerful in a variety of situations, the tree-based methods were not able to perform as well as the voting methods in detecting adversarial examples using SAD vectors. This may be because the SAD vectors fed into the tree algorithms discarded important voter-specific information. In particular, the vector of summed absolute differences effectively anonymizes the voters in the ensemble; it inherently considers each member of the ensemble equally.

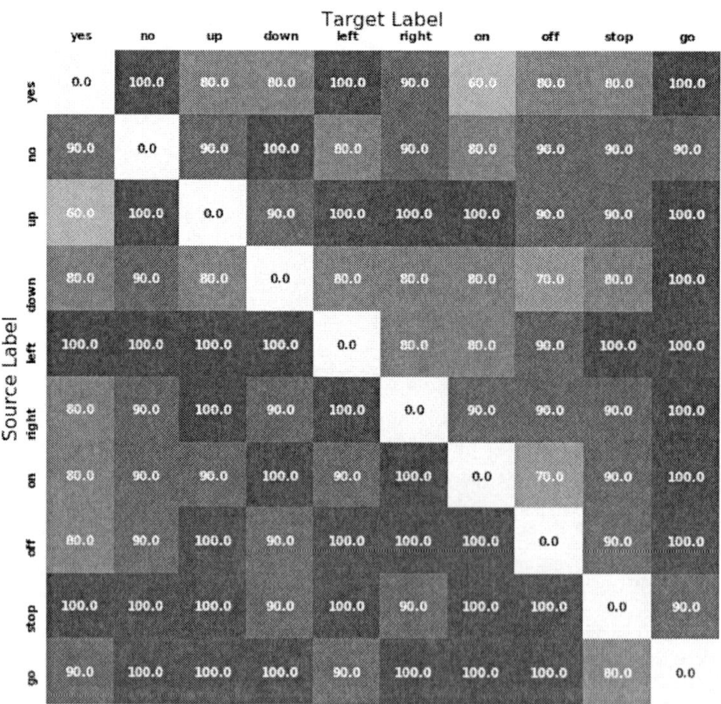



**Figure 1:** *A heat map detailing the rates (in percent) of detecting targeted adversarial examples with the Learned Threshold Voting method. The diagonal of zeroes correspond to trivial source-target pairs for which no adversarial examples were generated.*

This discarded information proved to be quite crucial for effectively detecting adversarial examples, as the tree-based classification methods performed significantly better with CP vectors (which are highly conservative). In particular, the extreme gradient boosting and adaptive boosting classification algorithms were able to yield the highest recall values for detecting adversarial examples out of all of the detection methods discussed in this research. Considering that the tree-based classification methods performed significantly better with the voter-specific information available in the CP vector, it is worth noting that the Learned Threshold Voting method, which yielded a higher $F_1$ score than any tree-based classification method, does not use voter-specific information; each vote carries equal weight towards breaking the learned threshold. As such, it may be possible that the tree-based classification methods outperform the Learned Threshold Voting method on larger datasets, as it could be that this training dataset was not sufficiently large enough for learning how to optimally use an 84-dimensional vector for classification. However, given the heavy reliance of training data that the tree-based classification methods exhibit, they are likely not as well-suited for flexibly handling different types of attacks as the voting methods.

As the Learned Threshold Voting method performed better over all other detection methods discussed in this paper, it can be helpful to examine the adversarial examples that remain undetected by this method and the benign signals that get incorrectly flagged as adversarial.

One method of analyzing the adversarial examples is by examining the average frequency level throughout the signal. Since we are able to recover the original, clean source for each adversarial example, we can examine the difference between the average frequencies of each adversarial example and its clean source. The means and standard deviations of this difference for undetected and detected adversarial examples are depicted in Table 3.

**Table 3:** *Mean and Standard Deviation of Differences of Average Frequencies for undetected and detected adversarial examples.*

| | Mean Difference (Hz) | Standard Deviation (Hz) |
|---|---|---|
| Undetected Adversarial Examples | 988 | 464 |
| Detected Adversarial Examples | 1176 | 590 |

Upon performing a Student's t-test, the difference in undetected adversarial examples was found to be less than the difference in detected adversarial examples with 99% statistical significance. This suggests that the frequencies of adversarial perturbations in the undetected adversarial examples were concentrated at lower frequencies than those of detected adversarial examples. As human speech is found within these lower frequencies, it is much more difficult to disrupt or detect these adversarial examples without distorting the speech in the signal. This may explain why these adversarial examples remained undetected under the Learned Threshold Voting method. As a side effect, these undetected adversarial examples with significant perturbation in the lower frequency bands would theoretically be more perceptibly noisy to humans, as the physiology of the inner ear is fine-tuned for picking up auditory information at these frequencies [16].

Benign examples that were falsely detected as adversarial also exhibited an interesting property. In particular, the Speech Commands model achieved a classification accuracy of 92.7% on raw benign examples that were not detected as adversarial, but that accuracy fell to 40.4% for raw benign examples that were falsely detected as adversarial. The relatively low classification accuracy for the benign examples flagged as adversarial suggests that even benign examples that are classified incorrectly by the model exhibits some volatility of outputted predictions upon preprocessing, similar to adversarial examples. For reference, the model achieved 90.3% classification accuracy in general over all benign examples.

## 5. Conclusion and Future Work

Although the results of this research suggest that ensembles of audio preprocessing can be highly effective for detecting adversarial examples, it is important to note the drawbacks of the defenses discussed in this paper. An analysis of adversarial examples that went undetected by the Learned Voting Threshold method implied that those examples had more adversarial perturbations in the lower frequency bands than the adversarial examples that were detected. This suggests that attacks can optimize adversarial examples robust to the Learned Threshold Voting method by concentrating adversarial perturbations within the frequency range of human speech.

Although using ensemble detection methods may provide marginal security over using isolated preprocessing detection methods, recent work has shown that adaptive attacks on image classifiers are able to bypass ensembles of weak defenses [17], including the feature squeezing ensemble of Xu, et al.; this work could be applied to attack speech recognition models. Future work can be done in investigating stronger ensembles for detecting audio adversarial examples and other defenses that can withstand adaptive attacks. Considering the faceted usefulness of Speex compression for detecting adversarial examples, perhaps further investigation into speech coding for defending against adversarial attacks is warranted.

Nevertheless, this paper demonstrated that methods of audio preprocessing can be used to detect adversarial examples produced by the attack of Alzantot et al. on Speech Commands. Additionally this paper examined the effectiveness of various ensembles of audio preprocessing detection methods for defending against adversarial examples. While these detection methods may not be extremely effective against more adaptive attacks, this research aimed ultimately to further discussion of defenses against adversarial examples within the audio domain: a field in desperate need of more literature.

**Acknowledgments**

We are thankful to the reviewers for helpful criticism, and the UCCS LINC and VAST labs for general support. This work is supported by the National Science Foundation under Grant No. 1659788. Any opinions, findings, and conclusions or recommendations expressed in the material are those of the author(s) and do not necessarily represent the views of the National Science Foundation.

**References**

[1] C. Szegedy, W. Zaremba, I. Sutskever, J. Bruna, D. Erhan, I. J. Goodfellow, and R. Fergus, "Intriguing properties of neural networks," in International Conference on Learning Representations, 2014.

[2] I. J. Goodfellow, J. Shlens, and C. Szegedy, "Explaining and harnessing adversarial examples," in International Conference on Learning Representations, 2015.

[3] M. Alzantot, B. Balaji, and M. Srivastava, "Did you hear that? adversarial examples against automatic speech recognition," in 31st Conference on Neural Information Processing Systems (NIPS), 2017.

[4] N. Carlini and D. Wagner, "Audio adversarial examples: Targeted attacks on speech-to-text," in 1st IEEE Workshop on Deep Learning and Security, 2018.

[5] A. E. Aydemir, A. Temizel, and T. T. Temizel, "The effects of JPEG and JPEG2000 compression on attacks using adversarial examples," arXiv preprint, no. 1803.10418,

2018.

[6] A. Graese, A. Rozsa, and T. E. Boult, "Assessing threat of adversarial examples on deep neural networks," in 15th IEEE International Conference on Machine Learning and Applications (ICMLA), 2016.

[7] A. Prakash, N. Moran, S. Garber, A. DiLillo, and J. Storer, "Deflecting adversarial attacks with pixel deflection," in IEEE/CVF Conference on Computer Vision and Pattern Recognition (CVPR), 2018.

[8] Z. Yang, B. Li, P.-Y. Chen, and D. Song, "Towards mitigating audio adversarial perturbations," 2018. [Online]. Available: https: //openreview.net/forum?id=SyZ2nKJDz

[9] D. Lemmond and R. Fitzgibbons, "Adversarial examples in audio," 2018, CS4860 Final Project Report, University of Colorado, Colorado Springs Spring 2018.

[10] J.-M. Valin, "Speex: A free codec for free speech," in Proceedings of linux.conf.au, 2006. [Online]. Available: https://arxiv.org/abs/1602. 08668

[11] J.-M. Valin, K. Vos, and T. B. Terriberry, "Definition of the Opus audio codec," RFC 6716, 2012.

[12] M. R. Schroeder and B. S. Atal, "Code-excited linear prediction (CELP): High-quality speech at very low bit rates," in IEEE International Conference on Acoustics, Speech and Signal Processing, 1985, pp. 937– 940.

[13] W. Xu, D. Evans, and Y. Qi, "Feature Squeezing: Detecting Adversarial Examples in Deep Neural Networks," 2018 Network and Distributed System Security Symposium (NDSS'18), Feb. 2018.

[14] P. Warden, "Speech commands: A dataset for limited-vocabulary speech recognition," arXiv preprint, no. 1804.03209, 2018.

[15] T. N. Sainath and C. Parada, "Convolutional neural networks for small-footprint keyword spotting," in INTERSPEECH, 2015.

[16] R. L. Warren, S. Ramamoorthy, N. Ciganović, Y. Zhang, T. M. Wilson, T. Petrie, R. K. Wang, S. L. Jacques, T. Reichenbach, A. L. Nuttall, and A. Fridberger, "Minimal basilar membrane motion in low-frequency hearing," Proceedings of the National Academy of Sciences, vol. 113, no. 30, Jul. 2016.

[17] W. He, J. Wei, X. Chen, N. Carlini, and D. Song, "Adversarial example defense: Ensembles of weak defenses are not strong," in 11th USENIX Workshop on Offensive Technologies, WOOT 2017, 2017.

The 2018 Conference on Computational Linguistics and Speech Processing
ROCLING 2018, pp. 31-45
©The Association for Computational Linguistics and Chinese Language Processing

# 使用性別資訊於語者驗證系統之研究與實作

# A study and implementation on Speaker Verification System using

# Gender Information

蘇俞睿　Yu-Jui Su
國立臺灣大學資訊工程學系
Department of Computer Science and Information Engineering
National Taiwan University
shikari.su@mirlab.org

張智星　Jyh-Shing Roger Jang
國立臺灣大學資訊工程學系
Department of Computer Science and Information Engineering
National Taiwan Normal University
jang@csie.ntu.edu.tw

詹博丞 Po-Cheng Chan
中華電信研究院
Chunghwa Telecom Laboratories, Taoyuan, Taiwan
cbc@cht.com.tw

## 摘要

在語者驗證領域中，在不改變聲學模型架構之前提下，以男性與女性之語料分別訓練
的性別相關模型取代性別不相關模型，是常見的提升系統辨識率作法之一。然而，在
實際運用情形中，由於測試語者的性別是未知的，因此性別分類器在此流程下便扮演
了非常重要的角色，其準確度更會直接影響語者驗證系統的表現；而確保系統面對不
同性別之仿冒者皆能正確拒絕，亦是此作法相當重要的一項訴求。為探討不同的「語
者性別資訊運用方法」對於語者驗證系統所產生的影響，本論文實作了以 i-向量與機
率性線性判別分析模型為語者特徵與評分器之語者驗證系統，與 2 種以 i-向量為基礎
的性別分類器。本論文在分析一般使用性別相關模型之語者驗證系統的弱點後，分別
於「性別分類器表現良好」與「性別分類器表現不良」之兩大狀況下提出其他不同的
性別資訊應用方法，並分析各方法在不同的仿冒者性別組成下之表現，最後亦達成了
在各種情況下皆能讓系統表現超越傳統作法之目標。

## Abstract

For speaker verification task, one way to improve system's accuracy without changing the algorithm of acoustic model is to use gender-dependent model instead of gender-independent one. However, since test speakers' genders are not available, gender classifier plays an important role since its accuracy directly affects the performance of the speaker verification system overall. Furthermore, ensuring that the system can maintain good performance under different gender composition of test speakers is also an important issue. To explore the impact of different gender information's usage on speaker verification system, this paper implemented a speaker verification system using i-vector and PLDA model as speaker feature and scoring model respectively, and 2 i-vector-based gender classifier. After analyzing the weakness of speaker verification system using gender-dependent model in a general way, we proposed different methods for the application of gender information under the conditions when gender classifier has good and poor performance respectively. Moreover, we analyze the performance of each method under different gender composition of test speakers as well. Finally, we reached the goal of improving our system to achieve better performance than tradition practice under different circumstances.

關鍵詞：語者驗證、性別資訊、性別分類器、i-向量、機率性線性判別分析

Keywords: Speaker Verification, Gender Information, Gender Classifier, i-vector, PLDA


一、緒論

語者辨識，或稱自動語者辨識（automatic speaker recognition），是一種將人類的語音透過電子設備轉換成電子訊號後，利用演算法分析不同語者之間的聲紋特性差異，來進行語者身份辨識的工作。語者辨識的應用領域相當廣泛，除了最常見的個人設備存取控制之外，舉凡門禁系統、信用交易、犯罪偵測、電子會議輔助、刑事案件舉證等皆屬於其應用範疇；且由於其需求不斷擴大，如何增進語者辨識技術的準確度與或提升系統演算法之速度，至今仍吸引學界與業界投入大量研究心力。本論文以語者驗證作為研究主軸，主要方向為探討「語者的性別資訊」對於語者驗證系統所產生的影響，探討的項目包括以下 3 點：第一，本論文將探討前人如何利用性別資訊提升語者驗證系統之辨識率，並分析該作法之弱點；第二，本論文將提出其他性別資訊應用方法之改良，並分析各種方法適用之情況；最後，本輪文將實作性別分類器，並實際將其應用於語者驗證系統中。

## 二、實驗語料與資料配置

本論文使用了 NIST SRE 2010 與 TIMIT 兩份語料庫分別進行實驗，以下將簡介此二語料庫與資料配置。NIST SRE 2010 [1] 是一場在 2010 年由美國國家標準技術研究所（National Institute of Standards and Technology, NIST）所舉辦的語者辨識（Speaker Recognition Evaluation, SRE）比賽，本論文取其訓練資料中的 3 種資料類型：「10sec」、「core」 與「8conv」，並除去重複的語者後進行實驗，其中「10sec」為長度約 10 秒的電話對話錄音，一共有 2,257 位（男 959／女 1,298）語者，每位語者提供 1 份錄音檔；「core」為長度約 3 至 15 分鐘的電話對話錄音或麥克風錄製的面試錄音，一共有 4,004 位（男 1,817／女 2,187）語者，每位語者提供 1 份錄音檔；「8conv」為長度約 2 至 3 分鐘的電話對話錄音，一共有 445 位（男 194／女 251）語者，每位語者提供 8 份錄音檔。3 種資料類型之音檔取樣頻率為 8,000 赫茲、樣本位元數皆為 16。資料配置方面，訓練資料是以 3 種資料類型各取 2／3 語者數量，一共 4,469 位（男 1,965／女 2,504）語者的集合；測試資料則是剩下的 1／3 語者數量，一共 2,237 位（男 1,005／女 1,232）語者的集合。而關於測試資料中註冊語料與驗證語料的分配，每位語者皆僅會註冊 1 組語者模型，其中「8conv」的每組模型皆以 7 份音檔註冊而成，剩下 1 份音檔作為驗證音檔；而由於「10sec」與「core」的每位語者皆只有 1 份音檔，因此這裡將每份音檔分割為 4 等份，每組模型皆以 3 份音檔註冊而成，剩下 1 份音檔作為驗證音檔。測試資料的每一位語者皆會自驗證語料中挑選 1,000 份音檔來測試自己的語者模型，1,000 份音檔中其中 1 份是會是正樣本（屬於此語者的聲音），而其他 999 份則是隨機挑選的負樣本（不屬於此語者的聲音），因此所有欲評測的樣本一共有 $2,237 \times 1,000 = 2,237,000$ 份。

TIMIT [2] 是由德州儀器（Texas Instruments, TI）、麻省理工學院（Massachusetts Institute of Technology, MIT）與斯坦福國際研究院（SRI International）聯合提供的語料庫，其一共包含了 630 位（男 438／女 192）語者。這些語者的腔調包含了美國 8 種主要地方方言腔調，每位語者皆提供 10 份錄音檔，每份錄音檔之取樣頻率為 16,000 赫茲、樣本位元數為 16，錄音內容則為指定內容、包含豐富音素（phoneme）的一句話，每句話平均長度約為 3 秒，最長不超過 8 秒。資料配置方面，訓練資料是以男性與女性各取 2／3 語者數量，一共 420 位（男 292／女 128）語者的集合；測試資料則是剩下的 1

／3 語者數量，一共 210 位（男 146／女 64）語者的集合。而關於測試資料中註冊語料與驗證語料的分配，每位語者皆會註冊 2 組語者模型，每組模型皆以 4 份音檔註冊而成，而剩下的 2 份音檔則作為測試音檔。測試資料的每一位語者皆會自驗證語料中挑選 100 份音檔來測試自己的語者模型，100 份音檔中其中 1 份是會是正樣本，而其他 99 份則是隨機挑選的負樣本，因此所有欲評測的樣本一共有 $210 \times 2 \times 100 = 42{,}000$ 份。

## 三、實驗一：對照組

實驗一將介紹本論文設定的對照組流程與實驗結果，此實驗為完全不使用語者性別資訊的傳統語者驗證方法，亦為本論文之後所有實驗之比較依據。本實驗之流程架構如圖 1 所示：

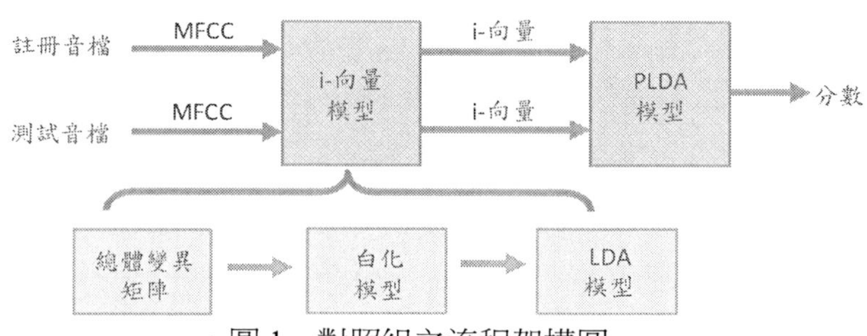


圖 1、對照組之流程架構圖

流程圖中之各項模型以 Bob toolbox [3]進行實作。由圖中可見，註冊音檔與測試音檔分別抽取 MFCC 特徵後，會經由 i-向量模型各自抽取 i-向量 [4] [5] [6]，最後經由 PLDA 模型算出分數 [7] [8] [9]；其中，此處所述之 i-向量模型裡除了包含原本用以將超向量轉化為 i-向量的總體變異矩陣之外，亦包涵了白化轉換模型 [10] 與線性判別分析模型 [11]。表 1 為對照組流程所使用的模型參數，而本論文其他語者驗證相關流程之模型參數設定亦與對照組相同：

表 1、語者驗證系統模型參數設定

| Model Parameter | | Value |
| --- | --- | --- |
| MFCC extraction | Frame size | 512 sample points |
| | Hop size | 128 sample points |
| UBM model | Number of mixture | 128 |
| | Number of training iteration | 10 |
| i-vector model | Dimension of i-vector | 300 |
| | Number of training iteration | 5 |
| LDA model | Reduced Dimension of i-vector | 50 |
| PLDA model | Dimension of speaker factor | 50 |
| | Dimension of channel factor | 50 |
| | Number of training iteration | 10 |

對照組流程的實驗結果如圖 2 所示：

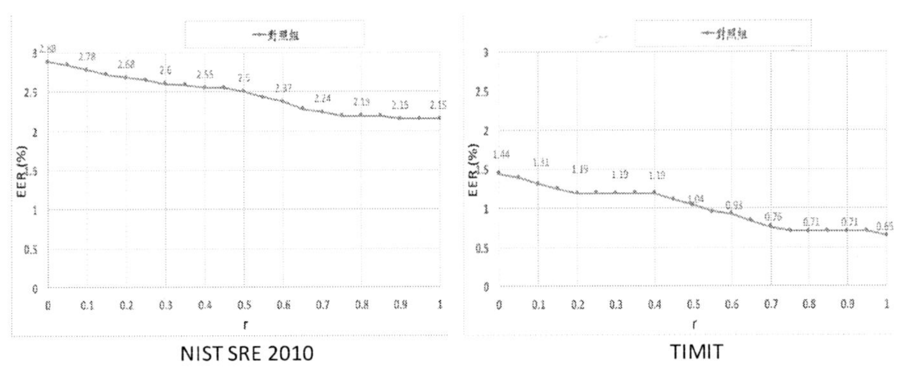


圖 2、對照組之流程架構圖

圖之左側與右側分別為 NIST SRE 2010 語料庫與 TIMIT 語料庫之實驗結果，兩張圖的縱軸為語者驗證系統之等錯誤率，單位為百分比；橫軸為 r，此 r 值代表的是「與註冊語者不同性別的仿冒者比例」，以下將簡單說明此實驗設計之意義。在前一章節中提及，本論文之資料配置形式為每一位註冊語者配對 1 份自己的音檔作為正樣本，並搭配許多其他仿冒者的聲音作為負樣本，而挑選仿冒者的一項重要考量，便是這些語者的性別。今假設語者驗證系統架設於使用者之行動裝置上，則可以考慮兩種情景，如圖 3 所示：

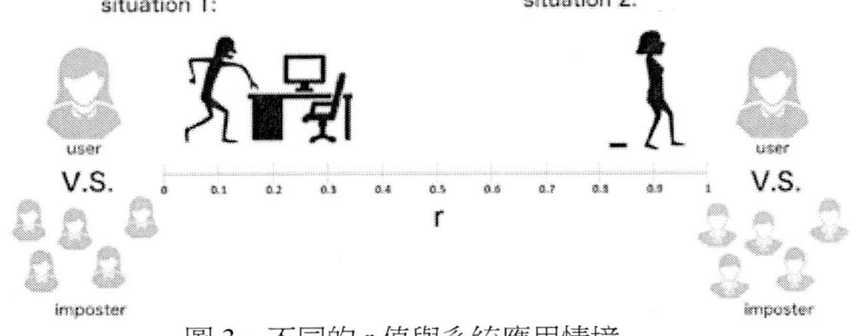


圖 3、不同的 r 值與系統應用情境

第一，當使用者到了教室或是工作場所時，若有同事或同學意圖在未經該使用者同意下存取其行動裝置，由於他們皆熟悉該使用者的聲音，因此勢必會找聲音與該使用者相像的人—至少會與該使用者同性別—來解鎖其語者驗證系統，在此情境下，我們可以假設絕大部分的仿冒者皆會和使用者同性別（事實上，NIST SRE 2010 比賽亦是設計成每個樣本的註冊方與測試方的性別皆相同，因此與此情境相同）。第二，當使用者的行動裝置（被陌生人）偷竊或不慎遺失時，由於拿到其行動裝置的人並不知曉該使用者的性別或聲音特性，因此此種情境下便不能假設仿冒者會和該使用者之性別相同，仿冒者和該使用者的性別相同的機率在此時只有 1／2，甚至更低。綜合以上兩種情境，我們便必須確保語者驗證系統在不同的 r 值，也就是不同的「仿冒者與使用者不同性別的機率」的情況下，皆應有良好的表現。因此，本論文所有的語者驗證相關實驗，皆會在不同的 r 值之下測量系統的表現。由圖 3 中可見，雖然對照組流程於 TIMIT 語料與 NIST SRE 2010 語料上的表現有明顯差距，但兩者的變化趨勢是相同的：從最左側的 r 等於 0 慢慢往最右側的 r 等於 1 移動時，系統的等錯誤率皆呈現近似線性下降的趨勢。造成此下降趨勢之原因其實非常直觀：與使用者不同性別的仿冒者，相較於同性別者，大多會與該使用者在聲紋特性上有較大的差別，造成其被系統拒絕的機率也相對高出許多，因此當 r 值越大，正樣本所得到的分數與其他負樣本相比便會相對高出許多，進而得到較低的等錯誤率。

## 四、實驗二：性別資訊應用方法 — 當性別分類器表現良好

實驗二將介紹若干種將性別資訊應用於語者驗證系統以提升其辨識率之方法，包括一般最常見作法，以及本論文提出的針對前者弱點所進行之改良方法。另外，本實驗之目的在於證明在性別分類器表現良好之前提下，藉由有效運用性別資訊，便能提升系統辨識率；因此本實驗中對於所有原本應假定為未知性別的測試語者，皆以其真實性別代替性別分類器的預測結果。

<u>前人作法（一般常見作法）</u>

本方法之流程架構如圖 4 所示：

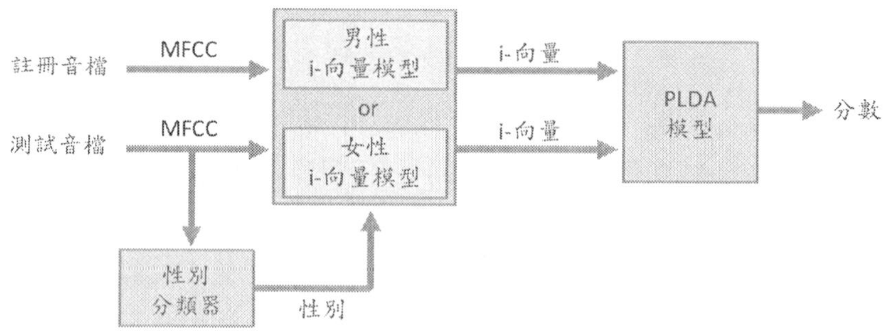


圖 4、前人作法之流程架構圖

其流程基本上與對照組流程類似，兩者不一樣的地方為：對照組之 i-向量模型是使用訓練資料中所有語者共同訓練而得來，而本作法之 i-向量模型則分為 2 個性別相關的模型，分別是使用訓練語者中的男性語者與女性語者進行訓練而得來，而所有註冊音檔或測試音檔，皆必須使用對應其語者性別之模型來抽取 i-向量。其中，註冊語者的性別可以假設是已知的，因為在實際運用情境中，我們可以要求所有使用者要註冊系統時提供自己的性別資訊；但是由於測試語者的性別是未知的，因此測試音檔必須先藉由性別分類器預測其性別，才能套入正確性別的 i-向量模型來抽取 i-向量。本做法的實驗結果如圖 5 所示：

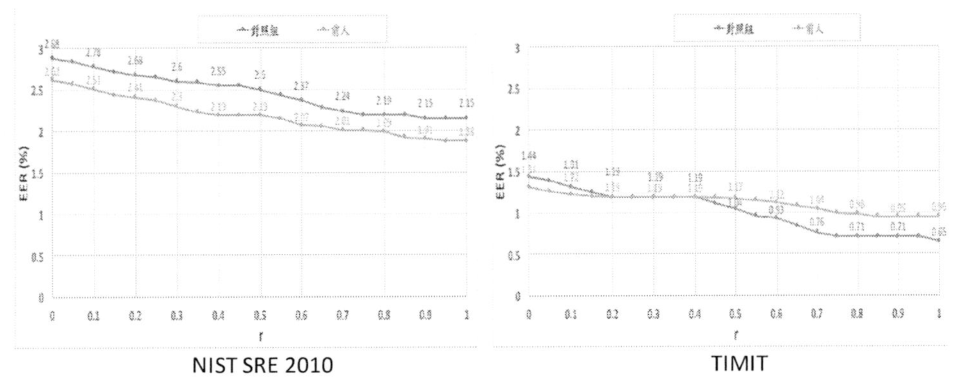


圖 5、前人作法之結果

同樣地，圖之左側與右側分別為 NIST SRE 2010 語料庫與 TIMIT 語料庫之實驗結果，兩張圖的藍線為方才對照組流程的結果，橘線則是本做法的結果。由圖中可以看到，在 NIST SRE 2010 語料中，本做法的結果從 r = 0 至 r = 1 始終都較對照組作法要進步，證明了其實用性；但反觀 TIMIT 語料，其實驗結果在最左側 r = 0 時尚較對照組進步一些，但慢慢往右側 r = 1 方向移動時，由於其等錯誤率的下降速率較對照組慢上許多，導致其結果逐漸被對照組超越，甚至被拉開距離。由於許多語者驗證比賽的樣本（如 NIST SRE 2010）並不包含註冊語者與測試語者性別不同的情形，因此許多以本作法實作的語者驗證系統，便沒能對此現象做進一部探討或進行補償措施。而本研究推測，造成上述現象的主因，是來自於本做法的一個缺陷：使用性別相關模型抽取的男性 i-向量與女性 i-向量，在空間分佈上可能存在重疊現象。圖 6 為 i-向量之理想二維點分佈圖：

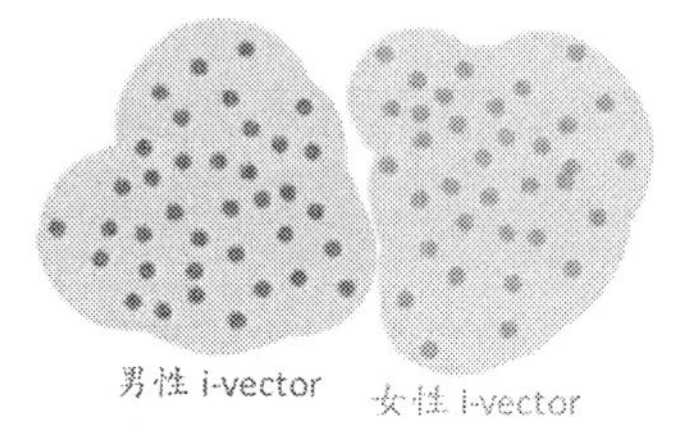


圖 6、i-向量之理想二維點分佈圖

在理想上，因為男性與女性的聲紋特性存在很大的差異，容易讓人以為 i-向量會在空間分佈上呈現男女各自群聚，且容易界定出兩群 i-向量之邊界的情形，正如同圖 6 所示。在此假設下，當一個樣本的註冊方與測試方擁有不同性別，因為兩者的 i-向量之間的距離很大，因此這個樣本便相當容易被系統拒絕。但實際情況中卻並非一定如此，尤其就男／女性 i-向量模型在訓練過程中並沒有接觸過女／男性的資料這個事實來看，我們更必須懷疑此假設之合理性。圖 7 左右兩圖是分別使用主成分分析（Principal Components Analysis, PCA）和 t-分佈隨機相鄰嵌入（T-distributed Stochastic Neighbor Embedding, TSNE），將訓練資料中的 i-向量降至二維平面所繪製的點分佈圖：

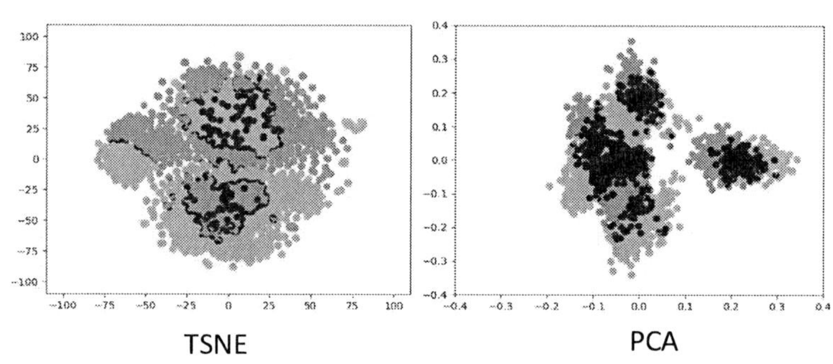


圖 7、i-向量之實際二維點分佈圖—以 TSNE 與 PCA 將 i-向量降為二維

由兩張圖我們能清楚看到，兩個性別的 i-向量群在空間分佈上確實存在重疊的情形。這種現象會造成語者驗證系統的錯誤率上升，尤其在當欲測試的樣本中含有大量註冊方與測試方不同性別的情形，即 r 有較大的值時更為顯著。為方便討論，此處假設系統之評分器僅以註冊方與測試方 i-向量之間的歐氏距離作為判斷是否為同一語者之唯一標準。在不分男、女資料所訓練出來的混合 i-向量模型，在訓練資料足夠的前提下，我們可以假定其會盡量將不同語者的 i-向量在空間上彼此分開；但是，正如方才所述，由於男／女性 i-向量模型在訓練過程中並沒有接觸過女／男性的資料，因此便很有可能產生特定男性語者與女性語者的 i-向量距離過度相近的現象，使得系統容易將他們誤判為同一

語者。此現象在訓練流程中，會使得系統的評分器─機率線性判別分析模型容易被混淆；在測試流程中，也容易會造成不同性別間語者被錯誤判斷成同一語者的比例較對照組流程還要高的現象。因此，針對因不同性別 i-向量空間重疊現象所造成的上述缺陷，本論文接下來將提出一種簡單的改良機制，以令結果獲得改善。

<u>方法一：拒絕與註冊者性別不符之測試者</u>
此改良方法之流程架構如圖 8 所示：

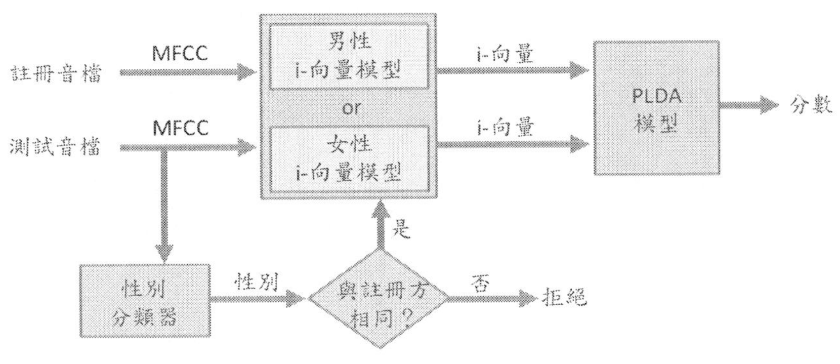


圖 8、方法一之流程架構圖

此版本之流程與前人作法類似，不同之處在於其多出了一個步驟：在以性別分類器判斷出測試語者之性別後，須檢視其是否與註冊語者之性別相同，若相同，則繼續進行原本的流程─以性別相關模型抽出雙方的 i-向量之後，以機率性線性判別分析模型計算出分數；若不同，則直接拒絕此測試語者（打上非常低的分數），因為不同性別的聲音不可能屬於同一位語者。如此一來，便能消除在前人作法中因不同性別的 i-向量在空間分佈上的重疊現象而造成的錯誤接受率攀升之問題。方法一流程的實驗結果如圖 9 所示。同樣地，藍線與橘線分別為對照組流程與前人作法流程之實驗結果，而新增的紅線則是

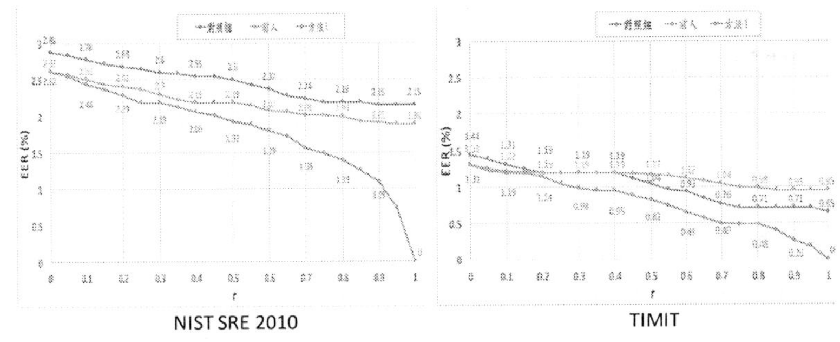


圖 9、方法一流程之結果

本方法一流程之實驗結果。在圖中，我們可以看到在最左側 r = 0 的時候，因為沒有註冊語者與測試語者性別不同的樣本，因此方法一與前人做法的表現是相同的；但慢慢往右側 r＝1 方向移動時，由於註冊方與測試方性別不同的樣本皆被系統拒絕，因此方法一在兩種語料的等錯誤率始終低於對照組，甚至越往右便越與對照組的結果拉開距離；到最後 r＝1 時，由於所有錯誤樣本皆成功被系統拒絕，等錯誤率便可達到 0%。此實驗結果除證明了前人做法確實存在著本論文所預測的缺陷與造成它的原因，亦證明了方法一流程在改善此種缺陷上的效果。

## 五、實驗三：性別分類器實作

<u>支持向量機性別分類器</u>

此分類器同樣以性別不相依模型產生的 i-向量作為特徵，並以支持向量機作為二元分類器，判斷音檔的性別。本分類器之實驗結果如圖 10 所示：

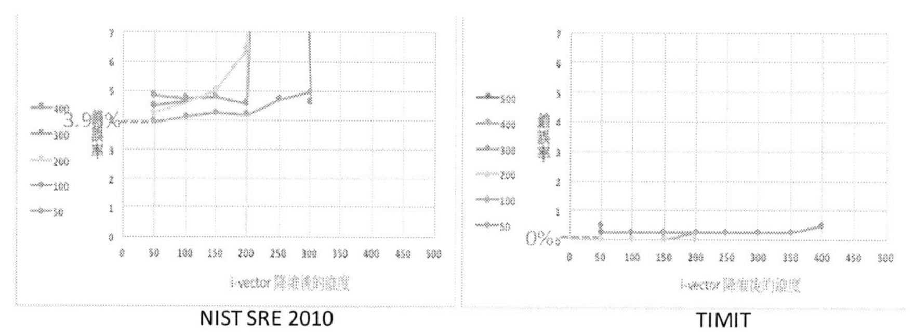


圖 10、支持向量機性別分類器之結果

本分類器之實驗與前者相同，調整了 i-向量模型中的 i-向量之初始維度與其降維後的維度，兩者分別在圖 10 中以不同顏色的線與圖之橫軸表示；此外，亦調整了支持向量機中最重要的 2 個參數：cost 與 gamma。在圖中，每一個數據點皆是將 cost 與 gamma 分別在集合{0.1, 1, 10, 100, 1000}與{0.01, 0.1, 1, 10, 100}內進行排列組合，並以網格搜尋法（grid search）所尋找到的最佳參數組合之結果。同樣地，圖中的紅色虛線所標記的是兩種語料庫中最佳參數所表現出的結果，NIST SRE 2010 語料庫的錯誤率可達 3.93%，而 TIMIT 語料庫則可以達到完全分類正確，即 0%錯誤率的結果。

<u>神經網路性別分類器</u>

此分類器同樣以性別不相依模型產生的 i-向量作為特徵，並以中間 4 層的神經網路模型作為二元分類器，判斷音檔的性別。而神經網路模型的參數（keras API）如表 2 所示：

| 模型參數 | 超參數 |
| --- | --- |
| batch_size = 128 | kernel_initializer='glorot_normal' |
| epochs = 200 | bias_initializer='zeros' |
| loss = binary_crossentropy | BatchNormalization() |
| optimizer = Adam(lr=3e-4) | Activation('relu') |
| metrics = 'accuracy' | Dropout(0.35) |

表 2、神經網路性別分類器之模型參數

其中，模型的每層節點數量由輸入至輸出端線性減少，舉例來說，若 i-向量維度數為 n，神經網路維中間層數為 4 層，則模型之各層結點數則如圖 11 所示：

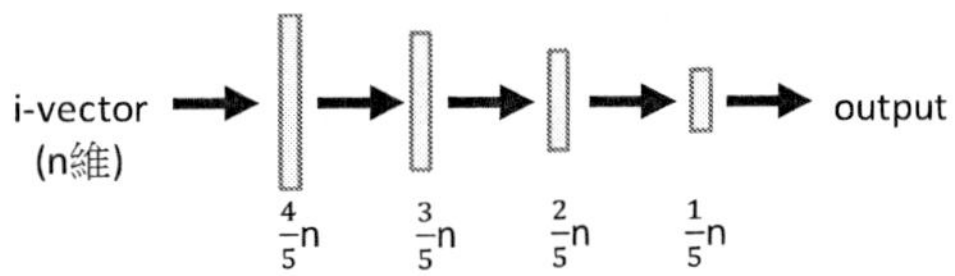



圖 11、神經網路模型之形狀

本分類器之實驗結果如圖 12 所示：

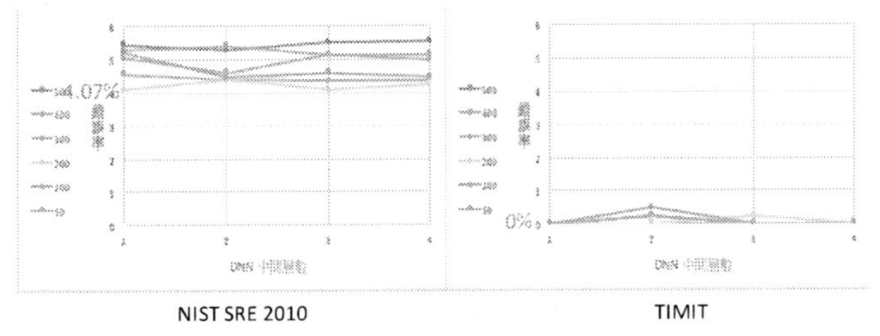



圖 12、神經網路性別分類器之結果

與前一個分類器不同的是，本實驗所使用的 i-向量一律維持初始維度，而不使用線性判別分析模型進行降維，而本分類器之實驗過程調整的兩個參數則改為是 i-向量之初始維度與神經網路模型的中間層數，兩者分別在圖 12 中以不同顏色的線與圖之橫軸表示。同樣地，圖中的紅色虛線所標記的是兩種語料庫中最佳參數所表現出的結果，NIST SRE 2010 語料庫的錯誤率可達 4.07%，而 TIMIT 語料庫則與支持向量機性別分類器一樣，可以達到完全分類正確，即 0%錯誤率的結果。

## 六、實驗四：性別資訊應用方法 — 當性別分類器表現不良

實驗四同樣將介紹若干種性別資訊應用於語者驗證系統之方法，但不同於實驗二以其真實性別代替性別分類器的預測結果，本實驗將使用在實驗三中實作的性別分類器，並特別針對當性別分類器表現不良的情況，介紹其他不同於實驗二的性別資訊應用方法。

<u>實際套用性別分類器所預測性別</u>

在實驗三中，因 TIMIT 語料庫在性別分類器上可以達到零錯誤率的效果，故其於語者驗證流程中套用實驗三所實作的性別分類器之結果，將與實驗二無異，因此本章節之實驗將僅包含 NIST SRE 2010 語料的部分。圖 13 是對照組流程與將在實驗三中於 NIST SRE 2010 語料中表現最好的支持向量機性別分類器套用於實驗二各流程之實驗結果：

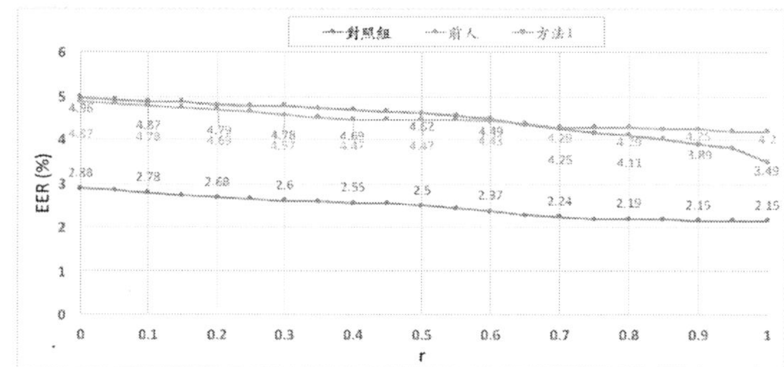


圖 13、各項語者驗證流程使用支持向量機性別分類器之實驗結果

同樣地，藍線、橘線、紅線分別代表對照組、前人作法與方法一的結果，由圖中可以見到，在實際套用真實性別分類器之後，實驗二中的所有流程在不同 r 值下的實驗結果產生了明顯的退步，甚至比對照組流程之結果更差。雖支持向量機性別分類器之錯誤率僅有 3.93%，但這些少量的錯誤卻會造成語者驗證系統之表現造成巨大影響，其原因一樣可分為錯誤接受與錯誤拒絕兩種情形來探討：我們可以想像，當註冊語者與測試語者為不同人時，即使性別分類器誤判了測試語者的性別，系統錯誤接受此負樣本的機率仍然不高。但當註冊語者與測試語者為同一人，一旦測試語者被誤判性別，使用前人作法的系統會分別以不同性別之模型為註冊方與測試方抽取 i-向量，此種情形幾乎必然會造成系統為此正樣本評出較非常低的分數；而使用方法一流程之系統，在檢測出註冊語者與

測試語者分屬不同性別後，便會對此樣本予以拒絕；最後，使用方法二流程之系統，由
於訓練資料中同一語者的 i-向量中用以代表性別的最後一維特徵皆有相同的數值，因此
當評分器見到註冊語者與測試語者在該維特徵之數值相異，自然同樣會評出非常低的分
數。綜上所述，實驗二的各種方法皆會為大量正樣本評出低落的分數，進而使得等錯誤
率跟著大幅提升。


方法二：檢查測試音檔的男女性別機率差

在先前的實驗中，我們可以見到圖 13 與圖 9 之差距來自於少數遭誤判性別的測試語者
被實驗二之各流程系統錯誤拒絕。倘若我們能將這些測試語者遭誤判性別的樣本與其他
樣本分別交由對照組流程與實驗二之改良流程進行判別，理論上便能得到近似於實驗二
之效果。若欲實際執行此概念，要如何預測性別分類器能否正確預測測試語者之性別，
必然是此方法必須面對的第一個問題，而本流程將提供一個較簡單的預測方法：以測試
音檔的性別機率來預測性別分類器能否正確預測其性別。實驗三所實做的性別分類器，
除了能預測一位語者之性別，更可以精確地計算出該語者屬於男性或女性的機率，而若
一份音檔的兩個機率值相差非常多，代表性別分類器對此音檔之性別預測結果有較大的
信心，因此便將此樣本交由方法一流程進行判別，反之，若一份音檔的兩個機率值相差
過小，則代表性別分類器的判斷有較大的機會出錯，因此便將此樣本交由對照組流程進
行判別。依此概念，便可以衍生出如圖 14 之流程：

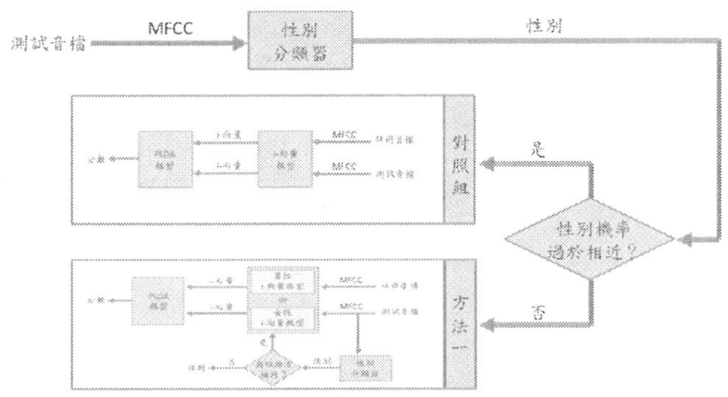

圖 14、方法二之流程架構圖

本流程使用實驗三中的支持向量機性別分類器為測試音檔進行性別預測，而系統之整體

表現與「測試音檔性別對數機率差之門檻值（t）」之關係則如圖 15 所示：

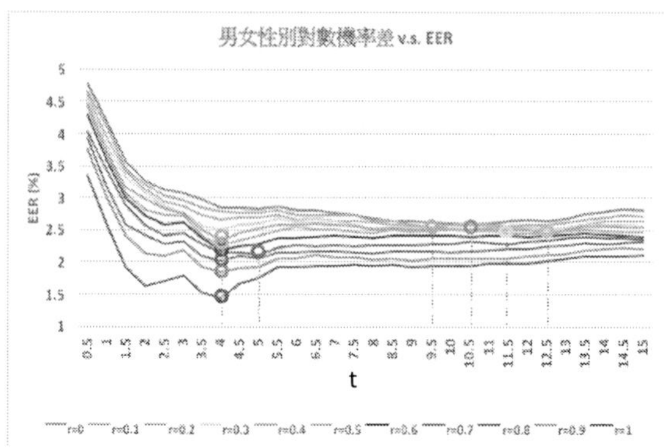

圖 15、方法二流程之選定測試音檔性別機率差門檻

由圖中可見，每條線皆呈現出兩側高、中間低的現象，而每條線的最低點位置（在圖中以圓圈標出）亦不相同，例如：當 r 值較小（0～0.3）時，這些線條之最低點出現在圖的右半部，顯示其最佳門檻值偏大；而當 r 值較大（0.4～1）時，這些線條之最低點出現在圖的左半部，顯示其最佳門檻值偏小。由此現象可以推斷，男女性別機率差之門檻並沒有最佳解，而是會隨著資料的 r 值而變動。圖 16 為方法二流程指定 t 值為 4 時之實驗結果：

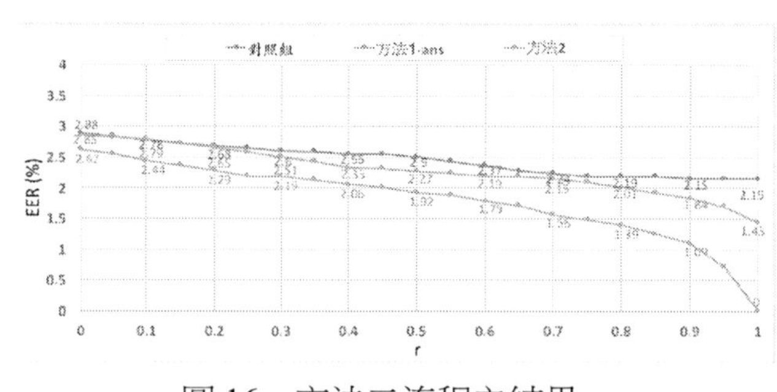

圖 16、方法二流程之結果

同樣地，藍線與橘線分別代表對照組與方法一流程使用真實性別代替性別分類器之結果，而新增的綠線則是本方法二流程之結果。我們可以看到，此方法二流程終於達到了最初的預期，也就是在性別分類器表現不良之前提下，仍然超越對照組流程的目標。

五、結論

本論文之各項實驗結果證實，無論性別分類器的表現或仿冒者的性別組成，皆會影響與者驗證系統的表現，因此不同的性別資訊運用方法，皆各有其適用的前提。以下整理本論文所使用的各種方法與其對應的適用情形作為總結：

(1) 當我們能確保系統的使用者可以提供品質良好的錄音，則性別分類器有較大機會表現良好，因此可選擇方法一。

(2) 當我們不能保證使用者能提供優良品質之錄音，則性別分類器有較大機會表現不良，因此在這種情況下，方法二為較合適之選項。

(3) 傳統作法的優點為不必花費額外時間進行性別預測，因此當我們對於系統的整體運算速度有較高的需求，則可以選擇維持原來的傳統作法。

## 參考文獻


[1] https://www.nist.gov/itl/iad/mig/speaker-recognition-evaluation-2010

[2] Garofolo, John S., et al. TIMIT Acoustic-Phonetic Continuous Speech Corpus LDC93S1. Web Download. Philadelphia: Linguistic Data Consortium, 1993.

[3] Anjos, André, et al. "Continuously reproducing toolchains in pattern recognition and machine learning experiments." (2017).

[4] Kenny, Patrick. "Joint factor analysis of speaker and session variability: Theory and algorithms." *CRIM, Montreal,(Report) CRIM-06/08-13* 14 (2005): 28-29.

[5] Kenny, Patrick, et al. "A study of interspeaker variability in speaker verification." *IEEE Transactions on Audio, Speech, and Language Processing* 16.5 (2008): 980-988.

[6] Dehak, Najim, et al. "Front-end factor analysis for speaker verification." *IEEE Transactions on Audio, Speech, and Language Processing* 19.4 (2011): 788-798.

[7] Prince, Simon JD, and James H. Elder. "Probabilistic linear discriminant analysis for inferences about identity." Computer Vision, 2007. ICCV 2007. IEEE 11th International Conference on. IEEE, 2007.

[8] Kenny, Patrick. "Bayesian speaker verification with heavy-tailed priors." Odyssey. 2010.

[9] Garcia-Romero, Daniel, and Carol Y. Espy-Wilson. "Analysis of i-vector length normalization in speaker recognition systems." *Twelfth Annual Conference of the International Speech Communication Association*. 2011.

[10]Mika, Sebastian, et al. "Fisher discriminant analysis with kernels." Neural networks for signal processing IX, 1999. Proceedings of the 1999 IEEE signal processing society workshop.. Ieee, 1999.

[11]Lyu, Siwei, and Eero P. Simoncelli. "Nonlinear extraction of independent components of natural images using radial gaussianization." *Neural computation* 21.6 (2009): 1485-1519.

The 2018 Conference on Computational Linguistics and Speech Processing
ROCLING 2018, pp. 46-60
©The Association for Computational Linguistics and Chinese Language Processing

# 會議語音辨識使用語者資訊之語言模型調適技術

# On the Use of Speaker-Aware Language Model Adaptation

# Techniques for Meeting Speech Recognition

陳映文　Ying-wen Chen，羅天宏　Tien-hong Lo，張修瑞　Hsiu-jui Chang，趙偉成
Wei-Cheng Chao，陳柏琳　Berlin Chen
國立臺灣師範大學資訊工程學系
Department of Computer Science and Information Engineering
National Taiwan Normal University
{cliffchen, teinhonglo, 60647028S,60647061S, berlin}@ntnu.edu.tw

## 摘要

本論文試圖減緩會議語音辨識時語者間用語特性不同所造成的問題。多個語者的存在可能代表有多種的語言模式；更進一步地說，人們在講話時並沒有嚴格地遵循文法，而且通常會有說話延遲、停頓或個人慣用語以及其它獨特的說話方式。但是，過去會議語音辨識中的語言模型大都不會針對不同的語者進行調整，而是假設不同的語者間擁有相同的語言使用模式，將包含多個語者的文字轉寫合成一個訓練集，藉此訓練單一的語言模型。為突破此假設，本研究希望針對不同語者為語言模型的訓練和預測提供額外的資訊，即是語言模型的語者調適。本論文考慮兩種測試階段的情境—「已知語者」和「未知語者」，並提出了對應此兩種情境的語者特徵擷取方法，以及探討如何利用語者特徵來輔助語言模型的訓練。我們分別在中文和英文會議語音辨識任務進行一系列語言模型的語者調適實驗，其結果顯示本論文所提出的語言模型無論是在已知語者，還是未知語者情境下都有良好的表現，並且比基礎類神經網路語言模型有較佳的效能。

## Abstract

This paper embarks on alleviating the problems caused by a multiple-speaker situation occurring frequently in a meeting for improved automatic speech recognition (ASR). There are a wide variety of ways for speakers to utter in the multiple-speaker situation. That is to say, people do not strictly follow the grammar when speaking and usually have a tendency to stutter while speaking, or often use personal idioms and some unique ways of speaking. Nevertheless, the existing language models employed in automatic transcription of meeting recordings rarely account for these facts but instead assume that all speakers participating in a meeting share the same speaking style or word-usage behavior. In turn, a single language model is built with all the manual transcripts of utterances compiled from multiple speakers that were taken holistically as the training set. To relax such an assumption, we endeavor to augment additional information cues into the training phase and the prediction phase of language modeling to accommodate the variety of speaker-related characteristics, through the process of speaker adaptation for language modeling. To this end, two disparate scenarios, i.e., "known speakers" and "unknown speakers," for the prediction phase are taken into consideration for developing methods to extract speaker-related information cues to aid in the training of language models. Extensive experiments respectively carried out on automatic transcription of Mandarin and English meeting recordings show that the proposed language models along with different mechanisms for speaker adaption achieve good performance gains in relation to the baseline neural network based language model compared in this study.

關鍵詞：會議語音辨識、語言模型、語者調適、遞迴式類神經網路

Keywords: speech recognition, language modeling, speaker adaptation, recurrent neural networks.

## 一、緒論

語音辨識技術越趨成熟，生活中隨處可見其應用；自動語音辨識技術(Automatic Speech Recognition, ASR)讓電腦能聽得懂人類的語言，也就是試圖理解人類在發音上和用語上的規則與內容。語言模型是一種將文字文本模型化的技術，在語音辨識任務上，語言模型可以判斷一條詞序列是否符合訓練文本的所隱含的規則或規律性。常用於語音辨識的 $N$ 連詞模型是利用 $N$ 連詞的發生機率模型化文本中詞彙共同出現的關係。但是 $N$ 連詞模型在面臨資料過於稀疏(Data Sparseness)時，便有難以估測的問題。原因是 $N$ 連詞模型假設每個詞有各自獨立的語意，僅從統計的觀點來考慮彼此共同出現關係並估測模型[1]。類神經網路便可以解決這個問題，因為類神經網路語言模型可以習得詞語的分布式表示(Distributed Representation) [2]，使得詞彙間的語意關係能被表示出來。據此，透過接續串接的前饋式神經網路(Feedforward Neural Networks, FNN)或是遞迴式神經網路(Recurrent Neural Networks, RNN)可以來做預測。近幾年已有許多的研究嘗試改良前饋式神經網路，並用應用到不同的自然語言處理和語音辨識任務上[3-8]。

會議語音語料和一般新聞、朗讀等，較為嚴謹的語料有非常大的差異[9]，會議語

料通常有著冷門用詞、短語句、語言混雜使用和個人用語習慣等特性；有鑑於此，本研究嘗試針對不同語者有著不同的說話習慣的特性，來發展改良的語言模型架構與訓練方式。從統計的觀點來看，每種語言都有一套文法，但是實際上人們說話時，並不會嚴格遵守文法，且會擁有習慣用語或是口吃等獨特的說話方式；但是現今常見的用於語音辨識的語言模型，並不會針對不同語者做不同的調整，而是將整份訓練資料當作一種語言模式。所以我們希望根據不同的語者，對語言模型的訓練與預測提供額外的資訊，也就是對語言模型作語者調適(Speaker Adaptation)。為此，本論文考慮兩種測試階段的情境—「已知語者」和「未知語者」，並提出了對應此兩種情境的語者特徵擷取方法，以及探討如何利用語者特徵來輔助語言模型的訓練。

## 二、類神經網路語言模型相關研究

至今，類神經網路應用在語言模型變化繁多，最早的應用可回溯於 Yoshua Bengio 在 2003 年提出的類神經網路語言模型，在[2]中將 $N$ 連詞的估測交由類神經網路來計算。另一方面，為了改善 $N$ 連詞無法應付資料太過稀疏的缺點，他也將一個重要的概念—詞嵌入(Word Embeddings)，應用在類神經網路語言模型中。在 2010 年，有學者提出了遞迴式類神經網路語言模型(Recurrent Neural Network Language Model, RNNLM)[10]，讓語言模型不再受到 $N$ 連詞的限制，歷史詞不再只能是 $N$-1 個詞。但是這個方法的缺點是模型難以訓練，並且容易遭受梯度消失或爆炸(Gradient Vanishing or Exploding)的問題[8]。Martin Sundermeyer 在 2012 年提出了利用長短期記憶(Long Short-Term Memory, LSTM)語言模型解決這個問題[11, 12]。從此，LSTM 語言模型一直是被視為最好的語言模型架構之一；但是也有些學者試圖使用其它架構建模，例如 Yann N. Dauphin 在 2016 年提出了在摺積式類神經網路上面加上閥門(Gate)，能稍微的改善語言模型效能，但是也因為它的網路過於複雜而產生訓練不易等問題[6]。

　　類神經網路語言模型因執行效率導致兩個問題，其一，難以用在語音辨識的第一階段解碼(First Pass Decoding)，所以通常用在第二階段的語言模型重新排序(Rescoring)；其二，只能將類神經網路應用在 $M$ 最佳候選詞序列($M$-best List)的重新排序，而不能應用在詞圖(Lattice)。為了解決這個問題，Xunying Liu 提出藉由減少詞圖的分支以加速詞圖中候選詞序列的重新排序。它屬於一種近似的方法，所以會使得結果略遜於候選詞序列重新排序，但卻能使類神經網路語言模型也可有效應用在詞圖重新排序[13]。

## 三、類神經語言模型應用於語音辨識

RNN 或 LSTM 語言模型在做預測時，需要經過數個矩陣運算，而不像傳統 $N$ 連詞語言模型僅需透過查表來完成。如前面所提到，因為它們在執行效能上的限制，所以多半是使用在第一階段解碼過產生詞圖，並將詞圖上可能的候選詞序列重新計分。另一方面，同樣因為執行效率，詞圖需經過候選詞序列的刪減(Pruning)才能直接重新計分，缺點是會喪失一些候選詞序列的部分路徑。或是藉由 $N$ 連詞語言模型產生 $M$ 最佳候選詞序列 (*M-best List*)，再將之重新排序。圖一是 AMI 英文會議語音辨識任務測試集(請參見第五節)中 1,000 候選詞序列被詞圖包含的查全率(Recall)。

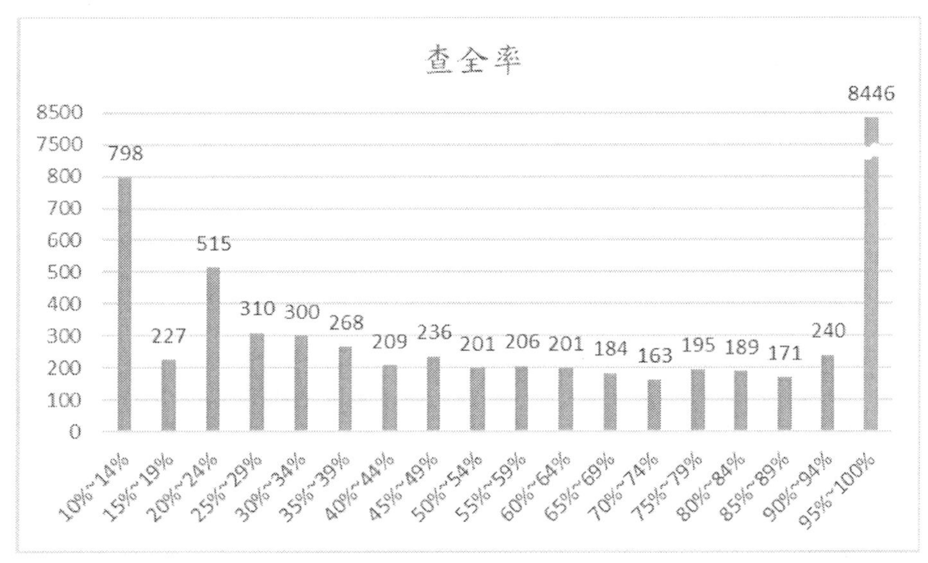


圖一、1,000 候選詞序列被詞圖包含的查全率

可以由圖一發現，1,000 候選詞序列中有許多詞序列並沒有在詞圖重新排序時被計算，95~100%只佔全部的 64.68%。另一方面，從表一所示(AMI 英文會議語音辨識任務)詞錯誤率數據也可以發現，就此會議語音語料庫，詞圖重新排序並不會比 $M$ 最佳候選詞序列重新排序的結果來的好。驗證過去研究的實驗一致 [13]。依據此結果，我們的語言模型調適實驗將會在 $M$ 最佳候選詞序列重新排序時進行。

表一、詞圖重新排序與 $M$ 最佳候選詞序列重新排序($M$=1,000)之比較

| 詞錯誤率 | 發展集 | 測試集 |
|---|---|---|
| 1,000 候選詞序列重新排序 | 21.17% | 20.41% |
| 詞圖重新排序 | 21.53% | 20.75% |

# 四、語者調適於會議語音辨識所使用之語言模型

## 4.1 問題解析

在會議語音辨識任務中，待轉寫的語音紀錄常會包含多個語者，不同語者間其實存在用語和講話習慣的差異，但是過去用於會議語音辨識的語言模型，並不會考慮不同語者所造成語言使用行為不同的問題。以下將探討如何運用「訓練語料中的語者資訊」來輔助語言模型的訓練以達到語者調適的效果。

在第一階段的語音辨識的過程，通常基於當語音訊號$X$發生時詞序列$W$的事後機率來進行語言解碼，並可化簡成依$P(X|W)P(W)$來決定詞序列$W$是最終語音辨識輸出的可能性(或所謂的排序分數)，如式(1)所示。

$$P(W|X) = \frac{P(X|W)P(W)}{P(X)} \propto P(X|W)P(W) \tag{1}$$

其中，$P(W)$通常以$N$連詞語言模型來估計，$P(X|W)$則可透過聲學模型來估計。藉由這兩個模型的相乘可算出候選詞序列$W$的分數，並經由語言解碼過程，適當地修剪候選詞序列而形成詞圖(Lattice)或$M$最佳候選詞序列($M$-best List)。接著，在第二階段語言模型重新排序時，我們可使用類神經網路語言模型重新估測$P(W)$，而達到候選詞序重新排序的目的(以$M$最佳候選詞序重新排序為例)：

$$W^* = \underset{W' \in M-best}{\operatorname{argmax}} P(X|W')P(W') \tag{2}$$

接著，我們將說明如何運用語者資訊輔助語言模型的訓練，以達到語者調適的效果。

(一) 已知每一條詞序列對應的語者為$k$時(假設總共有$K$位語者)：

$$P(W') = \sum_{k' \in K} P(W'|k')P(k') \tag{3}$$

若其中 $P(k') := \begin{cases} 1, & k' = k \\ 0, & k' \neq k \end{cases}$ ，則

$$P(W') = \sum_{k' \in K} P(W'|k')P(k') = P(W'|k) \tag{4}$$

依據全機率定理(Total Probability Theorem)，$P(W')$可以寫成$\sum_{k' \in K} P(W'|k')P(k')$，而當

已知詞序列對應的語者為$k$時，便可得到具有語者資訊的機率式(也就是語者調適過後的語言模型)$P(W'|k)$來估測詞序列$W'$的機率。

(二) 未知每一條詞序列對應的語者時：

$$P(W') = \sum_{k' \in K} P(W'|k')P(k') = \sum_{k' \in K} P(W'|k') \sum_{W''} P(k'|W'')P(W'') \tag{5}$$

若其中 $P(W'') = \begin{cases} 1, & W'' = W' \\ 0, & W'' \neq W' \end{cases}$，則

$$P(W') = \sum_{k' \in K} P(W'|k')P(k'|W') \tag{6}$$

當未知詞序列的語者時，同樣依據全機率定理將$P(W')$展開；但是此時$P(k)$因為是未知語者，所以再次依據全機率公式將$P(k')$拆解成$\sum_{W''} P(k'|W'')P(W'')$。因為詞序列已知是$W'$，所以當$W''$為$W'$時，$P(W'') = 1$，其餘為 0。更具體地說，進行第二階段語言模型重新排序時，我們先對每個候選詞序列$W'$估測各語者$k'$發生的機率$P(k'|W')$，並使語者調適過後的語言模型$P(W'|k')$來共同估測$P(W')$。在下一節，我將說明如何估測$P(k|W')$和$P(W'|k)$，其中$P(k|W')$涉及到語者特徵的擷取，而$P(W'|k)$是探討如何將語者特徵運用在具語者調適性的語言模型訓練和測試。

## 4.2 語者特徵的擷取

本篇論文提出兩種情境的語者特徵擷取方法。第一種情境是假設語者已知，可先用所有語者各自對應的訓練文本擷取出專屬的特徵；每個候選詞序列的語者特徵便是直接使用特定語者已擷取好的語者特徵，來做為語言模型額外的輸入資訊。此種預先擷取特徵的方法稱為「語者用詞特徵模型(Speaker Word-Usage Characteristics Model)」。而第二種情境是假設語者未知，所以必須動態地從每個候選詞序列擷取出隱藏的語者特徵，再該語者特徵來輔助語言模型。為此，我們提出了動態產生語者特徵的方法，即「語者慣用語模型(Speaker Slang Model)」。以下會對兩種情境的模型方法做進一步的介紹。

### 4.2.1 語者用詞特徵模型(Speaker Word-Usage Characteristics Model)

我們希望能夠擷取出不同語者使用詞彙的特性或頻率資訊。為此，我們提出三種產生語者特徵的單詞模型：分別為，詞頻模型(TF-based Model)、基於機率式潛在語意分析模

型(PLSA-based Model) [14]和語者特殊用詞模型(Speaker Specific Model, SSM)。

(一) 基於詞頻模型(TF-based Model)

此模型希望表現出某一位語者經常使用詞彙的頻率資訊，將此語者所說過的所有語句$s$基於其詞頻建模成語言模型：

$$P(t|s) = \frac{c(t,s)}{\sum_{t' \in s} c(t',s)} \tag{7}$$

其中$s$是語句，$c(t,s)$是計算詞$t$在語句$s$的出現次數。然後再將每一個語句的語言模型線性結合(Linear Combination)，其中每一個語句模型的權重相等。「基於詞頻模型」雖能表現每位語者不同的用詞，但是會有以下兩項缺點：

1. 此模型的維度是詞典的大小，過於龐大且稀疏。為了解決這個問題，我們提出第二種語者用詞模型，「基於機率式潛在語意分析的模型(PLSA-based Model)」，此模型可將語者詞彙使用資訊投影至潛在的語意空間，以達到降維的效果。

2. 此模型因為只計算詞頻，所以背景詞(Background Word)會使語者模型間差異不大。有鑒於此，我們提出「特殊用詞模型」，藉濾掉頻繁出現的背景詞，提升語者模型之間的鑑別度。

(二) 基於機率式潛在語意分析的模型(PLSA-based Model)

有別於基於詞頻模型，PLSA[14]是藉由找出潛在語意空間，以重新估測語者模型

$$P(t|s) = \sum_{k=1}^{K} P(t|z_k)P(z_k|s) \tag{8}$$

其模型參數可藉由期望值最大化(Expectation Maximization, EM)演算法來估測，其目標函數(Objective Function) $F_{\text{PLSA}}$表示如下：

$$F_{\text{PLSA}} = \sum_{s \in S} \sum_{t \in V} c(t,s) \log\left(\sum_{k=1}^{K} P(t|z_k)P(z_k|s)\right) \tag{9}$$

式(9)的目標是找出能最大化$F_{\text{PLSA}}$的$P(t|z_k)$與$P(z_k|s)$。為了達到降維的目的，所以我們取用估測得到的模型參數$p(z_k|s)$做為語者的特徵。

(三) 語者特殊用詞模型(Speaker Specific Word Model, SSWM)

為了提升語者模型之間的鑑別度，我們提出意在減少背景詞彙影響的特殊用詞模型。假
設每位語者模型間，詞彙使用規律可由語者特殊用詞模型和背景詞模型的組合表示：

$$P(t|s) = \sum_{x \in \{BG,SSWM\}} \lambda_x P(t|\theta_x) \tag{10}$$

其中$P(t|\theta_{BG})$代表背景詞模型，$P(t|\theta_{SSWM})$代表語者特殊用詞模型。而語者特殊用詞模
型的訓練目標函數$F_{SSWM}$可表示為

$$F_{SSWM} = \sum_{s \in S} \sum_{t \in V} c(t,s) \, log \left( \sum_{x \in \{bg,sswm\}} \lambda_x P(t|\theta_x) \right) \tag{11}$$

根據式(11)的訓練目標函數，我們同樣可使用期望值最大化(EM)演算法來估測參數。在
**E** 步驟以現有的模型參數求得$P(\theta_x)$的期望值，基於 E 步驟得到的期望值，在 **M** 步驟最
大化目標函數，重複直到收斂，便可以得到特殊用詞模型$P(t|\theta_{SSWM})$。

    **E** 步驟(Expectation Step)：

$$P(\theta_x) = \frac{\lambda_x P(t|\theta_x)}{\sum_{x' \in \{BG,SSWM\}} \lambda_{x'} P(t|\theta_{x'})} \tag{12}$$

    **M** 步驟(Maximization Step)：

$$P(t|\theta_{SSWM}) = \frac{\sum_{s \in S} c(t,s)\, P(\theta_{SSWM})}{\sum_{t' \in V} \sum_{s \in S} c(t',s)\, P(\theta_{SSWM})} \tag{13}$$

儘管單詞模型能夠表現語者的用詞習慣，但是這類單詞模型的方法具有兩項缺點：(1)
無法表現語者的前後文用語習慣；(2)測試語句(候選詞序列)也必須有對應的語者資訊。


### 4.2.2 語者慣用語模型(Speaker Slang Model, SSM)

上述的方法注重的是語者的用詞特徵，用單詞模型的結構描述語者。但是除了用詞外，
說話時人們也常會有習慣性的用語，且並不限於單一詞彙，例如：有的人說「對啊」時
會習慣性的講兩次變成，「對啊、對啊」。為此，我們希望設計出能表示慣用語特徵的語
者模型。在本研究，我們使用摺積式類神經網路(Convolutional Neural Network, CNN)對

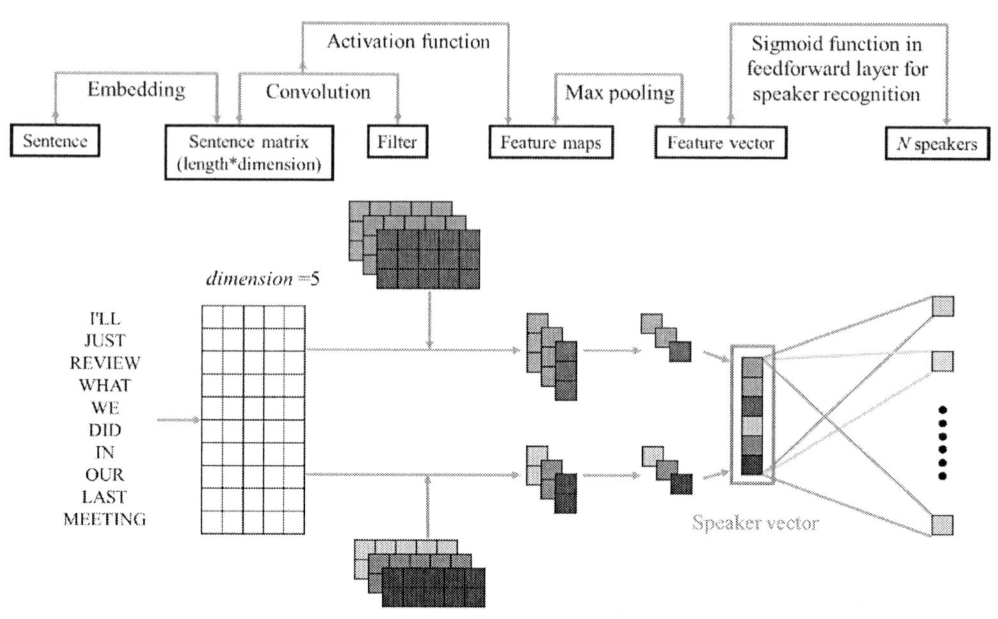



圖二、以摺積式類神經網路擷取語者慣用語特徵

每一個語句進行特徵擷取，並使用其隱藏層來做為語者慣用語特徵表示。

　　摺積式類神經網路的任務是語者識別。因為每個語句的內容並不一定會只來自某位語者(舉例來說，我們能確定某 A 句是由某語者所述，但是不能肯定 A 句不會出自其他語者)，所以在輸出層的設計上，我們不是選用分類的歸一化指數函數(Softmax)，而是針對每位語者對應各自的 S 函數(Sigmoid)。而在正例和反例上，正例為屬於該語者的語句；另一方面，我們藉由查詢相似度估計(Query Likelihood Estimation, QLE)計算與其相距最遠的語者，從中隨機挑選語句作為該語者的反例語句。圖二為以摺積式類神經網路擷取語者慣用語特徵的示意圖。

### 4.2.3 語者特徵用於語言模型調適

在獲得語者詞彙或慣用語特徵後，我們便可將之運用在語言模型的調適。過往常見於類神經網路的調適架構主要可分成兩類。第一類是添加輔助特徵到主任務的隱藏層（主任務為語言模型訓練），另一類則將特徵用於多任務學習(Multi-task Learning)的副任務。另一方面，在[15]的實驗結果卻指出，在輸入層添加輔助特徵可獲得更好的效果。其他神經網絡模型調適的相關研究也表明，將輔助特徵直接附加到主要特徵可帶來最佳效能，例如使用 i-vector 進行聲學模型語者調適[16]。因此在本研究中，我們採用的架構是將

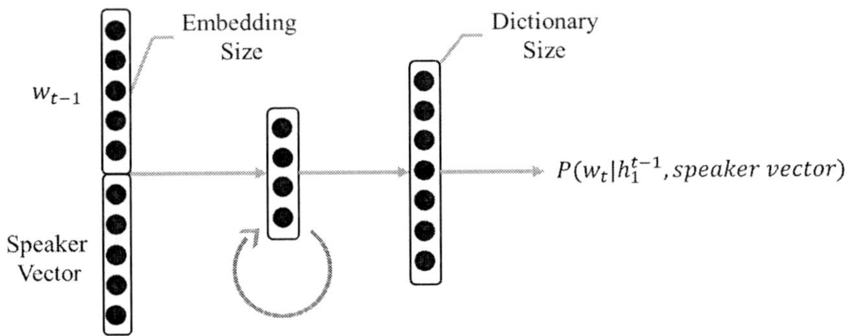


圖三、語者調適資訊融入 RNN(或 LSTM)為基礎的語言模型

語者特徵作為輔助特徵與主要特徵(一般詞彙特徵)共同輸入到隱藏層(如圖三所示)。

### 4.2.4 語者調適混和模型(Speaker Adaptive Mixture Model, SAMM)

相較於上述兩階段式方法,語者調適混和模型(SAMM)則是在訓練語言模型時,動態地擷取語者特徵,所以可直接使用於第二階段語言模型重新排序。SAMM 的主要想法是讓語言模型可自行動態地估測目前的語者,先訓練特定語者或具代表性語者(Specific or Representative Speakers)的各自語言模型,接著由組合器(Combinator)動態地為每個語句決定特定語者語言模型的權重,圖四為其示意圖。值得一提的是,在模型訓練時,特定語者的選取是基於語者們各自的 $N$ 連詞語言模型(使用對應到此語者的訓練語句訓練而成)與背景 $N$ 連詞語言模型(使用所有語者的訓練語句訓練而成)的差異來決定。在此研究,我們是選取差異最大的前 $L$ 位語者來訓練 $L$ 套特定語者語言模型。

從圖四可看出,在模型的測試階段,語者調適混和模型共用嵌入層和輸出層。當前一個時間點的詞輸入到此模型,先經過嵌入層投影至空間向量,接著經過各個特定語者語言模型和組合器的 LSTM 模型,然後輸出每位特定語者的隱藏層輸出以及組合權重,並再線性組合每位特定語者的隱藏層輸出和組合器輸出的權重。最後經過一個全連接層(Fully Connected Layer)與歸一化指數函數(Softmax)輸出下一個詞的機率。語者調適混和模型訓練階段可進一步分成下列幾個步驟:

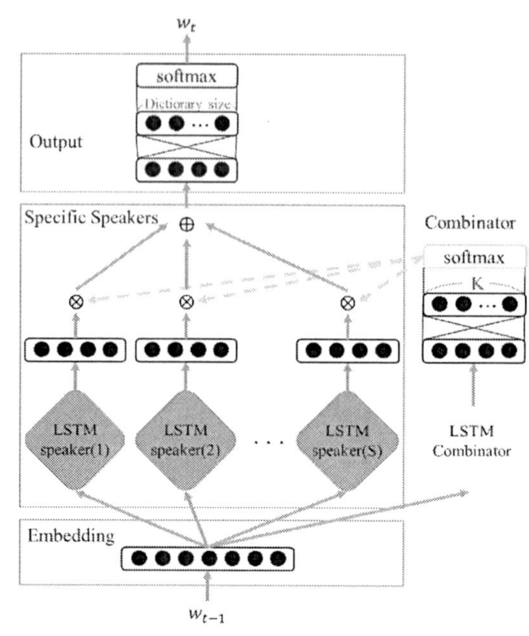


圖四、SAMM 語者特徵擷取

第一步：使用所有訓練語料來訓練背景 LSTM 語言模型。

第二步：以背景 LSTM 語言模型為基礎，使用其參數做為每一套特定語者語言模型的
初始化參數。接著，對於每一套特定語者語言模型固定其嵌入層和輸出層、保
持這些參數不變，並僅對應到此語者的訓練語句來訓練每一套特定語者 LSTM
語言模型的隱藏層間網路的參數。

第三步：獲取所有特定語者 LSTM 語言模型參數，輸入前一階段的嵌入和輸出參數以
初始化最終組合器模型，保持所有特定語者的 LSTM 語言模型參數以及嵌入
層參數不變，並在混合器 LSTM 上訓練所有數據，同時微調輸出層參數。

　　此方法中的組合器輸出可視為一種語者特徵，來輔助動態地產生最終的語言模型，
因為此模型的輸出是下一個詞的機率，所以也可以直接當作語音辨識第二階段語言模型
重新排序所需之語言模型。

## 五、實驗結果與分析

### 5.1 實驗語料與設定

表二、華語會議語料語言模型之訓練、發展與測試集

| 語料型別 | 訓練集 | 發展集 | 測試集 | 總計 |
|---|---|---|---|---|
| 小時數(小時) | 44.2 | 1.5 | 1.1 | 46.8 |
| 語句數(句) | 42,998 | 1,267 | 1,019 | 45,284 |
| 語者數(位) | 20 | 9 (1 無出現在訓練集) | 6 (1 無出現在訓練集) | 21 |

表三、AMI 會議之訓練、發展與測試集

| 語料型別 | 訓練集 | 發展集 | 測試集 | 總計 |
|---|---|---|---|---|
| 小時數(小時) | 70.29 | 7.81 | 8.71 | 95.79 |
| 語句數(句) | 97,222 | 10,882 | 13,059 | 133,775 |
| 語者數(位) | 155 | 21 (19 無出現在訓練集) | 16 (16 無出現在訓練集) | 173 |

我們所使用的語料庫為「華語會議語料」以及「AMI 會議語料」[9]。其中，華語會議語料庫為國內企業所整理的語料庫。華語會議語料對於會議談話內容與參與人員的對話方式並沒有經過設計，而是貼近一般公司在實際開會中將會面臨的問題。例如聊到專業技術時，常會出現中英文夾雜的對話；發表談話時可能有停頓、口齒不清或口吃的現象。相較於 AMI 語料庫，華語會議語料更具挑戰性；表二是華語會議語料的詳細統計資訊。AMI 會議語料是由歐盟資助開發，AMI 團隊致力於研究和開發輔助團體互動的技術，其主要的目的是開發會議瀏覽器，使得會議記錄易於索引。該團隊收集了 AMI 會議語料，一系列已記錄的會議現在已提供給大眾做為研究開發使用，雖然數據集是專門為該工作所設計的，但它可用於語言學、組織和社會心理學、語音和語言工程、影音處理和多模式系統等多種不同目的，表三是 AMI 的詳細統計資訊。本研究語音辨識系統的發展是使用 Kaldi 工具；聲學模型是 Lattice-free Maximum Mutual Information(LF-MMI) [17]，第一階段中的語言模型是三連詞語言模型。類神經網路語言模型是由 Pytorch 實現。

## 5.2 實驗結果與探討

本論文第一組的實驗是實作在華語會議語料；表四是在此語料上的語言模型複雜度(Perplexity)和語音辨識字錯誤率(Character error rate, CER)結果。首先，從訓練和測試語句正確轉寫(Reference Transcription)的語言模型複雜度的實驗結果可看出，使用基礎 LSTM 語言模型結合傳統三連詞語言模型(或單獨使用基礎 LSTM 語言模型，如括號內數值所示)均能較使用傳統三連詞語言模型有較低的語言模型複雜度，也就是說有較佳

表四、華語會議語料上語言模型複雜度和語音辨識結果

| 華語會議語料 | 發展集 | | 測試集 | |
|---|---|---|---|---|
| | 複雜度 | CER | 複雜度 | CER |
| 第一階段語音辨(三連詞語言模型) | 205.11 | 20.19 | 210.26 | 17.23 |
| 第二階段語言模型重新排序(基礎 LSTM 語言模型) | 161.20 (184.44) | 16.89 | 165.44 (191.97) | 15.91 |
| +基於 TF 的語者特徵 | 158.99 (202.35) | 16.84 | 163.26 (208.35) | 15.84 |
| +基於 PLSA 的語者特徵 | 156.20 (188.00) | 16.75 | 160.93 (194.16) | 15.86 |
| +基於 SSWM 的語者特徵 | 158.41 (199.51) | 16.84 | 162.94 (210.31) | 15.91 |
| +基於 CNN 的語者慣用語特徵 | 161.20 (255.85) | 16.88 | 165.44 (264.11) | 15.94 |
| 語者調適混和模型(SAMM) | 158.52 (184.45) | 16.75 | 161.71 (187.68) | 15.89 |

的語言模型預測能力。尤其使用基礎 LSTM 語言模型結合傳統三連詞語言模型能較僅使用傳統三連詞語言模型，不論是在發展集或是測試集均能提供超過 20%的相對複雜度降低。其次，從語音辨識第二階段使用基礎 LSTM 語言模型結合傳統三連詞語言模型來對於第一階段產生的 1000 最佳候選詞序列重新排序的實驗，這樣的結合能對於發展集和測試集的字錯誤率分別為 16.89%與 15.91%的改進。

再者，我們觀察以語者用詞特徵來輔助訓練語言模型在華語會議語料上的實驗結果；在表四呈現出分別使用基於 TF 的語者特徵、基於 PLSA 的語者特徵、基於 SSWM 的語者特徵和基於 CNN 的語者慣用語特徵在語言模型複雜度和 CER 降低的表現。融入這些語者相關的輔助特徵的 LSTM 語言模型均能較基礎 LSTM 語言模型在語言複雜度的表現上有些微的提升，其中基於 PLSA 的語者特徵有最好的表現；而經期望值最大化(EM)演算法估測所得之基於 SSWM 的語者特徵也會較基於 TF 的語者特徵的表現來的好，說明了使用期望值最大化演算法降低背景詞影響的重要性。接著，在辨識的結果，三種語者相關特徵在發展集上都能帶來些微的改善，尤其以 PLSA 的效果最好。而在測試集上，是使用基於 TF 的語者特徵的表現最好；使用基於 CNN 的語者慣用語特徵反而使

表五、AMI 會議語料實驗結果

| AMI 英文會議語料 | 發展集 | | 測試集 | |
|---|---|---|---|---|
| | 複雜度 | CER | 複雜度 | CER |
| 第一階段語音辨識(三連詞語言模型) | 85.19 | 23.25 | 76.44 | 23.02 |
| 第二階段語言模型重新排序(基礎 LSTM 語言模型) | 68.02 (73.40) | 21.17 | 60.61 (65.40) | 20.41 |
| +基於 CNN 的語者慣用語特徵 | 66.28 (104.1) | 21.07 | 59.05 (93.12) | 20.32 |
| 語者調適混和模型(SAMM) | 67.61 (99.80) | 21.04 | 60.43 (93.60) | 20.33 |

得 CER 有些許的上升，推測應是在 CNN 模型訓練時，反例語句檢索並沒有找到足以代表反例的語句，導致依其所建立之具語者調適性的語言模型沒有展現出期望中的效能。另一方面本論文所提出的語者調適混和模型(SAMM)不管是在複雜度或是 CER，均與上述方法旗鼓相當。

　　本論文第二組的實驗在 AMI 英文會議語料；表五是在此語料上的語言模型複雜度和 CER 結果。由於 AMI 英文會議語料的發展集與訓練集的語者重複極少、測試集與訓練集的語者完全不同，在表五僅呈現使用基於 CNN 的語者慣用語特徵和語者調適混和模型的實驗結果。使用基於 CNN 的語者慣用語特徵的語言模型在 AMI 英文會議語料的語言複雜度降低上並沒有預期中的表現，但是在語音辨識實驗卻有不錯的效能，可以降低約 0.5%的詞錯誤率。另一方面，語者調適混和模型在語言複雜度上，沒有預期中的表現，僅在 CER 些微下降；這可能是 AMI 英文會議語料語者較多，而本研究所選用的特定語者數(七位)占總語者數的比例太小，導致其表現沒有像在華語會議語料來的好。

## 六、結論與未來展望

本論文考慮了「已知語者」和「未知語者」兩種的情境，也以不同的角度考慮語者特徵擷取模型的建立，我們提出了三種語者特徵擷取模型，「語者用詞特徵模型」、「語者慣用語特徵模型」、「語者調適混和模型」，其中「語者慣用語特徵模型」以及「語者調適混和模型」適用於未知語者的測試階段，結果顯示語者調適混和模型不管在「已知語者」還是「未知語者」的情境都能達到一定的效果，但是語者慣用語特徵模型的表現較其它方法差，原因是所選取的反例語句無法很好的表現該語者的相反用語特性。

參考文獻

[1] M. Bacchiani and B. Roark, "Unsupervised language model adaptation," IEEE International Conference on Acoustics, Speech and Signal Processing, 2003.

[2] Y. Bengio et al., "A neural probabilistic language model," Journal of Machine Learning Research, 2003.

[3] X. Chen et al., "Future word contexts in neural network language models," IEEE Automatic Speech Recognition and Understanding Workshop, 2017.

[4] X. Chen et al., "Recurrent neural network language model adaptation for multi-genre broadcast speech recognition," The Annual Conference of the International Speech Communication Association, 2015.

[5] J. Chung et al., "Empirical evaluation of gated recurrent neural networks on sequence modeling," arXiv, 2014.

[6] Y. N. Dauphin et al., "Language modeling with gated convolutional networks," arXiv:1612.08083, 2016.

[7] Y. Kim, et al., "Character-aware neural language models," AAAI Conference on Artificial Intelligence, 2016.

[8] S. Kombrink et al., "Recurrent neural network based language modeling in meeting recognition," The Annual Conference of the International Speech Communication Association, 2011.

[9] J. Carletta et al., "The AMI meeting corpus: A pre-announcement," The International Workshop on Machine Learning for Multimodal Interaction, 2005.

[10] T. Mikolov et al., "Recurrent neural network based language model," The Annual Conference of the International Speech Communication Association, 2010.

[11] S. Hochreiter et al., "Long short-term memory," Neural Computation, 1997.

[12] M. Sundermeyer et al., "LSTM neural networks for language modeling," The Annual Conference of the International Speech Communication Association, 2012.

[13] X. Liu et al., "Efficient lattice rescoring using recurrent neural network language models," IEEE International Conference on Acoustics, Speech and Signal Processing, 2014.

[14] T. Hofmann, "Probabilistic latent semantic analysis," The Conference on Uncertainty in Artificial Intelligence, 1999.

[15] M. Ma et al., "Modeling non-linguistic contextual signals in LSTM language models via domain adaptation," IEEE International Conference on Acoustics, Speech and Signal Processing, 2018.

[16] T. Tan et al., "Speaker-aware training of LSTM-RNNs for acoustic modelling," IEEE International Conference on Acoustics, Speech and Signal Processing, 2016.

[17] D. Povey et al., "Purely sequence-trained neural networks for ASR based on lattice-free MMI," Annual Conference of the International Speech Communication Association, 2016.

The 2018 Conference on Computational Linguistics and Speech Processing
ROCLING 2018, pp. 61-75
©The Association for Computational Linguistics and Chinese Language Processing

# 繁體中文依存句法剖析器
## Traditional Chinese Dependency Parser

李彥璇  Yen-Hsuan Lee

國立交通大學電信工程研究所
Department of Communication Engineering
National Chiao Tung University
yh10305.cm05g@g2.nctu.edu.tw

王逸如 Yih-Ru Wang

國立交通大學電機工程系
Department of Electronic Engineering
National Chiao Tung University
yrwang@cc.nctu.edu.tw

## 摘要

近年來依存句法分析樹一直是 CoNLL 比賽的重要項目，其重要性可見一班，但其中參賽的隊伍並非以繁體中文為母語，若遇到繁體中文的語料通常會轉為簡體中文再做更進一步處理。因此，本研究以建立繁體中文依存句法分析樹為主要目的，透過目前相當熱門的深度學習模型，多層感知器及遞迴神經網路，與現有的斷詞器結合，得到繁體中文語句之句法分析樹。這樣的模型對於句法分析樹有相當好的成效，並比過去類似 Task 相比有高達 70%的成長。

## Abstract

Recently, dependency parser has been paid highly attention in CoNLL conference, in this case we can find how important it is. However, there is no native Taiwanese attend to this competition. Therefore, we aim to build a traditional Chinese dependency parser in this paper. Through different famous neural network structure , such as multilayer perceptron and recurrent neural network along with traditional Chinese segmentation, we are able to construct an efficient parser that could transfer a raw traditional Chinese sentences to a dependency tree. We have much better result than similar task that has been proposed at 2012.

關鍵詞：依存句法分析器，自然語言處理，多層感知器，遞迴神經網路

Keywords: dependency parser, natural language processing, MultiLayer Perceptron , Recurrent Neural Network

一、 緒論

在自然語言處理中，語意瞭解是很重要的一部分，而為了做語意瞭解，就必須做句法分析。早期學者們都使用樹狀結構句法分析(tree parsing)，如中研院的 CKIP Chinese Parser[1]。樹狀結構又稱短語結構(phrase structure)，主要是將句子拆解成不同的片語。近年來，學者們大多使用依存句法分析，依存句法分析中的資訊可由短語結構依照規則法轉換而來，儘管這兩種方式夾帶資訊類似，但在句法分析中可以直接表示詞與詞之間的相依關係。

由於近年來機器學習的技術一日千里，過去曾經做過的自然語言處理方式，又被提出來重新檢視，依存句法分析也不例外，並獲得相當好的成果。首先是 2013 年 Mikolov 提出新的詞向量表示法(Word Embedding)[2]，使句中的各詞可以存在一定的關聯，並能更好的利用每個輸入單詞，接著是不同機器學習架構，例如 MLP (Multilayer Perceptron) 和 LSTM (Long Short Term Memory)，將複雜的系統簡單化，像是 dependency parser 原本透過機率模型，需要設計不同規則來尋找詞與詞之間的可能關聯，在尋找的同時會耗費較多的苦工，然而使用深度學習技術，將選定好的特徵輸入，經過隱藏層後面的激活函數，可以直接學習出整個句子的語法，將規則比對與計算條件機率的部分簡化成學習神經網路中的權重。

依存句法分析深度學習的模型是使用監督式學習，因此正確的人工依存句法分析標示語料，是建立依存句法分析器不可或缺的訓練資料。這幾年，學術界組織了數個組織且訂定了依存句法分析的一套標準，並建立各個語言的依存句法標示語料庫。其中，由 Joakim Nivre 主持的 Universal Dependencies(UD)[3]是一個多人參與並建立資料較完整的組織，包含了全世界絕大數語言，2.1 版中新增了繁體與簡體中文。我們研究室在過去已發展有繁體中文的 word segmenter [4],、POS tagger 再加上依存句法的訓練工具及訓練語料應該可以達到很好的訓練效果。事實上，還有多問題需要解決，在 UD 繁體中文語料庫中的訓練語料僅有大約十萬詞，且其中使用的詞性與斷詞並沒有依照中研院的標準來建立。對於我們的現況來說 UD 語料庫並不適合建立一套 End-to-End 的系統。然而中研院也推出了自己的中文結構樹資料庫[1]，並且是以 dependency tree 的方式呈現，斷詞與 POS 標示都與中研院詞庫小組一致，且中研院的詞性標記種類多達 47 類，其中 P（介詞）更可細分成 66 類，而這些能提供句法分析更多資訊，使分析準確大為提升，以下圖一和圖二「與」為例，若沒有標示 POS 在句法判斷上，就無法知道他代表的是伴隨還是對等的意思，如圖一「與」POS 為 P35 代表的是伴隨，前面可以是人或其他事物；而圖二的「與」為 Caa，代表前後必須為對等的名詞片語或是動詞，然而在斷詞上，並無法分出這兩者的不同，故 POS 在訓練依存句法分析器中是個不可缺少的特徵。相較其他語言來說，中文的語法架構較為複雜，UD 語料庫中為了統一各個語言的 dependency type 只使用了 42 個，相較於中研院的 68 類，UD 可能無法涵蓋中文語意更深入的層面。

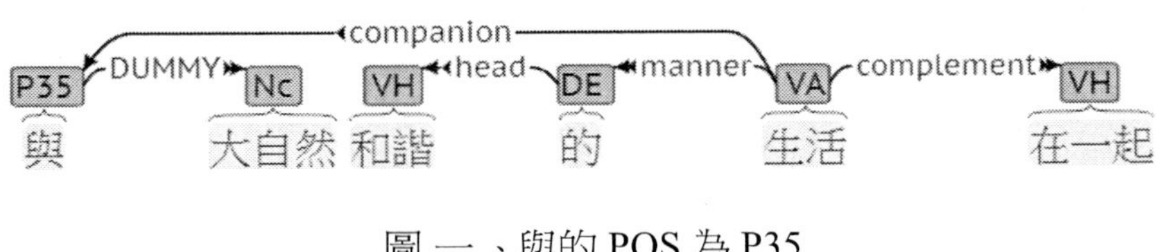

圖一、與的 POS 為 P35

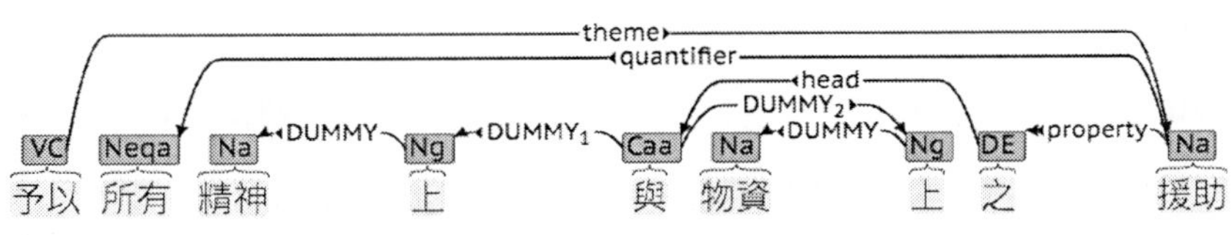

圖二、與的 POS 為 Caa

綜觀上面幾種情形，再加上我們實驗室現有的斷詞與 POS 標示都與中研院標準相同，以致於我們能更著重在訓練方法上。本研究提出了端到端的依存句法分析器，來提供未來自然語言處理發展上一項有利的工具。

後面小節中會提到依存句法分析器的做法，使用了 Joakim Nivre 提出的 Transition-based algorithm[5]，並結合 Stanford 提出的高效率剖析器[6]中的 Multilayer perceptron 架構，除了 Feedforward 外，也使用 Recursive Neural Networks 中的 Gated Recurrent Unit 來建立我們的依存句法分析器[7]，來彌補 MLP 中缺失的順序問題。

## 二、 方法

[1] http://www.aclclp.org.tw/use_conll_c.php

（一） 系統介紹

　　本研究中使用了交通大學語音處理實驗室的斷詞器與 POS 標示，斷詞器是繁體中文自然語言處理上很重要的一個元件，並不像其他語系，中文句子中沒有明確的詞語界線，需要有個明確的標準才能讓後續的使用更為靈活，而 POS 標示也十分依賴斷詞器的結果。透過高效能的斷詞器與 POS 標示，我們在多次 share task 中獲得亮眼的成績，因此我們有十分堅固的基礎來建立依存句法分析器。

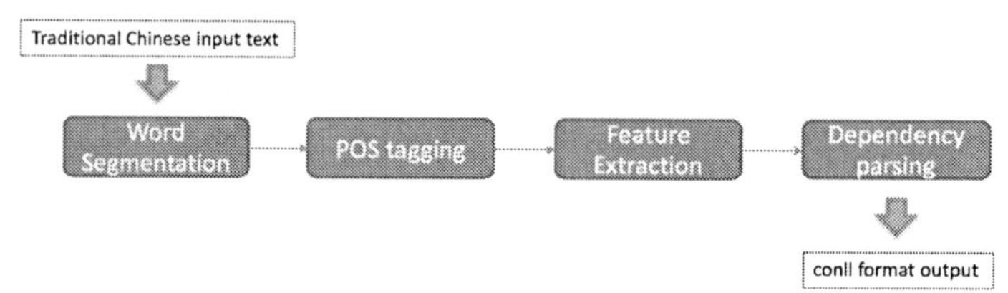


圖 三、End-to-End 架構中所包含的元件

　　在本篇論文，我們著重於圖三中的 Dependency Parsing，即為依存句法分析，在進入模型建立的方法前，先簡單介紹它的表示方式及代表意義：

　　在 dependency parser 輸出中(如圖四之範例)，會以弧 (arc) 來表示詞與詞間的相依性，圖中 arc 會從中心語(Head)指向修飾語，如："書架" 一詞會指向"一座座"。並且每一個 arc 會標示 dependency relation (如：quantifier(數量詞修飾語))。而"一座座書架"就組成一個詞組或片語。而再下一層，"一座座書架" 詞組修飾 "上"。如此，一層一層下去，最後，句中未修飾他詞的中心語(Head)則稱為 root (如句中"放"一詞)。

　　如此，dependency parser 以 head 和 dependent 來表示兩個詞之間的關聯，以 head 代表一個 phrase 的中心詞（名詞片語中的名詞，動詞片語中的動詞），剩下的詞可能與 head 有 direct、indirect 或 dependent 的關係。我們可以透過這樣的關聯，將 head-dependent 的配對做更進一步的分類，稱作 dependency relation 或 grammatical function。

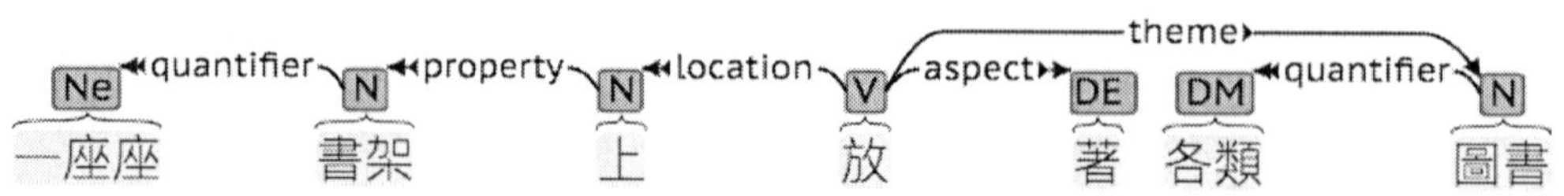


圖 四 、依存句法範例

而建構依存句法分析器尚需滿足三項限制，(1) 外加的 root，並沒有任何 arc 指向它，(2) root 以外的 node(詞或標點符號)，都會被一個 arc 指向，(3) root 到所有其他 vertex 只有一條唯一路徑。上述的 vertex 指的是在短語結構中（如圖五），詞組的中心語。短語結構樹也可稱為 constituency tree，並無上下文順序關係，僅以片語為分析重心。

以上面的邏輯，我們使用 Transition Based Parsing 的方式，來一一找出詞與詞的關聯，這個方法是來自於 shift-reduced parsing，使用了 stack 和即將被剖析的 word list。在 transition-based parsing 中有個重要的特徵組態（configuration）概念，其中有三個重要成分，stack、buffer 和 dependency relations 的集合。最初的特徵組態中，stack 只包含 ROOT，buffer 則是句子中的所有詞，而 dependency relations 一開始是空的。終止狀態中 stack 中僅剩下 ROOT 和 buffer 必須是空的，dependency relations 的集合代表最終的剖析結果。為了產生新的特徵組態，我們會使用三個 operator：

LeftArc：在最上層的詞和他下一層的詞中加入新的 head-dependent relations，並 pop 第二層的詞。

RightArc：在第二層的詞和最上層的詞中加入新的 head-dependent relations，並 pop 最上層的詞。

Shift：將 buffer 中最前面的詞 push 進 stack 後，將其移除。

在圖六中，我們可以將 Check dependency 分成不只 Left-arc 跟 Right-arc，加上 dependency relation，變成一個多類別的分類器，在判斷左右的同時也能判斷類別就能得到圖七帶有標籤的結果。

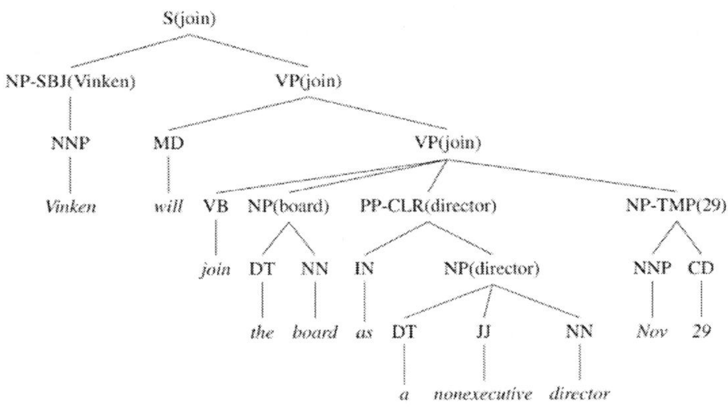

圖 五、Constituency Tree

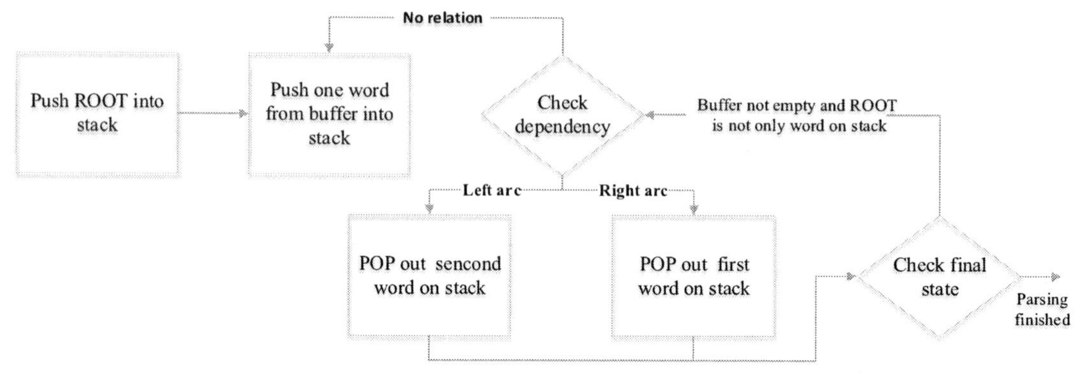


圖 六、transition-based 流程圖

　　將上述的流程套用在一個實際例子，由於句子的長度與 transition 為線性關係，我們選擇較短的句子「由四樓走上五樓」，斷詞完為四個詞，每個詞皆會被 pop 出 Stack 和 push 進 Stack 一次，因此只需要 4*2 步[2]就可以剖析完一句話。從表一我們可以知道，初始狀態從 ROOT 開始也到 ROOT 結束，每個詞也都會輪流進入 stack 檢視，直到所有關聯被建立。當執行完表一的所有步驟，將關聯圖像化即可得到如圖七

表 一、Transition based parsing 的過程

| Step | Stack | Word List | Action | Relation |
|---|---|---|---|---|
| 0 | [root] | [由,四樓,走上,五樓] | Shift | |
| 1 | [root,由] | [四樓,走上,五樓] | Shift | |
| 2 | [root,由,四樓] | [走上,五樓] | RightArc | (由→四樓) |
| 3 | [root,由] | [走上,五樓] | Shift | |
| 4 | [root,由,走上] | [五樓] | LeftArc | (由←走上) |
| 5 | [root,走上] | [五樓] | Shift | |
| 6 | [root,走上,五樓] | [] | RightArc | (走上→五樓) |
| 7 | [root,走上] | [] | RightArc | (root→走上) |
| 8 | [root] | [] | Done | |

---

[2] 視情況也可以為 n*2+1，若一開始將 ROOT 放在 word list，而非 stack，則需要將 ROOT push 至 stack

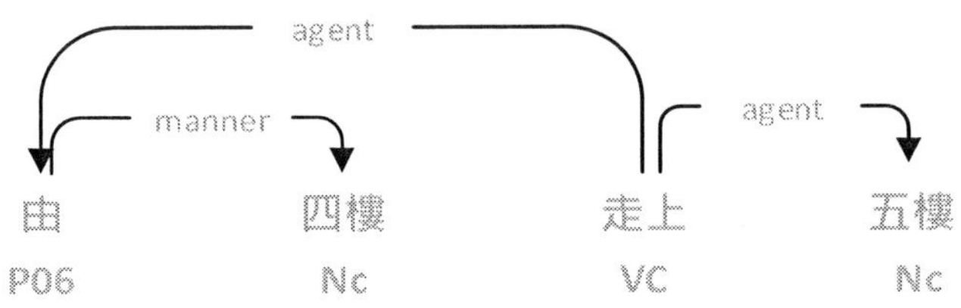


圖 五、表一的依存句法分析樹

## （二） 模型設計

　　自從 Mikolov 提出新的詞表達方式後，各式各樣的神經網路訓練模型，又成為自然語言處理界的寵兒，依存句法分析器當然也不例外，透過預先訓練好的詞向量，神經網路可以更有效地找出詞和詞之間的模式（pattern）。我們透過現在最常見的兩種模型——遞迴神經網路與多層感知器來實現依存句法分析器，由於 transition-based 是一種貪婪演算法，分類出當前的動作後，並無法使用回溯法更改前面判斷的動作。因此在這兩種深度模型中加入了定向搜索（Beam Search），產生多個句法分析樹，最後再以分數高的作為最終答案。

## 1. 多層感知器 Multilayer Perceptron

　　2014 年 Chen & Manning，提出了一種快速的 transition-based parsing 方法，保留了 stack 和 buffer 當作 input layer 的 feature，除了 word 以外也包含了 POS tags 和 arc label。在這當中如何選取 feature 是很重要的一個步驟，由於句子的長短並不一致，在 C&M 的論文中，選擇了 stack 和 buffer 最上層的 3 個 element、stack 上兩層個別的左一和一右修飾詞，以及最左關係詞下的最左修飾詞，最右修飾詞的最右修飾詞。總共會有 18 個 features，這些 words 的 POS tags 也有 18 個，還有 arc label 有 12 個（不包含 stack 和 buffer 中的六個詞），以上這些 features 皆拿來作為 dependency parsing 的輸入。以上介紹很可會過於抽象，因此以圖八為例，剖析完成的依存句法樹，transition-based 中每一個動作都是透過特徵組態(如表一的 step)來預測下一個動作。但輸入的特徵就像上面說的不僅僅只是拿當前狀態的 stack 和 buffer，還包括了已知的修飾關係組合。如圖九，「他」和「了」都在前面步驟被移出 stack，因為這兩者都修飾了「喝」這個詞，然而這項關係在下一步驟並沒有因此被忽略，進而成為我們的輸入特徵。

在圖九的架構中，我們將 features 分成三部分，詞、詞性和 Label，在輸入詞向量的時候，可能會出現 OOV (Out of Vocabulary)，因此將 POS 標記與詞向量合併做為新的詞向量來作訓練，而 POS 獨立出來訓練的目的，則是為了更有效的學習它在依存句法架構的重要性，在後面的一些實驗中，我們也發現 POS 在此模型中，有著舉足輕重的地位。

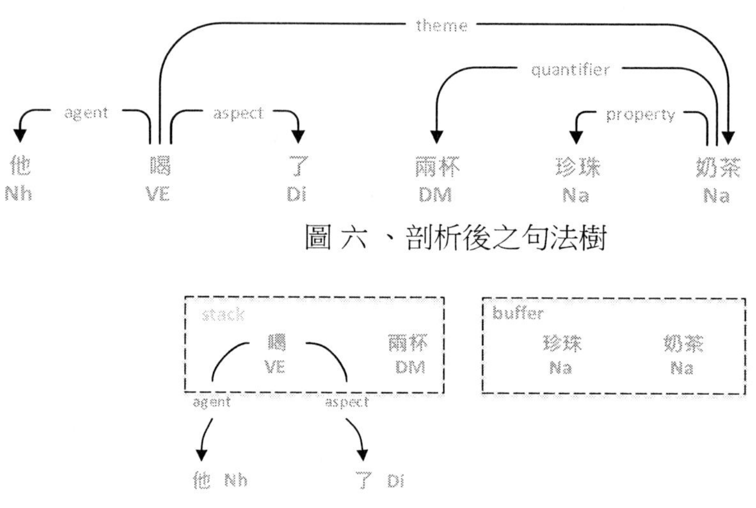


圖 六 、剖析後之句法樹



圖 七、預測下一個動作之特徵組態

## 2. 遞迴神經網路 Recurrent Neural Network

接著，在如此依賴字詞順序的架構上，2016 年，Marianas Labs 提出了一個基於 transition-based 的遞迴神經網路，又稱 Stack Long Short Term Memory 結合了 Stack、buffer 與 Action，擁有各自的 RNN 架構，Stack 的 RNN，夾帶了部分 parsing tree 的資訊，能更全面的預測當前的 action， 在 S-LSTM 中，多了 Action 這部份的資訊，將每個狀態預測出的 Action 變成時間序列，加以訓練。在部分 parsing tree 中，延用了 Stanford Parser 的 feature，將部分剖析樹合併到 Stack 的最上面兩層，由於剖析樹不只有詞其中還有 action 的 label，如此性質不同的情況下，會透過 composition 的方式各別訓練 label 和詞，再以線性轉換的方式，得到新的 stack 表達式。

在我們研究中，將上述的 LSTM 取代成 RNN 的另一種變種 GRU(Gated Recurrent Unit)將 LSTM 中的 forget gate 與 input gate 合成一個 update gate，另一個 gate 則與 cell state 合併成為 reset gate，依然能保存長短距離的資訊，在架構上 LSTM 與 GRU 的差異並不明顯，但在本研究中，會使用比英文更大維度的資料，希望降低權重數量，提升收斂速度。且在資料量不夠的狀態下，LSTM 學習效果並無法展現出來。在後面章節會直接稱我們的模型為 stack-GRU。

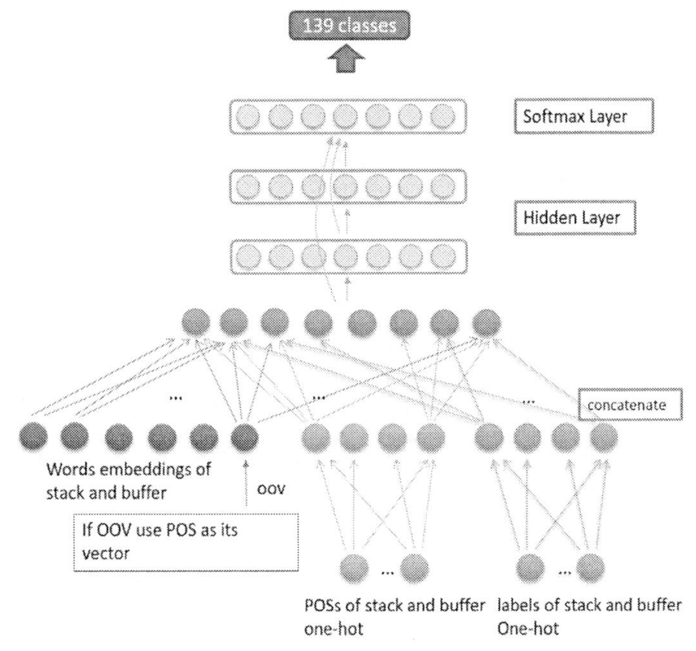


圖 八、MLP 架構

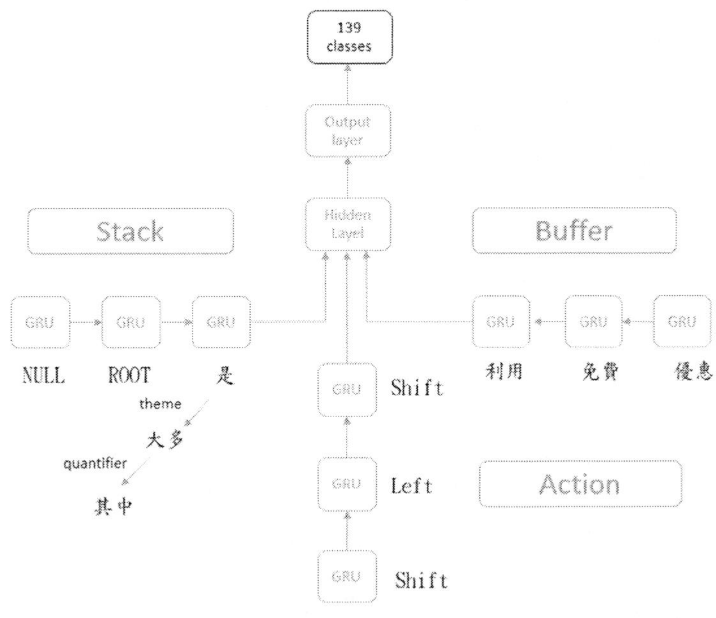


圖 九、Stack LSTM 架構

## 3. 定向搜索 Beam search

Transition-based 在前面提到是個計算上非常有效率的演算法，只要依據 stack 與 buffer 的狀態提供選擇，並一步一步剖析完整句話，然而這樣的做法，有個極大的缺點，一但做了決定，便無法回頭，即使後來發生難以判斷的狀態也無能為力。因此，我們希望能有系統地多看其他選項，並從中找出最適合的句法。而定向搜索則使用了橫向優先搜尋的策略以階層式的方法篩選使每一層只需要處理固定寬度（beam width）的資料。套用定向搜索至 transition-based 剖析上，我們需要稍微修改我們原本的演算法，原本僅需預測當前特徵組態的最適動作，現在則挑出機率前 N 高的動作，每個動作都會產生新的特徵組態，這些組態我們會列入 agenda（可能動作的集合），只要沒超過我們設定的寬度（beam width），就可以持續加入新的組態。當 agenda 達到預設的大小時，我們僅會加入比 agenda 中最差值機率高的組態。為了找到最好的句法樹，以迴圈的方式進行全局搜索直到終止狀態。其中機率為原本深度學習模型下，將最終輸出改成選擇的 N 個機率，而不使用單一的分類結果，下圖為本研究使用的定向搜索示意圖，每個節點都代表一個特徵組態，每個組態會輸入模型內並回傳前三高的機率，當達到終止狀態時，則計算機率總和最高作為最終答案。這樣一來我們便能較全面篩選每一個可能的句法。

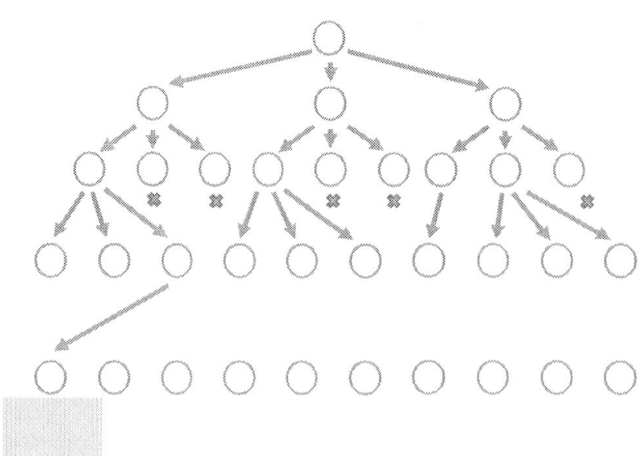

圖十、Beam-search

## 三、 結果與討論

## （一） 實驗配置

在評估標準上，依存句法較常使用 UAS( Unlabeled Attachment Score )及 LAS
( Labeled Attachment Score )，來確認 head-dependent 是否正確配對，Labeled 則更進一
步地表示 head-dependent 的關聯。如圖十三與十四，只看箭頭不看標籤可以看出 7 條
關聯中只有 4 條正確，而帶有標籤的情況則只有 3 條正確，因此這個範例中，UAS 為
4/7 而 LAS 為 3/7，儘管我們可以看到修飾「這場」的關聯是「quantifier」但修飾它的
詞不正確，故不能計算 LAS。

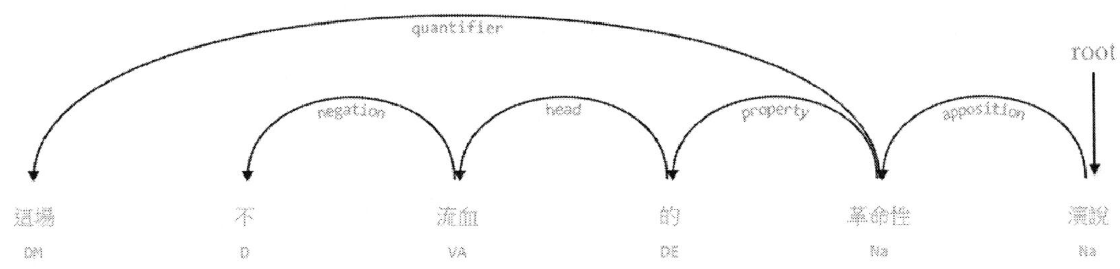



圖 十一、系統答案

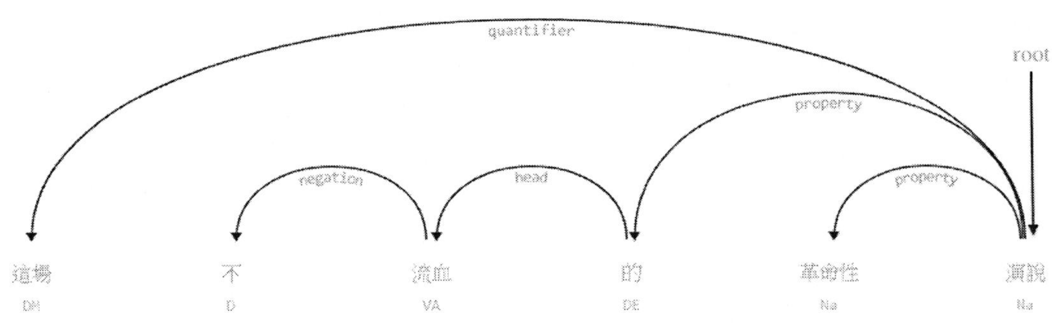



圖 十二、正確答案

除了基本的 UAS 與 LAS 外，中文多了一項評估標準以 f1-score 作為測試系統效能的
依據。f1-socre 的公式為

$$f1 = \frac{2 * precision * recall}{precision + recall}$$

而這裡的 precision（準確率）是以標準答案當作分母來計算，如下圖正確指向的箭頭
為 4 個，而標準答案共有 5 個，因此準確率為 4/5，然而 recall（召回率)是以我們的系
統輸出為分母計算，下圖系統輸出共有 8 個箭頭，召回率為 4/8，最後計算 f1-score 為
0.615。

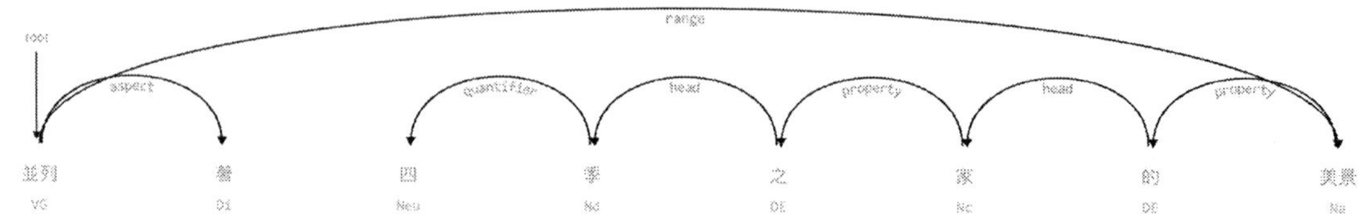


圖 十三、系統答案

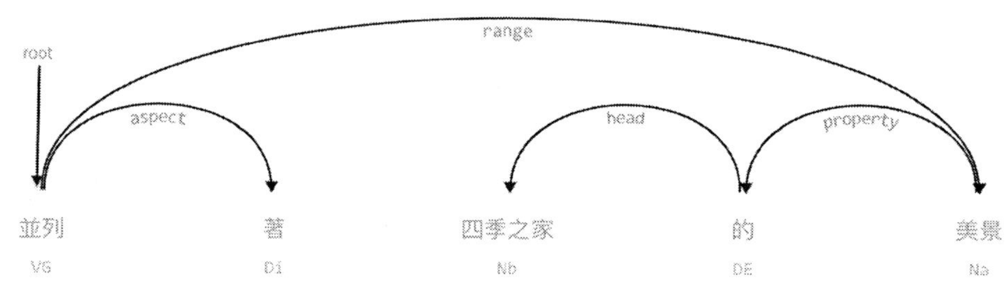


圖 十四、正確答案

在本研究討論了四種配置，Stack-GRU 與 MLP，以及各別加上 beam search 後的結
果。其中包含中研院提供的測試語料經過模型的準確度，與本實驗使用的斷詞器斷詞
後的結果，而我們使用的斷詞器與中研院斷詞有些許出入，因此使用 f1-score 作為分
析結果。

## （二） 實驗結果

目前繁體中文並沒有任何已知的基準提供我們做參考，因此以 2012 年 bake-offs 的
Traditional Chinese Parsing task[7]的評估結果來當我們的基準。此繁體中文剖析使用的
是短語的樹狀結構，如上面所說，短語句法樹可以轉換成依存句法結構，因此使用此
基準我們認為是可信的。如表二之一，2012 年所使用的資料集，與本次實驗訓練與測
試語料比率均為 1%左右。表二之一的測試語料佔 1.5%，表二之二則佔 1.2%。

表 二之一、2012 Traditional Chinese Parsing task 資料集

| Data Set | #Word | #Sent | Avg. Length |
|---|---|---|---|
| Training | 391,505 | 65,243 | 6 |
| Test | 8,565 | 1,000 | 8.57 |
| Validation | 341 | 37 | 9.2 |

表 三之二、中研院提供的資料集

| Data Set | #Word | #Sent | Avg. Length |
|---|---|---|---|
| Training | 337,174 | 56,957 | 5.92 |
| Test | 5,160 | 690 | 7.47 |

我們以當時各隊比賽的結果當作比較，由於斷詞可能與測試語料不一致，在此也看 F1 做為參考依據，其中分為微平均與宏平均，而宏平均與我們實驗的算法一致。表三中是以帶語意角色的短語結構剖析後的結果，相當於實驗中 LAS 的評估方式，表中最好的結果為 0.4287，故以此為基準。

表 四、帶語意角色的短語結構分析結果

| Submitted Runs | Micro-averaging | | | Macro-averaging | | |
|---|---|---|---|---|---|---|
| | Precision | Recall | F1 | Precision | Recall | F1 |
| NCU-Run1 | 0.3755 | 0.3429 | 0.3585 | 0.3506 | 0.3538 | 0.3522 |
| NEU-Run1 | 0.4358 | 0.4328 | 0.4343 | 0.4192 | 0.416 | 0.4176 |
| NEU-Run2 | 0.4409 | 0.4379 | 0.4394 | 0.4239 | 0.4209 | 0.4224 |
| CRF (Baseline) | 0.4382 | 0.4216 | 0.4297 | 0.4347 | 0.4229 | 0.4287 |

在本實驗中，多層感知器使用了 250 維的詞向量，詞性為 121 類的獨熱編碼（one-hot encoding）和依存關係 69 類的獨熱編碼作為輸入，各自乘上權重矩陣後再合併，並在後面使用兩層 RELU 隱藏層，如圖十，詞向量、詞性和依存關係的隱藏層神經元為 200 個，合併後則為 600 個，通過每一層隱藏層都逐漸減少 200 維，最後一層 Softmax 則輸出 139 類（transition-based action）。其中 Batch size 為 100，Epoch 為 5 就能收斂，因此在訓練上，MLP 十分有效率。

遞迴神經網路在架構上就與多層感知器有相當大的差別，所以在參數的設置也會有所不同，GRU 分成 stack 跟 buffer 兩部份，時間步數（time step）設為 3，由於我們的句長並不長，步數設少一點可以使整體模型執行更快。不同於 MLP，GRU 不是暴力地將特徵展開再餵進模型，stack 中，如我們在方法中所介紹的，會帶有部分剖析樹的資訊，分別有 stack 最上面兩層修飾的詞與依存關係，為了讓詞和依存關係可以有更好的學習效果，便各自加入隱藏層學習特定的權重矩陣，如此一來重要的依存關係特

徵可以被擷取出來。各自隱藏層的輸出會與 stack 前兩層的詞向量合併，再經過一層隱藏層得到該 stack 詞的新詞向量。這樣進入 GRU 的每個時間步數都為同樣維度。在此模型中，GRU 設置兩層隱藏曾，輸出為 200 維，stack 和 buffer 的 GRU 設置完全一樣，最後再將 stack 和 buffer 的輸出合併一起輸入 softmax 層，並得到與 MLP 一樣的輸出形式。

接著探討加入定向搜索的情況，在這裡為了減少運算量我們設置的定向寬度（Beam width）為 10，而每次輸出則取前 4 高，來分析可能的句法樹，因為定向寬度為 10 且取 4 個可能的動作，我們可以看 40 個不同動作造成的不同結果並得到對應的機率，再將 30 個超過定向寬度的節點刪除，以此循環直到終止狀態。

表 五 、不同配置的表現

|  | UAS | LAS | UAS f1-score | LAS f1-score |
|---|---|---|---|---|
| **Stack-GRU** | 88.5% | 83.1% | 80.66% | 74.17% |
| **+beam** | 89.8% | 84.5% | 81.05% | 74.54% |
| **MLP** | 87.5% | 82.7% | 79.28% | 73.24% |
| **+beam** | 88.3% | 83.5% | 80.45% | 74.71% |

表四為個別看 MLP 與 GRU 模型的結果，可以看出在多數情況 GRU 表現比 MLP 好，還沒加入定向搜索時，LAS 相差 0.4，但在加入定向搜索時則差距 1，可見遞迴神經網路較能找出過去的詞語當前詞的關聯。然而使用本研究中的斷詞器的結果，則是 MLP 加入定向搜索表現最好，原因是當斷詞錯誤或是詞性標示不一致，GRU 對於過去的詞性較為敏感，以至於過去的錯誤會隨著遞迴神經元中傳播至當前的預測結果。

四、 結論

在本研究中實現了完整的句法分析系統，結合交通大學語音實驗室的斷詞器以及詞性標示，跟過去的 share task 比從 0.42 至 0.74 有將近 70% 的進步幅度，顯示出在深度學習模型對於自然語言處理的功勞不可小覷。目前在此領域中尚未有人完整的整理出一套輸入句子（未斷詞）即可得到依存句法分析樹的系統，並且已建構線上系統提供學術使用。由於繁體中文的自然處理領域，才剛起步，對於這樣的系統上有十分多的改善空間，如使用 graph-based 方法，可獲得更好的長距離修飾關係，希望以此論文作為開頭，讓更多學者加入研究。

## 五、 致謝

感謝科技部計畫編號 MOST 107-2221-E-009-MY2 的支持與協助。

## 六、 參考文獻

[1] You, Jia-Ming, Keh-Jiann Chen, 2004, "Automatic Semantic Role Assignment for a Tree Structure", Proceedings of SIGHAN workshop.

[2] Mikolov, Tomas, Chen, Kai, Corrado, Greg, and Dean, Jeffrey. "Efficient Estimation of Word Representations in Vector Space ", In Proceedings of Workshop at ICLR 2013

[3] Joakim Nivre, Marie-Catherine de Marneffe, Filip Ginter, Yoav Goldberg, Jan Hajič, Christopher D. Manning, Ryan McDonald, Slav Petrov, Sampo Pyysalo, Natalia Silveira, Reut Tsarfaty, Daniel Zeman, 2016, "Universal Dependencies v1: A Multilingual Treebank Collection". In Proceedings of LREC.

[4] Yih-Ru Wang, 2003, "An Improvement on Chinese Parser"

[5] Joakim Nivre , 2003, "An Efficient Algorithm for Projective Dependency Parsing" In Proceedings of the 8th International Workshop on Parsing Technologies

[6] Danqi Chen, Christopher D. Manning , 2014, "A Fast and Accurate Dependency Parser using Neural Networks" in EMNLP

[7] Chris Dyer, Miguel Ballesteros, Wang Ling, Austin Matthews, Noah A. ,Smith, 2016, "Transition-Based Dependency Parsing with Stack Long Short-Term Memory"

[8] Yuen-Hsien Tseng, Lung-Hao Lee and Liang-Chih Yu, 2012, "Traditional Chinese Parsing Evaluation at SIGHAN Bake-offs 2012"

The 2018 Conference on Computational Linguistics and Speech Processing
ROCLING 2018, pp. 76-77
©The Association for Computational Linguistics and Chinese Language Processing

# 是非題之支持證據檢索

## Supporting Evidence Retrieval for Answering Yes/No Questions

吳孟哲　Meng-Tse Wu
中央研究院資訊科學研究所
Institute of Information Science
Academia Sinica
moju@iis.sinica.edu.tw


林一中　Yi-Chung Lin
中央研究院資訊科學研究所
Institute of Information Science
Academia Sinica
lyc@iis.sinica.edu.tw


蘇克毅　Keh-Yih Su
中央研究院資訊科學研究所
Institute of Information Science
Academia Sinica
kysu@iis.sinica.edu.tw

## 摘要

本篇論文提出了一個新的支持證據擷取方法，也就是給定一個文件，在回答是非問題時，從中找到相關的句子。本研究使用 n-gram 匹配的方法，根據問題的內容找到相關的課文片段。跟以前的方法相比，此種模型更有效率而且更容易實作。本研究以台灣小學社會課本的是非問題做測試。實驗結果顯示本方法的效果比知名的 Apache Lucene 搜尋引擎高 5%。

## Abstract

A novel approach for retrieving the supporting evidence, which is a question related text passage in the given document, for answering Yes/No questions is proposed in this paper. It locates the desired passage according to the question text with an efficient and simple n-gram matching algorithm. In comparison with those previous approaches, this model is more efficient and easy to implement. The proposed approach was tested on a task of answering Yes/No questions of Taiwan elementary school Social Studies lessons. Experimental results showed that the performance of our proposed approach is 5% higher than the well-known

Apache Lucene search engine.

關鍵詞：信息檢索，支持證據檢索

Keywords: Information Retrieval, Supporting Evidence Retrieval

# 探討聲學模型的合併技術與半監督鑑別式訓練於會議語音辨識之研究

## Investigating acoustic model combination and semi-supervised discriminative training for meeting speech recognition

羅天宏 Tien-Hong Lo, 陳柏琳 Berlin Chen

國立臺灣師範大學資訊工程學系

Department of Computer Science and Information Engineering

National Taiwan Normal University

{teinhonglo, berlin}@ntnu.edu.tw

## 摘要

近年來鑑別式訓練(Discriminative training)的目標函數 Lattice-free Maximum mutual information (LF-MMI)在自動語音辨識(Automatic speech recognition, ASR)上取得了重大的突破[1]，有別於傳統交互熵訓練 (Cross-Entropy training, CE) 和鑑別式訓練 (Discriminative training)的二階段訓練，LF-MMI 提供更快的訓練與解碼。儘管 LF-MMI 在監督式環境下斬獲最好的成果，然而在半監督式環境的表現仍有待研究。在半監督式環境最常見的訓練方法是自我學習(Self-training)[2][3][4]中，由於種子模型(Seed model)常因語料有限而效果不佳。且 LF-MMI 屬於鑑別式訓練之故，更易受到標記錯誤的影響。為了減緩上述的問題，過往常加入置信度過濾器(Confidence-based filter)[4][5][6]對訓練語料做挑選。過濾語料可在不同層級上進行，分為音框層級[7]、詞層級[8]、句子層級[3][8][9]。

本論文利用兩種思路於半監督式訓練。其一，引入負條件熵(Negative conditional entropy, NCE)權重與詞圖(Lattice)，前者是最小化詞圖路徑的條件熵(Conditional entropy)，等同對 MMI 的參考轉錄(Reference transcript)做權重平均，權重的改變能自然地加入 MMI 訓練中，並同時對不確定性建模。其目的希望無置信度過濾器(Confidence-based filter)也可訓練模型。後者加入詞圖，比起過往的 one-best，可保留更多假說空間，提升找到參考轉錄(Reference transcript)的可能性；其二，我們借鑒整體學習(Ensemble learning)

的概念[10]，使用弱學習器(Weak learner)修正彼此的錯誤，分為音框層級合併
(Frame-level combination)[11]和假說層級合併(Hypothesis-level combination)[12]。

　　本論文的實作目的便是在語料缺乏的半監督式環境下，利用負條件熵與詞圖輔助
LF-MMI 的訓練，並利用模型合併技術，進一步提升模型的辨識結果。我們希望即使在
語料不足的情況下，仍能達到不錯的辨識效果，甚至媲美原先有標記語料的訓練結果。
實驗結果顯示，加入 NCE 與詞圖皆能降低詞錯誤率(Word error rate, WER)，而模型合併
(Model combination)則能在各個階段顯著提升效能，且兩者結合可使詞修復率(Word
recovery rate, WRR)達到 60.8%。

關鍵詞：自動語音辨識、鑑別式訓練、半監督式訓練、模型合併


## 參考文獻


[1] D. Povey et al., "Purely sequence-trained neural networks for ASR Based on Lattice-Free MMI," in Proc. *INTERSPEECH*, 2016.

[2] K. Vesely et al., "Semi-supervised training of deep neural networks," in *ASRU*, 2013.

[3] F. Grezl et al., "Semi-supervised bootstrapping approach for neural network feature extractor training," in *ASRU*, 2013.

[4] P. Zhang et al., "Semi-supervised dnn training in meeting recognition," in Proceedings of. Sheffield, 2014.

[5] L. Lamel et al., "Lightly supervised and unsupervised acoustic model training," *Computer Speech & Language* , 2002.

[6] H. Y. Chan et al., "Improving broadcast news transcription by lightly supervised discriminative training," in *ICASSP*, 2004.

[7] S.-H. Liu et al., "Investigating data selection for minimum phone error training of acoustic models,"in *Multimedia and Expo*, 2007.

[8] K. Vesely et al., "Semisupervised training of Deep Neural Networks," in ASRU, 2013.

[9] S. Thomas et al., "Deep neural network features and semisupervised training for low resource speech recognition," in Proc. *ICASSP*, 2013.

[10] P. Zhang et al., "Semisupervised DNN training in meeting recognition," in *SLT*, 2014.

[11] L. Deng et al., "Ensemble deep learning for speech recognition," in *INTERSPEECH*, 2014.

[12] H. Xu et al., "Minimum bayes risk decoding and system combination based on a recursion for edit distance," *Computer Speech and Language*, 2011

The 2018 Conference on Computational Linguistics and Speech Processing
ROCLING 2018, pp. 81-95
©The Association for Computational Linguistics and Chinese Language Processing

# 基於基因演算法的組合式多文件摘要方法

## An Ensemble Approach for Multi-document Summarization using Genetic Algorithms

陳俊章 Chun-Chang Chen, 鍾羽凾 Yu-Hang Chung, 楊正仁 Cheng-Zen Yang
元智大學資訊工程學系
Department of Computer Science & Engineering
Yuan Ze University
Email: {ccc15,yhc17,czyang}@syslab.cse.yzu.edu.tw


范植昇 Jhih-Sheng Fan
中央研究院資訊科學研究所
Institute of Information Science, Academia Sinica
Email: fann1993814@iis.sinica.edu.tw


李肇元 Chao-Yuan Lee
妍發科技股份有限公司
Y-Fa Technology Inc.
Email: jason.lee@yfa.com.tw


## 摘要

多文件摘要研究在文件摘要工作中是一個重要的研究項目。透過多文件摘要，將可以減少人們閱讀許多內容相似但相同主題文件的時間。本研究中提出一個基於基因演算法的組合式多文件摘要模型，以四個網路摘要模型，以及四個機率主題網路摘要模型分別建構組合式多文件摘要模型。在這兩個組合式摘要模型中，以基因演算法找出最佳組合權重。在以DUC 2004年至2007年四個資料集的實驗中，這兩個組合摘要模型在ROUGE-1，ROUGE-2，ROUGE-SU4的評分項目上，相較於個別摘要模型都有最好的表現。

## Abstract

Multi-document summarization is an important research task in text summarization. It helps people to reduce much time in reading articles of similar contents but with the same topics. In this study, we propose an ensemble model based on genetic algorithms. Two ensemble summarization models are thus constructed, one for four network summarization models, and the other for four probabilistic topic network models. These two ensemble models use genetic algorithms to find the optimal weights. We use the datasets of DUC 2004 to DUC 2007 for performance evaluation. The experimental results show that these two ensemble models can achieve the best performance in ROUGE-1, ROUGE-2, and ROUGE-SU4 than other standalone network models and standalone probabilistic topic network models.

關鍵字：多文件摘要，組合摘要模型，基因演算法，效能評估

Keyword: Multi-document summarization, ensemble summarization models, genetic algorithms, performance evaluation

## 一、 緒論

文件摘要 (Text Summarization) 技術能從文件中擷取出重要資訊彙整成摘要，是相當受到重視的研究[7,11]。依照處理的文件數量，文件摘要技術可分為單文件摘要(Single Document Summarization)技術[4]與多文件摘要(Multi-document Summarization) 技術 [1,2,3,5,9,13,14,15]。近年來許多研究都在研討多文件摘要技術的發展。透過將許多相關的文件進行分析，產生精簡的摘要，能幫助人們快速了解重要資訊。在過往多文件摘要研究中，已提出許多方法。例如MEAD 使用Centroid-based Summarization 的技術，來計算語句的重要性[9]。Xiong與Luo提出以Latent Semantic Analysis (LSA)的技術來提升多文件摘要的效能[12]。Erkan與Radev提出LexRank[3]，以PageRank的網路模型計算語句重要性。Yang等人以Probabilistic Latent Semantic Analysis (PLSA)計算語句主題並結合網路模型來計算語句重要性[13]。

然而過往研究大多只集中討論在多文件摘要模型中如何使用某一類型特徵中哪一種特徵能被使用來分析這些文章的語句重要性，沒有考慮如何綜合這一類型特徵中的多種特徵來分析語句重要性。因此在本研究中，我們提出一個基於基因演算法(Genetic Algorithms)的組合式多文件摘要模型，以提升多文件摘要的效能表現。在過往多文件摘要研究中，Chali 等人以SVM (Support Vector Machines) 也曾提出一個組合式的摘要模型[2]。然而這個SVM組合式摘要模型則是針對特定方式的使用者需求來進行多文件摘要，並不是通用型多文件摘要(Generic Multi-document Summarization)。本研究所提出的

組合式多文件摘要模型則沒有考慮使用者需求，是通用型的多文件摘要方式。

為了評估所提出的組合式多文件摘要模型，我們使用DUC (Document Understanding Conference) 2004年至2007年四年的資料集進行實驗。在以四個網路摘要模型(Degree Centrality [3]，Normalized Similarity-based Degree Centrality [15]，PageRank Centrality [3]，iSpreadRank Centrality [14])構成的組合摘要模型中，無論是在ROUGE-1，ROUGE-2或ROUGE-SU4這些評分項目上，相較於個別單一摘要模型都能夠得到最好的表現。在以四個機率主題網路摘要模型(PL-Degree，PL-NSDC，PL-PageRank，PL-iSpreadRank)[13]構成的組合摘要模型中，在ROUGE-1，ROUGE-2或ROUGE-SU4這些評分項目上，相較於各別機率主題網路摘要模型，也能夠得到最好的表現。

本論文其餘內容安排如下：第二節將介紹多文件摘要的相關研究。第三節將說明基於基因演算法的組合式多文件摘要模型的設計。第四節將說明以DUC2004年至2007年四個資料集進行實驗的結果。最後，第五節是本論文的結論。

## 二、 相關研究

在過往多文件摘要技術相關研究上，Radev等人在2000年提出MEAD多文件摘要器[9]。他們使用Centroid-based Summarization (CBS) 質心計算技術，利用一個主題偵測追蹤(Topic Detection and Tracking, TDT) 的集群計算方法找出文件集的質心。他們將MEAD的質心值與Positional value 和First-sentence overlap三種特徵萃取出的摘要經過實驗比較後，實驗結果顯示質心值的效能最好。

潛在語義分析(Latent Semantic Analysis, LSA)也曾被使用在多文件摘要技術中。例如Ozsoy等人於2010年提出二種基於LSA的方法來改進Steinberger與Jezek的方法[10]，處理土耳其文多文件摘要[8]。他們發現所提出的方法中Cross作法能夠得到很好的效果，在實驗中比其他LSA作法的摘要模型都好。Hachey等人於2006年討論SVD對多文件摘要的效果[5]。他們發現SVD加上字詞共現特徵後，雖然摘要效果與TF-IDF的作法相比之下不分軒輕，但是比單純使用字詞共現特徵的效果要好。

Erkan與Radev於2004年提出Degree Centrality 與LexRank兩種網路摘要模型[3]。他

們利用網路模型計算語句重要性。在網路模型中，每個節點代表一個語句。節點之間的連結，則由語句TF-IDF 向量的Cosine Similarity 來決定。如果相似度超過一個門檻值，則兩個語句節點之間存在連結關係，建構出文章語句之間的關係網路。Degree Centrality方法會計算每個節點的對外連結數，對外連結數越多的節點代表越重要。計算方式如式(1)，其中α為相似度門檻值，$s_i$是語句，$\deg(s_i)$是$s_i$的Degree Centrality：

$$\deg(s_i) = \sum_{j:i \neq j \ and \ sim(s_i,s_j) \geq \alpha} 1 \tag{1}$$

但是當一些不重要的節點因彼此連結而有高的連結數時，Degree Centrality會將這些不重要的語句也納入摘要，降低摘要結果的品質。因此Erkan等人利用網路模型PageRank來計算出語句的重要性。因此對於$s_i$的PageRank分數$PR(s_i)$，計算方式如下：

$$PR(s_i) = \frac{d}{N} + (1 - d) \sum_{s_v \in adj[s_i]} \frac{PR(s_v)}{\deg(s_v)} \tag{2}$$

其中$N$是語句關係圖節點總數，$d$是阻尼因子，通常在0.1-0.2之間。$PR(s_i)$是節點$s_i$的LexRank向心性，$adj[s_i]$是$s_i$相鄰的節點集合，$deg(s_v)$是節點$s_v$的Degree Centrality分數。

2008年Yeh 等人提出另一個網路摘要模型iSpreadRank [14]。iSpreadRank利用了擴散活化理論，考慮節點的連結數量，並且考慮這些節點彼此之間的影響性。在iSpreadRank中，首先會將語句相似度網路轉成一個Sentence-by-Sentence矩陣A。

$$A = \begin{bmatrix} a_{1,1} & \cdots & a_{1,n} \\ \vdots & \ddots & \vdots \\ a_{n,1} & \cdots & a_{n,n} \end{bmatrix} \tag{3}$$

其中$a_{i,i} = 0$，$a_{i,j}$代表兩語句的相似度。接著使用擴散活化理論來擴散語句重要性給其他語句。網路中的每個節點都有一個活化級別。在離散時間內iSpreadRank反覆地更新所有節點的影響性，直到終止條件被滿足。在每次迭代中，所有節點在時間點$t$的iSpreadRank Centrality $X(t)$計算方式如下：

$$X(t) = X(0) + MX(t - 1), M = \sigma R^T \tag{4}$$

其中$X(0)$是一個$n \times 1$的向量，代表每個語句的初始向心性分數。$\sigma$為一擴散因子，設為0.7，控制節點影響性的程度。$R$是一隨機矩陣 (Stochastic Matrix)，其中$r_{i,j} = \frac{a_{i,j}}{\sum_k a_{i,k}}$：

$$R = \begin{bmatrix} r_{1,1} & \cdots & r_{1,n} \\ \vdots & \ddots & \vdots \\ r_{n,1} & \cdots & r_{n,n} \end{bmatrix} \tag{5}$$

擴散過程的終止條件設定為時間t與時間$t-1$的節點影響性差異總和是否小於一個門檻值$\epsilon$。若小於則結束擴散過程。計算方式如下，在[14]中 $\epsilon = 0.0001$：

$$\sum_i |X_i(t) - X_i(t-1)| \leq \epsilon \tag{6}$$

當iSpreadRank計算結束時，網路處於穩定狀態，每個節點用數字權重標記它們的最終重要程度。iSpreadRank便依照權重高低排名來選擇語句加入摘要。

2013年，Yeh等人討論了不同的網路模型多文件摘要技術[15]。他們同時討論兩個不同的關係網路：連續權重語句關係網路與離散權重語句關係網路，在連續權重語句關係網路中，節點之間的Cosine Similarity 值若高於門檻值，便為節點連結的權重，若沒有高過門檻值，則為0。在離散權重語句關係網路中，節點之間的連結關係則成為一種0或1的二元關係。接著，他們討論五種節點向心性計算方法在這二種關係網路上的表現，分別為：Degree，Normalized Similarity-based Degree，HITS，PageRank 及iSpreadRank。實驗結果顯示，連續權重語句關係網路較離散權重語句關係網路更佳，五種節點向心性的計算以iSpreadRank具有最高的效能。

機率式潛在語意分析(Probabilistic Latent Semantic Analysis, PLSA) 改善LSA不符合統計觀點和無法解決一詞多義的缺點，以機率計算並找出文件中潛在的重要主題，再以機率計算並找出符合該潛在主題的字詞，進而找到含有這些字詞的語句來當作摘要。2014年，Yang等人提出了機率主題網路模型(Probabilistic Topic-based Network Models)的多文件摘要技術[13]。在機率主題網路模型中，語句的主題特徵向量成為語句關係網路節點，再用不同的網路模型來處理主題網路。在實驗中分別討論PLSA與LDA (Latent Dirichlet Allocation)主題模型的效果。實驗結果顯示PLSA所強化的機率主題網路摘要模型能比原有的網路模型有更好的效能，且在不同的資料集中都有名列前茅的表現。

2009年Chali等人提出一個組合式摘要模型(Ensemble Summarization Model)[2]。這個組合摘要模型使用Support Vector Machines (SVM)的組合方法，並使用多個SVM建構一個交叉驗證委員會機制(Cross-Validation Committees, CVC) 來進行摘要。其策略是藉由使用其他SVM的輸出來校正其中一個SVM的錯誤。實驗結果證明組合的SVM摘要模型效能高於單一SVM摘要模型。

　　基因演算法(Genetic Algorithms) 是一種用於解決最佳化問題的搜索算法。對於一個最佳化問題，GA用染色體代表可能的解答，透過選擇、交配、突變等過程，來尋找最佳解。Bossard和Rodrigues在2011年提出Clustering Based Sentence Extractor for Automatic Summarization (CBSEAS)多文件摘要方法，將多文件摘要技術與GA結合[1]。CBSEAS依據與文件質心的相似度來排列所有語句，語句的相似度以Jaccard方式計算，接著建構相似矩陣，利用Fast Global K-means來將語句分成數個集合，並以四個加權方式：與用戶查詢或質心相似度、與集群中心相似度、重要的句子分數、得分句與期望句長之間的長度差異，來為每個集合選擇一個最具代表性的摘要。實驗結果顯示GA可以找到最佳的參數組合以提高摘要效能。

## 三、　組合式多文件摘要模型

　　在基因演算法組合式多文件摘要模型中，這個摘要模型的處理流程將說明如下。

## （一）、組合式多文件摘要處理流程

　　圖1是本研究所提出的基因演算法組合式摘要模型的處理流程。將多個單一摘要模型進行組合，然後由基因演算法來找出最佳權重。在處理流程中，首先會將文件進行前處理。前處理的項目分別為Sentence Segmentation，Tokenization，Stopword Removal 以及Stemming。然後按照不同的單一摘要模型分別計算出語句的分數。基因演算法組合摘要模型則依照線性組合公式，用基因演算法找出最佳組合權重，重新得到語句的最後加權分數。最後則用CSIS演算法[9]進行語句篩選，產生最後的摘要。

　　在組合的單一摘要模型中，分別考慮近年來有不錯表現的四個網路摘要模型，以及四個經過PLSA強化後的機率主題網路模型。這四個網路主題模型分別是Degree Centrality (Degree)摘要模型[3]，Normalized Similarity-based Degree Centrality (NSDC)摘

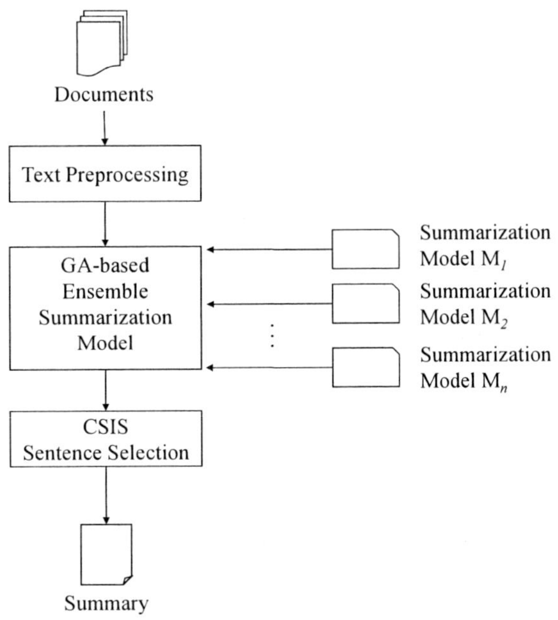



圖1、基因演算法組合摘要模型處理流程

要模型[15]，PageRank摘要模型[3]，以及iSpreadRank摘要模型[14]。它們的PLSA 主題強化摘要模型分別是PL-Degree，PL-NSDC，PL-PageRank 以及PL-iSpreadRank [13]。

## （二）、文件前處理

在進行多文件摘要前，每份文件都需要先進行文本的前處理。由於文件敘述中會有一些缺乏意義的詞彙，例如冠詞或Be動詞等所謂的停用詞(Stopword)，這些詞通常無法表現文件摘要的語句重要性，因此在前處理中會被移除。以下是前處理中進行的項目：

- Sentence Segmentation：文件中的每一個語句先需要被斷句分開。本研究使用 NLTK (Natural Language Toolkit)[1]工具來進行斷句。

- Tokenization：本研究使用NLTK以語句為單位，將語句中的單詞取出，以bag-of-words的方式來表示該語句。

- Stopword Removal: 我們使用Onix[2]停用詞表將語句中的停用詞移除。

- Stemming:在經過停用詞移除後，本研究再使用Porter Stemmer[3]進行詞根還原。

---

[1] https://www.nltk.org/

[2] http://www.lextek.com/manuals/onix/stopwords1.html

[3] https://tartarus.org/martin/PorterStemmer

經過上述前處理，如果語句的字數少於3個，該語句因為含有字詞過少，因此該語句極有可能缺乏重要語意，在本研究中將會捨棄而不予考慮。

## （三）、組合成員之單一摘要模型

### 1、語句關係網路建構

在本研究中，所組合的單一摘要模型為四個網路摘要模型與四個機率主題網路摘要模型。因此將先建構出語句關係網路(Sentence Relationship Network)。在網路摘要模型中，語句之間的關係是用語句之間的相似度(Sentence Similarity) 來考慮。在本研究中，語句以TF-IDF (Term Frequency-Inverse Document Frequency) 的向量表示。兩個語句$s_i$和$s_j$之間的相似度用Cosine Similarity 來計算，如式(7)所示。

$$\text{sim}(s_i, s_j) = \frac{\overrightarrow{s_i} \cdot \overrightarrow{s_j}}{|\overrightarrow{s_i}| \times |\overrightarrow{s_j}|} \tag{7}$$

在建構語句相似網路時，如果$sim\ (si,\ sj) < 0.1$，因為相似度太低，因此在網路模型中這兩個語句便不會有連結關係。

在機率主題網路摘要模型中，是以每個語句的主題字詞作為網路節點。語句之間的相似度是以主題機率的相似度來考慮。因此對於語句$s_i$和$s_j$，在主題空間z的情況下，它們的主題特徵向量$\overrightarrow{v_i} = \langle p(z_1|s_i), p(z_2|s_i), ..., p(z_K|s_i) \rangle$，$\overrightarrow{v_j} = \langle p(z_1|s_j), p(z_2|s_j), ..., p(z_K|s_j) \rangle$兩者的相似度用Cosine Similarity 計算，如式(8)：

$$\text{sim}(v_i, v_j) = \frac{\overrightarrow{v_i} \cdot \overrightarrow{v_j}}{|\overrightarrow{v_i}| \times |\overrightarrow{v_j}|} \tag{8}$$

在建構主題機率相似度網路時，也會設定門檻值來判斷語句之間的相似度關係是否存在。

### 2、單一摘要模型

在語句關係網路中，每個節點是各個語句的TF-IDF向量。在主題機率關係網路中，每個節點是各個語句的主題機率特徵向量。在本研究中，組合成員則是基於這兩種不同向量 上的四種網路摘要模型：Degree, NSDC, PageRank與iSpreadRank。Degree, PageRank與iSpreadRank如第2節中所介紹，在此便不重複說明。NSDC則是基於Degree模型但是考慮所有節點的相似度，然後就相似度總和來做正規化。在NSDC中，對語句$s_i$而言，它

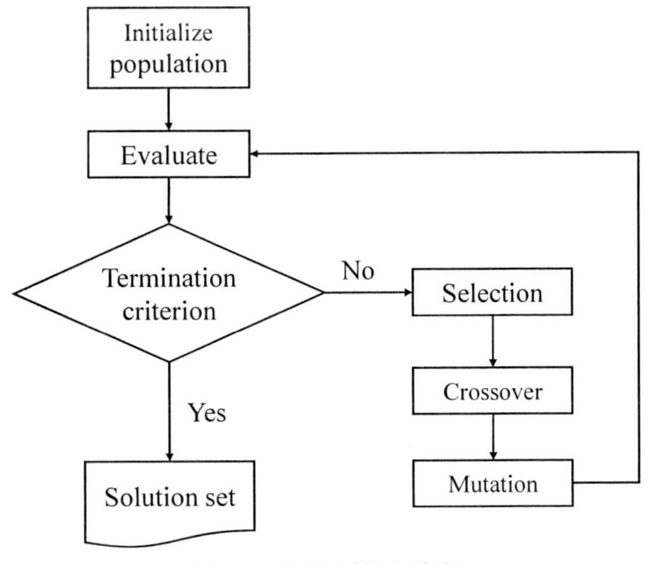

圖2、基因演算法流程

的NSDC Centrality $sim\ deg(s_i)$計算如下：

$$sim\ deg(s_i) = \sum_{j:i\neq k\ and\ sim(s_j,s_k)\geq\alpha} \frac{sim(s_i,s_j)}{\sum_{k:j\neq k\ and\ sim(s_j,s_k)\geq\alpha} sim(s_j,s_k)} \tag{9}$$

## （四）、基於基因演算法的組合摘要模型

在組合摘要模型中，組合的方式是每個單一摘要模型$M_j$先各別算出語句$s_i$語句重要性分數$I_{ij}$，然後用一個線性組合公式來算出語句$s_i$的最後排序分數$R_i$。在線性組合公式中，每個單一摘要模型的$I_{ij}$會分別乘上一個加權權重$w_j$。因此線性組合的計算公式如下：

$$R_i = \sum_{\forall j} w_j \times I_{ij} \tag{10}$$

為了要使語句排序的計算得到最佳結果，我們使用基因演算法來求得最佳組合權重。我們以摘要的目標函式作為GA適應函式。本研究分別以ROUGE-1，ROUGE2和ROUGE-SU4做為最佳化的目標函式來求得最佳的組合權重。

基因演算法的流程如圖2所示，以下將說明各個步驟。

1. Initialize population:

   本研究以$K$=50組染色體來進行計算。每組染色體有$N$個基因，$N$為單一摘要模型總數，代表單一摘要模型$M_j$的權重$w_j$。$w_j$的初始值範圍是$0 \leq w_j \leq 1$，取到小數點後4位，同時$\sum_{\forall j} w_j = 1$。在初代染色體中，保留代表各個單一摘要模型$(1, 0, ... , 0),(0, 1, ... ,$

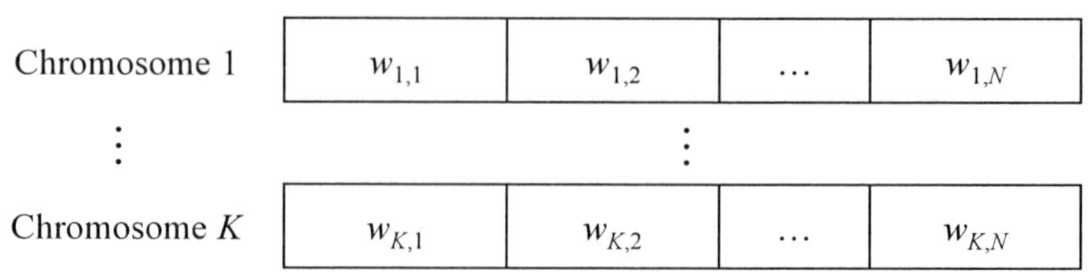



圖3、基因演算法中的染色體

0),...,(0, 0, ... , 1)的染色體。其餘染色體是隨機產生。圖3是此$K$組染色體的情況。

2. Evaluate:

在基因演算法評估時，會針對適應函式ROUGE-1，ROUGE-2，ROUGE-SU4 三種不同的摘要評分方式找出各自的最佳組合權重。GA 會以迴圈方式進行評估。中斷條件是當下面兩個條件其中之一滿足，GA便會結束。

- 連續5次的適應函數結果差距≤ 0.0001。
- 基因產生迴圈已進行1000次迭代。

3. Selection:

如果GA中止條件沒有滿足，GA便會進行Selection，Crossover和Mutation。在Selection中，如果該染色體的適應函式分數$F_k \geq F_{avg}$，就會被保留下來。如果$F_k < F_{avg}$，該染色體被目前所找到的最佳染色體所代替。$F_{avg}$是所有染色體的平均適應函式分數。

4. Crossover:

GA依據交配率決定是否進行交配。本研究設定交配率為0.5，進行$K$次交配，以單點交配法進行。交配時會隨機選2組染色體，並隨機決定1個切斷點，將這2組染色體切

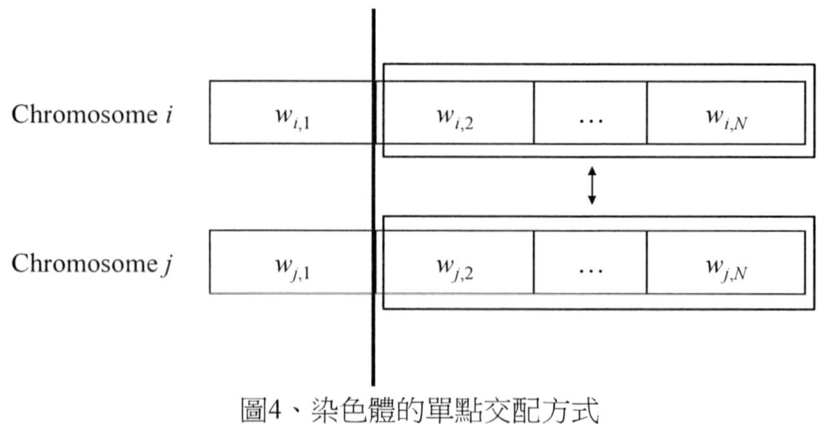



圖4、染色體的單點交配方式

```
Input: a rank list L of sentences
Output: the summary Sum
Initialize:
    set Sum = ∅
Summarize:
    while the required compression rate R is not met
        s_c ← the candidate sentence having the highest score in L
        if max sim(s_c, s_j) < C_R
           s_j∈Sum
                add s_i to Sum
        else
                omit s_i
        endif
        remove s_i from L
    output the summary Sum
```

圖5、CSIS語句選取方式

成兩部分，再將切開的部分重新組合成一對新的染色體。交配的方式如圖4所示。

5. Mutation:

GA交配完成後進入突變流程。本研究中突變率設0.25，希望能盡可能突破Local Optimal的情況。突變方式為單點突變，GA會隨機選擇該染色體的任一個基因突變，取一個在0到1之間的小數來取代，精確度到小數點後4位。

## （五）、語句選擇

經由組合計算後，將得到的語句分數排序，然後按此順序挑選摘要語句。為了去除重複多餘的資訊，我們採用CSIS (Cross-Sentence Information Subsumption)[9]來檢查候選語句是否與已選的摘要內容重複。CSIS演算法如圖5所示，相似度計算採用Cosine Similarity，$R$是摘要大小的限制，Sum是摘要集合，$C_R$門檻值決定語句是否重複，本研究設定為0.7。$L$是語句的排序列表。在計算相似度時，在網路摘要模型中是用語句的TF-IDF向量來計算，在機率主題網路摘要模型中，則是用語句的主題機率特徵向量來計算。

## 四、 實驗結果及分析

## （一）、實驗環境設定

表1、DUC資料集內容

|  | DUC 2004 | DUC 2005 | DUC 2006 | DUC 2007 |
|---|---|---|---|---|
| 文件集數 | 50 | 50 | 50 | 45 |
| 每個文件集的文件數 | 10 | 25-50 | 25 | 25 |
| 摘要長度要求 | 665 bytes | 250字 | 250字 | 250字 |

表2、實驗參數設定

| 主題數目($\tau$) | 256 (DUC 2004,DUC 2005), 128 (DUC 2006,DUC 2007) |
|---|---|
| 主題機率相似度門檻值($\gamma$) | 0.05 (NSDC:2007; iSpreadRank:2005, 2006),<br>0.2 (Degree:2004, 2007; NSDC:2006; PageRank:2004),<br>0.25 (Degree:2005, 2006; NSDC:2004, 2005; PageRank:<br>2005, 2006, 2007; iSpreadRank:2004, 2007) |
| 字詞向量相似度門檻值($S_t$) | 0.1 |
| PageRank阻尼因子($d$) | 0.15 |
| iSpreadRank擴散因子($\sigma$) | 0.001 |
| CSIS篩選門檻值 | 0.7 |

　　本實驗採用的資料集是來自於DUC (Document Understanding Conference)所提供
DUC 2004- 2007共4個資料集。它們的特性如表1所示。評估標準是採用ROUGE (Recall-
Oriented Understudy for Gisting Evaluation)作為評估工具[6]，ROUGE將人工所產生的摘
要作為參考答案，以$n$-gram為單位，計算人工摘要和 機器所產生摘要的同樣所包含的
字詞比例。本實驗將針對ROUGE-1，ROUGE-2，ROUGE-SU4來進行探討。

　　在不同的網路模型中，各項實驗參數設定如表2所示。這些參數的設定是參考自
[3]和[13]研究中的參數設定。

（二）、網路模型組合實驗

　　在網路摘要模型的組合實驗中，本研究所提出的基因演算法組合摘要模型(GA-
DNPI) 與另外四個網路摘要模型Degree，NSDC，PageRank，iSpreadRank 進行效能比
較。表3到表6是這五個摘要模型在四個資料集中的效能表現。我們可以看到GA-DNPI在
這四個資料集中都有最好的表現。

（三）、機率主題網路模型組合實驗

　　在機率主題網路模型的組合實驗中，本研究所提出的基因演算法組合摘要模型
(GA-PL-DNPI)與另外四個機率主題網路摘要模型PL-Degree, PL-NSDC, PL-PageRank,

表3、DUC 2004效能比較

|  | ROUGE-1 | ROUGE-2 | ROUGE-SU4 |
|---|---|---|---|
| Degree | 0.36264 | 0.08471 | 0.12636 |
| NSDC | 0.35068 | 0.06862 | 0.11376 |
| PageRank | 0.36482 | 0.08348 | 0.12539 |
| iSpreadRank | 0.36874 | 0.08882 | 0.12885 |
| GA-DNPI | **0.37009** | **0.08963** | **0.12993** |

表4、DUC 2005效能比較

|  | ROUGE-1 | ROUGE-2 | ROUGE-SU4 |
|---|---|---|---|
| Degree | 0.36444 | 0.06843 | 0.12342 |
| NSDC | 0.36255 | 0.06244 | 0.11850 |
| PageRank | 0.36891 | 0.06801 | 0.12455 |
| iSpreadRank | 0.36494 | 0.06693 | 0.12228 |
| GA-DNPI | **0.37235** | **0.06912** | **0.12575** |

表5、DUC 2006效能比較

|  | ROUGE-1 | ROUGE-2 | ROUGE-SU4 |
|---|---|---|---|
| Degree | 0.39174 | 0.08388 | 0.13943 |
| NSDC | 0.39216 | 0.07673 | 0.13450 |
| PageRank | 0.39867 | 0.08497 | 0.14187 |
| iSpreadRank | 0.39568 | 0.08491 | 0.14032 |
| GA-DNPI | **0.39929** | **0.08550** | **0.14204** |

表6、DUC 2007效能比較

|  | ROUGE-1 | ROUGE-2 | ROUGE-SU4 |
|---|---|---|---|
| Degree | 0.41209 | 0.09618 | 0.15271 |
| NSDC | 0.40988 | 0.08974 | 0.14645 |
| PageRank | 0.41561 | 0.09784 | 0.15332 |
| iSpreadRank | 0.41263 | 0.09741 | 0.15260 |
| GA-DNPI | **0.41781** | **0.09838** | **0.15422** |

PL-iSpreadRank 進行效能比較。由於在[13]中，主題數目也會影響效能，因此我們在實驗中，單一的機率主題摘要模型會用在 Rouge-1表現不錯的主題數目來處理。在實驗中，主題數目以64，128，256來考慮。表7到表10是這五個摘要模型在 DUC2004-DUC2007四年資料集中的效能表現，我們可以看到GA-PL-DNPI 也都有最好的表現。

五、 結論

多文件摘要是一件相當受到重視的研究工作，因為能夠幫助人們迅速掌握關鍵資料。本研究提出了基於基因演算法的組合摘要模型來處理自動多文件摘要問題，使用基因演算法來求得最佳組合。在 DUC 2004-2007資料集的實驗中，相較於個別單一摘要模型，

表7、DUC 2004不同主題數目效能比較

|  | τ值 | ROUGE-1 | ROUGE-2 | ROUGE-SU4 |
|---|---|---|---|---|
| PL-Degree | 256 | 0.38440 | 0.09010 | 0.13395 |
| PL-NSDC | 64 | 0.37878 | 0.08472 | 0.13024 |
| PL-PageRank | 256 | 0.38387 | 0.08978 | 0.13379 |
| PL-iSpreadRank | 64 | 0.38087 | 0.08297 | 0.13020 |
| GA-PL-DNPI | 256 | **0.38466** | **0.09165** | **0.13515** |

表8、DUC 2005不同主題數目效能比較

|  | τ值 | ROUGE-1 | ROUGE-2 | ROUGE-SU4 |
|---|---|---|---|---|
| PL-Degree | 256 | 0.38510 | 0.07269 | 0.13239 |
| PL-NSDC | 64 | 0.37368 | 0.06276 | 0.12402 |
| PL-PageRank | 256 | 0.38456 | 0.07145 | 0.13221 |
| PL-iSpreadRank | 64 | 0.37473 | 0.06389 | 0.12393 |
| GA-PL-DNPI | 256 | **0.38524** | **0.07289** | **0.13264** |

表9、DUC 2006不同主題數目效能比較

|  | τ值 | ROUGE-1 | ROUGE-2 | ROUGE-SU4 |
|---|---|---|---|---|
| PL-Degree | 128 | 0.41315 | 0.08642 | 0.14696 |
| PL-NSDC | 128 | 0.41296 | 0.08748 | 0.14743 |
| PL-PageRank | 128 | 0.41355 | 0.08629 | 0.14703 |
| PL-iSpreadRank | 128 | 0.41172 | 0.08795 | 0.14708 |
| GA-PL-DNPI | 128 | **0.41355** | **0.08854** | **0.14785** |

表10、DUC 2007不同主題數目效能比較

|  | τ值 | ROUGE-1 | ROUGE-2 | ROUGE-SU4 |
|---|---|---|---|---|
| PL-Degree | 128 | 0.42890 | 0.10150 | 0.15860 |
| PL-NSDC | 64 | 0.42889 | 0.10153 | 0.15933 |
| PL-PageRank | 128 | 0.42800 | 0.10516 | 0.16069 |
| PL-iSpreadRank | 64 | 0.42793 | 0.10065 | 0.15916 |
| GA-PL-DNPI | 128 | **0.43133** | **0.10645** | **0.16273** |

都能夠在ROUGE-1，ROUGE-2 和ROUGE-SU4這些評分項目上得到最好的表現。

## 六、 參考文獻

[1] A. Bossard and C. Rodrigues, "Combining a Multi-Document Update Summarization System –CBSEAS- with a Genetic Algorithm," in *Proceedings of the 2nd Inter-national Workshop on Combinations of Intelligent Methods and Applications (CIMA 2010)*, 2011, pp. 71–87.

[2] Y. Chali, S. A. Hasan, and S. R. Joty, "A SVM-Based Ensemble Approach to Multi-Document Summarization," in *Proceedings of the 22nd Canadian Conference on Artificial Intelligence (Canadian AI 2009)*, 2009, pp. 199–202.

[3] G. Erkan and D. R. Radev, "LexRank: Graph-based Lexical Centrality As Salience in Text Summarization," *Journal of Artificial Intelligence Research*, vol. 22, no. 1, pp. 457–479, Jul. 2004.

[4] Y. Gong and X. Liu, "Generic Text Summarization Using Relevance Measure and Latent Semantic Analysis," in *Proceedings of the 24th Annual International ACM SIGIR Conference on Research and Development in Information Retrieval (SIGIR '01)*, 2001, pp. 19–25.

[5] B. Hachey, G. Murray, and D. Reitter, "Dimensionality Reduction Aids Term Co-occurrence based Multi-document Summarization," in *Proceedings of the Workshop on Task-Focused Summarization and Question Answering (SumQA '06)*, 2006, pp. 1–7.

[6] C.-Y. Lin, "ROUGE: A Package for Automatic Evaluation of Summaries," in *Text Summarization Branches Out: Proceedings of the ACL-04 Workshop*, 2004, pp. 74–81.

[7] I. Mani, *Automatic Summarization*. John Benjamins Publishing Co., 2001.

[8] M. G. Ozsoy, I. Cicekli, and F. N. Alpaslan, "Text Summarization of Turkish Texts Using Latent Semantic Analysis," in *Proceedings of the 23rd International Conference on Computational Linguistics (COLING '10)*, 2010, pp. 869–876.

[9] D. R. Radev, H. Jing, and M. Budzikowska, "Centroid-based Summarization of Multiple Documents: Sentence Extraction, Utility-based Evaluation, and User Studies," in *Proceedings of the 2000 NAACL-ANLP Workshop on Automatic Summarization*, vol. 4, 2000, pp. 21–30.

[10] J. Steinberger and K. Ježek, "Using Latent Semantic Analysis in Text Summarization and Summary Evaluation," in *Proceedings of the 5th International Conference on Information Systems Implementation and Modelling*, Apr. 2004, pp. 93–100.

[11] J.-M. Torres-Moreno, *Automatic Text Summarization*, J.-C. Pomerol, Ed. John Wiley & Sons, Inc., 2014.

[12] S. Xiong and Y. Luo, "A New Approach for Multi-document Summarization Based on Latent Semantic Analysis," in *Proceedings of the 2014 7th International Symposium on Computational Intelligence and Design (ISCID '14)*, 2014, pp. 177–180.

[13] C.-Z. Yang, J.-S. Fan, and Y.-F. Liu, "Multi-document Summarization using Probabilistic Topic-based Network Models," *Journal of Information Science and Engineering*, vol. 32, no. 6, pp. 1613–1634, Nov. 2016.

[14] J.-Y. Yeh, H.-R. Ke, and W.-P. Yang, "iSpreadRank: Ranking Sentences for Extraction-based Summarization Using Feature Weight Propagation in the Sentence Similarity Network," *Expert Systems with Applications*, vol. 35, no. 3, pp. 1451–1462, Oct. 2008.

[15] J.-Y. Yeh, W.-P. Yang, H.-R. Ke, and P.-C. Cheng, "Extraction-based News Summarization Using Sentence Centrality in the Sentence Similarity Network," Journal of Information Management, vol. 21, no. 3, pp. 271–304, 2014.

The 2018 Conference on Computational Linguistics and Speech Processing
ROCLING 2018, pp. 96-110
©The Association for Computational Linguistics and Chinese Language Processing

# WaveNet 聲碼器及其於語音轉換之應用

## WaveNet Vocoder and its Applications in Voice Conversion

黃文勁*、羅振州*、黃信德*、曹昱**、王新民*

Wen-Chin Huang*, Chen-Chou Lo*, Hsin-Te Hwang*, Yu Tsao**, Hsin-Min Wang*

*中央研究院資訊科學研究所
Institute of Information Science
Academia Sinica

**中央研究院資訊科技創新研究中心
Research Center for Information Technology Innovation
Academia Sinica

## 摘要

多數語音轉換模型仰賴以傳統來源濾波器模型(source-filter model)為基礎之聲碼器(vocoder)對語音訊號進行語音參數抽取以及合成語音。然而，受限於傳統聲碼器的諸多理論與假設，以傳統聲碼器為架構進行語音轉換所生成的語音，其自然度以及與目標語者的相似度均無法進一步提升。在深度學習(deep learning)領域中，WaveNet 是現階段最成功的語音生成技術之一，能產生與過去方法相比自然度更高的語音。WaveNet 聲碼器為 WaveNet 的一個延伸，具備產生超越傳統聲碼器的高品質語音的能力，並已逐漸被從事語音轉換研究之國外團隊所採用。過去，國內研究團隊所開發的語音轉換模型多以傳統聲碼器為基礎進行語音轉換，本論文試圖將 WaveNet 聲碼器引入國內幾個新近提出的語音轉換模型，以評估 WaveNet 聲碼器在這些語音轉換模型上的應用潛力。於實驗中，我們比較了三種語音轉換模型分別使用傳統聲碼器與 WaveNet 聲碼器所得到的結果。其中，所比較的語音轉換模型包括 1)變分式自動編碼器(variational auto-encoder, VAE)、2)結合生成式對抗型網路之變分式自動編碼器、以及 3)跨特徵領域變分式自動編碼器(cross domain VAE, CDVAE)。實驗結果顯示，三個語音轉換模型在使用 WaveNet 聲碼器後，與目標語者的相似度均獲得顯著的改善。在自然度方面，則僅有以 VAE 為基礎之語音轉換模型在使用 WaveNet 聲碼器後有顯著的提升。

**關鍵詞**：WaveNet，聲碼器，語音轉換，變分式自動編碼器。

## Abstract


Most voice conversion models rely on vocoders based on the source-filter model to extract speech parameters and synthesize speech. However, the naturalness and similarity of the converted speech are limited due to the vast theories and constraints posed by traditional vocoders. In the field of deep learning, a network structure called WaveNet is one of the state-of-the-art techniques in speech synthesis, which is capable of generating speech samples of extremely high quality compared with past methods. One of the extensions of WaveNet is the WaveNet vocoder. Its ability to synthesize speech of quality higher than traditional vocoders has made it gradually adopted by several foreign voice conversion research teams. In this work, we study the combination of the WaveNet vocoder with the voice conversion models recently developed by domestic research teams, in order to evaluate the potential of applying the WaveNet vocoder to these voice conversion models and to introduce the WaveNet vocoder to the domestic speech processing research community. In the experiments, we compared the converted speeches generated by three voice conversion models using a traditional WORLD vocoder and the WaveNet vocoder, respectively. The compared voice conversion models include 1) variational auto-encoder (VAE), 2) variational autoencoding Wasserstein generative adversarial network (VAW-GAN), and 3) cross domain variarional auto-encoder (CDVAE). Experimental results show that, using the WaveNet vocoder, the similarity between the converted speech generated by all the three models and the target speech is significantly improved. As for naturalness, only VAE benefits from the WaveNet vocoder.

**Keywords:** WaveNet, Vocoder, Voice Conversion, Variational Auto-Encoder.

一、緒論

語音轉換(voice conversion)泛指在不改變來源語音的說話內容的條件下，將來源語音轉換成目標語音。語音轉換技術的應用廣泛，包括將聲音品質較差的窄頻語音訊號(narrowband speech)轉換成聲音品質較好的寬頻語音訊號(wideband speech) [1]、作為文字轉語音 (text-to-speech)系統之後處理 [2]、或是將發聲受損病患的語音轉為正常語音 [3] 等。其中，最基本及常見的應用為語者語音轉換(speaker voice conversion) (文獻中常泛稱語者語音轉換為語音轉換)，其目標為不改變來源語者(source speaker)的說話內容下，將來源語者的語音轉換成目標語者(target speaker)的語音 [4]。

多數的語音轉換方法是在聲碼器(vocoder)的框架下來實踐語音轉換，亦即需要先將語音波形進行分析(或稱參數化)，以求得聲碼器所需要的參數，例如：頻譜(spectrum)、韻律(prosody)、激發源(excitation)等特徵參數(通稱為語音參數)。接著，再對這些語音參數進行轉換，並將轉換過後的語音參數透過聲碼器還原回語音波形。簡而言之，一個典型的語音轉換系統可被拆解為三個部分：分析、轉換、合成。轉換後語音品質的好壞及與目標語者語音的相似程度，除了與語音轉換方法有密切關係外，也與聲碼器在進行分析與還原回語音波形的過程有關。過去，聲碼器的設計主要是基於來源濾波器模型(source-filter model)的理論，包括早期的線性預估編碼器 [5] 以及現今語音轉換與語音合成(文字轉語音)領域中廣被使用的高品質聲碼器，例如 STRAIGHT [6] 與 WORLD [7] 聲碼器。然而，基於來源濾波器模型理論所設計的聲碼器對人類發聲的過程有諸多的假設與簡化，使得聲音品質、自然度等無法進一步提升。

近年來，以深度類神經網絡(deep neural network, DNN)為基礎的技術被廣泛使用於語音生成相關主題上。其中，WaveNet [8] 是現階段最成功的語音生成技術之一。應用於文字轉語音，此網絡架構可從給定的語言參數及語音參數，直接產生出接近真實人聲的高品質語音波形 [8]。此外，基於 WaveNet 的聲碼器技術也已經被提出 [9, 10]。WaveNet 聲碼器為一種以資料驅動(data driven)之聲碼器，即透過大量訓練語料學習所得到的聲碼器。其扮演的角色主要用以取代傳統聲碼器在還原語音波形的過程。確切地說，給定傳統聲碼器中抽取而得的語音參數作為 WaveNet 聲碼器的輸入，則語音波形可直接透過 WaveNet 聲碼器的輸出端解碼得到。由於 WaveNet 聲碼器可直接產生語音波形(包含了頻譜與相位資訊)，避免了傳統聲碼器使用訊號處理的技術分開估測頻譜與相位資訊後再組合還原回語音波形的過程中所導致的誤差問題，因而可以產生比傳統聲碼器自然度更高的語音。

　　國內已有許多相當成熟的語音轉換技術[11, 12]，但多數仍使用傳統聲碼器，使得轉換的聲音品質無法繼續提升。WaveNet 聲碼器問世後，各國頂尖的語音轉換團隊紛紛開始使用。於 2018 年語音轉換挑戰賽(Voice Conversion Challenge 2018, VCC2018) [13] 中獲得前兩名的隊伍便是使用 WaveNet 聲碼器於他們的語音轉換系統中 [14, 15]，進而大幅提升轉換後語音的自然度及與目標語者語音相似度。本論文旨在對 WaveNet 聲碼器做一介紹，並展示其與國內研究團隊所開發的語音轉換技術結合後所帶來之正面效益，提供國內語音轉換、甚至其他語音生成任務研究者參考。

　　本論文的章節安排如下。於第二章，我們介紹 WaveNet 聲碼器。於第三章，我們介紹由國內團隊所開發的三種語音轉換技術。第四章則為實驗結果與分析。此篇論文的總結與未來展望則呈現於第五章。


## 二、WaveNet 聲碼器

### 2.1 網絡架構

WaveNet [8] 是一個深層自迴歸網絡，藉由以下條件機率式來逐點取樣，可以生成品質極高的語音波形：

$$P(X|h) = \prod_{n=1}^{N} P(x_n|x_{n-r}, \dots, x_{n-1}, h) \, , \tag{1}$$

其中$n$為當前取樣的樣本點編號，$r$為感知域大小，$x_n$為當前要生成的語音訊號樣本點，且此樣本點是以整數、有限的離散位階來表示(例如 16 bits量化位階，即$2^{16} = 65536$個整數值)，$h$則為輔助特徵向量。若將WaveNet作為聲碼器(例如 [9, 10])，則輔助特徵向量包含如傳統聲碼器STRAIGHT [6] 或World [7] 所抽取的語音參數等資訊，即頻譜特徵(spectral feature)、基頻(fundamental frequency)及描述激勵訊號的非週期性參數(aperiodicity)。給定輔助特徵向量，根據式(1)，WaveNet便可以估計出對應的語音樣本序列。如圖一所示，一個標準的WaveNet聲碼器包含了許多的殘差區塊(residual block)，每個殘差區塊中有一個2×1的空洞因果卷積層(dilated causal convolution)、一個門控激活函數(gated activation function)、以及一個1×1的卷積層。空洞因果卷積層可以擴大網路的感知域，而門控激活函數則被定義為：

$$\tanh\left(W_{f,k} * x + V_{f,k} * h\right) \odot \sigma\left(W_{g,k} * x + V_{g,k} * h\right) , \tag{2}$$

其中$x$為空洞因果卷積層的輸出，$W$和$V$為可被訓練的卷積核，$*$代表卷積運算，$\odot$代表點對點相乘，$\sigma(\cdot)$代表sigmoid函數。值得一提的是，WaveNet的訓練是將每個語音樣本點產生的過程視為分類問題，並使用交叉熵(cross entropy)目標函式來訓練網路。以16 bits量化位階的語音波形為例，每個語音樣本點可以表示成65536種有限的類別，而WaveNet的訓練目標即為正確分類每個語音樣本點。為了減少計算量與避免類別過多造成的分類錯誤，輸入的波形會先藉由傳統訊號處理編碼方法(例如$\mu$-law編碼法)進一步量化至較少位元的量化位階(例如8 bits，即每個語音樣本點僅有256個類別)。

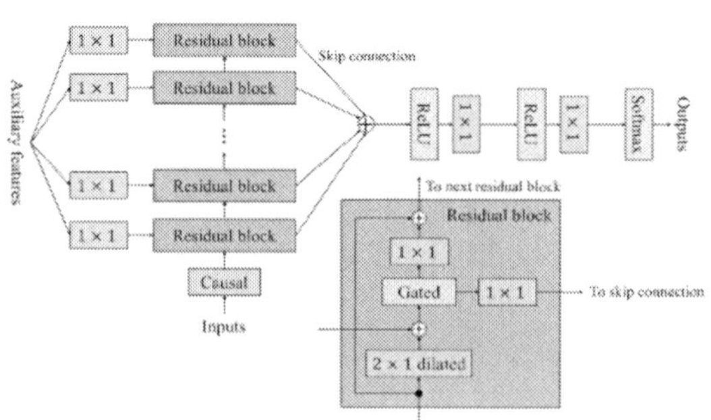


圖一、WaveNet 聲碼器示意圖。

## 2.2 多語者 WaveNet 聲碼器之語者調適

最早的 WaveNet 聲碼器是一種語者依賴(speaker dependent)的聲碼器，即使用單一語者的語料作為訓練資料集 [9]。由於訓練 WaveNet 聲碼器需要大量的訓練語料，而收集單一語者大量的語料顯得困難且不切實際，多語者 WaveNet 聲碼器(multi-speaker WaveNet vocoder)因而被提出，即在訓練階段使用多名語者的語料來訓練 WaveNet 聲碼器 [10]。將多語者 WaveNet 聲碼器應用於語音轉換時，必須針對目標語者進行語者調適(speaker adaptation)，亦即使用目標語者的語料，對多語者 WaveNet 聲碼器進行調適訓練。實驗證實，與多語者 WaveNet 聲碼器相比，此一語者調適的技巧可以有效提升輸出語音的品質及與目標語者的相似度 [14, 15, 16]。

## 三、語音轉換模型

### 3.1 基於變分式自動編碼器的語音轉換

變分式自動編碼器(variational auto-encoder, VAE) [17, 18] 可以將輸入至其編碼器(encoder)(或稱編碼函數)的語音音框(speech frame) $x$ 編碼成包含語音內容的隱藏編碼(latent code)，以 $z$ 表示。此編碼器被假設為語者獨立，亦即希望其所輸出之隱藏編碼 $z$ 僅包含語音內容，如音素等語音資訊，而不包含語者資訊。隱藏編碼 $z$ 與語者表示法 $y$ 串接後，透過解碼器(decoder)(或稱解碼函數)來還原回對應語者表示法相關的語音訊號，便可達到語音轉換的目的。VAE 的目標函數如下三式所示，而在 VAE 學習與建模過程之最大化目標函式即為最大化式(3)：

$$\log p_\theta(x) \leq -J_{vae}(x) = -J_{obs}(x) - J_{lat}(z) , \tag{3}$$

$$J_{lat}(\phi; z) = D_{KL}(q_\phi(z|x)||p_\theta(z)) , \tag{4}$$

$$J_{obs}(\phi, \theta; x) = -E_{q_\phi(z|x)}[\log p_\theta(x|z, y)] , \tag{5}$$

其中 $\phi$, $\theta$ 分別為編碼器、解碼器參數，$D_{KL}(\cdot || \cdot)$ 為 KL 散度(Kullback-Leibler divergence)。

　　VAE 架構如圖二所示，其中 $x$ 表示語音音框，$z$ 為該音框的隱藏編碼，$y$ 為語者表示法。在模型建模學習階段，VAE 對輸入語音拆解其語音內容然後還原，並且同時最佳化語者表示法，將此自我編碼與解碼還原過程應用於眾多語者的語音資料後，即可習得所有語者通用的編碼器、解碼器及各個語者各自之語者表示法。在使用階段係將輸入來源語者之每一語音音框$x$經由編碼器編碼得到隱藏編碼$z$後，結合建模學習階段所習得之目標語者的語者表示法$y$，透過解碼器來將該來源語者語音轉換成目標語者語音。由於 VAE 是藉由將語音內容$z$結合對應語者表示法$y$來達到語音轉換，將來源語音轉換成建模學習語料中的任意語者，表示編碼器在建模學習過程會習得整合不同的分佈特性，最後再透過不同語者表示法來形成對應的分佈。相較於傳統語者轉換方法需要不同語者的平行語料(即語者們的訓練文本相同)及需將不同語者之相同語句進行音框對齊，VAE 在模型訓練階段是透過自我還原的方式來習得編碼器、解碼器及語者表示法，故不需要平行語料，亦毋需對齊語句。換言之，VAE 是一種可以應用於無平行語料條件下的語音轉換技術。

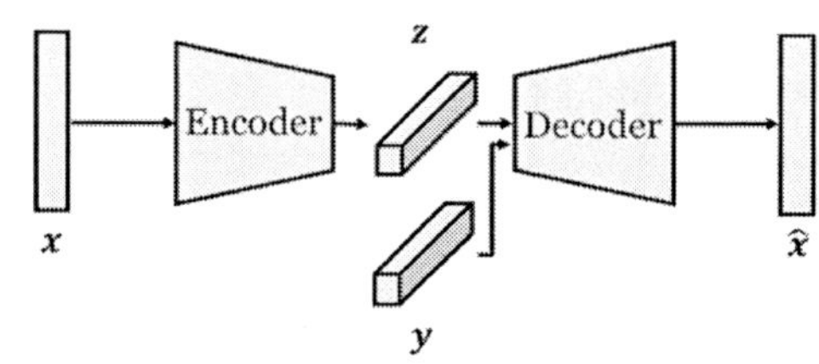


圖二、基於變分式自動編碼器的語音轉換示意圖。

## 3.2 引入生成式對抗型網路的語音轉換

生成式對抗型網路(generative adversarial network, GAN)的概念是透過讓生成模型(generator)以及鑑別模型(discriminator)互相對抗，而讓生成模型的輸出分佈最佳化 [19]。在訓練過程中，生成模型會依據不同的輸入資訊以及模型架構，來產生近似真實分佈的生成輸出分佈；鑑別模型則負責區分當前輸入的分佈究竟是屬於生成模型所生成的分佈，還是真實資料的分佈。在基於 VAE 的語音轉換中，其解碼函數所解碼生成的語音決定了最終轉換後語音的品質，而藉由引入 GAN 的目標函數，原 VAE 輸出的語音品質得以進一步被增強 [12]。

在諸多 GAN 的變形中，Wasserstein GAN(W-GAN)以訓練穩定為特色而被廣泛使用 [20]。W-GAN 是以推土機距離(earth mover's distance，或稱 Wasserstein distance)作為目標函數的一種 GAN 架構。於文獻 [12] 中，作者藉由計算模型所近似之分佈與原始分佈

的推土機距離來衡量語音轉換演算法的好壞，並透過 Discriminator 來增強原始 VAE 的
輸出語音品質。為了讓語音轉換在非對齊語料條件下實現，目標函數被定義為推土機距
離的對偶形式(Kantorovich-Rubinstein duality)，其定義如下式：

$$W\left(p_t^*, p_{t|s}\right) = \sup_{|D|_L \leq 1} \left(E_{x \sim p_t^*}[D(x)] - E_{x \sim p_{t|s}}[D(x)]\right), \tag{6}$$

其中，$D$ 為符合 1-Lipschitz continuity 的評分函數(critic function)，等價於 GAN 架構中的
鑑別模型，$p_t^*$為目標語者的真實機率分佈，$p_{t|s}$為轉換後語音的機率分佈。被用來近似
實現這個函數的深度神經網路為$D_\psi$，其中的真實分佈$p_t^*$可藉由取樣目標語者的語音求
得，而$p_{t|s}$則是透過原始的 VAE 來獲得，亦即由轉換後的語音輸出求得。在語音轉換的
應用上，推土機距離可寫為下式：

$$E_{x \sim p_t^*}[D_\psi(x)] - E_{z \sim q_\phi(z|x_s)}[D_\psi(G_\theta(z, y_t)], \tag{7}$$

其中，$G_\theta$為 VAE 的解碼函數。與上所述之 GAN 架構相同，評分函數$D_\psi$與解碼函數$G_\theta$(等
價於 GAN 架構中的生成模型)的目標是互相對抗的。在此需額外說明的是，這個架構是
讓評分函數對於真實目標語音以及 VAE 解碼函數所生成的轉換語音來做鑑別，希望給
真實的語音較高的分數，而給生成的語音較低的分數。然而，解碼函數的首要任務即為
讓解碼生成之語音的分佈可以盡量接近目標語者真實的語音分佈，亦即減少評分函數對
於真實語音與轉換語音的分數差值。透過結合 VAE 生成特性與 W-GAN 的對抗架構來達
到增強 VAE 轉換語音的品質，此演算法被稱作 VAW-GAN，如圖三所示。其目標函數如
下式：

$$J_{VAWGAN} = -D_{KL}(q_\phi(z|x)||p\_\theta(z)) + E_{q_\phi(z|x)}[log\, p_\theta(x|z, y)$$

$$+E_{x \sim p_t^*}[D_\psi(x)] - E_{z \sim q_\phi(z|x_s)}[D_\psi(G_\theta(z, y_t)]。 \tag{8}$$

圖三、引入生成式對抗型網路的 VAE 語音轉換示意圖。

## 3.3 跨特徵領域變分式自動編碼器的語音轉換

在VAE語音轉換中，假設編碼器能萃取出與語者資訊無關的語音內容。跨特徵領域變分式自動編碼器(cross domain VAE, CDVAE)的語音轉換之中心思想，即為充分利用從同一音框中抽取的、擁有不同屬性的頻譜特徵參數，來讓編碼器萃取出更純粹的語音內容 [21]。我們使用STRAIGHT編碼器 [6] 所求得的頻譜波封(簡稱STRAIGHT spectrum, SP)及梅爾倒頻譜係數(mel cepstral coefficients, MCCs) [22] 作為兩種不同的頻譜特徵參數。如圖四所示，CDVAE為一系列自編碼器的集合，每種特徵參數有其各自的一組編碼器及解碼器。對於每種特徵參數所對應的編碼器與解碼器組，除了要可以重建輸入特徵(圖四中的路徑(1)與(2))，編碼器還要能找出一個能讓其他特徵解碼器也可以成功重建的表示法；同樣的，解碼器要能從任意編碼器所編碼出的表示法重建出該特徵(圖四中的路徑(3)與(4))。我們更進一步在目標函數中加上一個相似誤差，讓不同特徵參數的編碼器所找出的表示法互相趨近(即$z_{SP}$與$z_{MCC}$要接近)。

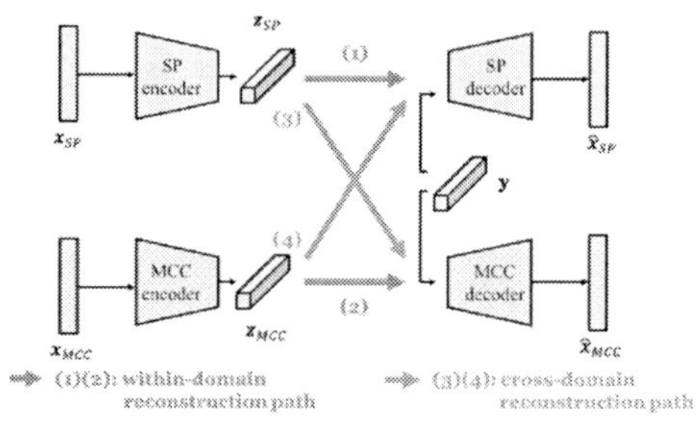


圖四、跨特徵領域的 VAE 語音轉換示意圖。

## 四、實驗

## 4.1 實驗設定

我們使用 Voice Conversion Challenge 2018 (VCC2018)比賽中大會所提供的語料，其中包括了 12 位專業英語語者的語音，每位語者錄製了 81 句訓練用語料以及 35 句測試用語料，取樣頻率為 22050 赫茲 [13]。我們使用 WORLD 聲碼器 [7] 作為抽取語音參數。語音訊號首先被切成長 25 毫秒、重疊 5 毫秒的音框。接著，我們從每個音框中抽取語音參數，包括 513 維的頻譜波封(spectral envelope)、513 維的非週期性訊號及基頻；35 維的梅爾倒頻譜係數(包括第 0 維的音框能量)則從頻譜波封中抽出。

在WaveNet聲碼器方面，我們以Hayashi 等人 [10] 所提出WaveNet聲碼器還原聲音波形，實作上也使用其提供的WaveNet聲碼器開源版本[1]。此外，所有模型及訓練參數都和此開源版本預設值相同。我們使用VCC2018中的所有訓練語料，總數為972句，總長度約為54分鐘來訓練多語者WaveNet聲碼器。WaveNet聲碼器所使用的輔助特徵向量(即輸入WaveNet聲碼器的語音參數)包括去除第0維的34維的梅爾倒頻譜係數、壓縮為2維的非週期性訊號、基頻，以及清音/濁音二元特徵。為了將這些輔助特徵向量使用在WaveNet聲碼器中，實作上採用了時間解析度調整(time resolution adjustment)的技巧 [9, 10]，即簡單地複製這些聲學特徵，使得他們和輸入的語音波形有同樣的時間解析度(亦即取樣頻率)。多語者WaveNet聲碼器的訓練迴圈數為200000，語者調適則是透過進一步使用目標語者的語料進行5000個迴圈的訓練完成。

在語音轉換模型的部分，我們使用公開的VAE及VAW-GAN語音轉換模型開源版本[2]，所有模型和訓練參數都和預設值相同。我們提出的CDVAE尚未開源，但其實作概念上相當於兩個VAE，因此我們使用兩個相同的VAE模型，訓練參數也仿照開源版本中的設定。我們同樣使用VCC2018的所有訓練資料。我們對頻譜波封取對數，並進行unit-sum的能量正規化，並將能量在訓練及轉換階段取出。在轉換階段，頻譜參數由語音轉換模型進行轉換，其在使用能量還原後，與不更動的非週期性訊號，以及在對數空間進行線性轉換後的基頻，一同輸入WORLD聲碼器或WaveNet聲碼器進行語音合成。詳細VAE、VAW-GAN及CDVAE關於語音參數、類神經網路架構與參數等設定可參考 [12, 18, 21]。

## 4.2 實驗結果與討論

我們針對 VCC2018 中 SF1 to TF1 這一個同性別轉換對，隨機從測試語料中選取 10 句語音，先利用 VAE、VAW-GAN、CDVAE 三種語音轉換模型進行語音轉換後，將其輸出特徵分別使用 WORLD 聲碼器以及 WaveNet 聲碼器合成語音。

---

[1] https://github.com/kan-bayashi/PytorchWaveNetVocoder
[2] https://github.com/JeremyCCHsu/vae-npvc

## 4.2.1 頻譜圖

圖五為轉換語音之頻譜圖。從圖中可發現，使用 WaveNet 聲碼器所生成之語音頻譜在中高頻的結構較接近真實語音(較為隨機)；而低頻的結構則過於模糊、雜訊較多，缺乏真實語音該有的共振峰結構(formant structure)。因此，WaveNet 聲碼器所產生的語音雖然較自然，但有較多的雜音。

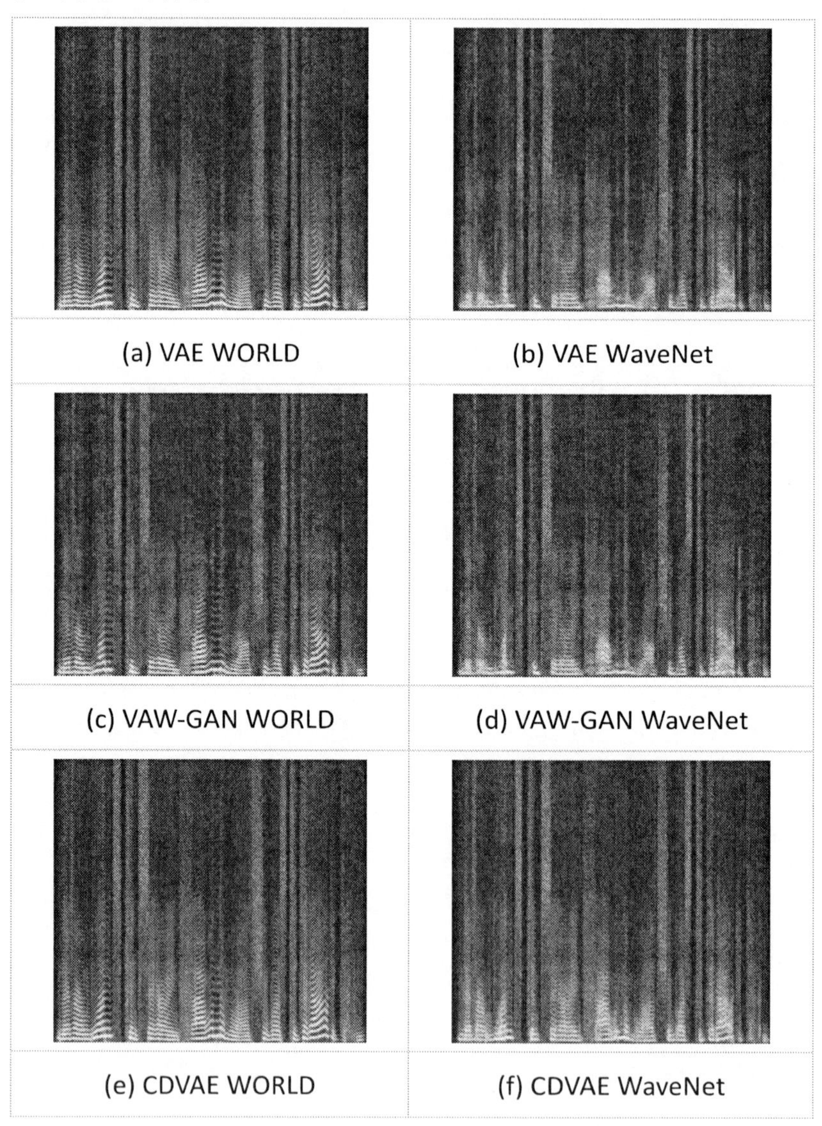


圖五、使用不同聲碼器生成之語音頻譜圖。

## 4.2.2 聽測實驗

此實驗邀請 9 位受試者來進行語音自然度及與目標語者相似度的聽測實驗。圖六為受試者針對轉換語音自然度所評估的平均意見分數(mean opinion score, MOS)之結果(包含目標語者之真實語音)。綜合平均分數及信心區間結果，可發現 WaveNet 聲碼器相對 WORLD 聲碼器在 VAE 語音轉換模型中有顯著的優勢，在 CDVAE 語音轉換模型中有些許但不顯著的優勢，在 VAW-GAN 中則是 WORLD 聲碼器相對於 WaveNet 聲碼器有些許但不顯著的優勢，這和 [23] 的結果類似。我們觀察到，WORLD 聲碼器傾向產生穩定但較糊的聲音，而 WaveNet 聲碼器雖然可以產生與 WORLD 聲碼器相比較清晰自然的語音，但有時所產生的聲音聽起來較為不穩定，含有抖音及些許雜音。我們認為可能的原因有二：其一為，在 VCC2018 語料庫中的語者彼此語音波形走勢(waveform trajectory)相差較大，造成 WaveNet 聲碼器難以有效擷取正確的走勢；其二為，WaveNet 聲碼器是以從真實語音所抽取之語音參數進行多語者訓練及語者調適，但實際進行語音轉換時卻是輸入轉換後的語音參數，這兩者間可能有落差(mismatch)。未來若能減少訓練及轉換間的落差，便可能產生自然度及品質更高的語音。

　　圖七為受試者針對轉換語音與目標語音之相似度的 ABX 測試結果。從圖中可以清楚地看到，相較於 WORLD 聲碼器，使用 WaveNet 聲碼器來合成語音可以有效的提高與目標語者間的相似度。綜合圖六與圖七之結果，我們可以發現 WaveNet 聲碼器所生成的語音在自然度上與 WORLD 聲碼器相似，但在與目標語者之相似度上則皆較優。值得注意的是，當把 WaveNet 聲碼器接在 VAW-GAN 後，不僅生成語音之自然度與 WORLD 聲碼器相較之下降低，在與目標語者之相似度所獲得的提升也不如 VAE 和 CDVAE。這將是未來需要被探討的。

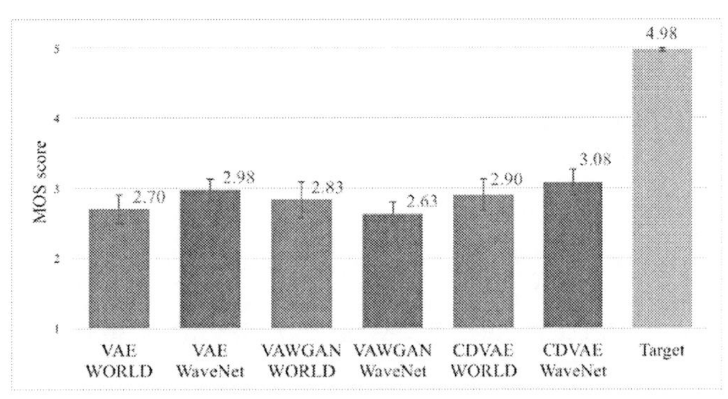

圖六、語音自然度之平均意見分數。誤差線代表 95%信心區間。

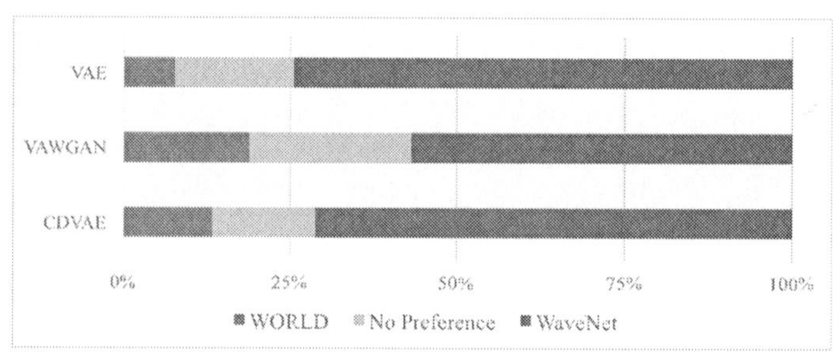

圖七、與目標語者相似度之偏好。

## 五、結論

在本論文中，我們對 WaveNet 聲碼器做了一簡單的介紹，並將其應用於數個國內研究團隊所研發之語音轉換模型。從聽測實驗的結果，WaveNet 聲碼器展現了其與傳統聲碼器相比之下，所能對現有語音轉換模型產生之正面效益。目前看到的效益主要在提升轉換後語音與目標語者語音之間的相似度，在語音自然度方面則與傳統 WORLD 聲碼器有相近的表現。在未來，我們希望能針對 WaveNet 聲碼器所合成語音之自然度進行優化，例如加大訓練語料，或者探討更有效的語者調適技巧，以縮小輸入 WaveNet 聲碼器之語音參數在訓練階段與實際轉換階段之間的落差等等。我們也期望國內語音研究者因為我們的引介，能方便快速地開始使用 WaveNet 聲碼器工具，讓生成語音的品質提升。

## 參考文獻


[1]　W. Fujitsuru, H. Sekimoto, T. Toda, H Saruwatari, and K. Shikano, "Bandwidth Extension of Cellular Phone Speech Based on Maximum Likelihood Estimation with GMM," Proc. NCSP2008

[2]　C. C. Hsia, C. H. Wu, and J. Q. Wu, "Conversion Function Clustering and Selection Using Linguistic and Spectral Information for Emotional Voice Conversion" *IEEE Trans. on Computers*, 56(9), pp. 1225–1233, September 2007.

[3]　H. Doi, T. Toda, K. Nakamura, H. Saruwatari, K. Shikano, "Alaryngeal Speech Enhancement Based on One-to-many Eigenvoice Conversion," *IEEE/ACM Trans. on Audio, Speech, and*

*Language Processing*, 22(1), pp. 172–183, January 2014.

[4]   Y. Stylianou, O. Cappe, and E. Moulines, "Continuous probabilistic transform for voice conversion," *IEEE Transactions on Speech and Audio Processing*, vol. 6, no. 2, pp. 131–142, Mar 1998.

[5]   B. S. Atal and S. L. Hanauer : "Speech analysis and synthesis by linear prediction of the speech wave", in J. Acoust. Soc. America , vol. 50, no. 2, pp.637–655, Mar. 1971.

[6]   H. Kawahara, I. Masuda-Katsuse, and A. de Cheveign, "Restructuring speech representations using a pitch-adaptive time-frequency smoothing and an instantaneous-frequency-based f0 extraction: Possible role of a repetitive structure in sounds," *Speech Communication*, vol. 27, no. 3, pp. 187 – 207, 1999.

[7]   M. Morise, F. Yokomori, and K. Ozawa, "WORLD: a vocoder-based high-quality speech synthesis system for real-time applications," IEICE Trans. Inf. Syst., vol. E99- D, no. 7, pp. 1877-1884, 2016.

[8]   A. van den Oord, S. Dieleman, H. Zen, K. Simonyan, O. Vinyals, A. Graves, N. Kalchbrenner, A. W. Senior, and K. Kavukcuoglu, "WaveNet: A generative model for raw audio," *CoRR*, vol. abs/1609.03499, 2016.

[9]   A. Tamamori, T. Hayashi, K. Kobayashi, K. Takeda, and T. Toda, "Speaker-dependent WaveNet vocoder," Proc. INTERSPEECH, pp. 1118–1122, 2017.

[10] T. Hayashi, A. Tamamori, K. Kobayashi, K. Takeda, and T. Toda, "An investigation of multi-speaker training for WaveNet vocoder," Proc. ASRU, 2017.

[11] J. Chou, C. Yeh, H. Lee, L. Lee, "Multi-target Voice Conversion without Parallel Data by Adversarially Learning Disentangled Audio Representations," Proc. INTERSPEECH, pp. 501-505, 2018.

[12] C.-C. Hsu, H.-T. Hwang, Y.-C. Wu, Y. Tsao, and H.-M. Wang, "Voice conversion from unaligned corpora using variational autoencoding wasserstein generative adversarial networks," in *Proc. Interspeech*, 2017, pp. 3364–3368.

[13] J. Lorenzo-Trueba, J. Yamagishi, T. Toda, D. Saito, F. Villavicencio, T. Kinnunen, and Z. Ling, "The voice conversion challenge 2018: Promoting development of parallel and nonparallel methods," in *Proc. Odyssey*, 2018, pp. 195–202.

[14] L. Liu, Z. Ling, Y. Jiang, M. Zhou, L. Dai, "WaveNet Vocoder with Limited Training Data for Voice Conversion," Proc. INTERSPEECH, pp. 1983-1987, 2018.

[15] P.L. Tobing, Y.-C. Wu, T. Hayashi, K. Kobayashi, and T. Toda, "NU voice conversion system for the voice conversion challenge 2018," in *Proc. Odyssey* 2018, pp. 219-226.

[16] Y.-C. Wu, P. L. Tobing, T. Hayashi, K. Kobayashi, and T. Toda, "The NU Non-Parallel Voice Conversion System for the Voice Conversion Challenge 2018," in *Proc. Odyssey*, 2018, pp. 211–218.

[17] D. P. Kingma and M. Welling, "Auto-encoding variational bayes," *CoRR*, vol. abs/1312.6114, 2013.

[18] C.-C. Hsu, H.-T. Hwang, Y.-C. Wu, Y. Tsao, and H.-M. Wang, "Voice conversion from non-parallel corpora using variational auto-encoder," in *Proc. APISPA ASC*, 2016, pp. 1–6.

[19] I. J. Goodfellow, J. Pouget-Abadie, M. Mirza, B. Xu, D. Warde- Farley, S. Ozair, A. C. Courville, and Y. Bengio, "Generative adversarial networks," *CoRR*, vol. abs/1406.2661, 2014.

[20] M. Arjovsky, S. Chintala, and L. Bottou, "Wasserstein GAN," *CoRR*, vol. abs/1701.07875, 2017.

[21] W.-C. Huang, H.-T. Hwang, Y.-H. Peng, Y. Tsao, and H.-M. Wang, "Voice Conversion Based on Cross-Domain Features Using Variational Auto Encoders," in Proc. ISCSLP 2018.

[22] T. Fukada, K. Tokuda, T. Kobayashi, and S. Imai, "An adaptive algorithm for mel-cepstral analysis of speech," *in Proc. ICASSP 1992*.

[23] K. Kobayashi, T. Hayashi, A. Tamamori, and T. Toda, "Statistical voice conversion with WaveNet-based waveform generation," Proc. INTERSPEECH, pp. 1138– 1142, 2017.

The 2018 Conference on Computational Linguistics and Speech Processing
ROCLING 2018, pp. 111-113
©The Association for Computational Linguistics and Chinese Language Processing

# 探討鑑別式訓練聲學模型之類神經網路架構及優化方法的改進

# Discriminative Training of Acoustic Models Leveraging Improved Neural Network Architecture and Optimization Method

趙偉成　Wei-Cheng Chao，張修瑞　Hsiu-Jui Chang，羅天宏　Tien-Hong Lo，

陳柏琳　Berlin Chen

國立臺灣師範大學資訊工程學系

Department of Computer Science and Information Engineering

National Taiwan Normal University

{60647028S, 60647061S, teinhonglo, berlin}@ntnu.edu.tw

## 摘要

本論文探討聲學模型上的改進對於大詞彙連續中文語音辨識的影響。近幾年來，語音辨識技術已有了長足的進步。其中，隨著深度學習技術以及電腦運算能力的突破性發展，聲學模型化技術已從傳統的高斯混合模型結合隱藏式馬可夫模型(Gaussian Mixture Model-Hidden Markov Model, GMM-HMM)[1][2]，轉變成以使用交互熵(Cross Entropy)作為損失函數的深度類神經網路結合隱藏式馬可夫模型(Deep Neural Network-Hidden Markov Model, DNN-HMM)[3]。DNN-HMM 將以往用 GMM 計算的生成機率透過 DNN 的輸出層所代表的事後機率來近似，輸入特徵使用當前幀還有相鄰的幀，輸出則和 GMM-HMM 常用的 Triphone 共享狀態相同，以得到更低的詞錯誤率(Word Error Rate, WER)或字錯誤率(Character Error Rate, CER)。另一方面，進一步透過鑑別式訓練估測的聲學模型在語音辨識的表現上往往比僅以交互熵做為深度類神經網路損失函數的訓練方式來的好。但由於傳統上進行鑑別式訓練需要使用先進行交互熵訓練的聲學模型來產生詞圖(Word Lattices)，才能再進行下一步聲學模型鑑別式訓練[4][5]。近年來為了減少時間及空間複雜度，有學者對於 Maximum Mutual Information (MMI)訓練，提出了所謂的 Lattice-free 的方式，使產生 Lattice 的步驟能夠在 GPU 上完成[6]，因而讓鑑別式訓

練得以做到端對端的訓練方式[7]，因而大幅縮減了聲學模型訓練所需時間。傳統 DNN-HMM 模型用於語音辨識的缺點在於無法充分利用語音信號之時間依賴性；相對來說時間延遲類神經網路(Time-Delay Neural Network, TDNN)[8]可以包含歷史和未來輸出、對長時間依賴性的語音訊號建模，使 TDNN-HMM 與傳統 DNN-HMM 訓練效率也相仿，因此在使用 LF-MMI 進行鑑別式訓練時，聲學模型的類神經網路部分通常是使用 TDNN。對於 TDNN 而言，增加層數可以說是擷取更長時間的特徵；我們希望加深 TDNN 的網路層數來達到更好的結果，但以往的實驗發現深度的網路常有退化問題，類神經網路的深度之增加準確率反而會下降。因此本篇論文將比較並結合當前先進的聲學模型訓練方法，例如[9]。對網路的矩陣分解訓練可以使網路訓練更穩定，以期達到更佳的語音辨識表現。另一方面，梯度下降是執行優化的最流行的算法之一，也是迄今為止優化類神經網絡的最常用方法。而常見的優化算法有隨機梯度下降法(Stochastic Gradient Descent, SGD)、RMSprop、Adam、Adagrad、Adadelta[10]。等演算法；其中，SGD 算法在語音辨識任務上最被廣為使用。而本論文則採用來回針法(Backstitch)[11]。做為模型優化的演算法；它是一種基於 SGD 上的改進，希望能夠藉由兩步驟的更新 Minibatch，以達到更好的效果。在中文廣播新聞的辨識任務顯示，上述改進方法的結合能讓 TDNN-LF-MMI 的模型在字錯誤率(Character Error Rate, CER)有相當顯著的降低。

關鍵詞：中文大詞彙連續語音辨識、聲學模型、鑑別式訓練、矩陣分解、來回針法

## 參考文獻


[1] Lawrence R. Rabiner et al., "A tutorial on hidden markov models and selected applications in speech recognition," *Proceedings of the IEEE, 1989*

[2] Mark Gales and Steve Yang, "The application of hidden markov models in speech recognition," *Foundations and Trends® in Signal Processing, 2008*

[3] Geoffrey Hinton et al., "Deep neural networks for acoustic modeling in speech recognition: the shared views of four research groups," *IEEE Signal processing magazine, 2012*

[4] Lalit Bahl et al., "Maximum mutual information estimation of hidden markov model parameters for speech recognition," *IEEE ICASSP, 1986*

[5] Karel Veselý, et al., "Sequence-discriminative training of deep neural networks," *Interspeech, 2013*

[6] Daniel Povey et al., "Purely sequence-trained neural networks for ASR based on lattice-free MMI," *Interspeech, 2016*

[7] Hossein Hadian et al., "End-to-end speech recognition using lattice-free MMI," *Interspeech, 2018*

[8] Alexander Waibel et al., "Phoneme recognition using time-delay neural networks," *IEEE Transactions on Acoustics Speech, and Signal Processing, 1989*

[9] Daniel Povey et al., "Semi-orthogonal low-rank matrix factorization for deep neural networks," *Interspeech, 2018*

[10] Sebastian Ruder, "An overview of gradient descent optimization algorithms," *arXiv*, 2016

[11] Yiming Wang et al., "Backstitch: counteracting finite-sample bias via negative steps," *Interspeech, 2017*

The 2018 Conference on Computational Linguistics and Speech Processing
ROCLING 2018, pp. 114-115
©The Association for Computational Linguistics and Chinese Language Processing

# 使用長短期記憶類神經網路建構中文語音辨識器之研究

## A study on Mandarin speech recognition using Long Short- Term Memory neural network

賴建宏　Chien-hung Lai
國立交通大學電信工程研究所
Institute of Communications Engineering
National Chiao Tung University
lsr950082@speech.cm.nctu.edu.tw


王逸如　Yih-Ru Wang
國立交通大學電機工程學系
Department of Electronic Engineering
National Chiao Tung University
yrwang@cc.nctu.edu.tw

## 摘要

近年來類神經網路(Neural network)被廣泛運用於語音辨識領域中，本論文使用遞迴式類神經網路(Recurrent Neural Network)訓練聲學模型，並且建立中文大辭彙語音辨識系統。由於遞迴式類神經網路為循環式連接(Cyclic connections)，應用於時間序列訊號的模型化(Modeling)，較於傳統全連接(Full connection)的深層類神經網路而言更有益處。

然而一般單純遞迴式類神經網路在訓練上隨著時間的遞迴在反向傳播(Backpropagation)更新權重時有著梯度消失(Gradient vanishing)以及梯度爆炸(Gradient exploding)的問題，導致訓練被迫中止，以及無法有效的捕捉到長期的記憶關聯，因此長短期記憶(Long Short-Term Memory, LSTM)為被提出用來解決此問題之模型，本研究基於此模型架構結合了卷積神經網路(Convolutional Neural Network)及深層類神經網路(Deep Neural Network)建構出 CLDNN 模型。

訓練語料部分，本研究使用了 TCC300(24 小時)、AIShell(162 小時)、NER(111 小時)，並加入語言模型建立大辭彙語音辨識系統，為了檢測系統強健度(Robustness)，使用三種不同環境之測試語料，分別為 TCC300(2.4 小時，朗讀語速)、NER-clean(1.9 小時，快語速，無雜訊)、NER-other(9 小時，快語速，有雜訊)。

關鍵詞：遞迴式類神經網路、長短期記憶、梯度消失(爆炸)、聲學模型、中文、大辭彙語音辨識、卷積類神經網路、深層類神經網路

## Abstract

In recent years, neural networks have been widely used in the field of speech recognition. This paper uses the Recurrent Neural Network to train acoustic models and establish a Mandarin speech recognition system. Since the recursive neural networks are cyclic connections, the modeling of temporal signals is more beneficial than the full connected deep neural networks.

However, the recursive neural networks have the problem of gradient vanishing and gradient exploding in the backpropagation, which leads to the training being suspended. And the inability to effectively capture long-term memory associations, so Long Short-Term Memory (LSTM) is a model proposed to solve this problem. This study is based on this model architecture and combines convolutional neural networks and deep neural networks to construct the CLDNN models.

Keywords: RNNs, LSTMs, gradient vanishing (exploding), acoustic model, Mandarin, LVCSR, CNNs, DNNs

The 2018 Conference on Computational Linguistics and Speech Processing
ROCLING 2018, pp. 116-125
©The Association for Computational Linguistics and Chinese Language Processing

# 探索結合快速文本及卷積神經網路於可讀性模型之建立

## Exploring Combination of FastText and Convolutional Neural Networks for Building Readability Models

曾厚強　Hou-Chiang Tseng
國立臺灣師範大學資訊工程學系 / 心理與教育測驗研究發展中心
Department of Computer Science and Information Engineering
National Taiwan Normal University
Research Center for Psychological and Educational Testing
ouartz99@gmail.com

陳柏琳　Berlin Chen
國立臺灣師範大學資訊工程學系
Department of Computer Science and Information Engineering
National Taiwan Normal University
berlin@ntnu.edu.tw

宋曜廷　Yao-Ting Sung
國立臺灣師範大學教育心理與輔導學系所
Department of Educational Psychology and Counseling
National Taiwan Normal University
sungtc@ntnu.edu.tw

## 摘要

可讀性模型可以自動估測文本的可讀性，幫助讀者去挑選符合自己閱讀能力的文件，以達到更好的學習效果。長久以來，研究人員致力於可讀性模型或特徵的研發，尤其近年來隨著表示學習法的蓬勃發展，使得訓練可讀性模型所需要的特徵可以不再需要仰賴專家，這也使得可讀性模型的發展有了一個嶄新的研究方向。然而，不同表示學習法所抽取出來的特徵各有所長，但過去的可讀性研究大多只用單一方法來訓練可讀性模型。因此，本論文嘗試利用類神經網路來融合卷積神經網路及快速文本兩種表示學習法，以訓練出一個能夠分析跨領域文件的可讀性模型，並可以因應文件內容多元主題的特性。從實驗結果可以發現本論文所提出的可讀性模型，其效能可略微勝出單一表示學習法所訓練的可讀性模型。

關鍵詞：可讀性，詞向量，卷積神經網路，表示學習法，快速文本

一、緒論

可讀性(Readability)是指閱讀材料能夠被讀者所理解的程度[1],[2],[3],[4]，當讀者閱讀高可讀性的文件時，會產生較好的理解及學後保留效果[2],[3]。由於文件的可讀性在知識傳遞扮演極為重要的角色，因此西方的可讀性公式發展的非常早[5],[6]，據 Chall 與 Dale[7]在 1995 年的統計，到 1980 年為止相關的可讀性公式就已經超過 200 多個。這些傳統的可讀性研究大多使用較淺層的語言特徵來發展線性的可讀性公式。然而，傳統可讀性公式所採用的淺層語言特徵，並不足以反映文件難度。Graesser、Singer 和 Trabasso[8]便指出，傳統語言特徵公式無法反映閱讀的真實歷程，文件的語意和語法只是文件的淺層語言特徵，並沒有考量文件的凝聚特性。Collins-Thompson[9]亦指出傳統可讀性公式僅著重在文件的表淺資訊，而忽略文件重要的深層特徵。這也讓傳統可讀性公式在預測文本可讀性的結果常遭受到質疑，甚至因為可讀性公式所採用的可讀性特徵過少，導致容易受到有心人士為了達到特定的可讀性數值，而刻意針對可讀性特徵的特性來修改文章，使得文章呈現許多簡短而破碎的句子，降低了文本的流暢度與連貫性，增加閱讀難度[10]。直至今日，可讀性的研究仍持續不斷。研究人員為了克服傳統可讀性公式的缺點，嘗試利用更細緻的機器學習演算法來發展出非線性的可讀性模型，並納入更多元的可讀性指標來共同評量文本的可讀性，除了可以提升可讀性模型的效能，亦可防止有心人士去操弄文本的可讀性[11],[12],[13]。

　　然而可惜的是，研究人員發現採用一般語言特徵的可讀性模型在應用到特定領域文時，一般語言特徵並無法判斷相同詞彙在不同領域文本時背後所代表的意義。其原因在於特定領域文本的內容著重在闡述領域的「知識概念」，而這樣子的描述方式有別於一般語文的敘述文或故事體的結構。Yan 等人[14]就明確指出美國大型醫學資料庫(Medical Subject Headings, MeSH)中的醫學專業術語的難度與語言特徵公式的音節數、字長無關。針對一般語言特徵無法表徵特定領域知識結構的問題，開始有學者針對這個議題進行研究。例如，Yan 等人[14]利用本體論的技術將美國國家醫學資料庫(Medical Subject Headings, MeSH)的醫學符號階層資料庫作為概念資料庫，從中找出每一個醫學類文件中的概念，並計算概念到此樹狀結構最底部的距離，得出每篇文件概念深度的指標(Document Scop)。Borst 等人[15]則是利用詞表的方式將每個詞彙的「類別複雜度」與「詞頻」兩個分數加總來計算詞彙複雜度，作為評估醫學線上文件的詞彙、句子及文件難度的依據。Tseng 等人[16]則是利用表徵學習(Representation Learning)方法(如：卷積神經網路、快速文本)自動從原始資料中抽取可讀性特徵，分別訓練出一個能夠分析跨領域文件的可讀性模型，以求可以更加貼近現實應用的需求。

　　根據過去的研究可以發現，多數的可讀性研究利用單一機械學習的模型來整合不同類型的可讀性特徵去訓練出可讀性模型，讓可讀性模型可以從更多面向來考量文本的可讀性。但若能夠進一步在訓練可讀性模型過程中就可以讓不同的演算法相互分享資訊，則在訓練可讀性模型的過程中便可以享有更多元的資訊，以提升可讀性模型的效能。基於這樣子的想法，本研究將基於類神經網路來融合兩種不同的表示學習法，訓練一個能夠分析跨領域文件的可讀性模型，其效能可優於單一表示學習法所訓練而成的可讀性模型。本論文的內容安排如下：第二節將描述兩種應用於中文可讀性模型的表示學習法。第三節將基於類神經網路來融合兩種不同的表示學習法，以訓練出一個能夠同時分析不同領域文件的可讀性模型。第四節將呈現本論文所提出可讀性模型的效能。最後第五節是總結及未來研究的方向。


## 二、基於表示學習技術之可讀性模型相關研究

表示學習法是指學習如何表徵資料的演算法，可以用來抽取有用的資訊來幫助建立預測模型[17]。對於可讀性的研究而言，透過表示學習技術可以自動抽取出訓練可讀性模型所需之可讀性特徵，是一個富有潛力的研究方向。以下將簡述兩個應用於中文可讀性模型的表示學習法。

## (一)、卷積神經網路

　　卷積神經網路(Convolutional Neural Network, CNN)是一種分層式的結構，每個模組都是由卷積層(Convolutional Layer)和池化層(Pooling Layer)來組成[18]，通過模組不斷的疊加或是加上多層的類神經網路後形成深度學習的模型。整個卷積神經網路透過三個重要的思想來幫助改進訓練的效率及效能：稀疏交互(Sparse Interactions)、參數共享(Parameter Sharing)及等變表示(Equi-variant Representations)[19]。稀疏交互又稱為稀疏連接(Sparse Connectivity)，主要是利用數個核(Kernel)基於自定核的大小(Kernel Size)來局部連結兩層網路，使得整個模型所要儲存的參數變少，可以有效減少計算量和提升計算效率。參數共享指的是在同一個核中，每一個元素在不同位置所作用的權重都是相同的。

這意味著在卷積運算的過程中，模型只需要學習一組固定的參數即可。因此這也將大幅度提高模型的訓練效能。而參數共享的機制再加上適當的池化策略，也讓卷積神經網路對於局部平移有一些不變的特性可以應用於圖像的處理或語音辨識，尤其是在關心某個特徵是不是有出現，而不是關心它出現的具體位置時[19]。這樣的特性也適用於文本可讀性的分析：在意的是對於文本中所提及的主題或知識概念的難度，而不是關心它在文本中具體的位置。因此，過去已有研究將卷積神經網路用來自動抽取可讀性模型所需要的特徵，並利用深層類神經網路訓練出可讀性模型[16]，其架構如圖一所示，在訓練的過程中，該研究使用到 Dropout[20]的技巧來避免模型過度適配(overfitting)外，並利用 rectified linear units (ReLU) [21]作為的激發函數(active function)，以避免典型的梯度消失(gradient vanish)問題。

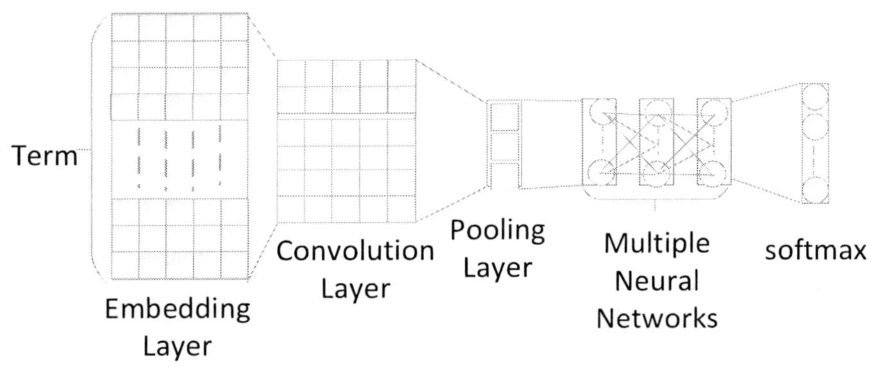


圖一、基於卷積類神經網路及深層類神經網路之可讀性模型架構

## (二)、快速文本 (fastText)方法

　　快速文本[22]是繼 Word2vec[23]之後，Joulin 等人持續發展出的架構，其架構如圖二(a)及圖二(b)所示，快速文本與 Word2vec 一樣有連續詞袋模型和略詞模型兩種訓練的架構。但不一樣的地方在於輸入層改為 n-gram 的方式來考慮句子或文章的詞序關係，並且將目標詞彙改換成訓練資料的類別。而這樣子的作法可以讓語意空間特別針對類別去進行優化，這將有助於區別語意或主題相近但實際上卻屬於不同類別的句子或文章。在過去，Tseng 等人[16]也嘗試將快速文本採用連續詞袋演算法來訓練出中文的可讀性模型。

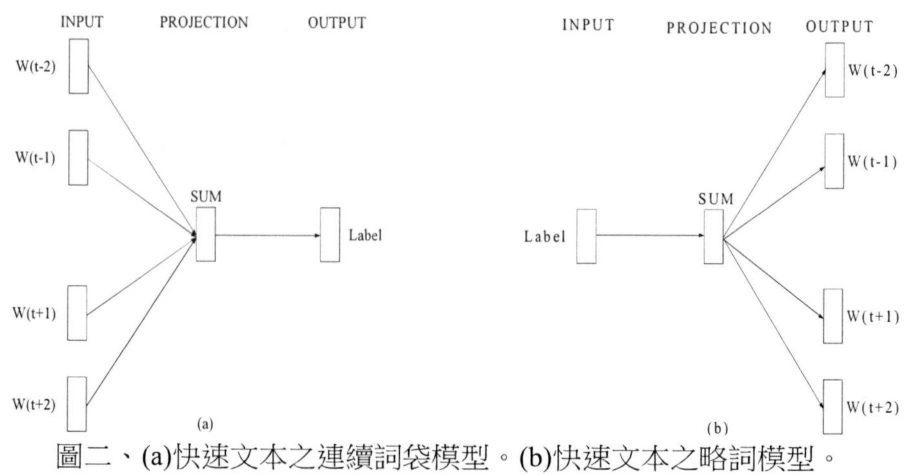



圖二、(a)快速文本之連續詞袋模型。(b)快速文本之略詞模型。

## 三、基於類神經網路融合不同表示學習法的可讀性模型

不同的表示學習法各有所長，例如卷積神經網路可以透過多個核來觀察文本中多個局部範圍的文本資訊來提取出特徵。有別於卷積神經網路，快速文本則是透過 n-gram 的方式來看同一個滑動視窗中詞彙與類別之間的關係，使其所訓練的詞向量所形成的語意空間可以特別針對類別去進行優化。假若在訓練可讀性模型的過程中可以同時融合這兩種演算法，其訓練可讀性模型的過程中就可以相互分享資訊，為可讀性模型帶來更豐富的資訊去評估文本的可讀性。基於這個想法，本研究利用類神經網路來融合卷積神經網路及快速文本兩種不同的表示學習演算法，其示意圖如圖三所示，在整個可讀性模型的訓練過程中，卷積神經網路和快速文本所產生的特徵會以向量的形式在融合層進行相加、相乘、平均或串聯等不同的運算方式進行融合，而融合後的特徵便可以讓可讀性模型在訓練的過程中享有不同表徵學習法所帶來資訊。

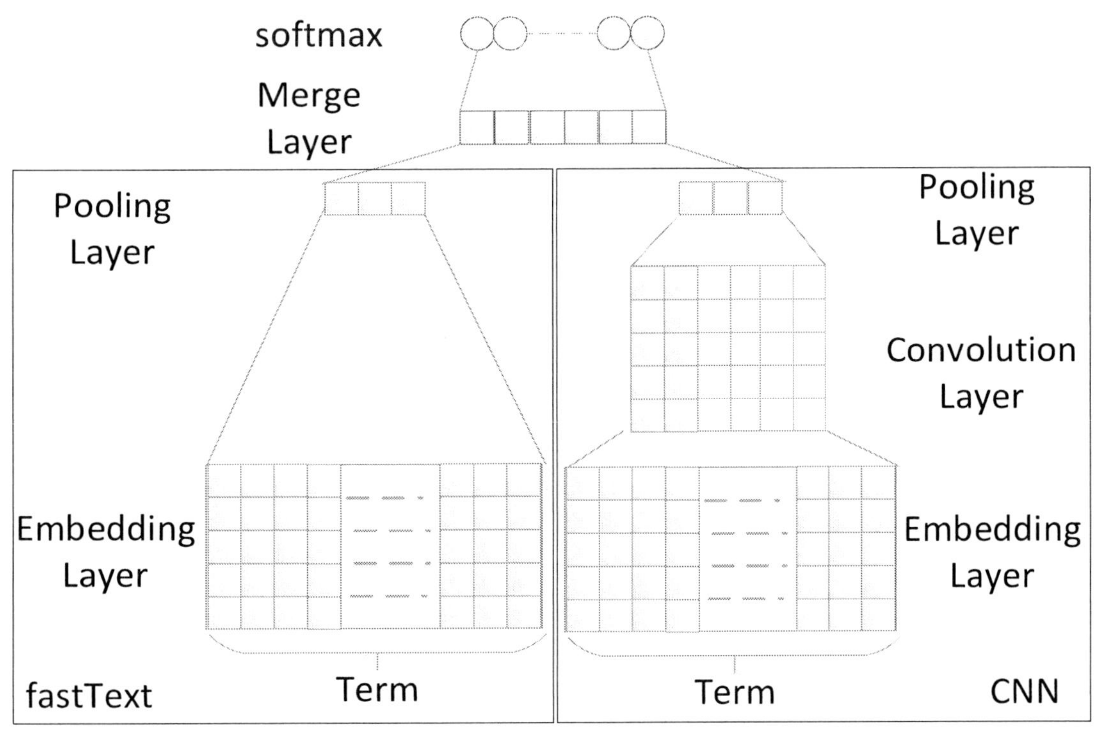


圖三、融合卷積神經網路及快速文本的可讀性模型架構

## 四、實驗及結果

### (一)、實驗材料

　　本研究材料選自98年度臺灣H、K、N三大出版社所出版的1-12年級審定版的國語科、社會科和自然科等三個領域的教科書全部共計4,648篇，各版本教科書均經由專家根據課程綱要編制而成，其實驗材料的年級分佈如表一所示。

表一、實驗材料在各年級的數量分佈

| 年級 | 1 | 2 | 3 | 4 | 5 | 6 | 7 | 8 | 9 | 10 | 11 | 12 |
|------|---|---|---|---|---|---|---|---|---|----|----|----|
| 社會科 | 0 | 0 | 80 | 74 | 85 | 81 | 389 | 407 | 325 | 340 | 331 | 270 |
| 自然科 | 0 | 0 | 72 | 67 | 67 | 62 | 172 | 175 | 157 | 211 | 355 | 295 |
| 國文科 | 24 | 67 | 61 | 71 | 69 | 70 | 37 | 34 | 28 | 84 | 41 | 47 |

## (二)、訓練可讀性模型

　　首先將實驗材料利用 WECAn[24]來進行中文斷詞的前處理程序，接著再以四比一的比例亂數從不同的年級去挑選訓練資料和測試資料。最後，將訓練資料輸入本研究所提出的架構來訓練可讀性模型，而可讀性模型所需的類別就是課文所屬的年級。待可讀性模型訓練完成後，將測試資料輸入至可讀性模型，可讀性模型便會自動預測該文本的可讀性。整體實驗利用 Keras[25]進行實作，流程如圖四所示。

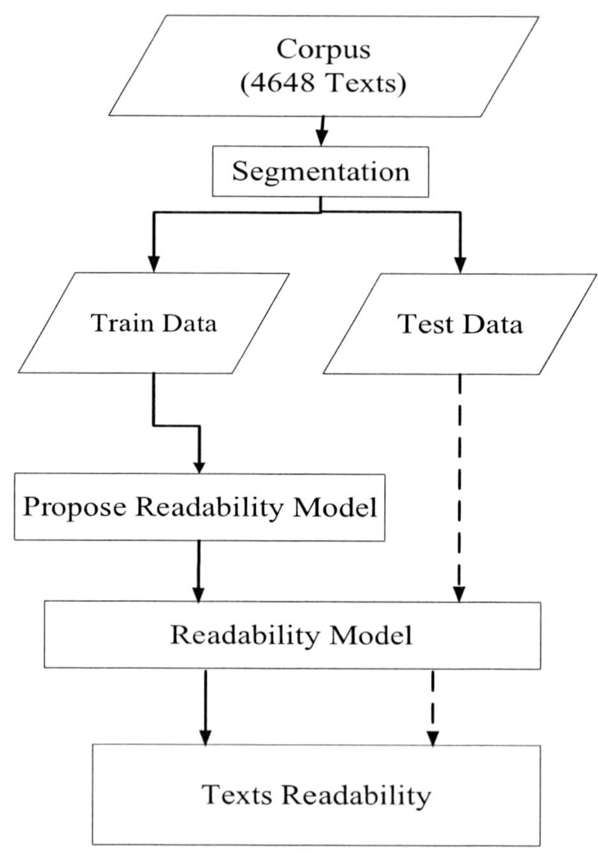


圖四、可讀性模型訓練及測試流程圖

## (三)、實驗結果

實驗結果如表二所呈，利用相乘方式所融合兩種表徵學習法的可讀性模型準確率為 79.42%，皆優於單一表徵學習法的可讀性模型，對於卷積神經網路而言準確率多了 3.77%，快速文本的準確率則微幅提升了 0.97%。若進一步將放寬上、下一個年級的標準來統計出相鄰準確率，以觀察可讀性模型錯誤預測的程度是否嚴重。從表二也可以發現以相乘方式融合的可讀性模型的相鄰準確率為 91.59%，仍是所有可讀性模型中相鄰準確率最高的。

此外，本研究亦將過去研究[13]成功應用於國語科文本的一般語言特徵利用深層類神經網路來訓練可讀性模型，以觀察其模型分析跨領域文件的能力為何。從表二的結果可以發現性其準確率與本研究所提出的可讀性模型相比差了 38.09%。而這樣子的結果也符合國外可讀性研究所得出的結論：一般語言特徵的確無法有效適用於評估特定領域文本的可讀性。

表二、基於卷積神經網路及快速文本之可讀性模型效能比較

| 適用年級 | 適用領域 | 可讀性模型 | 融合方式 | 準確率 | 相鄰準確率 |
|---|---|---|---|---|---|
| 1-12 年級 | 國語科、社會科、自然科共計 4,648 篇 | 卷積神經網路 | | 75.65% | 89.33% |
| | | 快速文本 | | 78.45% | 90.95% |
| | | 卷積神經網路 ＋ 快速文本 | 相加 | 74.89% | 87.93% |
| | | 卷積神經網路 ＋ 快速文本 | 相乘 | **79.42%** | **91.59%** |
| | | 卷積神經網路 ＋ 快速文本 | 串聯 | 76.40% | 90.30% |
| | | 卷積神經網路 ＋ 快速文本 | 平均 | 74.78% | 89.55% |
| | | 一般語言特徵 ＋ 深層神經網路 | | 41.33% | 69.11% |

## 五、結論

有鑑於過去的可讀性研究大多只用單一演算法來訓練可讀性模型，本研究利用類神經網路來融合卷積神經網路及快速文本兩種表示學習法，以訓練出一個能夠分析跨領域文件的可讀性模型。實驗結果顯示，雖然利用快速文本就已經可以達到不錯的模型效能，但若可以融合卷積神經網路，則不論是準確率或相鄰準確率都可以往上再提升。這個現象初步顯示在訓練可讀性模型的過程中，若可以找到適當的融合方式，是可以交織出更優質的特徵來提升可讀性模型的效能。在未來我們將以此為基礎，除了嘗試更多複雜的表徵學習演算法來進行橫向的融合外，也將進一步探討與縱向融合之間差異為何。

參考文獻

[1]E. Dale and J. S. Chall, "The concept of readability," *Elementary English,* vol. 26, pp. 19–26, 1949.

[2]G. R. Klare, "Measurement of Readability," 1963.

[3]G. R. Klare, "The measurement of readability: useful information for communicators," *ACM Journal of Computer Documentation (JCD),* vol. 24, pp. 107-121, 2000.

[4]G. H. McLaughlin, "SMOG grading: A new readability formula," *Journal of reading,* vol. 12, pp. 639–646, 1969.

[5]B. A. Lively and S. L. Pressey, "A method for measuring the vocabulary burden of textbooks," *Educational administration and supervision,* vol. 9, pp. 389–398, 1923.

[6]M. Vogel and C. Washburne, "An objective method of determining grade placement of children's reading material," *The Elementary School Journal,* pp. 373–381, 1928.

[7]J. S. Chall and E. Dale, *Readability Revisited: The new Dale-Chall Readability Formula,* Brookline Books, 1995.

[8]A. C. Graesser, M. Singer, and T. Trabasso, "Constructing inferences during narrative text comprehension," *Psychological Review,* vol. 101, pp. 371, 1994.

[9]K. Collins-Thompson, "Computational assessment of text readability: A survey of current and future research," *International Journal of Applied Linguistics,* vol. 165, pp. 97–135, 2014.

[10] B. Bruce, A. Rubin, and K. Starr, "Why readability formulas fail," *IEEE Transactions on Professional Communication,* pp. 50-52, 1981.

[11] S. E. Petersen and M. Ostendorf, "A machine learning approach to reading level assessment," *Computer Speech & Language,* vol. 23, pp. 89–106, 2009.

[12] L. Feng, M. Jansche, M. Huenerfauth, and N. Elhadad, "A comparison of features for automatic readability assessment," in *Proceedings of the 23rd International Conference on Computational Linguistics: Posters,* 2010, pp. 276–284.

[13] Y. T. Sung, J. L. Chen, J. H. Cha, H. C. Tseng, T. H. Chang, and K. E. Chang, "Constructing and validating readability models: the method of integrating multilevel linguistic features with machine learning," *Behavior research methods,* vol. 47, pp. 340–354, 2014.

[14] X. Yan, D. Song, and X. Li, "Concept-based document readability in domain specific information retrieval," in *Proceedings of the 15th ACM international conference on Information and knowledge management,* pp. 540–549, 2006.

[15] A. Borst, A. Gaudinat, C. Boyer, and N. Grabar, "Lexically based distinction of readability levels of health documents," *Acta Informatica Medica,* vol. 16, pp. 72–75, 2008.

[16] H. C. Tseng, B. Chen, and Y. T. Sung, "Exploring the Use of Neural Network based Features for Text Readability Classification," *International Journal of Computational Linguistics and Chinese Language Processing (IJCLCLP),* vol. 22, pp. 31–46, 2017.

[17] Y. Bengio, A. Courville, and P. Vincent, "Representation learning: A review and new perspectives," *IEEE transactions on pattern analysis and machine intelligence,* vol. 35, pp. 1798–1828, 2013.

[18] Y. LeCun, "Generalization and network design strategies," *Connectionism in perspective,* pp. 143–155, 1989.

[19] I. Goodfellow, Y. Bengio, and A. Courville, *Deep learning (adaptive computation and machine learning series).* MIT Press, 2016.

[20] N. Srivastava, G. E. Hinton, A. Krizhevsky, I. Sutskever, and R. Salakhutdinov, "Dropout: a simple way to prevent neural networks from overfitting," *Journal of machine learning research,* vol. 15, pp. 1929–1958. 2014.

[21] Nair, Vinod, and Geoffrey E. Hinton. "Rectified linear units improve restricted boltzmann machines," in *Proceedings of the International Conference on Machine Learning,* pp. 807–814. 2010.

[22] A. Joulin, E. Grave, P. Bojanowski, and T. Mikolov, "Bag of tricks for efficient text classification," *arXiv preprint arXiv:1607.01759.* 2016.

[23] T. Mikolov, K. Chen, G. Corrado, and J. Dean, "Efficient estimation of word representations in vector space," *arXiv preprint arXiv:1301.3781,* 2013.

[24] T. H. Chang, Y. T. Sung, and Y. T. Lee, "A Chinese word segmentation and POS tagging system for readability research," in *Proceedings of the Annual Meeting of the Society for Computers in Psychology,* 2012.

[25] F. Chollet, "Keras: Deep learning library for theano and tensorflow. *URL: https://keras.io.*" 2015.

The 2018 Conference on Computational Linguistics and Speech Processing
ROCLING 2018, pp. 126-139
©The Association for Computational Linguistics and Chinese Language Processing

# Weather Forecast Voice System

Thanh Do
Faculty of Information Technology, Ho Chi Minh City University of Foreign Languages and
Information Technology (HUFLIT)
*dodinhthanh@huflit.edu.vn*

## Abstract

This paper introduces Weather Voice System applied to information commands-responses system through Public Switched Telephone Network (PSTN). Being able to understand users' voice commands, our system would assist them during their searching weather forecast in Vietnamese towns and cities by communicating in Vietnamese through Telephone Network. What makes this system different from others consists of its ability to analyze syntax and semantics of voice commands after their being recognized by speech recognizer component. Weather Voice is composed of main components that are there: 1) Telephone network communicator, 2) Vietnamese speech recognizer, 3) Natural language processor, and 4) Vietnamese speech synthesizer. To the best of our knowledge, this is one of the first systems in Vietnam to combine text language processing and speech processing. This event could make voice applications more intelligent with aim to communicate with humans in natural language at high precision and at quick speed. The fact that experiments have proved our expectation as well as the friendliness of the system to users reveals the practicality of our research.

Keywords: Voice Application, Natural Language Processing, Voice Server, WeatherVoice

## 1. Introduction

In the recent years, Vietnamese voice processing researches have found themselves making significant progress. Among them, two which must be mentioned are Voice recognizing (transforming audible signals into visible text) and Voice synthesizing (transforming visible text into audible signals), their authors, Information Technology Institute (Vietnamese Science and Technology Institute) and Natural Science University (Vietnamese National University), have conducted and published many works high estimated [2],[4],[6],[8],[14]. Especially in 2012, the authors from Natural Science University succeeded in building Voice Server System [9] to explore potential applications of Voice Processing whose use was made of by media systems, such as Voice Information Providing System through mobile and fixed phones, this work was awarded the second prize of Vietnamese Gifted. However, the works above only focused on improving the processing of Vietnamese voice and still neglected the semantic analyzing of voice commands.

Weather Voice is Voice Server System built on the combination of speech language processing and text language one. It can recognize numerous patterns of Vietnamese voice commands in order to transform them into text, then analyze their syntax and semantics, afterwards carry out searching data base, and eventually answer to users with the data searched in Vietnamese voice.

The analyzing syntax and semantics of commands is assisted by DCG (Definite Clause Grammar) [3],[7],[11],[12],[17]. During the voice processing, we call for HTK (Hidden Markov Model Toolkit) [13] to recognize voices and apply Unit - selection [1] method to synthesizing voices.

## 2. System structure

The system is designed to achieve the following functions: Recognizing query statements through phones; analyzing them; searching data from database; answering to users through phones. Here is the scenario in details:

(0) Standby state

(1) User calls on the system and asks a command in Vietnamese.

(2) The system reasserts the content of the user's command.

_ (2.0) If the user confirms it, the system continues to carry out the step (3)

_ (2.1) If the user disapproves of it, the system returns to the step (0)

(3) The speech is transferred to the processing unit ASR and transformed into Vietnamese text.

(4) The system analyzes the command's syntax and processes its semantic meaning.

_ (4.0) If the command is grammatically correct

* The system conducts searching database and answers to the user in speech.

* When finishing, it returns to the step (0)

_ (4.1) If it is not the case, which means that the command is grammatically incorrect, the system will ask the user to redo a command in speech.

We will follow the example of a specific transaction:

- The system: Hello.

- The user: Please tell me what the weather is like in Can Tho tomorrow?

- The system: Do you want to know about the weather of tomorrow in Can Tho?

- The user: That's right.

- -The system: The temperature is between 24 degrees and 34 tomorrow, it is sunny in the daytime, it rains in the evening and at night.

For achieving the above functions, the system must require the following components:

- Voice recognizer component: to transform speech data which is human speech into data text.

- Vietnamese language processing component: to analyze commands' syntax and semantic meaning from users.

- Central processing component: to connect the other components each to another through such operations:

1. Transforming data text from speech recognizer into standard data to be executed by Prolog in Vietnamese language processing.

2. Transforming commands' semantic expressions into a file of select statements which is sent to database and executing them.

3. Filtering, arranging, and returning processed results via system to user.

o Database: contains selected data.

o Vietnamese language synthetizing component: transforms text data into speech.

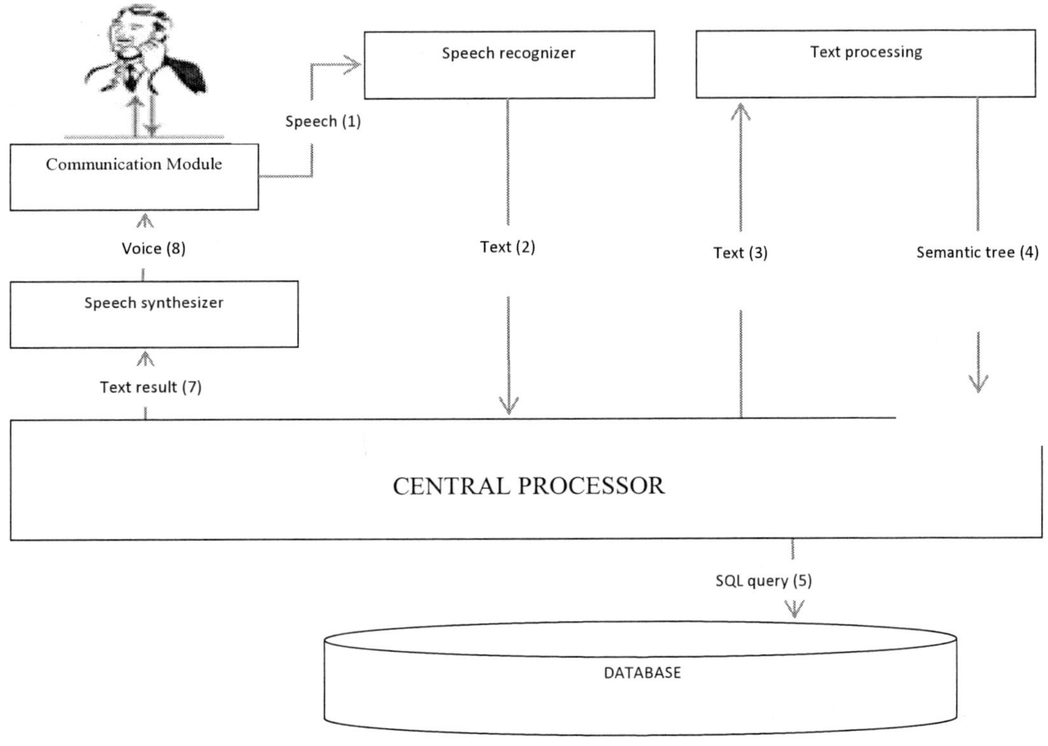


Figure 1: system structure.

# 3. Voice recognizer component

In the Weather Voice system, we use HTK to build the voice recognizer component. HTK provides us with instruments analyzing voice, specially the one recognizing voice, based on HMM [13]. According to approaches of [9], [10], [15], [16], [18] we implement a context-dependent model making use of triphone to recognize words from word list as well as to identify patterns' grammatical meaning which can happen in application context for the sake of recognizing sentences more correctly.

A. Steps in building voice recognizer component.

Building a voice recognizer component includes two main periods:

1. Training period:

- Preparing voice data file needs training and codifying this file.

- Labelling, building dictionary.

- Creating HMM prototypes for each of phone units.

The training period's output is the file of trained HMM prototypes.

2. Recognizing period:

- The file of trained HMM set is the result of the training period.

- Building dictionary.

- Extracting characteristics for voice series needing being recognized.

The recognizing period's output is the text series.

B. Data to train.

The file of data to train is recorded for 200 minutes in amount of 2,500 patterns. Those data must satisfy the criterion of 8,000 Hz, 16bit according to PCM format and be recorded in 50 different accents and in a quiet environment. The word list comprises 63 cities and towns' names over the country and key words concerning command sentences.

C. Building language grammar.

Our grammar is language prototypes providing information of sentences' syntax, semantics and word order. This component will help the system choose the best recognized results from the list of 'candidates' previously selected by the recognizing period.

Sentence structures are likely to exist in application contexts.

Building a language prototypes involves the determining its grammar. The complexity of grammar depends on that of the system needing being recognized.

Grammar structure is a generalized graphic which implicates pattern sentences possibly occuring in application context. In our application, a part of the grammar file will be displayed as:

$tinh_thanh= HOOF CHIS MINH | HAF NOOJI | DDAF NAWXNG | CAAFN THOW;

$ngay=HOOM NAY | NGAFY MAI | NGAFY MOOST;

...

$sentence1=THOWFI TIEEST $tinh_thanh $ngay(NHUW THEES NAFO | RA SAO);

D. Voice synthesizing (text-to-speech).

Text-to-speech system includes two main phases: text analyzing (processing phase, standardizing text input in order to synthesize it) and text -to - speech phase (building speech signals from the former's results). The second phrase can be implemented by Formant text-to-speech [8] or Unit-selection approach [1],[8]… For Weather Voice, we have chosen unit-selection, the phrase is undergone in the next procedure:

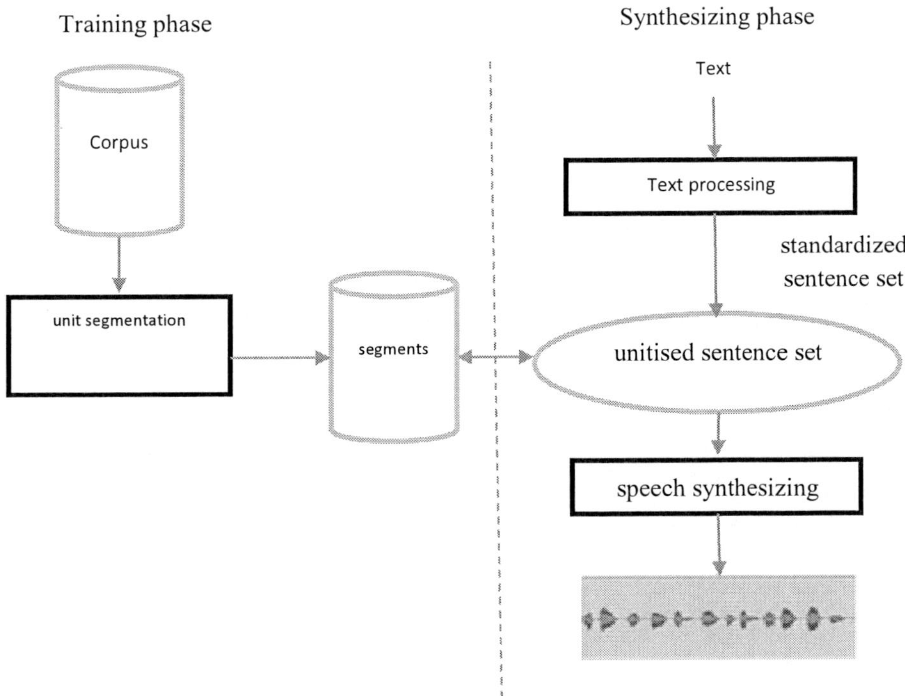


Figure 6: Text-to-speech procedure by connecting to unitise.

# 4. Vietnamese language processing

A. Query statement syntax.

Our system in all represents 18 query statement patterns as shown in the table 1.

Table 1: Some query statements classified according to them.

| Number | Query statement pattern | Example |
|---|---|---|
| 1 | [weather] [place] [time] | What is the weather like in Hanoi today? |
| 2 | [weather] [place] | What is the weather like in Hanoi? |
| 3 | [weather] [time] | What is the weather like today? |
| 4 | [place] [time] [weather] | In Hanoi tomorrow, what is the weather like? |
| 5 | [place] [weather] | In HCM city what is the weather like? |
| 6 | [time] [weather] | After tomorrow what is the temperature? |
| 7 | [time] [place] [weather] | After tomorrow in Can Tho what is the weather like? |
| 8 | [temperature] [place] [time] | What is the temperature in Hanoi today? |
| 9 | [temperature] [place] | What is the temperature in Hanoi? |
| 10 | [temperature] [time] | What is the temperature today? |
| 11 | [place] [temperature] [time] | In Hanoi what is the temperature tomorrow? |
| 12 | [place] [temperature] | In HCM city what is the temperature? |
| 13 | [time] [temperature] | After tomorrow what is the temperature? |
| 14 | [time] [place] [temperature] | After tomorrow in Can Tho what is the temperature? |
| 15 | [place] [time] [state] | In Da Nang tomorrow does it rain? |
| 16 | [time] [place] [state] | Tomorrow in Da Nang is it hot? |
| 17 | [place] [state] | In Sai Gon does it rain? |
| 18 | [time] [state] | After tomorrow does it rain? |

B. Analyzing statement semantic.

To represent query statement semantic, we use DCG [3],[7],[11],[12],[17] all nine representation patterns of query statement semantic are given in table 2:

Table 2. Representation patterns of query statement semantic.

| Number | Meaning representations | Query statement patterns |
|---|---|---|
| 1 | query(weather, place,  time) | Structure patterns from 1 to 7 coming from table 2 |
| 2 | query (weather, place) | |
| 3 | query (weather, time) | |
| 4 | query (temperature, place, time) | Structure patterns from 8 to 14 coming from table 2 |
| 5 | query (temperature, place) | |
| 6 | query (temperature, time) | |
| 7 | yesno (place, state, time) | Structure patterns from 15 to 18 coming from table 2 |
| 8 | yesno (place, state) | |
| 9 | yesno (state, time) | |

Example 1: What is the weather like in Hanoi tomorrow?

DCG syntactic and semantic order will be defined as follows:

query(query(Weather,Place,Time)) --> n_weather(Weather),prep_place,n_place(Place), n_time(Time),w_how.

prep_place --> [in].

n_weather(weather) --> [weather].

n_place(place(cần_thơ)) --> [cần_thơ].

n_time(time(tomorrow )--> [tomorrow].

w_how --> [how].

DCG syntactic and semantic order has defined semantic pattern of example 1's query statement as:

$$query(\ weather(thoi\_tiet),\ place(can\_tho),\ time(ngay\_mai)).$$

This pattern is the pattern number 1 in the table 3.

We carry out transforming these semantic patterns into corresponding SQL statements in order to search corresponding weather information in the database. These data are automatically extracted from Yahoo Weather APL.

## 5. Experiments and evaluations

The experiments, at first, were conducted by each of system's components, which comprised voice recognizer, Vietnamese language processor and central processor. Afterwards, we experimented the entire system as well as performed surveys on users' reviews of the system including text-to-speech component.

A. Speech recognizer component.

The performance of speech recognizer is often evaluated by the metric WER (Word Error Rate), it is computed as the next formula:

$$WER = (S+D+I) / N \text{ x } 100\%$$

Where:

- N is the number of words,
- S is the number of substitutions,
- I is the number of insertions,
- D is the number of deletions.

But here, we used the metric WAR (Word Accuracy Rate) in the evaluation of the system's performance by the formula:

$$WAR = (1 - (S + D + I) / N) \text{ x } 100\%$$

We gradually carried out the experiments classified in accordance to areas, sexes, ages, and trained participants. The system's accuracy is shown in the following tables 3, 4, 5 and 6.

Table 3: Based on areas.

| WAR | | |
|---|---|---|
| North | Center | South |
| 90% | 88% | 93% |

Table 4: Based on sexes.

| WAR | |
|---|---|
| **Female** | **Male** |
| 91% | 94% |

Table 5: Based on ages.

| WAR | |
|---|---|
| 18-30 | Others |
| 95% | 90% |

Table 6: Based on trained participants and non-participants.

| WAR | |
|---|---|
| Trained participants | Non-participants |
| 98% | 93% |

## B. Natural language processing component.

Thanks to this component, we succeeded in experimenting 50 statements, the results for the statements involved exactly corresponded to our expectation. These statements are circumscribed within the syntastic structures having been built for the system. The system's ability to correctly process all these standard statements attests its stability and accuracy.

The amplitude: For the statements which do not fall within the syntastic structures' circumscription, when returned by the system they will be assessed to be false. This evidence demonstrates our synstatic regulations DCG is incomplete and yet our grammar cannot cover every case which is likely to occur.

If words grammar is added to it and synstatic regulations are improved, the system's amplitude will significantly expand.

C. Surveys on users' reviews.

During these surveys, users were asked the question coming from the system: "Is the system easy to use?". The answers are ranked in order of usefulness as mentioned in the table 7.

Table 7: Indication of levels of the system's usefulness.

| Very useful | Quite useful | Slightly useful | Useless |
|---|---|---|---|
| 25% | 27% | 23% | 25% |

D. Experimenting the entire system.

The system is built in PC environment with Java language and SWI-Prolog version 6.6.5.

Table 8: Experiment parameter.

| | |
|---|---|
| Number of query statements | 100 |
| Environment | indoor |
| Sample rate | 8kHz |
| Quantization | 16bits |
| Format | PCM |
| Device | mobile phone |

The results given by the system are correct for 48 out of 50 Vietnamese query statements. As seen above, all the unexpected results happened during the identifying period. The feedback time is 2.6 seconds on average.

E. Assessment

Throughout the experiment, voice recognizer component has incorrectly identified 6 out of 50 experimented statements. But syntactically, among them 4 statements have always kept their initial meanings and then correctly been processed by natural language processing component; only the two left ones have received the wrong meanings because of the identifying period. By that, we have found that the important part is played by the natural language processing component, it can even rectify errors resulting from the identifying period.

## 6. Conclusion

The paper has offered the presentation of the Weather Voice system's structure and the approaches to build it. In the system, the Vietnamese language processing component, responsible for analyzing the statements' syntax and semantic meaning, assumes the central part. According to our knowledge, this is one of the first systems in Vietnam to be equipped with effective natural language processing mechanism of voice application, this priority has made the system more intelligent and flexible. This research has also opened a new development to building and expanding question-answer systems which can understand Vietnamese and communicate with users in this language. In the future, we are also interested in developing voice applications for emotional analysis based on studies by Thien et al. [19,20].

## 7. References


[1] Hunt, A. Black and W. Alan, "Unit selection in a concatenative speech synthesis system using a large speech  database," Pro c. ICASSP-96, 1, pp. 373, 1996.

[2] Duong Dau, Minh Le, Cuong Le and Quan Vu, "A Robust Vietnamese Voice Server for Automated Directory  Assistance Application," RIVF-VLSP 2012, Ho Chi Minh City, Viet Nam, 2012.

[3] Fernando C. N. Pereira and Stuart M. Shieber, Prolog and Natural-Language Analysis. Microtome Publishing, pp.1 – 284, Massachusetts, 2005.

[4] Hue Nguyen, Truong Tran, Nhi Le, Nhut Pham, Quan Vu, "iSago: The Vietnamese Mobile Speech Assistant for  Food-court and Restaurant Location," RIVF-VLSP 2012, Ho Chi Minh City, Viet Nam, 2012.

[5] Michelle Quinton, Windows NT 5.0 Brings You New Telephony Development Features with TAPI 3.0, Microsoft Systems Journal. [Online]. Available: http://www.microsoft.com/msj/1198/tapi3/tapi3.aspx, 1998.

[6] Nhut Pham, Quan Vu, "A Spoken Dialog System for Stock Information Inquiry," in Proc. IT@EDU, Ho Chi Minh City, Viet Nam, 2012.

[7] Patrick Blackburn, Johan Bos, "Representation and Inference for Natural Language: A First Course in Computational Semantics". CSLI Press, pp. 1 – 376, Chicago, 2007.

[8] Quan Vu, "VOS: The Corpus-based Vietnamese Text-to-speech System," Journal on Information, Technologies, anh Communications, 2010.

[9] Quan Vu et al., (2012). "Nghiên cứu xây dựng hệ thống Voice Server và ứng dụng cho các dịch vụ trả lời tự động qua điện thoại". Technical report, Research project, HCM City Department of Science and Technology, Viet Nam.

[10] Tran, T.K., Phan, T.T.: An upgrading SentiVoice-a system for querying hotel service reviews via phone. 2015 International Conference on Asian Language Processing (IALP). Pp.115-118.

[11] Richard Montague, Formal Philosophy: Selected Papers of Richard Montague. Bell & Howell Information & Lea, pp. 1 – 119, New Haven, 1974.

[12] Sandiway Fong, "LING 364: Introduction to Formal Semantics. www.dingo.sbs.arizona.edu/~sandiway ", 2012.

[13] Steve Young et al, The HTK Book (version 3.4). Available: htk.eng.cam.ac.uk/docs/docs.shtml, 2006.

[14] Thang Vu, Mai Luong, "The Development of Vietnamese Corpora Toward Speech Translation System," RIVF- VLSP 2012, Ho Chi Minh City, Viet Nam, 2012.

[15] Thien Khai Tran, Dang Tuan Nguyen (2013). "Semantic Processing Mechanism for Listening and Comprehension in VNSCalendar System". International Journal on Natural Language Computing (IJNLC) Vol. 2, No.2, April 2013.

[16] TK Tran, TCK Tran, TA Mai, NMH Nguyen, HT Vu. EDUVoice - a system for querying academic information via PSTN. The Third Asian Conference on Information Systems (ACIS 2014). Nha Trang.

[17] Tran, T.K., Phan, T.T.: An upgrading SentiVoice-a system for querying hotel service reviews via phone. Asian Language Processing (IALP), 2015 International Conference on, 115-118.

[18] TK Tran, DM Pham, B Van Huynh. Towards Building an Intelligent Call Routing System International Journal of Advanced Computer Science and Applications 7 (1).

[19]   Tran, T.K., Phan, T.T.: A hybrid approach for building a Vietnamese sentiment dictionary. J. Intell. Fuzzy Syst. 35(1), 967–978 (2018).

[20]   Tran, T.K., Phan, T.T.: Mining opinion targets and opinion words from online reviews. Int. J. Inf. Technol. 9(3), 239–249 (2017).

The 2018 Conference on Computational Linguistics and Speech Processing
ROCLING 2018, pp. 140-141
©The Association for Computational Linguistics and Chinese Language Processing

# 未登錄詞之向量表示法模型於中文機器閱讀理解之應用

## An OOV Word Embedding Framework
## for Chinese Machine Reading Comprehension

羅上堡  Shang-Bao Luo
國立臺灣科技大學資訊工程系
Department of computer science and information engineering
National Taiwan University of Science and Technology
M10615012@mail.ntust.edu.tw


李青憲  Ching-Hsien Lee
工業技術研究院巨資中心
Computational Intelligence Technology Center
Industrial Technology Research Institute
C.H.Lee@itri.org.tw


陳冠宇  Kuan-Yu Chen
國立臺灣科技大學資訊工程系
Department of computer science and information engineering
National Taiwan University of Science and Technology
kychen@mail.ntust.edu.tw

## 摘要

在使用深度學習(Deep Learning)方法於自然語言處理的問題時，通常會先將每一個詞以一個相對應的詞向量(Word Embedding)表示，再輸入至各式神經網路模型。當遭遇未登錄詞(Out-of-Vocabulary, OOV)的問題時，常見的處理方式是略去該未登錄詞、以一個零向量表示或是用一個隨機產生的向量表示這個未登錄詞。就我們所知，在目前的研究裡，似乎仍未有一套合理且快速的做法，用於產生未登錄詞的詞向量表示法，並進一步地探討未登錄詞的詞向量對於各式任務成效的影響性。因此，本論文嘗試提出一套新穎的詞向量表示法學習技術，其目標是為未登錄詞產生一個較為合理且可靠的低維度向量表示法；除此之外，本研究進一步地把此一技術運用於中文機器閱讀理解任務之中，探究未登錄詞對於中文機器閱讀理解任務之影響，並驗證本論文所提出的詞向量表示法學習技術之成效。

關鍵詞：深度學習、詞向量表示法、未登錄詞、機器閱讀理解。

# 致謝

This research was partially supported by the Project H367B83300 (ITRI) under the sponsorship of the Ministry of Economic Affairs, Taiwan.

The 2018 Conference on Computational Linguistics and Speech Processing
ROCLING 2018, pp. 142-156
©The Association for Computational Linguistics and Chinese Language Processing

# 智慧手機客語拼音輸入法之研發-以臺灣海陸腔為例

## Research and Implementation of Hakka Pinyin Input Method for Mobile Cell - An Example of Taiwan HioLiuk Accent

黃豐隆, 劉名峻

Feng-Long Huang, Ming-Chan Liu

國立聯合大學資訊工程學系

Department of Computer Science and Information Engineering, National United University

ncat70, gn01932987@gmail.com

## 摘 要

根據客委會 105 年度所進行的全國客家人口暨語言基礎資料調查資料，全國最新客家人口比例為 19.3％，總數為 453 萬 7 千多人，成為台灣第二大族群，因研究者本身為新竹客家人，新竹客語以海陸腔為主，故以海陸腔為基礎。

本文開發智慧手機平台上客語拼音輸入法之海陸腔系統，在客語海陸腔輸入法中，除了基礎功能使用者偏好輸入、客語拼音字首快速輸入、前後詞預測、並提出了解決客語特殊字在智慧手機上無法顯示的問題之方法，讓客語特殊字以其拼音方式顯示。為讓完全無客語基礎之使用者也可以打出客語文章，我們增加中轉客輸入法，中文轉客語輸入法設計給毫無客語語言基礎或是尚在學習客語的使用者，讓使用者使用注音符號無聲調方式來輸入，輸入中文後、系統會自動比對其中文的客語詞彙，再進一步將輸入的中文轉成客語詞彙顯示。

在系統客語語料庫中，包含客語單字拼音字庫 5366 筆、客語詞彙拼音字庫 19351 筆、客語前後詞字庫 8505 筆與中文客語對照字庫 1679 筆；語音合成系統縮需之語音檔有單詞 2949 個、詞彙 1566 個，這些資料為客委會和教育部所提供。

在使用者評估調查中，在客語海陸腔輸入法的總平均 4 分，中文轉客語輸入法總平均分數為 4.46 分，客語語音總平均分數為 4.3 分，在台灣大多數使用者使用注音做拼音輸入，所以使用者的輸入習慣大大的影響其評估分數，在語音調查方面，使用者認為此系統有助於學習客語海陸腔的發音，也有助於數位學習的發展。

關鍵字: 智慧型手機，客語海陸腔輸入法、中文轉客語輸入法、語言模型。

# Abstract

According to a survey data about the Hakka dialect made by Hakka Affairs Council in 2016, Hakka people in Taiwan is a population ratio of 19.3%, with 4.537 million peoples, making it the second largest cultural group in Taiwan. Coincidentally, the researcher of this thesis is a Taiwanese from Hsinchu city with a Hakka origin. Also, the Hakka accent in this area in Hsinchu is called HioLiuk accent. Thus, this thesis is based on HioLiuk accent.

The Hakka input method not only has the basic functions such as Preference, Quick-type, words- prediction, but also displays a pinyin selection on the smart phone monitor for the user to key-in the desired word and instantly provides the special Hakka characters. This input method is designed for people who do not understand Hakka language well, and allows the users to use phonetic notation (without tones) as input. After keying in, the system will check its meaning and output the Hakka characters to finally choose from.

There are 5,366 records in Hakka Single Word Pinyin database (table), 19,351 records in Hakka Word Pinyin database (table), 8,505 records in Hakka Previous and Successive Word database (table) and 1,679 records in Chinese To Hakka database (table). Speech synthesis system requires many voice files: 2,949 word files and 1,566 phrases provided by Hakka Affairs Council and Ministry of Education.

In the survey questionnaire filled-out by users, HioLiuk input method got 4.0 points on average. Chinese To Hakka input method got 4.5 points on average, Hakka Language pronunciation got 4.3 points on average. Most users in Taiwan use pinyin input method, which has the big influence on the points. In the questionnaire about voice input, users believe that this system is conducive to those people who are learning Hakka and effective for the development of e-learning.

**Keyword: Mobile Cell, Hakka Input Methods, Chinese-Hakka Input Methods, Language Model.**

# 一、概論

　　台灣客家人是指具有漢族客家人血統的臺灣人，為臺灣第二大族群。其母語為台灣客家話，歷經明鄭時期、清治時期，數百年來通行於臺灣的客家地區，日治、光復時期至今，仍是多數客家族群的母語。「逢山必有客、凡客必住山」西部的丘陵與山區漸形成客家人為主的村莊，保有濃厚的客家文化，亦有客家人居住在平原或沿海鄉鎮等地。在客家委員會根據「客家基本法定義」調查顯示，臺灣客家人口比例較高的客家地區即桃竹苗、高屏、花東縱谷地區。

## 臺灣客語與輸入法現況

　　根據客委會 105 年度所進行的全國客家人口暨語言基礎資料調查資料[25]，全國最新客家人口比例為 19.3％，總數為 453 萬 7 千多人，而有子女的客家人中，子女和父母交談使用的語言以國語占大多數，造就現在客語有逐漸失傳的現象。

　　目前台灣的３Ｃ產品普及率高，幾乎人手一機，如果能在智慧型手機上推廣客語，應能提升客家語言，並傳承發揚客語文化。基於四縣腔客語輸入法[2]，本文進一步開發出海陸腔版本之輸入法。再以二十六個羅馬拼音方式[4]作為客語輸入，並提出一種替代字的拼音，解決臺灣客語中十分特別之「特殊字」，原本無法顯示於手機平台的問題，將文句中的特殊字以其拼音方式顯示。

　　語言與文字是人們溝通方式中最常使用的方法，如果可以更有效率使語言的學習與流傳，勢將有助於語言與文字的推展有益，進而促使文化的推展更加順暢。如前所述，臺灣的客語使用率不高，導致客語與客家文化面臨嚴重流失，未來甚至可能消失。因此，在手機環境中研發客語的拼音輸入法，提供一種具效率方式，使用者可以直接輸入客語文字，並且具有語音輸出，提供便利學習客語的方式，這是研發本輸入法的目的。

　　在「中轉客輸入法」中，以教育部的注音符號標示[5]為基準作為其輸入，以輸入中文詞的無聲調注音符號後，系統會以對應之客語詞做轉換，將其客語做輸出，也就是輸入中文詞輸出為客語詞；為讓使用者能快速的選出想要的字，提出與實作注音字首縮寫輸入，以減少使用者的操作動作。這兩套輸入法的研開目的都是為了使客語能夠永續與易於推廣，經由手機的便利性與流通性以提升客語的使用與傳承。

目前在電腦平台上已有的輸入法：教育部台灣客語拼音輸入法[5]，客語無聲調拼音輸入法[6]，信望愛客語輸入法[7]。相關拼音輸入法相關的研究與成果有:閩南語拼音輸入之台語兒[20]，手機實體按鍵與觸控介面之新式輸入法[10]，開發新式輸入法改善手機現有輸入問題;智慧手機平台四縣客語拼音輸入法，客語四縣腔輸入法;客語語音合成之初步研究[12];客語文章翻語音系統之實作[13];行動電話注音輸入法鍵盤配置之研究[21]中文文轉音系統中韻律階層的求取[29];以及客語《陸豐方言》百年語言演變析探[30]等。

# 二、智慧手機平台好客輸入法

自 Android 平台 1.5 版本以後，Google 已開放 Android 平台輸入法框架 (Input Method Framework, IMF)，IMF 是 Android 平台的特色設計，大大推動不具實體鍵盤之設備的產生。IMF 結構中包含三個主要的部分，如圖一所示：

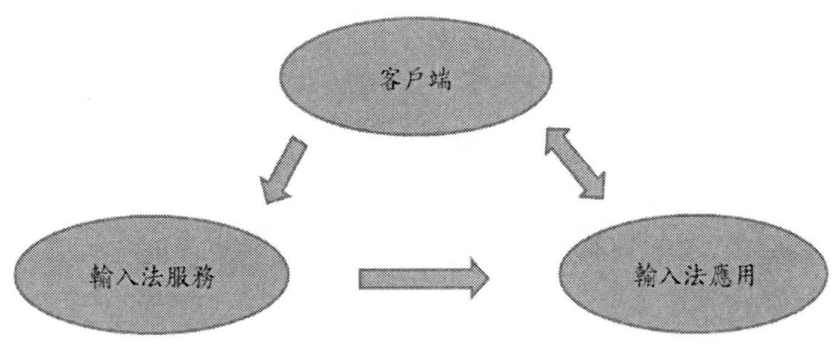


圖一： 輸入法整體架構

輸入法是用戶、應用程序之間的互動的渠道，所有的輸入法應用都需要繼承特定的 Android 平台提供的服務，Android 平台的輸入法框架為輸入法應用定義一個父類 InputMethodService，InputMethodService 提供一個輸入法的標準實現流程，定義輸入法生命周期內的重要函數，以方便開發人員對 Android 輸入法進行擴展。

## 手機鍵盤介面

在 Android 系統平台裡，輸入法編輯器（Input Method Editor，IME）是一個 Android app，也是輸入法框架（Input Method Framework，IMF）的組件之一，允許應用程式向用戶提供其他輸入的方法，例如螢幕上的鍵盤，甚至語音的輸入。系統模組包含好客輸入法 APP（Application，APP）、語音合成雲端伺服器兩部分，在 APP 部分，為一基於 Android IMF 設計的智慧客語拼音輸入法，使用者能在任何 APP 需要輸入客語文字、英文或標點符號時，鍵盤進行切換並輸入客語文字，0 一為我們設計智慧型手機的鍵盤介面，本 APP 開發完成後即可加入手機，新增為使用者的客語拼音輸入法。

圖二：輸入法鍵盤介面

使用者鍵入欲輸出的客語單字拼音或客語詞彙拼音縮寫，輸入法便會以使用者輸入進行搜尋，搜尋儲存於 Android 上的 SQLite 資料庫的單字拼音對照字庫和詞彙拼音縮寫對照詞庫，根據搜尋的結果產生候選字或候選詞彙，供使用者選擇並輸出。

## 一)客語詞典及功能

目前針對客語斷詞做標記的論文不多，交大電信工程蔡依玲的碩士論文[9]運用隱藏式馬可夫模型，我們採用客家委員會[11][12][13]和教育部[14][15]提供之客語例句與詞彙，並參考林昕緯斷詞標記模組工具[10]，如圖七所示，以結合人工標記與中文斷詞功能半自動式之客語斷詞及詞性等資訊而取得語料，並用該語料來建置客語辭典。

本文客語輸入法中，海陸腔客語語料詞典包含：

**1）單字拼音對照字庫**

**2）前後詞對照詞庫**

**3）縮寫詞拼音對照字庫**

在手機 SQLite 內的結構以資料表呈現。在單字拼音對照字庫資料表，含有 5366 個字數，包含了 Val、Key、Cnt、Pref 四個欄位，分別代表了客語單字（Val）、拼音（Key）、字頻（Cnt）、偏好（Pref），如表八所示。

輸入法會依照使用者輸入查詢【單字拼音】資料表，藉由輸入的客語拼音，查詢資料表拼音（Key）的欄位，列出所有可能的字詞，並依照字頻和使用者偏好輸入計算優先權重，然後按照優先權重進行排序；在字頻（Cnt）是將所有蒐集的文章以字為單位，進行斷詞所統計出的數量；在偏好（Pref）則是記錄使用者習慣輸出的字詞。

【前後詞對照詞庫】資料表，有 8505 個詞彙數，則包含了 Uniq、Prev、Next、Cnt 及 Pref 五個欄位，分別代表了客語詞彙（Uniq）、上一個詞（Prev）、下一個詞（Next）、次數總和（Cnt）及偏好（Pref），如表九所示。前後詞對照詞庫資料表資料來源為客語能力認證基本詞彙-初級、中級、高級之例句做斷詞，再加以合成前後詞後，統計其在例句中出現之次數(Cnt)

臺灣客家語言中，因應客語文化的獨特性，另定一些自創之特殊字型，稱為「客語特殊字」。為了可以正確顯示出字型，客委會已電腦平台上提供造字編碼表及造字檔**錯誤! 找不到參照來源。**，供使用者下載安裝，約有 300 個特殊字，例如：「房間□」的「□」字，或者中文「我」的客語「偃」等。現在手機平台並無客語輸入法，導致手機上不易普遍使用客語文章，客語文句中的特殊字勢必增加客語使用與推廣的難度。手機作業系統中，客委會或相關軟體目前尚無提供相關的造字檔，因此無法於手機平台上顯示任何特殊字字彙。

# 三、輸入法之功能設計與結果分析

　　海陸腔輸入法的三個資料庫是藉由蒐集來的客語字及客語詞彙，在大量的客語文章內進行斷字及斷詞所整理來，因此提供四種功能：

1. **客語無聲調輸出模式：** 讓使用者更快輸出客語詞及客語文句。

2. **前後詞預測模式：** 鍵入客語客客、詞時，快速正確顯示下一個客語詞彙。

3. **使用者偏好輸入：** 目的讓使用者能依照自己偏好快速將常用的字輸出。

4. **客語特殊字的處理：** 解決手機端客語特殊字無法顯示之問題。

5. **中轉客輸入法：** 中文輸入轉客語的功能可提供一般人不會客語、想學習客語的使用者，一個友善學習環境。

## 一）無聲調輸入模式

　　客語單字與詞彙是蒐集大量的客語文章，進行斷字與斷詞的動作，在提供在輸入法框架內，並做輸出單字與詞彙的功能，表十四為輸入「向」客語拼音時，候選詞窗會顯示相關聯的拼音，目的輸入客語拼音時，將相對應的客語字詞更快顯示在候選詞窗中，並提供使用者輸出。

## 二）前後詞預測模式

　　在前後詞模式中，提供使用者能以最少操作動作來達成想要輸出的句子。在大量的客語文章及客語的句子做斷詞的動作後，在資料庫內設（uniq）客語詞彙、前一個詞（prev）、下一個詞（next）、個數（cnt）及偏好（pref）等五個欄位，將斷詞完成的結果歸類在資料庫內。

　　*n*-gram model 是一種機率統計式的語言模型，依據樣本語料庫之文句序列（sequence）文字(character)或詞彙（wrod）單元加以訓練，獲得文句上下文文字與詞彙出現的機率值。*n*-gram 語言模型是自然語言處理技術的基礎，已廣泛應用於機器翻譯、語音識別與合成、手寫體識別、拼寫糾錯、漢字輸入，以及文獻分類與查詢等研究。

設 S 序列包含 m 個詞彙 $w_1, w_2,..., w_m$, S 出現的機率 $P(w_1, w_2,..., w_m)$ ,為每一個詞出現的條件機率相乘：

$$P(S)=P(w_1, w_2,..., w_m)=P(w_1)*P(w_2|w_1) *...*P(w_m|w_1, w_2,..., w_{m-1}) \tag{1}$$

其中 $P(w_1)$ 表示第一個詞 $w_1$ 出現的機率；$P(w_2|w_1)$ 則是已知第一個詞 $w_1$、第二個詞 $w_2$ 出現的條件機率；同理，第 $m$ 詞 $w_m$ 出現的機率決定 S 序列開頭起至 $w_m$ 之前面所有($m$-1)的詞彙 $w_1, w_2,... w_{m-1}$。

依拜氏定理(Bayes theorem)，條件機率 $P(B|A)$ 可以計算求得機率值，惟面臨參數空間過太模型不易訓練以及資料嚴重稀疏(Data sparsity)，雖然可以運用平滑化（data Smoothing）方法克服部份問題，惟這些問題導致模型效益大大降低。實際上，任意一個詞的出現的機率僅僅與它前面出現的有限的一個或者幾個詞有關。

如果一個詞的機率僅限於它前面出現的 $n$ 個詞有關，公式(2)即可化簡如下：

$$P(S)=P(w_1,w_2,...,w_m)=P(w_1)*P(w_2|w_1)* ...*P(w_m|w_{m-n+1},w_{m-n+2},..., w_{m-1}) \tag{2}$$

在 $n$-gram, 一般常用的模型多見 $n$=1, 2, 3,

如果一個詞的出現的機率僅於它前面出現的一個詞有關，那麼我們就稱之為 bigram model，公式(2)可表示如下:

$$P(S)= P(w_1,w_2,...,w_m)=P(w_1)*P(w_2|w_1)* P(w_3|w_2)*\cdots*P(w_m|w_{m-1}) \tag{3}$$

本文在 $n$-gram 語言模型，目前訓練客語單字與客語詞之 1-gram 與 2-gram 語言模型，以計算出前後字或前後詞出現之條件機率。

## 三）偏好輸入

每個人輸入文句時，會有個人常用的字或詞，這些常用字或詞會因為每個人的使用習慣而不同，因此提供有為個人使用習慣而建立的偏好功能，減少使用者在輸入時尋找的時間，此即個人化的使用詞彙環境。

為了將使用者常用的詞，更快輸出，因此在資料庫欄位上設置 pref（偏好），紀錄使用者平常輸入的字或詞的頻率；在系統內的 pref 一開始的初始值為 0，每當輸入一個字或詞時，將紀錄在資料庫上的 pref 欄位做加 1 的動作，以此類推，並依照 pref 排列在作搜尋，排列出下一個可能習慣輸出的客語單字或詞彙，並提供在候選詞窗中的前面供使用者選取做輸出，

## 四）客語特殊字顯示處理

客家委員會之客家語言有自創之特殊字型，為了可以正確顯示出字型，在電腦平台客委會有提供造字編碼表及造字檔[17]，供使用者安裝，但礙於智慧手機市面上並無客語輸入法，導致客語在手機上不盛行，因此客委會目前尚未提供智慧手機上相關的造字檔呈現字型。

在徵詢多位客委會「客語薪傳師」後，我們採用此方式解決手機平台顯示客語特殊字的問題。

智慧手機中因為有特殊字無法顯示的問題，在這裡我們將特殊字以其「無聲調拼音」方式顯示，智慧手機能顯示出來，讓使用者能夠辨別，而不再是無法顯示的亂碼，圖三為客語特殊字(1)「𠊎（ngai）」與(2)「𥊌」拼音顯示。

圖三：　特殊字顯示示意圖(1) (2)

## 五)中轉客輸入法

在目前臺灣的社會，年輕客家一輩多不會說自己母語，導致客語能力只剩聽的能力，甚至連聽的能力也已流失；此外，對於非客家的朋友，常因身旁沒會講客語者可以請教，因此學習客語成為一件困難的事。為此，我們提出中文輸入轉成客語的功能，可提供一般人不會客語、想學習客語的使用者，一個友

善學習環境，並且在數位學習上新增客語學習方式。這項功能整合於我們的客語拼音的系統，以鍵盤的功能鍵切換「客語／中文」輸入法。

## 中文注音無聲調輸入

本輸入法設定使用對家為一般客語初學者，由於初學者大多數不會客語拼音，為此，我們特別設計使用「中文注音方式」輸入，並自動轉譯成客語輸出顯示於手機畫面上，如此可以讓不知客語詞彙的情形下，以替代方式輸入客語語彙。

在中轉客辭典只有中轉客注音對照料表，有 5853 個詞彙數，包含了 Val、Chunese、Key、Pinyin、afterabber 及 Pref 六個欄位，分別代表了客語詞彙(Val)、中文意義(Chunese)、注音縮寫(Key)、完整注音(Pinyin)、第一個字完整後面都縮寫(afterabber)及偏好偏好 Pref。

中轉客注音對照料表之建立，資料來源為客語能力認證基本詞彙-初級、中級、高級，將其正規劃後(如:E3)，並利用重編國語辭典修訂本[15]建立客語的中文意義注音，在建立中文注音的字首縮寫與第一個字拼音完整其他都字首縮寫(如:E4、E5)，並轉成對映按鍵之注音編碼其注音編碼方式，如表二所示。

在中轉客輸入法中，也運用在海陸腔無聲調輸入模式使用的資料探勘中的聚類分析的觀點。其目的為輸入中文注音拼音時，將中文對應的客語詞能更快顯示在候選詞窗中，並提供使用者輸出，圖七為輸入中文無聲調「土地公生日」之注音拼音轉成客語詞彙之過程。中文:土地公生日=>客語:伯公生。

首先輸入中文「土」字之注音拼音「ㄊㄨ」，其後選欄位將列出所有有關"ㄊㄨ"注音拼音之轉換客語後相關詞彙，當使用者輸入的關鍵拼音越多時，所顯示在候選欄的相關詞彙，將越接近使用者想輸入的詞彙，提供使用者做輸入動作。當輸入動作到第四步時，已經顯示出我們預先想要輸入的中文轉成客語詞彙「伯公生」。惟中文輸入詞如找不到合適客語詞，則無法轉換客語詞。

# 四、輸入法評量分析

本文在 Andorid 手機平台上研發海陸腔客語拼音輸入法，希望提供 3C 使用者具效率之客語輸入法，可以快速便利輸入客語文句，並且具有單字與詞彙之客語語音輸出，提供一種手機平台上經由聽語音學習客語的方式。簡而言之，本輸入法的特色可以歸納如下表所示。

表一：本輸入法的特性說明

| 本輸入法功能 | 說　明 | 備　註 |
|---|---|---|
| 1　手機平台 | 可在 Andorid 手機或 PAD 平台環境輸入客語文句。 | 以海陸腔為主 |
| 2　輸入單字與詞彙 | 可以輸入單字、詞彙 | |
| 3　邊輸入邊搜尋 | 使用者一面鍵入拼音符號，即開始比對可能的單字或詞彙。 | 邊鍵入邊搜尋客語詞典 |
| 4　前後字預測 | 確定一字之後，可以預測該字之後可能的下一個字。 | |
| 5　前後詞預測 | 確定一個詞彙之後，可以預測該字之後可能的下一個詞。 | 運用統計式語言模型 bigram |
| 6　客語特殊字呈現 | 目前客語單字中有數百個特殊字，以拼音顯示出來。 | 特殊字無法正常顯示在手上 |
| 7　語音學習 | 可對一個單字或一個詞彙作語路輸出。 | |
| 8　記憶個人化輸入語彙環境 | **可以記憶個人化輸入語彙環境** | 個人常用單字與詞彙，其出現順序往前遞增。 |
| 9　中轉客輸入法 | 本輸入法對於客語初學者或某些忘記的客語拼音，提供輸入中文轉換為客語的功能，可提供所需之客語拼音與詞彙。 | |

　　本輸入法具有上述之功能，為提供正確、效率化的輸入法，需經使用者的測試，作為修正與改進的依據。本文有關海陸腔客語輸入法的評量測試，採用平均主觀分數(Mean Opinion Score, MOS)的方式做為操作滿意度之分析，操作調查的受測者為懂客語拼音並且擁有客語初級、中級或高級其中之一認證者:客家委員會人員含客家薪傳師[18]羅文生、張旭英、何惠美等老師，

與懂客語但不會客語拼音的新竹在地海陸腔之使用者 10 人，總共合計 13
人，這些受測者使用客語海陸腔最少都有 20 年以上。

　　這些使用者提供五句客語句子跟五句中文句子輸入，操作完成後，依
照受測者自己對者兩套輸入法做滿意度評分，滿意度評分分數為 1~5 分。

## 一)客語海陸腔輸入法之滿意度評量

　　由圖八可知，受測者在使用客語海陸腔輸入法後的滿意程度，大部分
受測者覺得此輸入法入門門檻有點高，因為使用客語海陸腔輸入法所採用
的拼音，需要經過相關的訓練才能使用此輸入法，因此覺得對不懂客語拼
音的使用者來說很難操作，其總平均分數為 4.0 分, 達良好的程度。

　　受測者之意見，主要有：本輸八法操作上滿順手，對於平常使用倉頡
或注音輸入，反而比較慢，建議考慮具有操作者習慣的輸入方式；使用者
必須具備客語能力能能操作使用；很直覺化的拼音系統，感覺非常實用。

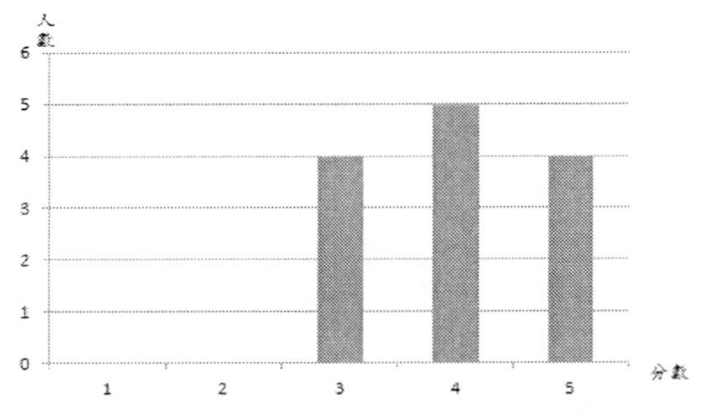

圖四: 海陸腔輸入法使用者評分

## 二）中轉客輸入法之滿意度評量

　　由圖九所示，因臺灣人的輸入習慣大部分都是使用注音符
號，因此中轉客輸入法對使用者來說，比較親切與順手，故大
部分使用者的評分分數都較使用拼音方式的海陸腔輸入法高，
其總平均分數為 4.46 分，接近很好的程度，這亦顯示提供「中
文學習客語」之數位學習功能受到測試者肯定。

受測者意見主要有，本系統構想、做法很好，可讓想學習客語的人
容易上手；希望後端詞彙庫能多點，讓系統能夠更佳完整發揮功能；希望
能將海陸腔輸入法與中轉客輸入法兩套系統整合在一起，才不用做麻煩的
切換動作。

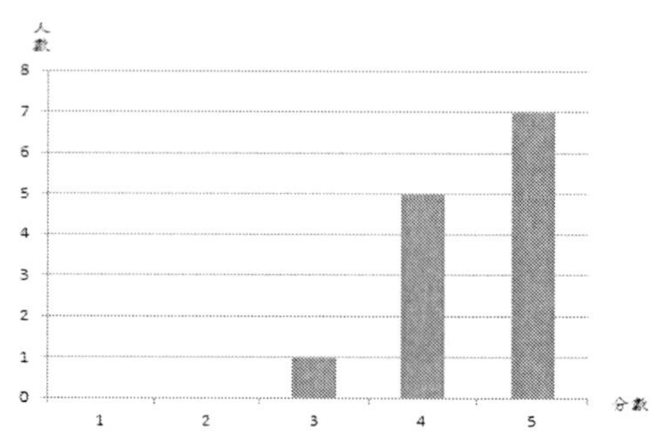

圖五: 中轉客輸入法使用者評分

# 五、結論與未來方向

本文提出的智慧型手機客語海陸腔輸入法及中轉客輸入法，希望熟悉客語
和不熟悉客語的使用者能夠使用，對於現在眾多輸入法當中，缺少的就是客家
語言的輸入法，本文以研發海陸腔客語輸入法與相關應用為主，客語使用族群
能夠運用母語在手機上交談，進一步達到客語的傳承與發揚。

在語料庫的收集過程中，我們使用客委會提供的初級、中級、高級基本詞
彙及教育部台灣客家語常用詞辭典，總共 19315 個客語詞彙、5366 個客語單
字、8050 筆客語前後詞詞彙，並使用中興大學資訊科學與工程學系林昕緯的
斷詞標記模組工具[10]，做大量的客語文章斷詞做業來建立前後詞對照詞庫。

海陸腔輸入法及中轉客輸入法都以聯合大學資訊工程學系劉桂森的論文為
基底，並加以提出使用客語特殊字的拼音解決客語特殊字無法顯示之問題，中
轉客輸入法，以輸入客語詞之對應中文注音來達成輸入中文輸出客語之功能，
並且加入散打功能，讓使用者能夠快速的找出想輸入的字詞。

在使用者評估調查中，調查了十三位客語海陸腔的使用者，其中有 3 位為
現任客家薪傳師；在海陸腔輸入法的總平均 4 分，中轉客輸入法總平均分數為
4.46 分。由評估調查中可以發現，在中轉客輸入法分數較高，很可能因國人的

輸入使用習慣所造成的，在台灣大多數使用者使用注音輸入文句，所以使用者的輸入習慣大大的影響其評估分數。

對於本論文之研發與相關研究尚有需多待改進之部分，因此，在未來可進行的研究方向:

1. 將客語拼音輸入法與中轉客輸入法做整合，可省去切換輸入法之間的時間與操作。

2. 海陸腔相關資料較四縣腔來的少，因此還需要收集並整理出更多海陸腔相關資料，並建立出更加完整的資料庫系統。

3. 新增錯誤提示功能，藉由建議選字，使用者無須再打一次，可自動修正成正確的客語字詞。

4. 持續擴充客語語料庫內容，並訓練語言模型。

# 參考文獻


[1] 黃河、陳信木，全國客家認同與客家人口之抽樣調查研究，台北：行政院客家委員會，2002。

[2] 劉桂森，智慧手機平台中四縣客語拼音輸入法之研究與應用，聯合大學資訊工程學系碩士論文，2017。

[3] 教育部客委會出版，客家語言拼音方案，2012。

[4] 教育部，重修國語詞典修訂本，2015。

[5] 教育部客委會出版，台灣客家語言拼音輸入法，2013。

[6] 魏俊瑋，客家無聲調拼音輸入法之研究與實作，國立中興大學資訊工程系碩士論文，2013。

[7] 信望愛台語客語輸入法，2005，http://taigi.fhl.net/TaigiIME/，[存取日期：10.1.2018]。

[8] 維基百科，客家裔臺灣人，https://zh.wikipedia.org/wiki/客家裔臺灣人。

[9] 蔡依玲，基於隱藏式馬可夫模型之客語文具轉語音系統，國立交通大學電信成所碩士論文，2009。

[10] 林昕緯，中文轉客文語音合成系統中的文句分析模組之研究，國立中興大學資訊科學與工程學系碩士論文，2014。

[11] 客家委會出版，105 年客語能力認證基本詞彙-中級暨中高級[海陸腔]-上冊，2016。

[12] 客家委員會出版，105 年客語能力認證基本詞彙-中級暨中高級[海陸腔]-下

冊，2016。

[13]    客家委員會，105 年度客語能力認證基本詞彙-初級【海陸腔】，2016

[14]    教育部客委會出版，教育部台灣客家語常用詞辭典。

[15]    教育部客委會出版，重編國語辭典修訂本。

[16]    DATA MINING Concepts and Techniques(3th ed.). (2011). Morgan Kaufmann, Jiawei Han, MichelineKamber, Jian Pei.

[17]    哈客網路學院出版，客語造字檔，2009，http://elearning.hakka.gov.tw/ver2015/kaga/dontseehakkafont.aspx，[存取日期：15/1/2018]。

[18]    客家委員會-客語薪傳師，https://master.hakka.gov.tw/，[存取日期：15/1/2018]。

[19]    FFmpeg，2011，https://ffmpeg.org/about.html，[存取日期：15/1/ 2018]

[20] BaconBao，台語兒，google chrome store，2015，[存取日期：15 /1/2018]

[21] 吳孟龍，手機實體按鍵與觸控介面之新式輸入法，國立成功大學工業設計學系碩士論文，2011。

[22] 周宇軒，行動電話注音輸入法鍵盤配置之研究，華梵大學資訊管理學系碩士論文，2010。

[23]    Yabin Zheng, Chen Li & Maosong Sun,2011 "CHIME:An Efficient Error-Tolerant Chinese Pinyin Method", IJCAI'11 Proceedings of the Twenty-Second international joint conference on Artificial Intelligence – Volume Three pp. 2551-2556.

[24]    Yabin Zheng, Lixing Xie, Zhiyuan Liu, Maosong Sun, Yang Zhang & Liyun Ru, 2011"Why Press Backspace? Understanding User Input Behaviors in Chinese Pinyin Input Method", HLT '11 Proceedings of the 49th Annual Meeting of the Association for Computational Linguistics Volume 2 pp. 485-490.

[25] 客家委員會，2016，http://www.ihakka.net/epaper/1060203/epaper.htm，[存取日期：22 /1/2018]

[26] 五南圖書出版，" 客語發音學"，2006。

[27] 李雪貞，客語語音合成之初步研究"，國立臺灣科技大學資訊工程所，碩士論文，2002。

[28] 林東毅，客語文句翻語音系統之實作，國立交通大學電信工程所，碩士論文，2007。

[29] 蔡育和，中文文轉音系統中韻律階層的求取，國立中興大學資訊科學與工程所，碩士論文，2005。

[30] 呂嵩雁，客語《陸豐方言》的百年語言演變析探，國立東華大學台灣語文學系，研究計畫報告書，2007。

The 2018 Conference on Computational Linguistics and Speech Processing
ROCLING 2018, pp. 157-157
©The Association for Computational Linguistics and Chinese Language Processing

# 以深層類神經網路標記中文階層式多標籤語意概念

# Hierarchical Multi-Label Chinese Word Semantic Labeling using

# Deep Neural Network

周瑋傑　　Wei-Chieh Chou
國立交通大學電機工程學系
Department of Electrical Engineering
National Chiao Tung University
m0450743.eed04g@g2.nctu.edu.tw


王逸如　　Yih-Ru Wang
國立交通大學電機工程學系
Department of Electrical Engineering
National Chiao Tung University
yrwang@mail.nctu.edu.tw

## 摘要

傳統上對超過 100 個階層式標籤分類可以使用扁平 (flatten) 標籤做分類，但如此會喪失架構樹 (taxonomy) 的階層資訊。本研究旨在對廣義知網中文詞彙做概念分類與標記，提出考慮廣義知網架構樹階層關係之深層類神經網路訓練方法，其輸入為詞彙樣本點的詞向量，詞向量方面本研究亦提出考慮上下文前後關係之 2-Bag Word2Vec，而各階層的訓練結果有不同的重要性，所以在模型的最後使用最小分類誤差法，賦予各階層在測試階段時不同的權重。實驗結果顯示階層式 (hierarchical) 分類預測正確率會比扁平分類還高。

## Abstract

Traditionally, classifying over 100 hierarchical multi-labels could use flatten classification, but it will lose the taxonomy structure information. This paper aimed to classify the concept of word in E-HowNet and proposed a deep neural network training method with hierarchical relationship in E-HowNet taxonomy. The input of neural network is word embedding. About word embedding, this paper proposed order-aware 2-Bag Word2Vec. Experiment results shown hierarchical classification will achieved higher accuracy than flatten classification.

關鍵詞：詞向量、類神經網路、最小分類誤差、廣義知網、階層式分類、多標籤分類

Keywords: Word2Vec、neural network、minimum classification error、E-HowNet、hierarchical classification、multi-label classification

The 2018 Conference on Computational Linguistics and Speech Processing
ROCLING 2018, pp. 158-168
©The Association for Computational Linguistics and Chinese Language Processing

# LENA computerized automatic analysis of speech development from birth to three

Li-Mei Chen

National Cheng Kung University, leemay@mail.ncku.edu.tw

D. Kimbrough Oller

University of Memphis, USA, koller@memphis.edu

Chia-Cheng Lee

University of Wisconsin-Eau Claire, USA, jiajiajanejane@gmail.com

Chin-Ting Jimbo Liu

National Chin-Yi University of Technology, jimbo@ncut.edu.tw

## Abstract

This study investigated the relationship between the linguistic input children receive and the number of children's vocalizations by using computerized LENA (Language Environment Analysis) system software which is able to collect and analyze the data automatically, instantly, and objectively. Data from three children (two boys and one girl) at ages of 10, 20, and 30 months were analyzed. The results indicated that: 1) child vocalizations (CV) and child-caregiver conversational turns (CT) increased with time while adult word counts (AWC) children overheard in the background decreased; 2) CT is highly correlated with CV. LENA automatic device can substantially shorten the time of data analysis in the study of child language, and provide preliminary results for further analysis.

## 1. Introduction

This paper explores the relationship between children's vocalization and the linguistic input they received by using LENA (Language Environment Analysis https://www.lena.org/), a computer system of automatic, objective and inexpensive device that collects and analyzes data for up to 16-hour-long recordings. It has been shown that the audio input children exposed to might largely affect their vocalizations [1], [2], [3], which in turn serve as an essential indicator of their later language development [4], [5].

## 1.1 Volubility as early indicators of future language development

Infants' volubility can be defined as the number of speech-like utterances made by infants within a certain period of time. Vocalizations appear with a variety of forms, including but not limited to cooing, vocal play and canonical babbling (e.g., "ba", "ma"). The forms of vocalizations vary from time to time, depending on the maturation of the speech motor control ability.

Studies have shown that infants' vocalization was associated with their later speaking ability. Typically developing (TD) children produced 41% more vocalizations than those with cleft lip and palate [6]. Similarly, children with severe-to-profound hearing loss were reported to have their onset of canonical babbling later than those of TD children [7]. In short, it has been confirmed that infants' early vocalizations are an essential indicator of their later language development.

## 1.2 Audio input and later language development

Input from adults is identified as one of the most influential factors affecting children's verbal performances [8]. However, it is still inconclusive whether children can acquire language by overhearing. In other word, it is still debatable if the linguistic input in the background plays a significant role in children's language development. Many scholars claimed that language acquisition takes place even when the linguistic materials, which children are exposed to, are not addressed to them directly [9]. On the other hand, other scholars concluded that, in comparison to adult conversations overheard by children, speech addressed directly to children have stronger effect on children's vocabulary learning [10]. Studies investigating the relationship among adults' speech in the background, adults' speech directly addressed to children and children's vocalizations will shed light on our understandings of the relationship between different types of linguistic input and language development.

## 1.3 Coding efficiency and length of observation

Due to the laborious measurements required for measuring the linguistic input in the ambient environment, studies focusing on infant's vocal developments are usually based on limited data [11]. In view of this, LENA, an innovative recording device with automatic analyzing capacities, is adopted for data collection in the present study. The device weighs about 70 grams and can be put into children's vest pocket. More importantly, the device is able to run for a consecutive of 16 hours to record the holistic picture of the input a child receives when s/he is awake. LENA is able to calculate the number of the words adults produce in the background (i.e. input by overhearing) and to calculate the number of the conversational turns between the child and the interlocutor (i.e. speech addressed directly to the child). Additionally, the vocalizations made by the child are counted automatically, too. It has been shown that the results from LENA are accurate and reliable [12].

## 1.4 Present study

The goal of the present study is to examine the contributions from two sorts of input (i.e. overhearing and speech addressed directly to the child) to children's vocalizations. The specific questions are:

a.  Do adult word counts in the background (AWC), conversational turns (CT) and number of child vocalizations (CV) produced by children increase as they grow older?

b.  Are both AWC and CT effective contributors to the number of CV at the ages of 10, 20 and 30 months?

## 2. Method

## 2.1 Participants

Data from three children (two boys and one girl) growing up in a Chinese-speaking family were recorded and analyzed by LENA. Each child participated in the 16-hour-long recording session twice in a month. In the current study, data at tenth, twentieth, and thirtieth months were reported. According to the reports from the parents, all the children were full-term and were without hearing and speech-related disorders.

## 2.2 Equipment, procedures and data analysis

LENA was the equipment used to collect and analyze the data. The recording device, digital language processor (DLP), was put in a vest specially designed for children (Figure 1). The caretaker turned the device on to start a session. The caretakers were instructed and understood how to operate, interrupt and recharge the device. After the recording sessions were completed, DLP was sent back to the experimenters and the device was connected with a computer of LENA system software which automatically uploaded and processed the audio file (Figure 2) and developed the reports (Figure 3).

The adult word counts measure the total number of adult words the child hears per hour, per day and per month. The conversational turns display the total number of conversational turns the child engages in with an adult per hour, per day and per month. The child vocalizations array the total number of vocalizations the child produces per hour, per day and per month.

The core design of LENA system is the algorithmic models which is capable to segment and identify sounds of different amplitude and intensity. The audio data were categorized into eight categories with different sources: the key child (wearing LENA DLP), other child, adult male and adult female, overlapping sounds, noise, electronic sounds (e.g., TV), and silence. Each category is further identified as clear and unclear (or quiet and distant) subcategories. In order to identify a variety of audio signals efficiently and accurately, LENA audio processing models are trained by audio transcriptions of each category first. For example, the speech processing algorithms need to recognize the differences between adult speech and child speech, and between the key child and other children [13].

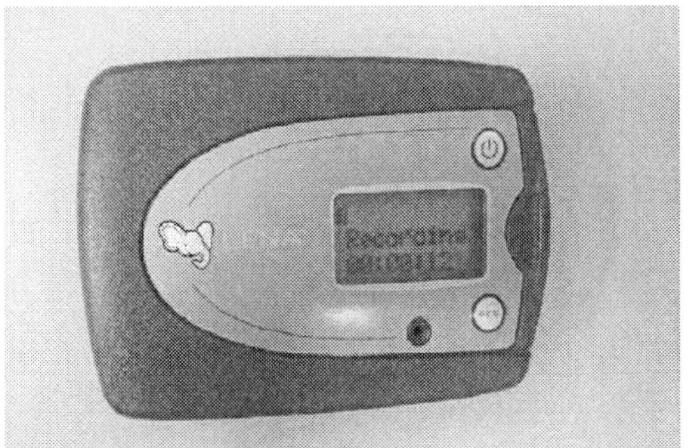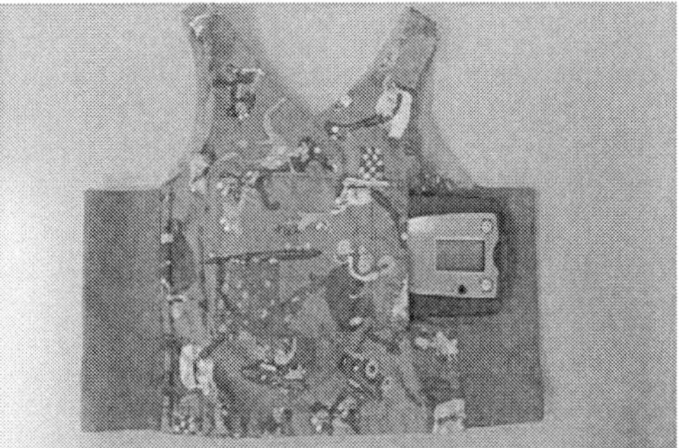

Figure 1. The LENA digital language processor (DLP) placed in the pocket of LENA vest.

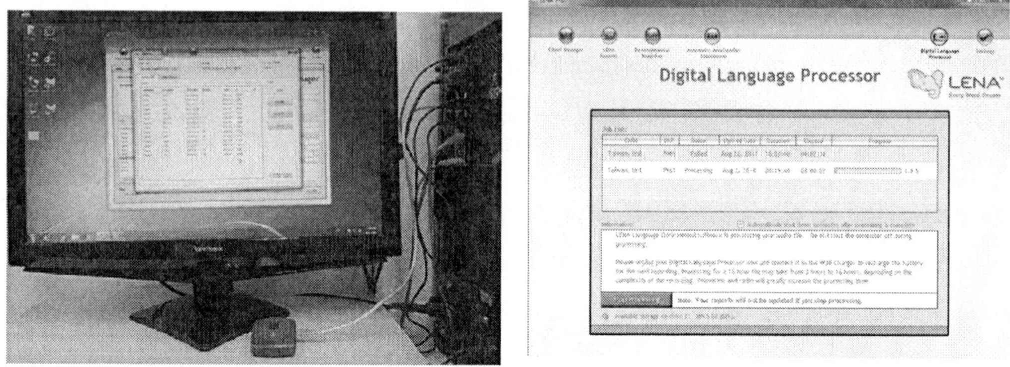

Figure 2. Data transfer from DLP to LENA system software

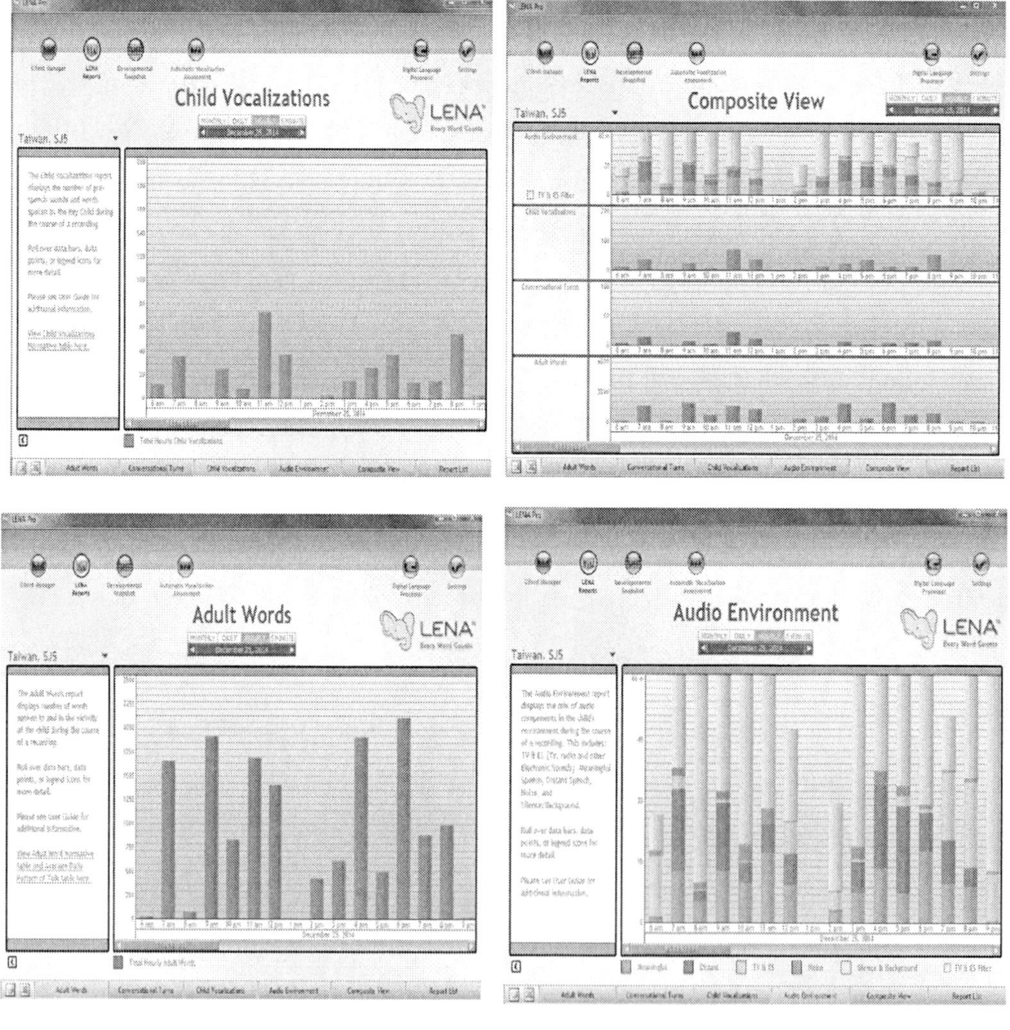

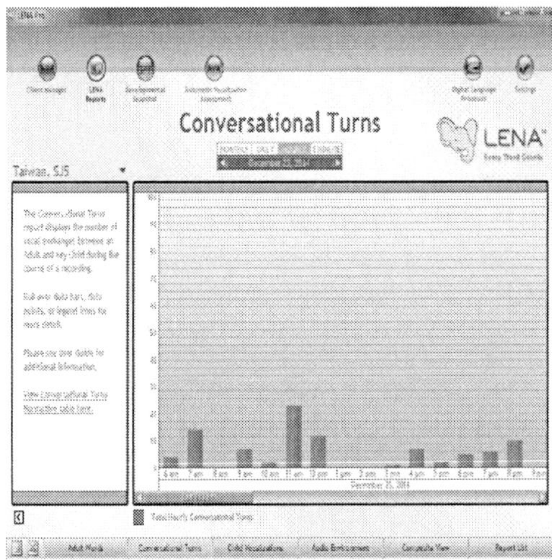


Figure 3. Reports from LENA system software

In order to answer the research questions, two statistical measures were performed, First, three one-way repeated measures ANOVAs were performed to explore if there were any changes of the three variables, (adult word counts, conversational turns, and child vocalizations) along the time. Next, multiple regressions were performed at the ages of 10, 20 and 30 months to examine how much AWC and CT contribute to CV at each age.

## 3. Results and Discussion

Figure 4 shows the average number of child vocalizations (CV), adult word counts (AWC), and conversational turns (CT) from the recordings made at 10, 20, and 30 months. The average number of CV gradually increased from 10, 20, and 30 months. The average number of CT also showed a gradual increase from 10, 20, and 30 months although the increase was small. However, the average number of AWC showed a decrease from 10, 20, and 30 months. Results of the three one-way repeated measures ANOVAs did not show significant differences among the three ages (AWC: $F_{(2, 10)}=1.89$, $p = 0.20$; CT: $F_{(2,10)}=0.43$, $p = 0.67$; CV: $F_{(2,10)}=1.03$, $p = 0.39$) , suggesting that the results of the mean of AWC, CT, CV were similar across the three ages.

The results of multiple regressions showed that CT and CV were highly correlated at all the three ages (10 months p<.001, $\beta = 3.746$; 20 months p<.001, $\beta = 3.600$, 30 months p<.01, $\beta = 4.829$). However, AWC and CV were not correlated at any of the ages (10 months $p = 0.08$, $\beta = -0.15$; 20 months $p = 0.06$, $\beta = -0.08$; 30 months $p = 0.1$, $\beta = -0.18$). Since a CT can be calculated when a child speaks and an adult responds, or when an adult speaks and the child responds, it is hard to identify if the increase in CT reported in Figure 4 was a result of the adult's responses to the child's vocalizations or vice versa.

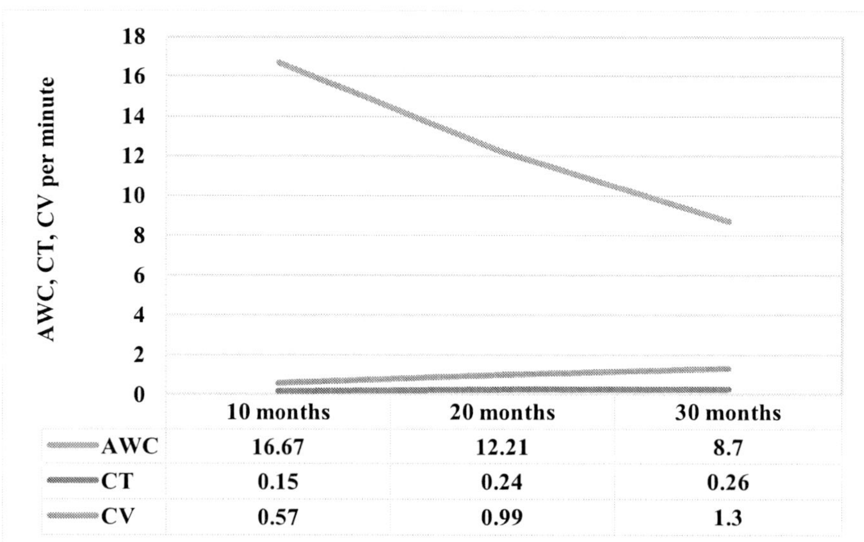

Figure 4. Average adult words (AWC), conversational turns (CT), child vocalizations (CV) per minute at 10, 20, and 30 months

It was also found that AWC decreased with child's ages. One possible explanation is that parents or other people may have been very voluble when addressing their 10-month-old child even when the child's utterances were not meaningful words or when the child did not vocalize. As the child grew up and started to produce words and sentences, parents may talk or respond only when their child produced meaningful utterances.

Figure 5 shows AWC per minute from recordings of individual child at three ages. SJ5's AWC was overall higher than YC6's and CC8's AWC. SJ5's and YC6's AWC deceased from 10 to 30 months. However, CC8's AWC showed an increase from 10 to 20 months and a slight decrease from 20 to 30 months.

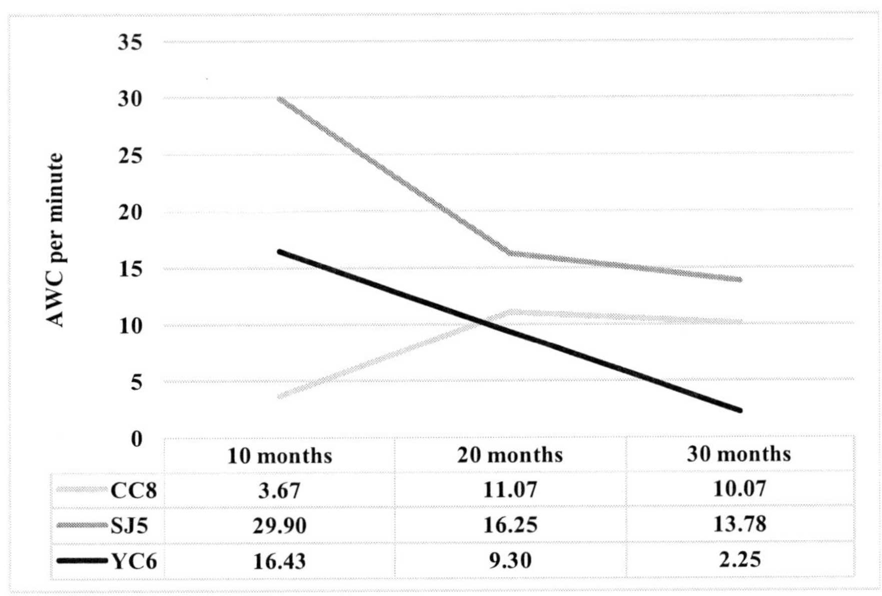

| | 10 months | 20 months | 30 months |
|---|---|---|---|
| CC8 | 3.67 | 11.07 | 10.07 |
| SJ5 | 29.90 | 16.25 | 13.78 |
| YC6 | 16.43 | 9.30 | 2.25 |

Figure 5. Adult words (AWC) per minute by individual child and age

Figure 6 and 7 shows CT and CV per minute from recordings of each individual child at three ages. The results of CT and CV showed a similar pattern. For example, CC8's and SJ5's CT and CV increased from 10 to 30 months. YC6's CT and CV decreased from 10 months to 30 months. Although SJ5's AWC was the highest of the three children, his CT and CV were the lowest among the three children.

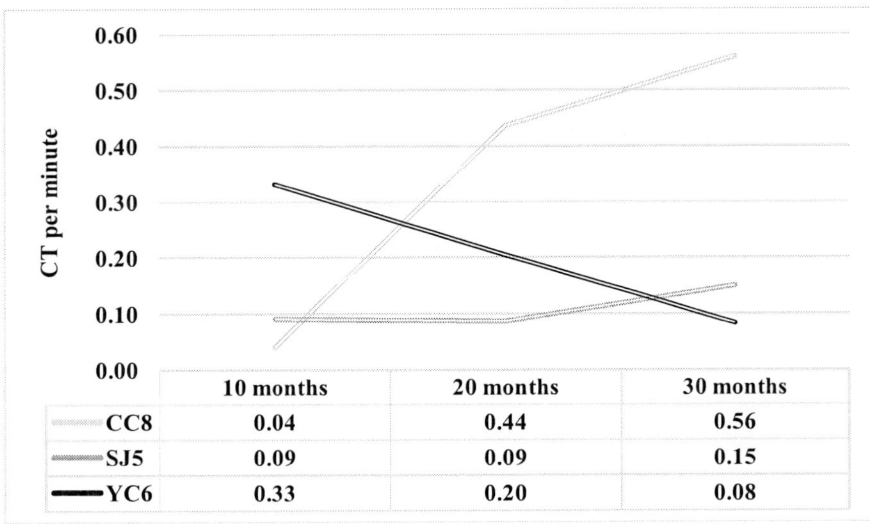

| | 10 months | 20 months | 30 months |
|---|---|---|---|
| CC8 | 0.04 | 0.44 | 0.56 |
| SJ5 | 0.09 | 0.09 | 0.15 |
| YC6 | 0.33 | 0.20 | 0.08 |

Figure 6. Conversational turns (CT) per minute by individual child and age

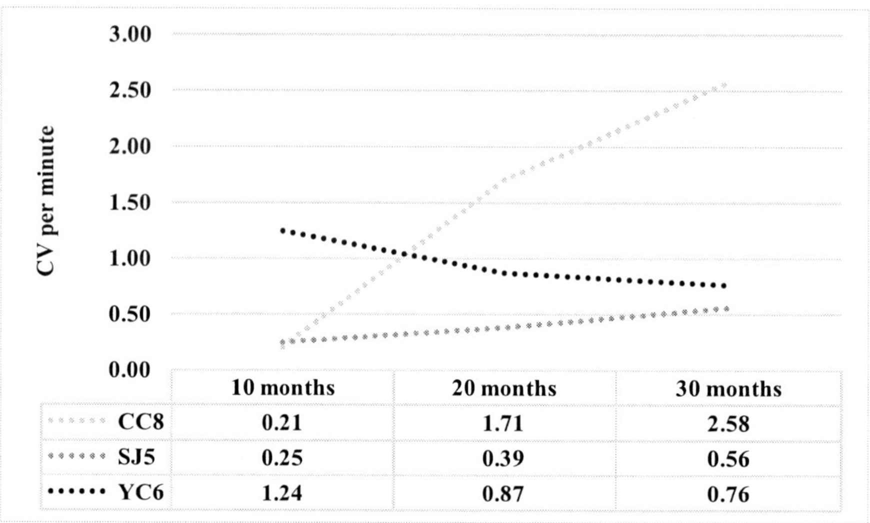


| | 10 months | 20 months | 30 months |
|---|---|---|---|
| CC8 | 0.21 | 1.71 | 2.58 |
| SJ5 | 0.25 | 0.39 | 0.56 |
| YC6 | 1.24 | 0.87 | 0.76 |

Figure 7. Child vocalizations (CV) per minute by individual child and age

## 4. Summary

(1)  LENA system software is an objective, efficient, and reliable device to display profile of child's speech and the linguistic inputs.

(2)  Child vocalizations and conversational turns increased with time, but the numbers among the three ages were not statistically different.

(3)  Adult word counts decreased as the child grows older, the counts among the three ages were not statistically different either.

(4)  There was a high correlation between child vocalizations and conversational turns.

(5)  No correlation was found between child vocalizations and adult word counts.

(6)  The preliminary findings suggested that speech directed to children (i.e. CT) exerted much stronger influence to children's vocalizations than speech overheard by children (i.e. AWC) did. That is, the findings supported the view proposed in [10], but not in [9]. However, cautions should be taken in this interpretation as only limited participants were included. Therefore, more data from more ages and from more children are crucial to verify the current findings.

# 5. Acknowledgement

This research was supported by Chiang Ching-Kuo Foundation for International Scholarly Exchange in Taiwan to Li-Mei Chen. A special thank you is extended to the families of the children in this longitudinal study for their support of this project.

# 6. References

[1] D. Suskind, K. Leffel, M. Hernandez, S. Sapolich, E. Suskind, E. Kirkham and P. Meehan, "An Exploratory Study of 'Quantitative Linguistic Feedback'", *Communication Disorders Quarterly*, vol. 34, no. 4, pp. 199-209, 2013.

[2] M. Rowe, "A Longitudinal Investigation of the Role of Quantity and Quality of Child-Directed Speech in Vocabulary Development", *Child Development*, vol. 83, no. 5, pp. 1762-1774, 2012.

[3] M. Caskey, B. Stephens, R. Tucker and B. Vohr, "Importance of Parent Talk on the Development of Preterm Infant Vocalizations", *Pediatrics*, vol. 128, no. 5, pp. 910-916, 2011.

[4] B. Franklin, A. Warlaumont, D. Messinger, E. Bene, S. Nathani Iyer, C. Lee, B. Lambert and D. Oller, "Effects of Parental Interaction on Infant Vocalization Rate, Variability and Vocal Type", *Language Learning and Development*, vol. 10, no. 3, pp. 279-296, 2014.

[5] E. Patten, K. Belardi, G. Baranek, L. Watson, J. Labban and D. Oller, "Vocal Patterns in Infants With Autism Spectrum Disorder: Canonical babbling status and vocalization frequency", *Journal of Autism and Developmental Disorders*, vol. 44, no. 10, pp. 2413-2428, 2014.

[6] N. Scherer, A. Williams and K. Proctor-Williams, "Early and Later Vocalization Skills in Children With and Without Cleft Palate", *International Journal of Pediatric Otorhinolaryngology*, vol. 72, no. 6, pp. 827-840, 2008.

[7] S. Iyer and D. Oller, "Fundamental Frequency Development in Typically Developing Infants and Infants With Severe To Profound Hearing Loss", *Clinical Linguistics & Phonetics*, vol. 22, no. 12, pp. 917-936, 2008.

[8] M. Caskey, B. Stephens, R. Tucker and B. Vohr, "Importance of Parent Talk on the Development of Preterm Infant Vocalizations", *PEDIATRICS*, vol. 128, no. 5, pp. 910-916, 2011.

[9] N. Akhtar, J. Jipson and M. Callanan, "Learning Words Through Overhearing", *Child Development*, vol. 72, no. 2, pp. 416-430, 2001.

[10] A. Weisleder and A. Fernald, "Talking to Children Matters: Early language experience strengthens processing and builds vocabulary", *Psychological Science*, vol. 24, no. 11, pp. 2143-2152, 2013.

[11] D. Oller, P. Niyogi, S. Gray, J. Richards, J. Gilkerson, D. Xu, U. Yapanel and S. Warren, "Automated Vocal Analysis of Naturalistic Recordings from Children With Autism, Language Delay, and Typical Development", *Proceedings of the National Academy of Sciences*, vol. 107, no. 30, pp. 13354-13359, 2010.

[12] J. Gilkerson, Y. Zhang, D. Xu, J. Richards, X. Xu, F. Jiang, J. Harnsberger and K. Topping, "Evaluating Language Environment Analysis System Performance for Chinese: A pilot study in Shanghai", *Journal of Speech Language and Hearing Research*, vol. 58, no. 2, p. 445, 2015.

[13] M. Ford, C. T. Baer, D. Xu, U. Yapanel and S. Gray, "The LENA Language Environment Analysis System: Audio specifications of the DLP-0121, LTR-03-2", LENA Foundation, 2008.

The 2018 Conference on Computational Linguistics and Speech Processing
ROCLING 2018, pp. 169-183
©The Association for Computational Linguistics and Chinese Language Processing

# Using Statistical and Semantic Models
# for Multi-Document Summarization

**Divyanshu Daiya**

Department of Computer Science Engineering

LNM Institute of Information Technology

Jaipur, INDIA

daiyadivyanshu@gmail.com

**Anukarsh Singh**

Department of Computer Science Engineering

LNM Institute of Information Technology

Jaipur, INDIA

anukarshsingh1@gmail.com

**Abstract.** We report a series of experiments with different semantic models on top of various statistical models for extractive text summarization. Though statistical models may better capture word co-occurrences and distribution around the text, they fail to detect the context and the sense of sentences /words as a whole. Semantic models help us gain better insight into the context of sentences. We show that how tuning weights between different models can help us achieve significant results on various benchmarks. Learning pre-trained vectors used in semantic models further, on given corpus, can give addition spike in performance. Using weighing techniques in between various statistical models too further refines our result. For Statistical models, we have used TF/IDF, TextRAnk, Jaccard/Cosine Similarities. For Semantic Models, we have used WordNet-based Model and proposed two models based on Glove Vectors and Facebook's InferSent. We tested our approach on DUC 2004 dataset, generating 100-word summaries. We have discussed the system, algorithms, analysis and also proposed and tested possible improvements. ROUGE scores were used to compare to other summarizers.

**Keywords.** Extractive Text Summarization, Semantic Summarization Models, Statistical Summarization Models, Multi Document Summarization

# 1. Introduction

Automatic Text Summarization deals with the task of condensing documents into a summary, whose level is similar to a human-generated summary. It is mostly distributed into two distinct domains, i.e., Abstractive Summarization and Extractive Summarization. Abstractive summarization( Dejong et al. ,1978) involves models to deduce the crux of the document. It then presents a summary consisting of words and phrases that were not there in the actual document, sometimes even paraphrasing [20]. A state of art method proposed by Wenyuan Zeng [25] produces such summaries with length restricted to 75. There have been many recent developments that produce optimal results, but it is still in a developing phase. It highly relies on natural language processing techniques, which is still evolving to match human standards. These shortcomings make abstractive summarization highly domain selective. As a result, their application is skewed to the areas where NLP techniques have been superlative. Extractive Summarization, on the other hand, uses different methods to identify the most informative/dominant sentences through the text, and then present the results, ranking them accordingly. In this paper, we have proposed two novel stand-alone summarization methods.The first method is based on Glove Model [17],and other is based on Facebook's InferSent [4]. We have also discussed how we can effectively subdue shortcomings of one model by using it in coalition with models which capture the view that other faintly held.

# 2. Related Work

A vast number of methods have been used for document summarization. Some of the methods include determining the length and positioning of sentences in the text [19], deducing centroid terms to find the importance of text [19] and setting a threshold on average TF-IDF scores. Bag-of-words approach, i.e., making sentence/Word freq matrix, using a signature set of words and assigning them weights to use them as a criterion for importance measure [10] have also been used. Summarization using weights on high-frequency words [14] describes that high-frequency terms can be used to deduce the core of document.

While semantic summarizers like Lexical similarity is based on the assumption that important sentences are identified by strong chains [6, 2, 13]. In other words, it relates sentences that employ words with the same meaning (synonyms) or other semantic relation. It uses WordNet [12] to find similarity among words that apply to Word Frequency algorithm.POS(Part of Speech) Tagging and WSD(Word Sense Disambiguation) are common among semantic summarizers. Graphical summarizers like TextRank have also provided great benchmark results.TextRank assigns weights to important keywords from the document using graph-based model and sentences which capture most of those concepts/keywords are ranked higher) [2, 11] TextRank uses Google's PageRank (Brin and Page, 1998) for graphical modeling. Though semantic and graphical models may better capture the sense of document but miss out on statistical view. There is a void of hybrid summarizers; there haven't been many studies made in the area.Wong [23] conducted some preliminary research but there isn't much there on benchmark tests to our knowledge. We use a mixture of statistical and semantic models, assign weights among them by training on field-specific corpora. As there is a significant variation in choices among different fields. We support our proposal with expectations that shortcomings posed by one model can be filled with positives from others. We deploy experimental analysis to test our proposition.

## 3. Proposed Approach

For Statistical analysis we use Similarity matrices, word co-occurrence/ n-gram model, andTF/IDF matrix. For semantic analysis we use custom Glove based model, WordNet based Model and Facebook InferSent [4] based Model. For Multi-Document Summarization,after training on corpus, we assign weights among the different techniques .We store the sense vector for documents, along with weights, for future reference. For Single document summarization, firstly we calculate the sense vector for that document and calculate the nearest vector from the stored Vectors, we use the weights of the nearest vector. We will describe the flow for semantic and statistical models separately.

### 3.1. Prepossessing

We discuss, in detail, the steps that are common for both statistical and semantic models.

### 3.1.1. Sentence Tokenizer

We use NLTK sentence tokenizer sent_tokenize(), based on PUNKT tokenizer, pre-trained on a corpus. It can differentiate between Mr. , Mrs. and other abbreviations etc. and the normal sentence boundaries. [7]
Given a document $D$ we tokenize it into sentences as $<s_1, s_2, s_3, s_4 ... s_n>$.

### 3.1.2. Word Tokenizer

Replacing all the special characters with spaces for easier word-tagging and Tokenizing. We use NLTK word tokenizer, which is a Penn Treebank–style tokenizer, to tokenize words.We calculate the total unique words in the Document. If we can write any sentence as:-

$$s_i \rightarrow \; <\mathbf{w_I}, \mathbf{w_J}, \mathbf{w_K}, \mathbf{w_L}, ..>, \; \mathrm{i} \in (1, n)$$

Then the number of unique words can be represented as:-

$$(\mathrm{I}, \mathrm{J}, \mathrm{K}, \mathrm{L}....) \subset (1, ..M) \;, n \rightarrow Total\, sentences, M \rightarrow Total\, unique\, words$$

## 3.2. Using Stastical Models

### 3.2.1. Similarity/Correlation Matrices

**Frequency Matrix generation:** Our tokenized words contain redundancy due to digits and transitional words such as "and", "but" etc., which carry little information. Such words are termed stop words. [22] We removed stop words and words occurring in $<0.2\%$ and $>15\%$ of the documents (considering the word frequency over all documents). After the removal, the no. of unique words left in the particular document be p where p$<$m (where m is the total no. of unique words in our tokenized list originally). We now formulate a matrix $F_{\mathrm{n \times p}}$ where n is the total number of sentences and p is the total number of unique words left in the document. Element $e_{ij}$ in the matrix $F_{\mathrm{n \times p}}$ denotes frequency of $j^{th}$ unique word in the $i^{th}$ sentence.

**Similarity/Correlation Matrix generation:** We now have have sentence word frequency vector $\mathbf{Sf_i}$ as $<\mathbf{f_{i1}}, \mathbf{f_{i2}}, \mathbf{f_{i3}}, ...\mathbf{f_{i4}}>$ where $f_{ia}$ denotes frequency of $a^{th}$ unique word in the $i^{th}$ sentence. We now compute,

$$\mathtt{Sentence\_similarity(Sf_i, Sf_j)}$$

We use two similarity measures : We generate the similarity matrix $Sim_{n \times n}^{j}$ for each of the similarity Measure, where j indexes the similarity Measure. Element $E_{ij}$ of $Sim_{n \times n}^{j}$ denotes similarity between $\mathrm{i^{th}}$ and $\mathrm{j^{th}}$ sentence. Consequentially, we will end up with $Sim_{n \times n}^{1}$ and $Sim_{n \times n}^{2}$, corresponding to each similarity measure.

1. Jaccard Similarity: For some sets A and B, $<$a,b,c,... $>$and $<$x,y,z,... $>$respectively, the Jaccard Similarity is defined as:-

$$\mathtt{Jaccard\_similarity(A,B)} \leftarrow \frac{n(A \cap B)}{n(A \cup B)}$$

2. Cosine Similarity: The Cosine distance between 'u' and 'v', is defined as:-

$$\mathtt{Cosine\_similarity(A,B)} \leftarrow 1 - \frac{u \cdot v}{||u|| \, ||v||}$$

where '$u \cdot v$' is the dot product of '$u$' and '$v$'.

### 3.2.2. PageRank

PageRank algorithm [15], devised to rank web pages, forms the core of Google Search. It roughly works by ranking pages according to the number and quality of outsourcing links from the page. For NLP, a PageRank based technique ,TextRank has been a major breakthrough in the field. TextRank based summarization has seeded exemplary results on benchmarks. We use a naive TextRank analogous for our task.

Given $n$ sentences $<s_1, s_2, s_3, ..s_n>$, we intend to generate PageRank or probability distribution matrix $\mathbf{R_{n \times 1}}$,

$$\begin{bmatrix} Pr(s_1) \\ Pr(s_2) \\ \vdots \\ Pr(s_n) \end{bmatrix}$$

, where $Pr(s_k)$ in original paper denoted probability with which a randomly browsing user lands on a particular page. For the summarization task, they denote how strongly a sentence is connected with rest of document, or how well sentence captures multiple views/concepts. The steps are as:

1. Initialize $\mathbf{R}$ as,

$$\begin{bmatrix} Pr(s_1) \\ Pr(s_2) \\ \vdots \\ Pr(s_n) \end{bmatrix} = \begin{bmatrix} \frac{1}{n} \\ \frac{1}{n} \\ \vdots \\ \frac{1}{n} \end{bmatrix}$$

2. Define $\mathbf{d}$, probability that randomly chosen sentence is in summary and $\varepsilon$ as measure of change i.e. to stop computation when difference between to successive $\mathbf{R}$ computations recedes below $\varepsilon$.

3. Using cosine-similarity matrix $Sim^2_{n \times n}$, we generate the following equation as a measure for relation between sentences:-

$$\mathbf{R} = \begin{bmatrix} (1-d)/n \\ (1-d)/n \\ \vdots \\ (1-d)/n \end{bmatrix} + \mathbf{d} \times \mathbf{Sim^2_{n \times n}} \times \mathbf{R}$$

4. Repeat last step until $|R(t+1) - R(t)| > \varepsilon$.

5. Take top ranking sentences in $\mathbf{R}$ for summary.

### 3.2.3. TF/IDF

Term Frequency(TF)/Bag of words is the count of how many times a word occurs in the given document. Inverse Document Frequency(IDF) is the number of times word occurs in complete corpus. Infrequent words through corpus will have higher weights, while weights for more frequent words will be depricated.

Underlying steps for TF/IDF summarization are:

1. Create a count vector

$$Doc_1 \leftarrow <fr_{Word_1}, fr_{Word_2}, fr_{Word_3}, ..>$$

2. Build a tf-idf matrix $W_{M \times N}$ with element $w_{i,j}$ as,

$$w_{i,j} = tf_{i,j} \times log(\frac{N}{df_i})$$

Here, $tf_{i,j}$ denotes term frequency of $\mathtt{ith}$ word in $\mathtt{jth}$ sentence, and $log(\frac{N}{df_i})$ represents the IDF frequency.

3. Score each sentence, taking into consideration only nouns, we use NLTK POS-tagger for identifying nouns.

$$Score(S_{o,j}) \leftarrow \frac{\sum No_{i,j}}{\sum\limits_{p=1}^{N} N_{p,j}}$$

4. Applying positional weighing .

$$Scores[S_{o,j}] = Score(S_{o,j}) \times (\frac{o}{T})$$

$$\mathtt{o} \rightarrow \mathtt{Sentence\ index} \quad \mathtt{T} \rightarrow \mathtt{Total\ sentences\ in\ document\ j}$$

5. Summarize using top ranking sentences.

### 3.3. Using Semantic Models

We proceed in the same way as we did for statistical models. All the pre-processing steps remain nearly same. We can make a little change by using lemmatizer instead of stemmer. Stemming involves removing the derivational affixes/end of words by heuristic analysis in hope to achieve base form. Lemmatization, on the other hand, involves firstly POS tagging [21], and after morphological and vocabulary analysis, reducing the word to its base form. Stemmer output for 'goes' is 'goe', while lemmatized output with the verb passed as POS tag is 'go'. Though lemmatization may have little more time overhead as compared to stemming, it necessarily provides better base word reductions. Since WordNet [16] and Glove both require dictionary look-ups, in order for them to work well, we need better base word mappings. Hence lemmatization is preferred.

### 3.3.1. Additional Pre-processing

1. **Part of Speech(POS) Tagging:** We tag the words using NLTK POS-Tagger.

2. **Lemmatization:** We use NTLK lemmatizer with POS tags passed as contexts.


### 3.3.2. Using WordNet

We generated Similarity matrices in the case of Statistical Models. We will do the same here, but for sentence similarity measure we use the method devised by Dao. [5] The method is defined as:

1. **Word Sense Disambiguation(WSD):** We use the adapted version of Lesk algorithm [9], as devised by Dao, to derive the sense for each word.

2. **Sentence pair Similarity:** For each pair of sentences, we create semantic similarity matrix $S$. Let $A$ and $B$ be two sentences of lengths $m$ and $n$ respectively. Then the resultant matrix $S$ will be of size $m \times n$, with element $s_{i,j}$ denoting semantic similarity between sense/synset of word at position $i$ in sentence $A$ and sense/synset of word at position $j$ in sentence $B$, which is calculated by path length similarity using $\texttt{is-a}$ (hypernym/hyponym) hierarchies. It uses the idea that shorter the path length, higher the similarity. To calculate the path length, we proceed in following manner:-
   For two words $W_1$ and $W_2$, with synsets $s_1$ and $s_2$ respectively,

   $$sd(s_1, s_2) = 1/distance(s_1, s_2)$$

   $$S_{m \times n} = \begin{bmatrix} sd(s_1, s_1) & \cdots & sd(s_1, s_n) \\ sd(s_2, s_1) & \ddots & \vdots \\ \vdots & sd(s_i, s_j) & \\ sd(s_m, s_1) & \cdots & sd(s_m, s_n) \end{bmatrix}$$

   We formulate the problem of capturing semantic similarity between sentences as the problem of computing a maximum total matching weight of a bipartite graph, where X and Y are two sets of disjoint nodes. We use the Hungarian method [8] to solve this problem. Finally we get bipartite matching matrix $B$ with entry $b_{i,j}$ denoting matching between $A[i]$ and $B[j]$. To obtain the overall similarity, we use Dice coefficient,

   $$Sim(A, B) = \frac{|A \cap B|}{|A| + |B|}$$

   with threshold set to 0.5, and $|A|$ ,$|B|$ denoting lengths of sentence $A$ and $B$ respectively.

3. We perform the previous step over all pairs to generate the similarity matrix $Sim^3_{N \times N}$.

### 3.3.3. Using Glove Model

Glove Model provides us with a convenient method to represent words as vectors, using vectors representation for words, we generate vector representation for sentences. We work in the following order,

1. Represent each tokenized word $w_i$ in its vector form $<a_i^1, a_i^2, a_i^3, \ldots a_i^{300}>$.

2. Represent each sentence into vector using following equation,

$$SVec(s_j) = \frac{1}{|s_j|} \sum_{w_i \in s_j} f_{i,j}(a_i^1, a_i^2, \ldots a_i^{300})$$

   where $f_{i,j}$ being frequency of $w_i$ in $s_j$.

3. Calculate similarity between sentences using cosine distance between two sentence vectors.

4. Populate similarity matrix $Sim_{N \times N}^4$ using previous step.


### 3.3.4. Using Facebook's InferSent

Infersent is a state of the art supervised sentence encoding technique [4]. It outperformed another state-of-the-art sentence encoder SkipThought on several benchmarks, like the STS benchmark ($http://ixa2.si.ehu.es/stswiki/index.php/STSbenchmark$). The model is trained on Stanford Natural Language Inference (SNLI) dataset [3] using seven architectures Long Short-Term Memory (LSTM), Gated Recurrent Units (GRU), forward and backward GRU with hidden states concatenated, Bi-directional LSTMs (BiLSTM) with min/max pooling, self-attentive network and (HCN's) Hierarchical convolutional networks. The network performances are task/corpus specific.
Steps to generate similarity matrix $Sim_{N \times N}^5$ are:

1. Encode each sentence to generate its vector representation $<l_i^1, l_i^2, l_i^3, \ldots l_i^{4096}>$.

2. Calculate similarity between sentence pair using cosine distance.

3. Populate similarity matrix $Sim_{N \times N}^5$ using previous step.


### 3.4. Generating Summaries

TF-IDF scores and TextRank allows us to directly rank sentences and choose $k$ top sentences, where $k$ is how many sentences user want in the summary. On the other hand, the similarity matrix based approach is used in case of all Semantic Models, and Similarity/correlation based Statistical models. To rank sentences from Similarity matrix, we can use following approaches:-

1. **Ranking through Relevance score**

   For each sentence $s_i$ in similarity matrix the Relevance Score is as:-

   $$RScore(s_i) = \sum_{j=1}^{N} Sim[i,j]$$

   We can now choose $k$ top ranking sentences by RScores. Higher the RScore, higher the rank of sentence.

2. **Hierarchical Clustering**

   Given a similarity matrix $Sim_{N \times N}$, let $s_{a,b}$ denote an individual element, then Hierarchical clustering is performed as follows:-

   (a) Initialize a empty list $R$.

   (b) Choose element with highest similarity value let it be $s_{i,j}$ where, $i \neq j, s_{i,j} \neq 0$

   (c) Replace values in column and row $i$ in following manner:-

   $$s_{d,i} = \frac{s_{d,i} + s_{d,j}}{2}, d \in (1,N), \quad s_{i,d} = \frac{s_{i,d} + s_{j,d}}{2}, d \in (1,N)$$

   (d) Replace entries corresponding to column and row $i$ by zeros.

   (e) Add $i$ and $j$ to $R$, if they are not already there.

   (f) Repeat steps 2-5 until single single non-zero element remains, for remaining non-zero element apply Step 5 and terminate.

   (g) We will have rank list $R$ in the end.

   We can now choose $k$ top ranking sentences from $R$.

## 3.5. Single Document Summarization

After generating summary from a particular model, our aim is to compute summaries through overlap of different models. Let us have $g$ summaries from $g$ different models. For $p_{th}$ summarization model, let the $k$ sentences contained be:-

$$Sum_p \leftarrow \left( s_{(1,p)}, s_{(2,p)} \cdots, s_{(k,p)} \right)$$

Now for our list of sentences $< s_1, s_2, s_3, ...s_n >$ we define **cWeight** as weight obtained for each sentence using $g$ models.

$$cWeight(s_i) = \sum_{j=1}^{g} W_i B(j, s_i)$$

Here, $B(j, s_i)$ is a function which returns 1 if sentence is in summary of $j_{th}$ model, otherwise zero. $W_i$ is weight assigned to each model without training, $W_i = \frac{1}{g}, i \in (1,g)$

### 3.6. Multi-Document/Domain-Specific Summarization

We here use machine learning based approach to further increase the quality of our summarization technique. The elemental concept is that we use training set of $u$ domain specific documents, with gold standard/human-composed summaries, provided we fine tune our weights $W_i \forall i \in (1, g)$ for different models taking F1-score/F-measure. [18] as factor.

$$F1Score = \frac{2.precision.recall}{precision + recall}$$

We proceed in the following manner:-

1. For each document in training set generate summary using each model independently, compute the $F_1 Score$ w.r.t. gold summary.

2. For each model, assign the weights using

$$W_i = \frac{\sum_{j=1}^{v} f_1^{(j,i)}}{u}, i \in (1, g)$$

Here, $f_1^{(j,i)}$ denotes $F_1 Score$ for $j_{th}$ model in $i_{th}$ document.

We now obtain **cWeight** as we did previously, and formulate cumulative summary, capturing the consensus of different models. We hence used a supervised learning algorithm to capture the mean performances of different models over the training data to fine-tune our summary.

### 3.7. Domain-Specific Single Document Summarization

As we discussed earlier, summarization models are field selective. Some models tend to perform remarkably better than others in certain fields. So, instead of assigning uniform weights to all models we can go by the following approach.

1. For each set of documents we train on, we generate document vector using bidirectional GRU ( [1] as described by Zichao Yang [24]for each document. We then generate complete corpus vector as follows:-

$$cDocs = \sum_{i=1}^{v} (a_i^1, a_i^1, a_i^1, \ldots, a_i^p,)$$

where,$v$ is total training set size, $p$ is number of features in document vector.

2. We save $cDocs$ and $weights$ corresponding to each corpus.

3. For each single document summarization task, we generate given texts document vector, perform nearest vector search over all stored $cDocs$, apply weights corresponding to that corpus.

### 3.8. Experiments

Table 1: Average ROUGE-2 Scores for Different Combination of Models.

| Models | | | | | | Score |
|---|---|---|---|---|---|---|
| A | B | C | D | E | F | $ROUGE2(95\%)$ |
|  |  | • |  | • |  | 0.03172 |
| • |  |  |  | • |  | 0.03357 |
| • |  | • |  | • |  | 0.03384 |
|  | • | • |  | • |  | 0.03479 |
| • | • |  |  | • |  | 0.03572 |
| • | • | • |  | • |  | 0.03519 |
|  |  | • |  |  | • | 0.03821 |
| • |  |  |  |  | • | 0.03912 |
| • |  | • |  |  | • | 0.03822 |
|  | • | • |  |  | • | 0.03986 |
| • | • |  |  |  | • | **0.04003** |
| • | • | • |  |  | • | 0.03846 |
|  |  | • | • |  |  | 0.03312 |
| • |  |  | • |  |  | 0.03339 |
| • |  | • | • |  |  | 0.03332 |
|  | • | • | • |  |  | 0.03532 |
| • | • |  | • |  |  | 0.03525 |
| • | • | • | • |  |  | 0.03519 |
|  |  | • | • |  | • | 0.03721 |
| • |  |  | • |  | • | 0.03689 |
| • |  | • | • |  | • | 0.03771 |
|  | • | • | • |  | • | 0.03812 |
| • | • |  | • |  | • | 0.03839 |
| • | • | • | • |  | • | 0.03782 |
|  |  | • |  | • | • | 0.03615 |
| • |  |  |  | • | • | 0.03598 |
| • |  | • |  | • | • | 0.03621 |
|  | • | • |  | • | • | 0.03803 |

*Continued on next page*

| Models | | | | | | Score |
| --- | --- | --- | --- | --- | --- | --- |
| A | B | C | D | E | F | *ROUGE*2(95%) |
| • | • |  |  | • | • | 0.03819 |
| • | • | • |  | • | • | 0.03784 |
|  |  | • | • | • |  | 0.03314 |
| • |  |  | • | • |  | 0.03212 |
| • |  | • | • | • |  | 0.03426 |
|  | • | • | • | • |  | 0.03531 |
| • | • |  | • | • |  | 0.03544 |
| • | • | • | • | • |  | 0.03529 |
|  |  | • | • | • | • | 0.03712 |
| • |  |  | • | • | • | 0.03713 |
| • |  | • | • | • | • | 0.03705 |
|  | • | • | • | • | • | 0.03821 |
| • | • |  | • | • | • | 0.03829 |
| • | • | • | • | • | • | 0.03772 |

We evaluate our approaches on 2004 DUC(Document Understanding Conferences) dataset(`https://duc.nist.gov/`). The Dataset has 5 Tasks in total. We work on Task 2. It (Task 2) contains 50 news documents cluster for multi-document summarization. Only 665-character summaries are provided for each cluster. For evaluation, we use ROGUE, an automatic summary evaluation metric. It was firstly used for DUC 2004 data-set. Now, it has become a benchmark for evaluation of automated summaries. ROUGE is a correlation metric for fixed-length summaries populated using n-gram co-occurrence. For comparison between model summary and to-be evaluated summary, separate scores for 1, 2, 3, and 4-gram matching are kept. We use ROUGE-2, a bi-gram based matching technique for our task.

In the *Table 1*, we try different model pairs with weights trained on corpus for Task 2. We have displayed mean ROUGE-2 scores for base Models. We have calculated final scores taking into consideration all normalizations, stemming, lemmatizing and clustering techniques, and the ones providing best results were used. We generally expected WordNet, Glove based semantic models to perform better given they better capture crux of the sentence and compute

---

[1]**A**→ *Jaccard/Cosine Similarity Matrix* **B**→ *TextRank* **C**→ *TFIDF* **D**→ *WordNet Based Model* **E**→ *Glove-vec Based Model* **F**→ *InferSent Based Model*

similarity using the same, but instead, they performed average. This is attributed to the fact they assigned high similarity scores to not so semantically related sentences. We also observe that combinations with TF/IDF and Similarity Matrices(Jaccard/Cosine) offer nearly same results. The InferSent based Summarizer performed exceptionally well. We initially used pre-trained features to generate sentence vectors through InferSent.

Table 2: Average ROUGE-2 scores for base methods.

| Model | $ROUGE-2$ |
| --- | --- |
| Jaccard | 0.03468 |
| Cosine | 0.02918 |
| TextRank | 0.03629 |
| TFIDF | 0.03371 |
| WordNet Based Model | 0.03354 |
| Glove-vec Based Model | 0.03054 |
| InferSent Based Model | 0.03812 |

### 3.9. Conclusion/Future Work

We can see that using a mixture of Semantic and Statistical models offers an improvement over stand-alone models. Given better training data, results can be further improved. Using domain-specific labeled data can provide a further increase in performances of Glove and WordNet Models.

Some easy additions that can be worked on are:

1. Unnecessary parts of the sentence can be trimmed to improve summary further.
2. Using better algorithm to capture sentence vector through Glove Model can improve results.
3. Query specific summarizer can be implemented with little additions.
4. For generating summary through model overlaps, we can also try Graph-based methods or different Clustering techniques.

### References

[1] D. Bahdanau, K. Cho, and Y. Bengio, "Neural machine translation by jointly learning to align and translate," *arXiv preprint arXiv:1409.0473*, 2014.

[2] A. Barrera and R. Verma, "Combining syntax and semantics for automatic extractive single-document summarization," in *International Conference on Intelligent Text Processing and Computational Linguistics*. Springer, 2012, pp. 366–377.

[3] S. R. Bowman, G. Angeli, C. Potts, and C. D. Manning, "A large annotated corpus for learning natural language inference," *arXiv preprint arXiv:1508.05326*, 2015.

[4] A. Conneau, D. Kiela, H. Schwenk, L. Barrault, and A. Bordes, "Supervised learning of universal sentence representations from natural language inference data," *arXiv preprint arXiv:1705.02364*, 2017.

[5] T. N. Dao and T. Simpson, "Measuring similarity between sentences," *The Code Project*, 2005.

[6] P. Gupta, V. S. Pendluri, and I. Vats, "Summarizing text by ranking text units according to shallow linguistic features," in *Advanced communication technology (ICACT), 2011 13th international conference on*.   IEEE, 2011, pp. 1620–1625.

[7] T. Kiss and J. Strunk, "Unsupervised multilingual sentence boundary detection," *Computational Linguistics*, vol. 32, no. 4, pp. 485–525, 2006.

[8] H. W. Kuhn, "The hungarian method for the assignment problem," *Naval Research Logistics (NRL)*, vol. 2, no. 1-2, pp. 83–97, 1955.

[9] M. Lesk, "Automatic sense disambiguation using machine readable dictionaries: how to tell a pine cone from an ice cream cone," in *Proceedings of the 5th annual international conference on Systems documentation*.   ACM, 1986, pp. 24–26.

[10] C.-Y. Lin and E. Hovy, "The automated acquisition of topic signatures for text summarization," in *Proceedings of the 18th conference on Computational linguistics-Volume 1*.   Association for Computational Linguistics, 2000, pp. 495–501.

[11] R. Mihalcea and P. Tarau, "Textrank: Bringing order into text," in *Proceedings of the 2004 conference on empirical methods in natural language processing*, 2004.

[12] G. A. Miller, R. Beckwith, C. Fellbaum, D. Gross, and K. J. Miller, "Introduction to wordnet: An on-line lexical database," *International journal of lexicography*, vol. 3, no. 4, pp. 235–244, 1990.

[13] V. G. Murdock, "Aspects of sentence retrieval," MASSACHUSETTS UNIV AMHERST DEPT OF COMPUTER SCIENCE, Tech. Rep., 2006.

[14] A. Nenkova, L. Vanderwende, and K. McKeown, "A compositional context sensitive multi-document summarizer: exploring the factors that influence summarization," in *Proceedings of the 29th annual international ACM SIGIR conference on Research and development in information retrieval*.   ACM, 2006, pp. 573–580.

[15] L. Page, S. Brin, R. Motwani, and T. Winograd, "The pagerank citation ranking: Bringing order to the web." Stanford InfoLab, Tech. Rep., 1999.

[16] T. Pedersen, S. Patwardhan, and J. Michelizzi, "Wordnet:: Similarity: measuring the relatedness of concepts," in *Demonstration papers at HLT-NAACL 2004*. Association for Computational Linguistics, 2004, pp. 38–41.

[17] J. Pennington, R. Socher, and C. Manning, "Glove: Global vectors for word representation," in *Proceedings of the 2014 conference on empirical methods in natural language processing (EMNLP)*, 2014, pp. 1532–1543.

[18] D. M. Powers, "Evaluation: from precision, recall and f-measure to roc, informedness, markedness and correlation," 2011.

[19] D. R. Radev, H. Jing, M. Styś, and D. Tam, "Centroid-based summarization of multiple documents," *Information Processing & Management*, vol. 40, no. 6, pp. 919–938, 2004.

[20] T. Rocktäschel, E. Grefenstette, K. M. Hermann, T. Kociský, and P. Blunsom, "Reasoning about entailment with neural attention," *CoRR*, vol. abs/1509.06664, 2015. [Online]. Available: http://arxiv.org/abs/1509.06664

[21] B. Santorini, "Part-of-speech tagging guidelines for the penn treebank project (3rd revision)," *Technical Reports (CIS)*, p. 570, 1990.

[22] W. J. Wilbur and K. Sirotkin, "The automatic identification of stop words," *Journal of information science*, vol. 18, no. 1, pp. 45–55, 1992.

[23] K.-F. Wong, M. Wu, and W. Li, "Extractive summarization using supervised and semi-supervised learning," in *Proceedings of the 22nd International Conference on Computational Linguistics-Volume 1*. Association for Computational Linguistics, 2008, pp. 985–992.

[24] Z. Yang, D. Yang, C. Dyer, X. He, A. Smola, and E. Hovy, "Hierarchical attention networks for document classification," in *Proceedings of the 2016 Conference of the North American Chapter of the Association for Computational Linguistics: Human Language Technologies*, 2016, pp. 1480–1489.

[25] W. Zeng, W. Luo, S. Fidler, and R. Urtasun, "Efficient summarization with read-again and copy mechanism," *CoRR*, vol. abs/1611.03382, 2016. [Online]. Available: http://arxiv.org/abs/1611.03382

The 2018 Conference on Computational Linguistics and Speech Processing
ROCLING 2018, pp. 184-198
©The Association for Computational Linguistics and Chinese Language Processing

# 台語古詩朗誦系統

蔡育霖 黃兆湘 林川傑
國立臺灣海洋大學資訊工程學系
Department of Computer Science and Engineering
National Taiwan Ocean University
{yltsai.cse, 10657025, cjlin}@ntou.edu.tw

## 摘要

本論文提出一個能用台語朗誦古詩的系統的建造方法。以台語朗讀古詩會碰到兩大問題，一個是文讀音的挑選，尤其當一個字有多種讀音時；另一個問題則是變調的位置，台語句中有大量變調的情形，全用本調唸會不自然而且無法聽懂。

在選擇讀音的策略上，我們採用了來自紙本台語字典所提供的資訊，包含了文白讀音以及常用讀音等。選擇字典所提供的第一讀音就能達到 89%左右的正確率。此外，我們也嘗試統計各資料集的最常見讀音，搭配文讀音標記可達到 96.44%的正確率。

變調位置會依句中字數而不同。分別以五言詩與七言詩統計各位置最常出現的本調或變調情形，依此結果當判斷規則即可達到 96.71%及 95.60%的正確率。雖然我們也提出了斷詞組合提供的特徵值，但僅在五言詩實驗中有微幅的提昇。

關鍵詞：古詩朗誦、文讀音、台語變調、台語字轉音

## 一、緒論

本土語言的研究越來越成為重要的課題。台語已被列入「國家語言法」草案之中，對於台語的各種研究與推廣越會被受到重視。

目前已有許多台語處理相關研究，但是多是以生活口語型態的台語為主。包括國台語翻譯系統 [1][2]、台語朗讀系統 [3][4][5][6][7]，語音辨識[8][9]、台語輸入法[10]等等。由於大部份的系統都在處理現代台語，我們有興趣開發一個能以台語朗誦古文的系統，可用以推廣台語教學。雖然用台語朗誦古文時，只需將每個中文字以一個台語音讀出，但仍有幾個課題需要先克服，包括選音、文讀音、變調等等問題，分別說明如下。

首先在市面上各式台語辭典中，許多中文字都對應有多種讀音，主要原因有三。第一是文白讀的問題，許多中文字在平常口語對話中的讀音 (稱做「白讀音」) 與誦讀詩文時所用讀音 (稱做「文讀音」) 不同，像「水」白讀為 chui2，文讀為 sui2。第二是破音字，若一個字在國語有多個讀音和語義，它在台語通常也會有不同讀音，像「為」在「因為」中讀音為 ui7，在「成為」中讀音為 ui5。第三則是腔調，例如「張」就有 tiuN1 和 tiouN1 兩種不同的腔調。

要解決文白讀問題，字典本身必須提供相關資訊。我們採用[2]的方法，將楊青矗的「國台雙語辭典」裡收錄的中文字及其讀音繕打成電子檔，做為系統選音依據的單字音典。這部字典提供了文白讀、漳泉各腔調的標記，適合本系統開發所用。

值得一提的是，在建立資料集的過程中，我們發現詩句中有不少中文字或是它們的古音並沒有收錄在「國台雙語辭典」裡面。為了系統的完整性，我們參考了另一部出版於 1954 年、沈富進所著「彙音寶鑑」，將這些缺字或缺音加入，並加上 h 標記其來源。未來會試著將整本彙音寶鑑完整收錄。

但要解決破音字問題就不是很容易。目前常見解法是先將文本斷詞，多字詞發音可直接參考字典，單字詞則必須進行語意解歧義，需要大型語料庫做為訓練語料。以上方案在現代漢語較有可能找到資源，古漢語不論斷詞、訓練語料庫、語意資源都相對缺乏，更不易找到台語資源，只能留待未來研究。

變調現象在台語發音中相當重要，因為用台語說出一句話時，裡面大部份的字都會變調，只有句尾、名詞詞組結尾等字會讀做本調[2][4]。但這也是現代漢語的研究結果，在古文朗讀時變調位置是否與現代規則相同仍不清楚。在朗讀古詩時，變調不完全和詞性相關。例如「東園 載酒 西園 醉」這句詩句，其中 "西園" 是名詞，按照現代變調系統會判斷 "園" 字該讀本調，但實際上 "西園" 兩個字都會變調。

要正確判斷變調位置似乎需要好的古漢語斷詞及詞性標記系統，困難度更高。本論文於是轉向採用韻律較規律的格律體古詩做為研究對象，先了解如何以台語朗誦唐詩中的律詩和絕句，未來再推向古文的朗讀。

本論文第二節介紹台語朗誦古詩資料集的建立方法，第三節提出各種選音策略，第四節則是探討變調位置的決定方法，最後第五節是結論。

## 二、台語朗誦古詩資料蒐集

為了要研究台語朗誦古詩時會如何決定讀音以及變調的位置，我們尋找的資料必須包含 1) 詩句的台語讀音、2) 標有朗讀時所使用的調 (變調結果)。可是網路上這樣的資料並不多，文字版大多只寫出本調 (亦即平常台語書寫法)，語音或影像則許多都是吟唱的版本而失去原本的聲調資訊。以下幾個網站是我們這次研究的主要資料來源。

### (一) 鯤島園地

鯤島園地[1]是一個推廣台語的網站，在其中「古典詩」(如圖一所示) 收錄了千家詩裡面許多首五言及七言的律詩和絕句。台語拼音系統採用通用拼音，所標出的聲調都是變調以後的結果。

由於原始檔案是 HTML 檔，裡面的文字以 HTML 格式來呈現，而非視覺所見的字母。例如 cūn 是寫成 cūn、gun 是寫成 g<u>u</u>n、而鼻化音 ⁿ 和輕聲調 ⁰ 則會以上標字<sup>…</sup>來表示。在準備純文字版本的實驗資料時，都必須額外處理這些特殊

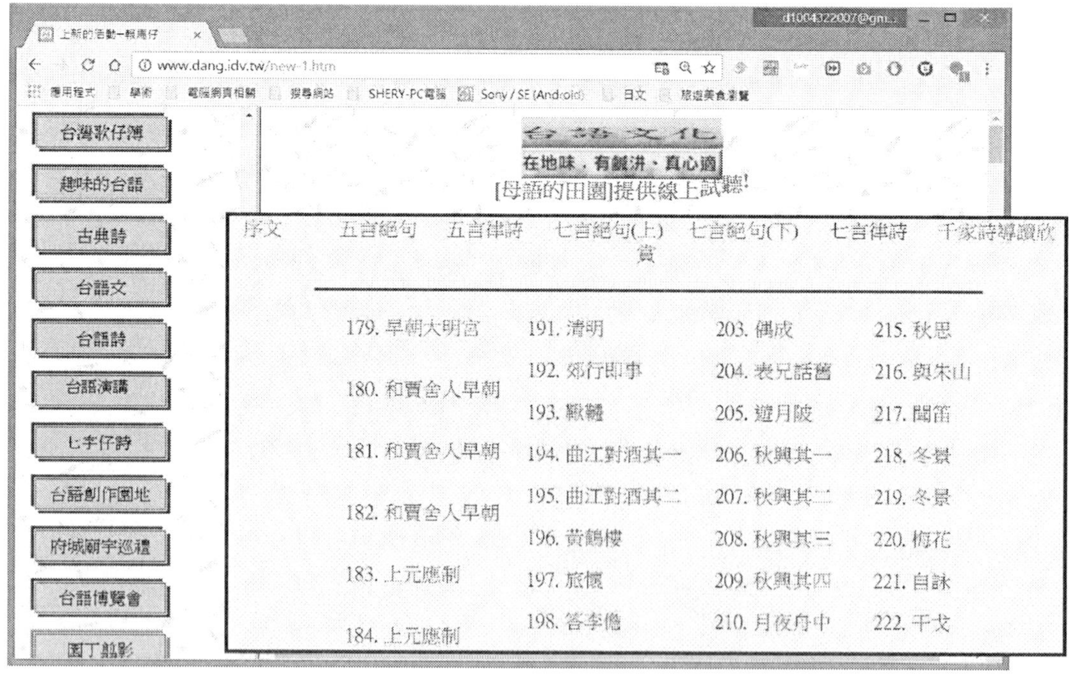


| 五言律詩 | 七言絕句(上) | 七言絕句(下) | 七言律詩 |
|---|---|---|---|
| 179. 早朝大明宮 | 191. 清明 | 203. 偶成 | 215. 秋思 |
| 180. 和賈舍人早朝 | 192. 郊行即事 | 204. 表兄話舊 | 216. 與朱山 |
|  | 193. 轆轤 | 205. 遊月陂 | 217. 聞笛 |
| 181. 和賈舍人早朝 | 194. 曲江對酒其一 | 206. 秋興其一 | 218. 冬景 |
| 182. 和賈舍人早朝 | 195. 曲江對酒其二 | 207. 秋興其二 | 219. 冬景 |
|  | 196. 黃鶴樓 | 208. 秋興其三 | 220. 梅花 |
| 183. 上元應制 | 197. 旅懷 | 209. 秋興其四 | 221. 自詠 |
| 184. 上元應制 | 198. 答李儋 | 210. 月夜舟中 | 222. 干戈 |

圖一、鯤島園地首頁，及其「古典詩」中「七言律詩」列表

---

[1] http://www.dang.idv.tw/memo.htm

字元。此外，因為帶有調號的字母、上標文字在電腦處理上較麻煩，因此我們改用數字來表示調號等等替代方案。像是 cūn 改成 cun7、gun 改成 gun3、tiaⁿ 則改成 tiaN7。

雖然網頁中提供了難得的變調後讀音，相反地卻沒有本調資訊。我們於是查詢第 1 節介紹過的單字音典，選擇各字在字典中帶有相同聲母及韻母的讀音做為其本調音。但由於單字音典是採用教會羅馬字拼音系統，因此需先將通用拼音轉為教羅拼音。所幸幾個主要的台語拼音系統都是一對一對應，可以很容易地以程式進行拼音系統的轉換，未來也預計將所有台語資料統一轉為台羅拼音系統。

但如果相同聲母及韻母的讀音有兩種以上的選擇，就需以人工判斷。像是「渭城朝雨浥輕塵」和「銀燭朝天紫陌長」句中的「朝」在朗誦時都變調為 tiau7 (註：教羅拼音)，但在「朝雨」中是 "早晨" 的意思、本調是 tiau1，而在「朝天」是 "面向" 的意思、本調是 tiau5。以下是「早朝大明宮」第一句「銀燭朝天紫陌長」的通用拼音、教羅拼音本調、與教羅拼音變調的處理結果。

詩句文字：銀燭朝天紫陌長

通用拼音：ghūn　ziōk　　diāu　tian　　zi　　bhǐk　doing

教羅本調：gun5　chiok4　tiau5　thian1　chi2　bek8　tiong5

教羅變調：gun7　chiok4　tiau7　thian1　chi1　bek4　tiong5

(二) 瑞峰國小

台南市南化區瑞峰國小的網站之前維護有許多個台語教學相關的網頁，包括「台語吟唐

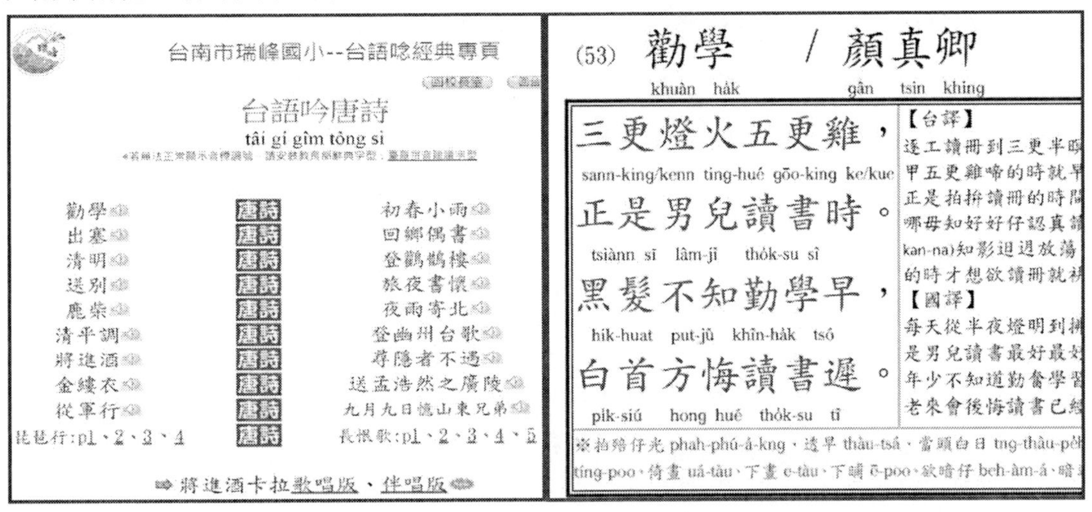


圖二、瑞峰國小「台語吟唐詩」及所收錄唐詩「勸學」網頁範例

詩」[2]以及「台語唸經典」。「台語吟唐詩」網頁如圖二所示，收錄的唐詩 (如圖二中的「勸學」) 以圖片檔顯示，因此我們必須將圖片的文字轉成文字檔。拼音系統採用台羅拼音，而且都是本調。因為需要正確的變調結果，我們僅選擇了有提供朗誦版錄音檔的詩 (在圖二中有音量圖示者)，並以聽打方式記下變調結果。其中「將進酒」和「登幽州台歌」因為各句字數不一所以先不算，「清平調」分成三首。所錄者多是絕句，僅「旅夜書懷」是五言律詩。拼音系統也先轉為教羅拼音以方便實驗。

至於「台語唸經典」[3]收錄有許多古文、古詩詞、經文等等，同樣地並不是每首都有朗讀音檔。由於我們希望先處理古詩的朗誦，因此只收錄了「滿江紅」(各句字數不一)、「正氣歌」(五言排律)、「陋室銘」(各句字數不一且應算古文)、「將進酒」(各句字數不一)、「登幽州台歌」(各句字數不一) 和「短歌行」(四言排律)。其他古文留待未來研究。

(三) YouTube 影片

在觀察前兩種資料後，發現他們在一些讀音和變調策略上偶有差別。為了看看是否不同朗誦者會有不同讀法，我們試著再找其他的來源。

在 YouTube 上有幾個頻道主上傳過幾部用台語朗讀詩詞的影片，但是數量都不夠多。這其中，spwang1000 頻道[4]是一位父親教兒子唸唐詩的影片，讀了王維、李白、杜牧共 22 首詩。我們決定將這些詩聽打下來做為第三種來源，拼音就採教羅拼音。因為聽打得到的是變調後結果，也需如處理鯤島園地資料一樣將本調資料補上。

順帶一提的是，我們也找到了 JaniceWu 這個頻道，頻道主是社團法人臺灣瀛社詩學會的常務理事吳秀真老師，在她的頻道中收錄有許多用台語朗誦詩詞的影片，據稱是以康熙字典所載之中古音為基準。我們原本找了許多部林正三老師朗誦唐詩的影片。但聽打後發現，林老師在讀詩時完全用本調，和其他人大部份字都會變調不同，所以暫不使用。

表一列出了本實驗用到的三種來源的資料集的統計數據，最後一欄列出各資料集中出現的相異中文字數。鯤島園地資料量最大，瑞峰國小台語吟唐詩與 YouTube spwang1000 影片的資料集大小差不多，瑞峰國小台語唸經典雖然只有 6 首詩，因為有正氣歌這類長

---


[2]　http://www.rfes.tn.edu.tw/master/tong5-si.html
[3]　http://www.rfes.tn.edu.tw/master/taigi.html
[4]　王維　https://www.youtube.com/watch?v=2kUxcP9mThA
　　　李白　https://www.youtube.com/watch?v=ZPGUkS1CPE4
　　　杜牧　https://www.youtube.com/watch?v=W61aLUCRH6Y

詩，因而字數也不少。

表一、各來源的台語詩文朗誦資料集的統計數據

| 資料集 | 詩數 | 句數 | 字數 | 來源種類 | 詩數 | 句數 | 字數 | 相異 |
|---|---|---|---|---|---|---|---|---|
| 鯤島園地_五絕 | 34 | 156 | 780 | spwang1000_五言 | 12 | 56 | 280 | |
| 鯤島園地_五律 | 45 | 360 | 1800 | spwang1000_七言 | 10 | 40 | 280 | |
| 鯤島園地_七絕 | 94 | 376 | 2632 | 鯤島園地_全部 | 226 | 1276 | 7900 | 1655 |
| 鯤島園地_七律 | 48 | 384 | 2688 | 瑞峰吟唐詩_全部 | 18 | 76 | 484 | 307 |
| 瑞峰吟唐詩_五言 | 5 | 24 | 120 | 瑞峰唸經典_全部 | 6 | 164 | 800 | 491 |
| 瑞峰吟唐詩_七言 | 13 | 52 | 364 | spwang1000_全部 | 22 | 96 | 560 | 334 |

## 三、古詩朗讀選音策略與實驗

朗誦古詩的第一步是要先決定每個中文字的台語讀音。這裡提出查詢單字音典以及統計資料集最常見讀音的兩種策略來進行選音的實驗。

### (一) 依據單字音典的規則式選音策略

第一個選音實驗直接採用單字音典所提供的讀音。如前所提，一個中文字在單字音典中可能有許多種讀音。為了瞭解選擇讀音實驗的難度，表二統計了各資料集中文字所用的讀音在單字音典中排在第幾位，最糟的情形正解出現在第 8 名。有趣的是，光選擇第一讀音，正確率就可以達到 88.57% (496/560) 到 89.75% (7090/7900)。

表二、各中文字讀音在單字音典中排名位置統計

| 位置 | 鯤島園地 | 瑞峰吟唐詩 | 瑞峰唸經典 | spwang1000 |
|---|---|---|---|---|
| 第 1 讀音 | 7090 | 430 | 716 | 496 |
| 第 2 讀音 | 618 | 41 | 64 | 45 |
| 第 3 讀音 | 104 | 10 | 15 | 12 |
| 第 4 讀音 | 41 | 2 | 2 | 1 |
| 第 5 讀音 | 8 | 0 | 1 | 0 |
| 第 6 讀音 | 4 | 0 | 0 | 0 |
| 第 7 讀音 | 2 | 0 | 0 | 0 |
| 第 8 讀音 | 1 | 0 | 0 | 0 |
| 輕聲調 | 20 | 0 | 1 | 0 |
| 不在字典 | 12 | 1 | 1 | 6 |

單字音典裡能用的資訊，還有有文讀音 (標為 b)、白讀音 (標為 p)、和來自彙音寶典的

讀音 (標為 h) 這些標記。其中白讀音不應做為候選音，其他標記則會有選擇優先順序
的問題。表三列出四種不同選音策略的正確率，策略分別是：

- ◆ "1st"：全部選擇單字音典中第一個發音
- ◆ "b > h > 1st"：優先選擇文讀音，其次是來自彙音寶鑑的讀音，都沒有就選擇第一個發音
- ◆ "h > b > 1st"：優先選擇來自彙音寶鑑的讀音，其次是文讀音，都沒有就選擇第一個發音
- ◆ "rand"：隨機選擇單字音典中任一種發音

表三、依單字音典選音實驗的正確率

| 資料集 | 總字數 | 1st | b > h > 1st | h > b > 1st | rand |
|---|---|---|---|---|---|
| 鯤島園地_全 | 7900 | **7090 (89.75%)** | 7022 (88.89%) | 6986 (88.43%) | 4075 (59.56%) |
| 瑞峰吟唐詩_全 | 484 | **430 (88.84%)** | 428 (88.43%) | 428 (88.43%) | 278 (57.44%) |
| 瑞峰唸經典_全 | 800 | **716 (89.50%)** | 712 (89.00%) | 709 (88.63%) | 509 (63.63%) |
| spwang1000_全 | 560 | **496 (88.57%)** | 492 (87.86%) | 489 (87.32%) | 331 (59.11%) |

由表三數據來看，令人驚訝的是，選第一讀音比其他策略效果好很多。經過觀察，單字
音典中有一半的字第一讀音不帶有任何標記 (表示該字常用文白讀相同)，另一半有分
文白讀者都先列出文讀音，因此選擇第一讀音會有很好的效果。

錯誤的主要來源是破音字，以及朗誦者習慣讀音與第一讀音不同。另在表二中可注意的
是，有 21 個字讀為輕聲調。還有 20 (=12+1+1+6) 個字是朗誦者的特別發音，像是「梅」
字為了押韻，不唸 mui5 而改唸 moai5。這些都不是字典音所以會產生錯誤。


(二) 來自相同資料集的最常見讀音策略

為了提高選音的正確率，另一個常用的策略就是選擇最常見的讀音。因為同一來源的朗
誦者相同，預期來自同一來源的統計資料會有較好的效果，本節先進行以相同來源資料
集的統計數據做為選音依據的實驗。

實驗針對各資料集進行留一法交叉驗證 (leave-one-out cross-validation)，亦即每個字的
讀音採用同資料集裡同中文字 (不包含自己) 出現最多次的讀音。若次數相同，採用在
單字音典中順位在前者。若某個中文字只出現過一次 (因此沒有參考對象)，改採用單字
音典的音，選音策略與前節所述相同。

表四、相同資料集最常見讀音的選音實驗結果

| 資料集 | 總字數 | 1st | Frq > 1st | Frq > b > h > 1st | Frq > h > b > 1st |
|---|---|---|---|---|---|
| 鯤島園地_全 | 7900 | 89.75% | 7611 (96.34%) | **7619 (96.44%)** | 7618 (96.43%) |
| 瑞峰吟唐詩_全 | 484 | 88.84% | **455 (94.01%)** | **455 (94.01%)** | 454 (93.80%) |
| 瑞峰唸經典_全 | 800 | 89.50% | 732 (91.50%) | 732 (91.50%) | **733 (91.63%)** |
| spwang1000_全 | 560 | 88.57% | 526 (93.93%) | **527 (94.11%)** | 523 (93.39%) |

表四列出了選擇最常見讀音策略的正確率，可看見在 4 個資料集都有大幅的改善。而且不在訓練集的中文字因較罕見所以也大多只有一個讀音，因此搭配各種單字音典選音策略沒有太大差異。

為了觀察最常見讀音所帶來的選音歧異性，表五列出各資料集中各中文字出現的讀音數量。僅有約 4% 的中文字有兩種以上的讀音，平均每個字有 1.04 種讀音。

表五、各資料集中各中文字出現的讀音數量

| 字數 | 鯤島園地 | 瑞峰吟唐詩 | 瑞峰唸經典 | spwang1000 |
|---|---|---|---|---|
| 相異字數 | 1654 | 306 | 491 | 334 |
| 1 種讀音 | 1574 | 301 | 473 | 325 |
| 2 種讀音 | 75 | 5 | 18 | 9 |
| 3 種讀音 | 5 | 0 | 0 | 0 |

(三) 來自不同資料集的最常見讀音策略

前節實驗中，鯤島園地因為數量最多，正確率最高。我們於是想看看某個大型資料集的最常見讀音，是否可用來決定其他小型資料集的讀音。表六列出以各資料集做為訓練集去測試其他資料集的選音實驗結果，其中對角線列出的是相同資料集最常見讀音的實驗正確率，因為採用留一法，因此結果不能直接相比較，僅供參考。

表六、不同資料集最常見讀音的選音實驗結果

| 測試 \ 訓練 | 鯤島園地 | 瑞峰吟唐詩 | 瑞峰唸經典 | spwang1000 |
|---|---|---|---|---|
| 鯤島園地 | *96.44* | 92.58 | 92.22 | 92.84 |
| 瑞峰吟唐詩 | 95.04 | *94.01* | 92.98 | 92.36 |
| 瑞峰唸經典 | 91.88 | 91.38 | *91.50* | 92.13 |
| spwang1000 | 93.75 | 91.79 | 91.96 | *94.11* |

與預期結果相同的是，以鯤島園地做訓練集，可以提高來自瑞峰國小資料集的選音正確率。但實際觀察後發現，跨資料集實驗還無法做出明確結論。原因是各資料集收錄的詩

很少重複，彼此重疊的中文字常僅佔一半比例，另一半在單字音典中能否選對讀音又有點看運氣。這都是資料集不夠大的緣故。


## 四、古詩朗讀變調策略與實驗

朗誦古詩的第二步則是要決定各字讀本調或需變調。在此提出各種規則及機器學習可用的特徵來進行判斷。

### (一) 僅考慮位置資訊的變調決定規則

在實驗準備初期我們就觀察到，若是字數很規律的詩像是律詩或絕句等，維持本調的字大多出現在固定的位置上。因此我們猜測光依照位置來決定本變調，應該有極高的正確率。

表七統計了各實驗資集中五言律詩和五言絕句的本變調情形，列出各詩句中位在第一字到第五字的本變調最大宗情形所佔比例，其中 "位 1 變" 表示在詩句第一個字變調的情形、"位 2 本" 表示在詩句第二個字維本調的情形，以此類推。同理，表八統計了各實驗資集中七言律詩和七言絕句的本變調情形。請注意，瑞峰國小「台語唸經典」並不在統計表中，因為它收錄的是古詩或古文、經典，句中字數並不規則，從 3 個字到 8 個字都有，這會在後面的實驗再做處理。

表七、各資料集五言詩各位置本變調最大宗情形所佔比例

| 資料集 | 位 1 變 | 位 2 本 | 位 3 變 | 位 4 變 | 位 5 本 | 全部 |
|---|---|---|---|---|---|---|
| 鯤島園地 | 94.96 | 96.32 | 96.51 | 97.87 | 97.87 | 96.71 |
| 瑞峰吟唐詩 | 91.67 | 95.83 | 95.83 | 83.33 | 100.00 | 93.33 |
| spwang1000 | 89.29 | 92.86 | 89.29 | 69.64 | 98.21 | 87.86 |
| 總和 | 94.30 | 95.97 | 95.81 | 94.63 | 97.99 | 95.74 |

表八、各資料集七言詩各位置本變調最大宗情形所佔比例

| 資料集 | 位 1 變 | 位 2 本 | 位 3 變 | 位 4 本 | 位 5 變 | 位 6 變 | 位 7 本 | 全部 |
|---|---|---|---|---|---|---|---|---|
| 鯤島園地 | 96.18 | 91.97 | 97.63 | 97.24 | 92.50 | 95.13 | 98.55 | 95.60 |
| 瑞峰吟唐詩 | 94.23 | 76.92 | 98.08 | 98.08 | 92.31 | 84.62 | 100.00 | 92.03 |
| spwang1000 | 97.50 | 90.00 | 100.00 | 92.50 | 90.00 | 95.00 | 100.00 | 95.00 |
| 總和 | 96.13 | 90.96 | 97.77 | 97.07 | 92.37 | 94.48 | 98.71 | 95.36 |

表七和表八驗證了我們的猜測：五言詩在第二和第五位置多讀本調，其餘位置多會變調；七言詩在第二、第四和第七位置多讀本調，其餘位置多會變調。依此規則決定本變調的話，五言詩的整體正確率是 95.74%，七言詩的整體正確率則是 95.36%。

請注意除了本調和變調兩種可能性之外，有些字會讀成輕聲調 (調號 0)，像是 "來"、"去" 在某些位置 (例如句尾) 常會變成輕聲調，但又不是百分百如此。這些字的前一個字會讀本調，因此具決定性角色。可惜輕聲調情形少於 1%，無法撰寫推測輕聲調的規則。底下為輕聲調範例詩句，其中 "去" 讀輕聲調，因此 "鶴" 讀本調。

昔人已乘黃鶴去　　　sek8 jin5 i1 seng5 hong5 hok8 khu0

(二) 機器學習訓練變調分類器

雖然依照位置來決定本變調已有不錯的正確率，想達到更高的正確率就需要研究其他方法。我們提出了幾個可能用來判斷是否變調或維持本調的特徵，並且以機器學習、交叉驗證方法來進行實驗。

1.　判斷本變調相關特徵

本節介紹所有我們用來猜測本變調或輕聲調的特徵，分類器輸出類別包含變調 (Y)、本調 (N)、和輕聲調 (0)。

首先介紹一個本論文新提出的特徵：**斷詞詞中比例**與**斷詞詞尾比例**。在處理一個詩句的時候，先請現代斷詞系統提供句中所有出現的合法詞彙，而不是只提供一種斷詞方式。這些合法詞彙的最後一個字算「詞尾」情形 (標記為 E)，其他字算「詞中」情形 (標記為 I)。對於句中某一個位置而言，定義**斷詞詞中比例** $f_{mid,k}$ 為出現在這個位置所有詞彙屬 I 的比例，**斷詞詞尾比例** $f_{end,k}$ 則為出現在這個位置所有詞彙屬 E 的比例。

以詩句「昔人已乘黃鶴去」為例，句中除了每個字都可各自形成單字詞外，另有 "昔人"、"乘黃"、"黃鶴" 這三個合法詞彙，詞中各字標記情形如表九所列。由於詩句中 "黃" 字的位置，是 "黃鶴" 這詞的詞中，各斷詞詞中比例 $f_{mid,0}$ 是 1/3；"黃" 字位置是 "黃" 和 "乘黃" 兩詞的詞尾，各斷詞詞尾比例 $f_{end,0}$ 是 2/3。

表九、「昔人已乘黃鶴去」詩句計算斷詞中尾比例範例

| 詩句 | 昔 | 人 | 已 | 乘 | 黃 | 鶴 | 去 |
|---|---|---|---|---|---|---|---|
|  | 昔_E |  | 已_E |  | 黃_E |  | 去_E |
|  | 昔_I | 人_E |  | 乘_E |  | 鶴_E |  |
|  |  | 人_E |  | 乘_I | 黃_E |  |  |
|  |  |  |  |  | 黃_I | 鶴_E |  |
| $f_{mid,0}$ | 1/2 | 0 | 0 | 1/2 | 1/3 | 0 | 0 |
| $f_{end,0}$ | 1/2 | 1 | 1 | 1/2 | 2/3 | 1 | 1 |

由於還沒出現品質夠好的古文斷詞系統，我們打算以斷詞詞中尾比例來估算一個位置維持唸本調的機率有多大 (即斷詞詞尾比例)，反之也可找到一定需要變調的位置 (即斷詞詞中比例為 1 的時候)。以下為本論文使用之所有特徵定義。

(1) 第一類特徵：位置資訊 $f_{pos}$

既然位置資訊能達到不錯的正確率，自然要採用這種特徵。請注意五言和七言的位置資訊無法互用，因此我們把特徵值設計為 "5_1"、"5_2"、… "7_7" 這樣的字串，前面的數字代表詩句中總字數，後面的數字代表目標字在詩句中的位置。

(2) 第二類特徵：類別大宗 $f_{maj}$

使用位置資訊特徵所訓練出來的分類器只能處理五言詩和七言詩，而且無法互相支援。更無法支援其他字數，從唐詩訓練所得的分類器無法用來處理宋詞或字數不規律的古詩，有些可惜。

我們於是提出一種替代特徵，直接標示目標字在詩句中的位置最常出現哪種情形，特徵值包括最常讀本調 (O)、最常變調 (C)、位在句尾 (E) 這三種。以七言詩為例，出現在第一、第三、第五、第六位置的字，此特徵值是 C (較常變調)，出現在第二、第四位置的字，此特徵值是 O (較常讀本調)，出現在第七位置的字，此特徵值是 E (句尾)。設計 E 這個特徵值的用意是，位在句尾的字有極大機率要讀本調，因此需獨立出來。

(3) 第三類特徵：詞中尾比例 $f_{mid,k}$、$f_{end,k}$

此特徵即本節一開始所定義的斷詞詞中比例及斷詞詞尾比例兩種特徵。而前一個字和下一個字的資訊也很值得參考，特徵代碼 $f_{xxx,k}$ 中 $k = \{-1, 0, 1\}$ 分別目標字前一字、本身、

後一字的詞中尾比例特徵。第一個字並沒有前一個字，$f_{xxx,-1}$ 特徵值設為 0。同理，句尾字沒有後面的字，$f_{xxx,1}$ 特徵值也設為 0。

這裡我們再提出另一套新的特徵。觀察發現，古詩在寫作時，常會出現對仗的句子。兩句字數相同，句中名詞動詞、實字虛字的對仗常常很工整。因此若能同時考慮對仗句對方的斷詞組合情形，對本變調判斷應該也很有幫助。因此將對句的前中後斷詞詞中尾比例特徵一併納入考慮，代碼為 $pf_{mid,k}$ 和 $pf_{end,k}$。以詩句「昔人已乘黃鶴去」為例，這些特徵值來自它的對句「此地空餘黃鶴樓」。(註：以絕句為例，第一、三句的對句分別是第二、四句，反之第二、四句的對句分別是第一、三句。)

(4)　第四類特徵：輕聲調用字 $f_{0tn}$ 和 $f_{0tnE}$

觀察鯤島園地資料集時，發現會讀為輕聲調的字不多，只有 "去"、"是"、"裡"、"否"、"來"、"時"、"矣" 這七個字。我們想要同時判斷各字是要維持本調、變調、還是讀輕聲調，因此加上了 $f_{0tn}$ 這個特徵，標記目標字是不是一個輕聲調用字，值為 Y 或 N。

此外，根據固定輕聲調變調規則，這幾個輕聲調字前一字會維持本調。因此也同時考慮 $f_{0tnE}$ 這個特徵，標記下一個字是否為輕聲調用字且位在大宗本調位置，值為 Y 或 N。

2.　本變調判斷實驗

本節介紹所有本變調判斷系統，各使用不同的特徵組合如下。

- ◆ 系統一 $S_{p,me\pm1,t0}$：$f_{pos}$、$f_{mid,0\pm1}$、$f_{end,0\pm1}$、$f_{0tn}$
- ◆ 系統二 $S_{p,me\pm1,pf,t0}$：$f_{pos}$、$f_{mid,0\pm1}$、$f_{end,0\pm1}$、$pf_{mid,0\pm1}$、$pf_{end,0\pm1}$、$f_{0tn}$
- ◆ 系統三 $S_{j,me\pm1,pf,t0}$：$f_{maj}$、$f_{mid,0\pm1}$、$f_{end,0\pm1}$、$pf_{mid,0\pm1}$、$pf_{end,0\pm1}$、$f_{0tn}$
- ◆ 系統四 $S_{p,me\pm1,pf,t0E}$：$f_{pos}$、$f_{mid,0\pm1}$、$f_{end,0\pm1}$、$pf_{mid,0\pm1}$、$pf_{end,0\pm1}$、$f_{0tn}$、$f_{0tnE}$
- ◆ 系統五 $S_{j,me\pm1,pf,t0E}$：$f_{maj}$、$f_{mid,0\pm1}$、$f_{end,0\pm1}$、$pf_{mid,0\pm1}$、$pf_{end,0\pm1}$、$f_{0tn}$、$f_{0tnE}$

實驗採用以詩為單位切分、依字數平衡的十等分交叉驗證法來進行。資料集僅採用鯤島園地，因為它的詩題數量才足夠進行實驗。機器學習方法使用了 Weka 系統[5]，採用了決策樹 (J48)、隨機森林 (Random Forest)、支持向量機 (Support Vector Machine) 以及自適應增強 (AdaBoost) 這幾種方法，另外再找尋 CRF++[6]一起比較。正確率列在表十和表十一，表格左上角列出依位置規則的變調判斷正確率以供比較。

---


[5]　https://www.cs.waikato.ac.nz/ml/weka/
[6]　https://taku910.github.io/crfpp/

表十、以鯤島園地資料集測試之五言詩本變調判斷正確率

| 規則 | 96.71 | J48 | RandF | SVM | AdaBst | CRF |
|---|---|---|---|---|---|---|
| 系統一 | $S_{p,me\pm1,t0}$ | 96.71 | 96.55 | 96.71 | 96.63 | 96.64 |
| 系統二 | $S_{p,me\pm1,pf,t0}$ | 96.78 | 96.59 | 96.74 | 96.63 | 96.78 |
| 系統三 | $S_{j,me\pm1,pf,t0}$ | 96.78 | 96.59 | 96.78 | 96.71 | 96.78 |
| 系統四 | $S_{p,me\pm1,pf,t0E}$ | 96.71 | 96.71 | 96.78 | 96.63 | **96.82** |
| 系統五 | $S_{j,me\pm1,pf,t0E}$ | 96.74 | 96.71 | 96.78 | 96.71 | **96.82** |

表十一、以鯤島園地資料集測試之七言詩本變調判斷正確率

| 規則 | **95.60** | J48 | RandF | SVM | AdaBst | CRF |
|---|---|---|---|---|---|---|
| 系統一 | $S_{p,me\pm1,t0}$ | **95.60** | 95.41 | **95.60** | 85.26 | 95.58 |
| 系統二 | $S_{p,me\pm1,pf,t0}$ | **95.60** | 95.21 | **95.60** | 87.29 | 95.58 |
| 系統三 | $S_{j,me\pm1,pf,t0}$ | **95.60** | 95.38 | **95.60** | **95.60** | 95.58 |
| 系統四 | $S_{p,me\pm1,pf,t0E}$ | **95.60** | 95.11 | **95.60** | 87.29 | 95.56 |
| 系統五 | $S_{j,me\pm1,pf,t0E}$ | **95.60** | 95.23 | **95.60** | **95.60** | 95.58 |

由於依位置判斷變調的規則式系統正確率已經很高，我們所提的其他特徵幾乎沒有效果，決策樹 (J48) 常獲得最佳效能，且學到的規則正是位置大宗情形。決策樹在五言詩中比規則式系統多猜對了 2 個字，所依據的規則是「位置 5_2 若是輕聲調用字，且對句 $pf_{mid,0}$ 大於 0，則猜為輕聲調」，無法說明意義。CRF 在五言也是多猜對一個字而已。

此外，表十一的實驗有個可以探討的地方。在採用位置特徵 $f_{pos}$ 時，AdaBoost 大受影響而降低正確率。然而改採類別大宗特徵 $f_{maj}$ 後，AdaBoost 就恢復與規則式及決策樹一樣好的效能。可見類別大宗特徵較具廣用性。

我們原本還規劃了兩個實驗。一個是跨資料集的變調判斷，但因為最佳系統與規則式系統相當，因此結果會與表七、表八相同。另一實驗則是以類別大宗特徵來判斷非五言及七言的詩句變調位置，現在也變成僅是目前資料集所能得到的統計結果。表十二將「台語唸經典」的統計結果列出以供參考。

我們也嘗試過以複製方式增加小眾訓練資料，但是反而會遽烈降低效能，結果就不列出。可想見要解決變調問題，正確斷詞資訊才可能有幫助，期待未來能加入古文或古詩的斷詞系統提供斷詞資訊以供判斷。

表十二、「台語唸經典」各字數各位置本變調最大宗情形判斷正確率

| 位置 | 句數 | 位 1 | 位 2 | 位 3 | 位 4 | 位 5 | 位 6 | 位 7 | 位 8 | 正確率 |
|---|---|---|---|---|---|---|---|---|---|---|
| 三言 | 19 | 13 變 | 18 變 | 19 本 | | | | | | 87.72 |
| 四言 | 43 | 35 變 | 38 本 | 38 變 | 43 本 | | | | | 89.53 |
| 五言 | 70 | 60 變 | 63 本 | 63 變 | 66 變 | 68 本 | | | | 91.43 |
| 六言 | 5 | 5 變 | 4 變 | 4 本 | 3 變 | 4 變 | 5 本 | | | 83.33 |
| 七言 | 25 | 25 變 | 24 本 | 25 變 | 24 本 | 23 變 | 25 變 | 25 本 | | 97.71 |
| 八言 | 2 | 1 變 | 2 變 | 2 本 | 2 變 | 1 本 | 2 變 | 2 變 | 2 本 | 87.50 |

## 五、結論

本論文提出了一個能用台語朗讀古代格律詩的系統，並以網路上搜集所得的台語朗讀資料集進行實驗。選擇資料集中最常見讀音、搭配單字音典中第一讀音或是標有文讀的音，選音正確率可達到 96.44%。依位置判斷變調正確率則可達到 96.78%。

未來希望加強輕聲調出現的判斷，同時可解決選音及變調的問題。此外在選音實驗部份，本論文並未針對古文的破音字提出策略。也可嘗試其他辭典或斷詞資訊來判斷變調位置，這些都是未來的研究方向。

## 參考文獻


[1] 黃志超 (2015) <u>範例為本的國語—台語翻譯之研究</u>，碩士論文，國立臺灣海洋大學。

[2] Chuan-Jie Lin and Hsin-Hsi Chen (1999) "A Mandarin to Taiwanese Min Nan Machine Translation System with Speech Synthesis of Taiwanese Min Nan," *IJCLCLP*, Vol. 4, No. 1, pp. 59-84.

[3] Wei-Chih Kuo, Chen-Chung Ho, Xiang-Rui Zhong, Zhen-Feng Liang, Hsiu-Min Yu, Yih-Ru Wang, and Sin-Horng Chen (2007), "Some Studies on Min-Nan Speech Processing," *International Journal of Computational Linguistics and Chinese Language Processing*, Vol. 12, No. 4, pp. 391-410.

[4] Yih-Jeng Lin, Ming-Shing Yu, and Chin-Yu Lin (2008) "Using Chi-Square Automatic Interaction Detector to Solve the Polysemy Problems in a Chinese to Taiwanese TTS

System," *Proceedings of the 8th International Conference on Intelligent Systems Design and Applications*, pp. 362-367.

[5] 林義証, 余明興, and 林尉綸 (2012) "利用關聯式規則解決台語文轉音系統中一詞多音之歧異," *Proceedings of ROCLING 2012*, pp. 276-291.

[6] 黃偉杰, 林志柔, 呂仁園, 江永進, and 張智星 (2012) "台語朗讀資料庫之自動切音技術應用於音文同步有聲書之建立," *Proceedings of ROCLING 2012*, pp. 214-230.

[7] Chen-Yu Chiang (2018), "Cross-Dialect Adaptation Framework for Constructing Prosodic Models for Chinese Dialect Text-to-Speech Systems", *IEEE/ACM Transactions on Audio, Speech, and Language Processing*, Vol. 26, Issue 1, pp.108-121.

[8] Ren-Yuan Lyu, Chi-Yu Chen, Yuang-Chin Chiang, and Min-Shung Liang (2000) "A bilingual Mandarin/taiwanese (min-nan), large vocabulary, continuous speech recognition system based on the tong-yong phonetic alphabet(TYPA)," *Proceedings of the 6th International Conference on Spoken Language Processing (ICSLP 2000) / INTERSPEECH 2000*, pp. 226-229.

[9] 李毓哲, 王崇喆, 陳亮宇, 張智星, and 呂仁園 (2013) "使用語音評分技術輔助台語語料的驗證," *Proceedings of ROCLING 2013*, pp. 37-38.

[10] 余明興 and 蔡承融 (2008) "國台語無聲調拼音輸入法實作," *Proceedings of ROCLING 2008*, pp. 137-150.

The 2018 Conference on Computational Linguistics and Speech Processing
ROCLING 2018, pp. 199-213
©The Association for Computational Linguistics and Chinese Language Processing

# On the Semantic Relations and Functional Properties of Noun-Noun Compounds in Mandarin

Shu-Ping Gong
Department of Foreign Languages
National Chiayi University
spgong@mail.ncyu.edu.tw


Chih-Hung Liu
Department of Foreign Languages
National Chiayi University
joker150258@hotmail.com

## Abstract

The goal of this research was to determine the distribution of compounds in Mandarin Chinese from the aspect of semantics. In particular, the focus was on two types of compounds: compounds interpreted by semantic relations or by functional properties between constituents. We collected 880 compounds from a dictionary and categorized them into two types of noun-noun compounds in Mandarin, including relation-based compounds (e.g., 中國菜 *zhōngguócài* "Chinese food") and functional property-based compounds (e.g., 柳葉眉 *liǔyèméi* "arched eyebrows"). Finally, the frequency of occurrence of the two types of compounds was determined. The results showed that relation-based compounds occurred much more frequently than property-based compounds in our data (96.1% vs. 3.8%). In addition, it was found that within the relation-based compounds, noun-noun compounds using the FOR relation (e.g., 信紙 *xìnzhǐ* "letter paper") had the highest rates of occurrence (37.6%), while the CAUSE relation (e.g., 刀傷 *dāoshāng* "wounds by a knife") had the lowest rates of occurrence (0.7%). On the other hand, the functional property-based compounds, almost always referring to objects in the NATURAL KIND domain, take metaphorical meanings from individual constituents. Our study suggests that the relation-based meanings for interpreting compounds are common in daily conversation, which could be the dominant strategy people use to interpret novel compounds. This research has practical implications for natural language processing in dealing with segmentation of compounds and multiword expressions in Mandarin and even recognition of novel word combinations.

Keywords: Relation-based Compounds, Property-based Compounds, Natural Kind, Artifact, Corpus, Mandarin.


## 1. Introduction

Compounds are frequent and pervasive in daily language. Compounds, which are lexemes that consist of two or more words, are not interpreted with ease. Indeed, even though compounds are highly frequent, sometimes it is not easy to interpret (novel) compounds for several reasons. First, the semantic relations within compounds are complex [1]. For example, Gagne & Shoben [2] found that people used more than ten semantic relations to interpret compounds, such as 日月潭紅茶 *rìyuètán hóngchá* "Black Tea of Sun Moon Lake" as interpreted by the PLACE relation. Second, the meanings of some compounds are idiosyncratic, which cannot be inferred from the literal meanings of individual constituents [3]. For example, the compound 片花 *piànhuā* indicates "trailers of movies" and does not refer to "a piece of flower". Third, some compounds have more than one meaning and the appropriate meanings are determined by the context [1]. For example, the compound 出爐 *chūlú* refers to something "freshly baked". This can be food (e.g., bread) or written/innovative products (e.g., theses, books, or movies).

In this study, we focus on compounds. In particular, it is found that compounds can be interpreted by semantic relations or by functional property principles. First, when compounds are interpreted by semantic relations among constituents, these kinds of compounds are called relation-based compounds [2]. Such compounds are derived from the thematic relation between morphemes/words. For example, the compound 檸檬汁 *níngméngzhī* "lemon juice" in Mandarin Chinese belongs to this type. Second, when compounds are interpreted by using the functional properties involved in the meanings of words, these types of compounds are the property-based ones [4] that are constructed via mapping a property from one word to another word. For example, the compound 蝴蝶蘭 *húdiélán* "Phalaenopsis orchid" is this type.

In previous studies, two theories were proposed for accounting for how compounds are understood: The competition-among-relations-in-nominals (CARIN) and the dual-process theory. The CARIN theory proposed by Gagne and Shoben [2] accounted for relation-based compounds, suggesting that these compounds were interpreted based on the semantic relations between modifiers and head nouns. A high frequency of relations between words facilitated the processing of compounds, whereas a low frequency of relations between words inhibited the interpretation of compounds.

On the other hand, the dual-process theory, proposed by Wisniewski [4], involved two independent operations: relation-linking and property-mapping in the process of interpreting compounds. In particular, compounds were first interpreted using the relation-linking operation. If this operation did not yield a meaning, property-mapping was activated and used to interpret the meaning of the compound.

Even though past studies have discussed how the two types of compounds were understood, most have only investigated these compounds in English. In fact, little research has determined the frequency of occurrence of the two types of compounds in Mandarin. Compounds in Mandarin are very pervasive in daily language. Compounds, one kind of multiword expression, are constructed according to some semantic principles, i.e., semantic features and functional property mapping. It is necessary to know the distribution of compound types in order to know how people process compounds. Therefore, the current research intends to examine the distribution of relation-based and property-based compounds in Mandarin Chinese.


## 2. Background

As mentioned above, two theories have been proposed to describe how compounds are interpreted and understood, namely the competition-among-relations-in-nominals (CARIN) theory [2] and the dual-process theory [4]. The CARIN theory proposes that the meaning of compounds can be unified by a particular thematic relation between modifiers and head nouns, while the dual-process theory proposes that compounds can be interpreted via two independent operations, either relation-linking or property-mapping. In the following sections, each theory will be presented in detail.


2.1 Relation-based Compounds

Gagne and Shoben [2] proposed the CARIN theory to deal with how compounds are interpreted and comprehended. They proposed that speakers will select a specific thematic relation, connecting the modifier and the head noun, to unify the ultimate interpretation. Three experiments testing compounds with three thematic relations supported their theory: highly frequent for both constituents (HH, e.g., "mountain bird"), highly frequent only for the modifier (HL, e.g., "mountain magazine"), and highly frequent only for the noun (LH, e.g., "gas cloud cloud"). Their experimental results demonstrated that the typical usages of modifiers (i.e., HH and HL) can ease the comprehension of the combinations, as the CARIN theory predicted. Moreover, knowledge of highly frequent thematic relations can also influence the ease of comprehending modifier-noun compounds, though the relational information of the modifier is not the sole factor in the ease of interpretation.

Gagne [5] investigated whether property-based compounds were as common as relation-based compounds, and whether the similarity between the modifier and the head noun would affect the interpretation of property-based compounds. Two kinds of novel compounds were tested (Table 1).

Gagne [5] showed that: (1) relation-based compounds were processed more readily and that some properties were added to the newly conceptual combination after the selection of the general relation in the unitary meaning; (2) as predicted by the CARIN theory [2], the general relation of the modifier was the basis for unifying the relation-based compound; and

(3) relation-based compounds were easily adopted by speakers, which suggests that speakers

tended to interpret novel compounds through a relation-based approach. For example, people

tend to interpret the compound "mountain bird" as "a bird living on a mountain", instead of "a

large bird". Nevertheless, the current research found that the selection of compounds for the

corpus-based studies might have been influenced by the unbalanced proportion of

relation-based and property-based compounds.

Table 1. Examples from Gagne's (2000) Experiment

| Property-based | | Relation-based | |
|---|---|---|---|
| Similar Nouns | Dissimilar Nouns | High Relation Frequency | Low Relation Frequency |
| Coat, shirt | Coffee, sword | Plastic toy | Water bird |

Gagne and Spalding [6] conducted experiments to discover the effect of the lemma frequency

and the family frequency of each constituent's position. They found that both the lemma

frequency and the positional family frequency affected the processing of compounds. For

example, people's interpretation of the compound "doghouse" was affected by the family

members of the structures "dog + __" and "__ + house", but not by the family members of the

structures "__ + dog" and "house + __".

To conclude, the CARIN theory proposes that compounds connected via thematic

relations between modifiers and head nouns are easier to interpret and comprehend. Past

studies [2, 5-6] have supported this proposition. In addition, other factors, including the

frequency of the modifiers and the types of head nouns, play an important role in compound

processing.


2.2 Property-based Compounds

As proposed by Wisniewski [4] and Wisniewski and Love [7], property-based compounds are interpreted by mapping a property from one word to another word. They found that people mainly interpreted noun-noun compounds via aligning the property with the head noun to acquire the combined meaning, or by extracting a property from one constituent and transferring it to another constituent to obtain the compound. For example, the compound "shark lawyer" should be interpreted as "a lawyer is as truculent as a shark", not as "a lawyer for a shark".

Wisniewski [4] conducted a study to investigate the hypothesis of relation-linking via novel noun-noun compound interpretations and the distribution of relation-based compounds via two interpretation tasks. In addition, Wisniewski (1996) tested whether the higher similarity between constituents within the compound would promote the adoption of a property-based interpretation and found that although the relation-based approach might have facilitated the interpretation of compounds, property-based interpretations were not rare. Wisniewski [4] also suggested that speakers might possess a two-process mechanism for processing compounds. Moreover, the higher similarity between the constituents within the compound might have promoted the adoption of property-based interpretation.

Furthermore, Wisniewski and Love [7] discussed whether speakers first considered the relational information of the constituents and then mapped the property of the modifier to obtain the compound meaning if the semantic relation failed to interpret the meaning. For example, the compound "robin hawk" can be interpreted as "a hawk that preys on robins" or "a small hawk". They found that the higher the similarity between the constituents, the easier it was to interpret property-based compounds.

Wisniewski and Love [7] suggested that the relation-based approach and the property-based approach were both adopted by speakers. Finally, although there was a significant difference between the relation-based approach (70.9%) and the property-based approach (29.1%), this result also revealed that property-based interpretations of compounds occurred frequently, which was different from the findings of the CARIN theory [2].

To conclude, although the relation-based approach to interpreting compounds was dominant in comprehending noun-noun compounds, the property-based approach was often used to interpret compounds when the relation-based approach failed to produce the meanings of compounds.

## 3. Goals of This Study

How people construct different concepts to form a novel compound word is still debatable. Some have supported the relation-based approach, while others have suggested the property-based approach. One area that has yet to be investigated is whether processing may have something to do with the frequency of compound usages in daily language. While previous studies have focused on the processing of compounds, few studies have investigated the distribution of compounds from the perspective of corpus linguistics. In particular, no studies have determined the distribution of the types of compounds in Mandarin Chinese. Therefore, this research collected compounds from a dictionary and counted the frequencies of the compounds using both relation-based and property-based theories.

Accordingly, our research question is as follows: What is the distribution of relation-based and property-based compounds in Mandarin Chinese? In particular, we would like to know whether relation-based compounds occur more frequently than property-based ones in Mandarin.

## 4. Methods

The goal of this corpus-based study was to investigate the distribution of relation-based and property-based noun-noun compounds in Mandarin Chinese. Noun-noun combinations were collected from a dictionary and then categorized into relation-based and property-based categories. Finally, the frequency of occurrence of the relation-based and property-based compounds was examined.

## 4.1 Data Collection and Analysis

This corpus-based study replicated Gagne's [5] analysis of compounds. Compounds were collected from a Chinese classifier dictionary [8]. The reason for using a classifier dictionary was that the compounds listed in this type of dictionary were more concrete than normal compounds, since compounds in Mandarin Chinese can have abstract meanings. That is, compounds preceded by classifiers were considered evidence that the meaning of these compounds could be either objects or referring to something concrete in the real world.

In addition, noun-noun compounds were selected according to the following four principles. First, one-character nouns preceded by classifiers were excluded, such as 人 *rén* "people", 棋 *qí* "chess", and 玉 *yù* "jade". Second, if the noun-noun compounds could not be segmented into two parts, or the head noun was followed by a modifier, they were removed; for example, in the Chinese compound 雪花 *xuěhuā* "snowflakes", the head noun precedes the modifier. Third, binding words such as 葡萄 *pútáo* "grape" and 蝴蝶 *húdié* "butterfly" and reduplicative words such as 星星 *xīngxīng* "stars" were removed from the data. Fourth, if one constituent of the compound did not belong to the syntactic category of the noun, the compound was deleted from the data; for example, the Chinese phrase 釣魚 *diàoyú* "fish" acts as a verbal phrase in the Chinese compound 釣魚竿 *diàoyúgān* "fishing rod", so it was deleted from the data.

According to these four principles, 880 compounds were collected. Next, a concreteness rating test was conducted to exclude all the compounds that carried abstract meanings. Thirty-two undergraduate students participated in the rating test, which required them to rate compounds as having either abstract meanings or concrete meanings. Compounds were classified as concrete when 75% agreement was reached among the participants. After the rating task, 417 compounds were collected.

The 417 compounds were classified into two word-formation categories: relation-based compounds [2, 5] and property-based compounds [4]. If a Chinese compound could be interpreted by relation, it was placed into the relation-based category. For example, 書桌 *shūzhuō* "desk" is interpreted by the relation FOR, as this is a table for working or for studying. On the other hand, if one or more properties of a constituent were mapped to the other constituent, it was classified as property-based. For example, the Chinese compound 貝殼機 *bèikéjī* "clamshell phone" is a type of mobile phone, and the opening shape (i.e., a functional property) of the noun 貝殼 *bèiké* "shell" is transferred to the other noun to interpret this compound.

Table 2. Eleven Thematic Relations for Noun-Noun Combinations used in this study

| Thematic Relations between words | Examples |
| --- | --- |
| MAKE | 木椅 *mùyǐ* "wooden chairs" |
| IS | 蘭花 *lánhuā* "orchid" |
| DERIVE | 米酒 *mǐjiǔ* "rice wine" |
| LOCATE | 田鼠 *tiánshǔ* "voles" |
| HAVE | 繪本 *huìběn* "picture books" |
| CAUSE | 高山症 *gāoshānzhèng* "altitude sickness" |
| FOR | 窗簾 *chuānglián* "curtain" |
| USE | 兒童椅 *értóngyǐ* "children's chairs" |
| ABOUT | 山雜誌 *shānzázhì* "mountain magazine" |
| DURING | 冬雨 *dōngyǔ* "winter rain" |
| BY | 學生故事 *xuéshēnggùshì* "student story" |

Sixteen property-based compounds were obtained, and of the 401 compounds classified as relation-based, they were further divided into 11 thematic categories (Table 2) according to Gagne's classification [5].

Table 2 shows Chinese examples in the 11 thematic categories, such as the compound

田鼠 *tiánshǔ* "voles", which is classified into the category LOCATE because it is interpreted as "a kind of mouse located in the mountains". Another example is the compound 木椅 *mùyǐ* "wooden chairs", which is a lexical item in thematic relation to the noun (i.e., "chair") modified by what it is made of (i.e., "wood"). Finally, these 401 compounds were further grouped into eight categories. In the following section, the distribution of thematic relations between the constituents in Chinese compounds will be reported.


4.2 Results and Discussion

Of the 417 compounds collected, 401 (96.2%) compounds were classified as relation-based and 16 (3.8%) compounds were classified as property-based. The frequency of occurrence and the corresponding percentages of the 401 relation-based compounds are shown in Table 3. The FOR relation occurred the most frequently in Chinese compounds (37.6%), while the MAKE relation occurred the second most frequently (12.2%), and the BY and CAUSE relations occurred the least frequently.

For the 16 functional property-based interpretations, six categories were discovered, including FARMING AND PLANT, ANIMAL, PHYSICAL APPEARANCE, UNIVERSE, ARTIFACT, and PAPER DOCUMENT. Then, these six categories were placed into one of two domains, the NATURAL KIND domain (i.e., FARMING AND PLANT, ANIMAL, PHYSICAL APPEARANCE, and UNIVERSE), and the ARTIFACT domain (i.e., ARTIFACT and PAPER DOCUMENT; see Table 4). Moreover, findings similar to Wisniewski and Love (1998) were obtained.

The ARTIFACT category occurred the most frequently in Chinese compounds via the property-based strategy, such as 鞭炮 *biānpào* "firecracker". The FARMING AND PLANT category occurred the second most frequently, including 蝴蝶蘭 *húdiélán* "Phalaenopsis orchid", 黃金扁柏 *huángjīn biǎnbǎi* "Oriental arborvitae", 黃金葛 *huáng jīn gě* "centipede tongavine", and 梯田 *tītián* "terraced fields". These findings are in line with those proposed by Wisniewski and Love [7].

Table 3: Distribution of Thematic Relations between Constituents

| Thematic Relations | Examples | Frequency (%) |
| --- | --- | --- |
| FOR | 保險金 *bǎoxiǎnjīn* "insurance claims" | 157 (37.6%) |
| MAKE | 鐵門 *tiěmén* "iron gate" | 51 (12.2%) |
| LOCATE | 山豬 *shānzhū* "wild boar" | 40 (9.5%) |
| IS | 蘭花 *lánhuā* "orchid" | 63 (15.1%) |
| USE | 汽車 *qìchē* "automobile" | 15 (3.5%) |
| ABOUT | 卡通片 *kǎtōngpiàn* "cartoon film" | 17 (4.0%) |
| HAVE | 帆船 *fānchuán* "sailboat" | 26 (6.2%) |
| DURING | 年輕人 *niánqīngrén* "youngster" | 10 (2.3%) |
| DERIVED | 蜂蜜 *fēngmì* "honey" | 15 (3.5%) |
| BY | 中國菜 *zhōngguócài* "Chinese food" | 4 (0.9%) |
| CAUSE | 刀傷 *dāoshāng* "wounds by a knife" | 3 (0.7%) |
| Total | | 401 (100%) |

The third most frequently occurring category was PHYSICAL APPEARANCE, including 柳葉眉 *liǔyèméi* "arched eyebrows", 硃砂痣 *zhūshāzhì* "cinnabar mole", and 大花臉 *dàhuāliǎn* "painted face". Moreover, within the top three categories, the properties of SHAPE and COLOR were transferred from one constituent to another. For example, in the compound 蝴蝶蘭 *húdiélán* "Phalaenopsis orchid", the property of SHAPE is transferred from butterflies to describe the shape of the flowers. In another instance, in the compound 黃金葛 *huángjīngě* "centipede tongavine", the property of COLOR is transferred from gold to describe the color of the plant. These results show that the properties of SHAPE and COLOR were adopted as modifiers.

Table 4: Domains and Categories of Property-based Compounds

| Domains | Categories | Examples |
|---|---|---|
| NATURAL KIND | FARMING AND PLANT | 蝴蝶蘭 *húdiélán* "Phalaenopsis orchid" |
| | ANIMAL | 金魚 *jīnyú* "gold fish" |
| | PHYSICAL APPEARANCE | 柳葉眉 *liǔyèméi* "arched eyebrows" |
| | UNIVERSE | 彗星 *huìxīng* "comet" |
| ARTIFACT | ARTIFACT | 原子筆 *yuánzǐbǐ* "ball-point pen" |
| | PAPER DOCUMENT | 黑函 *hēihán* "poison-pen letter" |

In addition, the property-based compounds were classified according to the properties of the modifiers. As Table 5 shows, modifiers with the SHAPE property were the most frequently occurring (50%), while the second most frequently occurring was the COLOR property (31.2%), and the METAPHORICAL property occurred the least (18.7%).

Table 5: Distribution of Property-based Modifiers

| Properties | Examples | Frequency (%) |
|---|---|---|
| COLOR | 黃金扁柏 *huángjīn biǎnbǎi* "Oriental arborvitae" | 5 (31.2%) |
| SHAPE | 蝴蝶蘭 *húdiélán* "Phalaenopsis orchid" | 8 (50.0%) |
| METAPHORICAL | 黑函 *hēihán* "poison-pen letter" | 3 (18.7%) |
| Total | | 16 (100%) |

The corpus results showed that there were very few property-based compounds. This could have resulted from the stimuli collected. Most of the stimuli (i.e., relation-based compounds) analyzed in this study belonged to the ARTIFACT domain, while property-based compounds occurred more often in the NATURAL KIND domain.

## 5. Conclusion and future work

The goal of this study was to determine the distribution of relation-based and property-based compounds in Mandarin Chinese. Our study intended to determine the frequency of occurrence of relation-based and property-based compounds in Mandarin Chinese. The results showed that relation-based compounds occurred much more frequently than property-based compounds (96.1% vs. 3.8%). Furthermore, it was found that within the relation-based compounds, noun-noun compounds using the FOR relation (e.g., 信紙 *xìnzhǐ* "letter paper") had the highest rates of occurrence (37.6%), while the CAUSE relation (e.g., 刀傷 *dāoshāng* "wounds by a knife") had the lowest rates of occurrence (0.7%). Thus, our study suggests that relation-based word formations were the most commonly found compounds in Mandarin Chinese. Finally, it was found that the property-mapping principles were likely applied to interpret compounds in the ARTIFACT domain.

To answer our research question of "What is the distribution of relation-based and property-based compounds in Mandarin Chinese?", it was found that the frequency of relation-based compounds was much higher than property-based compounds. This distribution is consistent with the prediction of the CARIN theory [2].

Our findings show that there is a tendency that the compounds in the NATURAL KIND domain would likely be interpreted by property-mapping between constituents, while the ones in the ARTIFACT domains would likely be interpreted by relation-linking between constituents. However, our data have insufficient compounds to further analyze this hypothesis. In the future, a study will be conducted in order to collect more compounds from more categories, including ANIMAL, PLANT, and FOOD, to determine whether more property-based compounds occur in the NATURAL KIND than in the ARTIFACT domains.

To conclude, this research has shown that relation-based compounds occurred more frequently than property-based compounds. In addition, the property-based compounds were more likely to occur in the NATURAL KIND domain. These corpus findings suggest that the CARIN theory [2] can better predict the distribution of compound types compared with the dual-process theory [4].

It is hoped that this research will offer more cross-linguistic evidence with which to evaluate the CARIN theory and the dual-process theory regarding compounds. This study has implications for computer processing in dealing with how machines learn to recognize compounds and even novel word combinations. This study has shown that many thematic relations or property-mapping strategies exist in the search for compounds or word combinations, which can help machines to acquire possible thematic relations to interpret novel compounds or concept combinations.


## Acknowledgments

This research was supported by grants from the Ministry of Science and Technology (MOST 105-2410-H-415-025) to the first author. We would like to thank the anonymous reviewers for their comments on this work. Remaining errors are our sole responsibility.

References

[1]  R. Girju, D. Moldovan, M. Tatu, and D. Antohe, "On the semantics of noun compounds", Computer Speech and Language, vol. 19, pp. 479–496, 2005.

[2]  C. L., Gagne and E. J. Shoben, "Influence of Thematic Relations on the Comprehension of Modifier-Noun Combinations". *Experimental Psychology: Learning, Memory, and Cognition,* vol. 23, no. 1, pp. 71-87, 1997.

[3]  M. Constant , G. Eryiğit , J.. Monti , L. V. D. Plas , C. Ramisch , M. Rosner and A. Todirascu, "Multiword Expression Processing: A Survey", Computational Linguistics, vol. 43, no. 4, pp. 837-892, 2017.

[4]  E. J., Wisniewski, "Construal and Similarity in Conceptual Combination", *Memory and Language*, vol. 35, no. 24, pp. 434-453, 1996.

[5]  C. L., Gagne, "Relation-Based Combinations versus Property-Based Combinations: A Test of the CARIN Theory and the Dual-Process Theory of Conceptual Combination", *Memory and Language,* vol. 42, no. pp. 365-389, 2000.

[6]  C. L., Gagne and T. L. Spaldin, "Constituent Integration during the Processing of Compound Words: Does It Involve the Use of Relational Structures?" *Memory and Language,* vol. 60, pp. 20-35, 2009.

[7]  E. J., Wisniewski and B. C. Love, "Relations versus Properties in Conceptual Combination" *Memory and Language,* vol. 38, pp. 177-202, 1998.

[8]  C.-R., Huang, K.-J., Chen, and Q.-X. Lai, *Chinese Classifier Dictionary.* Taipei: Mandarin Daily News, 1996.《黃居仁、陳克健、賴慶雄 (1996)。*常用量詞詞典。* 臺北市：國語日報。》

The 2018 Conference on Computational Linguistics and Speech Processing
ROCLING 2018, pp. 214-223
©The Association for Computational Linguistics and Chinese Language Processing

# An LSTM Approach to Short Text Sentiment Classification with Word Embeddings

Jenq-Haur Wang
Department of Computer Science and Information Engineering
National Taipei University of Technology, Taipei, Taiwan
jhwang@csie.ntut.edu.tw

Ting-Wei Liu
PChome eBay Co., Ltd., Taipei, Taiwan
s5548765@gmail.com

Xiong Luo, Long Wang
School of Computer and Communication Engineering
University of Science and Technology Beijing, Beijing, China
xluo@ustb.edu.cn, lwang@ustb.edu.cn

## Abstract

Sentiment classification techniques have been widely used for analyzing user opinions. In conventional supervised learning methods, hand-crafted features are needed, which requires a thorough understanding of the domain. Since social media posts are usually very short, there's a lack of features for effective classification. Thus, word embedding models can be used to learn different word usages in various contexts. To detect the sentiment polarity from short texts, we need to explore deeper semantics of words using deep learning methods. In this paper, we investigate the effects of word embedding and long short-term memory (LSTM) for sentiment classification in social media. First, words in posts are converted into vectors using word embedding models. Then, the word sequence in sentences are input to LSTM to learn the long distance contextual dependency among words. The experimental results showed that deep learning methods can effectively learn the word usage in context of social media given enough training data. The quantity and quality of training data greatly affects the performance. Further investigation is needed to verify the performance in different social media sources.

Keywords: Sentiment Classification, Deep Learning, Long Short-Term Memory, Word2Vec Model.

# 1. Introduction

Sentiment classification has been used in analyzing user-generated contents for understanding users' intent and opinions in social media. Conventional supervised learning methods have been extensively investigated such as bag-of-words model using TF-IDF, and probabilistic model using Naïve Bayes, which usually need hand-crafted features. For social media content which are very short and diverse in topic, it's difficult to obtain useful features for classification. Thus, a more effective method for short text sentiment classification is needed.

Deep learning methods have gradually shown good performance in many applications, such as speech recognition, pattern recognition, and data classification. These methods try to learn data representation using a deeper hierarchy of structures in neural networks. Complicated concepts are possible to learn based on simpler ones. Among deep feedforward networks, Convolutional Neural Networks (CNNs) have been shown to learn local features from words or phrases [1], while Recurrent Neural Networks (RNNs) are able to learn temporal dependencies in sequential data [2]. Given the very short texts in social media, there's a lack of features. To obtain more useful features, we further utilize the idea of distributed representation of words where each input is represented by many features and each feature is involved in many possible inputs. Specifically, we use the Word2Vec word embedding model [3] for distributed representation of social posts.

In this paper, we want to investigate the effectiveness of long short-term memory (LSTM) [4] for sentiment classification of short texts with distributed representation in social media. First, a word embedding model based on Word2Vec is used to represent words in short texts as vectors. Second, LSTM is used for learning long-distance dependency between word sequence in short texts. The final output from the last point of time is used as the prediction result. In our experiments of sentiment classification on several social datasets, we compared the performance of LSTM with Naïve Bayes (NB) and Extreme Learning Machine (ELM). As the experimental results show, our proposed method can achieve better performance than conventional probabilistic model and neural networks with more training data. This shows the potential of using deep learning methods for sentiment analysis. Further investigation is needed to verify the effectiveness of the proposed approach in larger scale. The remainder of this paper is organized as follows: Sec. 2 lists the related works, and Sec. 3 describes the proposed method. The experimental results are described in Sec. 4. And some discussions of the results are summarized in Sec.5. Finally, Sec. 6 lists the conclusions.

## 2. Related Work

Artificial neural network is a network structure inspired by neurons in human brains. Nodes are organized into layers, and nodes in adjacent layers are connected by edges. Computations are done in a feed-forward manner, and errors can be back-propagated to previous layers to adjust the weights of corresponding edges. Extreme Learning Machines (ELMs) [5] are a special type of neural networks in which the weights are not adjusted by back propagation. The hidden nodes are randomly assigned and never updated. Thus, the weights are usually learned in one single step, which is usually much faster.

For more complex relations, deep learning methods are adopted, which utilize multiple hidden layers. With deeper network structures, it usually takes more computing time. These methods were made feasible thanks to the recent advances of computing powers in hardware, and the GPU processing in software technologies. Depending on the different ways of structuring multiple layers, several types of deep neural networks were proposed, where CNNs and RNNs are among the most popular ones. CNNs are usually used in computer vision since convolution operations can be naturally applied in edge detection and image sharpening. They are also useful in calculating weighted moving averages, and calculating impulse response from signals. RNNs are a type of neural networks where the inputs of hidden layers in the current point of time depend on the previous outputs of hidden layer. This makes them possible to deal with a time sequence with temporal relations such as speech recognition. According to previous comparative study of RNN and CNN in natural language processing [6], RNNs are found to be more effective in sentiment analysis than CNNs. Thus, we focus on RNNs in this paper.

As the time sequence grows in RNNs, it's possible for weights to grow beyond control or to vanish. To deal with the vanishing gradient problem [7] in training conventional RNNs, Long Short-Term Memory (LSTM) [4] was proposed to learn long-term dependency among longer time period. In addition to input and output gates, forget gates are added in LSTM. They are often used for time series prediction, and hand-writing recognition. In this paper, we utilize LSTM in learning sentiment classifiers of short texts.

For natural language processing, it's useful to analyze the distributional relations of word occurrences in documents. The simplest way is to use one-hot encoding to represent the occurrence of each word in documents as a binary vector. In distributional semantics, word embedding models are used to map from the one-hot vector space to a continuous vector space in a much lower dimension than conventional bag-of-words model. Among various word embedding models, the most popular ones are distributed representation of words such as Word2Vec [3] and GloVe [8], where neural networks are used to train the occurrence relations between words and documents in the contexts of training data. In this paper, we adopt the Word2Vec word embedding model to represent words in short texts. Then, LSTM classifiers are trained to capture the long-term dependency among words in short texts. The sentiment of each text can then be classified as positive or negative.

## 3. The Proposed Method

In this paper, the overall architecture include three major components: pre-processing & feature extraction, word embedding, and LSTM classification, as shown in Fig. 1.

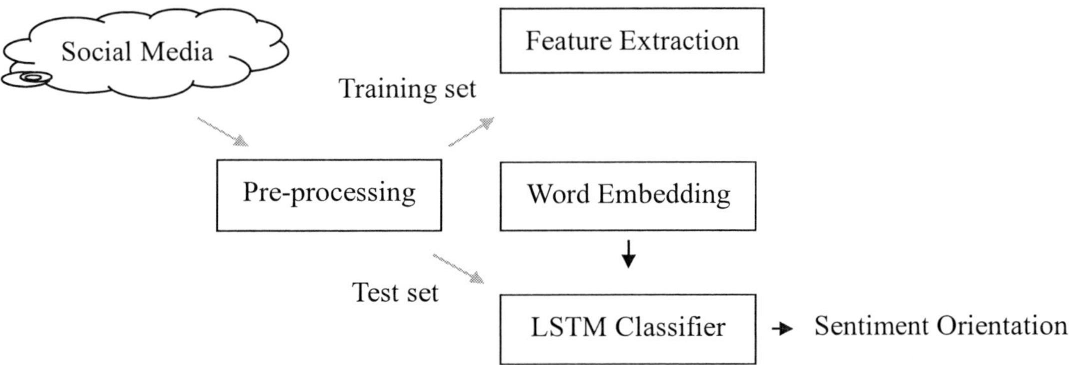


Figure 1. The system architecture of the proposed approach

As shown in Fig.1, short texts are first preprocessed and word features are extracted. Second, the Word2Vec word embedding model [3] is used to learn word representations as vectors. Third, LSTM [4] is adopted for sequence prediction among words in a sentence. The details of each component are described in the following subsections.

## 3.1. Preprocessing and Feature Extraction

First, short texts are collected with custom-made crawlers for different social media. Then, preprocessing tasks are needed to cleanup post contents. For example, URL links, hashtags, and emoticons are filtered. Also, stopword removal is performed to focus on content words. For Chinese posts, we used Jieba for word segmentation. Then, we extract metadata such as poster ID, posting time, and the number of retweets and likes. These will be used as additional features for classification.

## 3.2. Word Embedding

In bag-of-words model, it's very high dimensional, and there's a lack of contextual relations between words. To better represent the limited content in short texts, we use Word2Vec word embedding model [3] to learn the contextual relations among words in training data. Also, the fixed number of dimensions in word embedding model can facilitate more efficient computations. There are two general models in Word2Vec, Continuous Bag-of-Words (CBOW) and Skip-gram. Since much better performance for skip-gram model in semantic analysis can be obtained [3], we use word vectors trained via Word2Vec Skip-gram model as the inputs to the following stage of classification.

## 3.3. Long Short-Term Memory (LSTM)

After representing each word by its corresponding vector trained by Word2Vec model, the sequence of words $\{T_1, \ldots, T_n\}$ are input to LSTM one by one in a sequence, as shown in Fig.2.

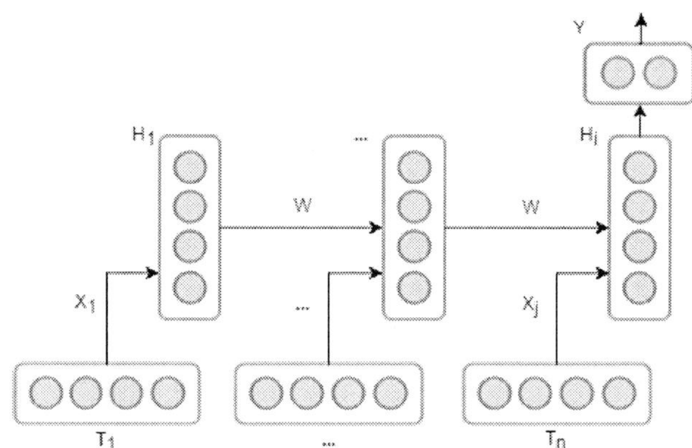


Figure 2. The idea of LSTM

In Fig.2, each term $T_i$ is first converted to the corresponding input vector $x_i$ using Word2Vec model and input into LSTM one by one. At each time $j$, the output $W$ of the hidden layer $H_j$ will be propagated back to the hidden layer together with the next input $x_{j+1}$ at the next point of time $j+1$. Finally, the last output $W_n$ will be fed to the output layer.

To comply with the sequential input of LSTM, we first convert posts into three-dimensional matrix M(X, Y, Z), where X is the dimension of Word2Vec word embedding model, Y is the number of words in the post, and Z is the number of posts. To avoid the very long training time, we adopt a single hidden-layer neural network. The number of neurons in input layer is the same as the dimension of Word2Vec model, and the number of neurons in output layer is the number of classes, which is 2 in this case. By gradient-based back propagation through time, we can adjust the weight of edges in hidden layer at each point of time. After several epochs of training, we can obtain the sentiment classification model.

## 3.4. Sentiment Classification

After sentiment classification model is trained using LSTM, all posts in test set are preprocessed with the same procedure as the training set, and represented using the same word embedding model. Then, for testing step, the same processes of LSTM in Fig. 2 are followed, except for the weights update. The output of LSTM model will then be evaluated with the labels of each post in test data in the experiments.

## 4. Experiments

In order to evaluate the performance of our proposed approach, we conducted three different experiments. First, we used English movie reviews from IMDB. Second, we tested Chinese movie review comments from Douban. Finally, we evaluated the performance for Chinese posts in the PTT discussion forum.

In the first dataset, there are 50,000 review comments in IMDB Large Movie Review Dataset [9], where 25,000 were used as training and 25,000 as test data. To avoid influence from previous comments of the same movie, we collected no more than 30 reviews for each movie. The rating of each movie was used as the ground truth, where a rating above 7 as positive, and a rating below 4 as negative.

In the second dataset, we collected top 200 movies for each of the 10 categories in Douban Movies. The top 40 to 60 review comments were extracted from each movie according to their popularity. The ground truth of this dataset was set as follows: a rating of 1-2 as negative, and a rating of 4-5 as positive. The comments with a rating of 3 or no ratings are ignored. After removing these comments, there are 12,000 comments where 6,000 were used as training and 6,000 as test data.

In the third dataset for the most popular social media platform PTT in Taiwan, we collected 3,500 posts during Aug. 31 and Sep. 1, 2015 and the corresponding 34,488 comments as the training data, and 1,000 posts during Sep. 2 and Sep. 3, 2015 and the 6,825 comments as the test data. The user ratings of like/dislike are used as the ground truth of this dataset.

To evaluate the classification performance, standard evaluation metrics of precision, recall, F-measure, and accuracy were used to compare three classifiers: Naïve Bayes (NB), Extreme Learning Machine (ELM), and Long Short-Term Memory (LSTM). Word2Vec model is applied for all three classifiers.

For the first dataset of IMDB movie reviews, the performance comparison among three classifiers are shown in Fig.3.

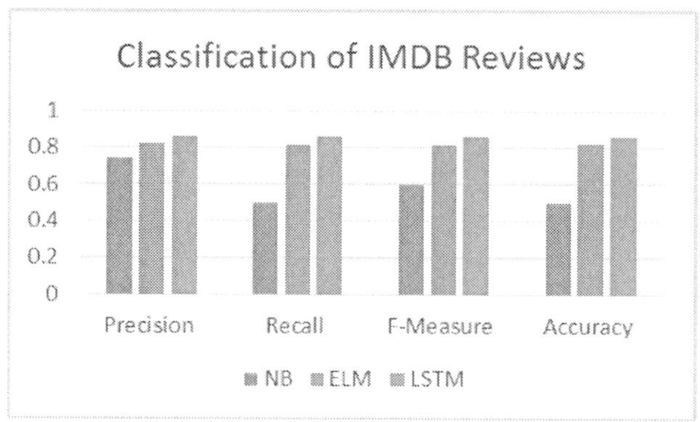


Figure 3. The performance comparison of three classifiers for IMDB reviews

As shown in Fig.3, the best performance can be achieved for LSTM with a F-measure of 0.859. We can see the consistently better performance for LSTM than NB and ELM. Naïve Bayes is the worst due to its high false positive rates. This shows the better performance for neural network methods, especially for deep learning methods. Next, the performance for more casual comments in Douban Movies is shown in Fig.4.

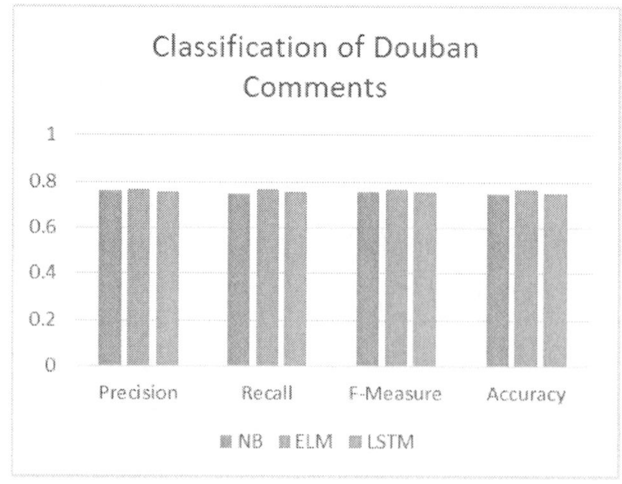


Figure 4. The performance comparison of classification for Douban comments

As shown in Fig.4, the performance of all three classifiers are comparable with slight differences. The best performance can be achieved for ELM with a F-measure of 0.765, while LSTM obtained a comparable F-measure of 0.754. Since the comments are less formal and shorter in lengths, they are more difficult to classify than longer reviews in IMDB. To further evaluate the effects of training data size on the performance, we include more training data from 6,000 reviews to 10,000 and 20,000 in the next experiment. The test data size remains unchanged. The results are shown in Fig.5.

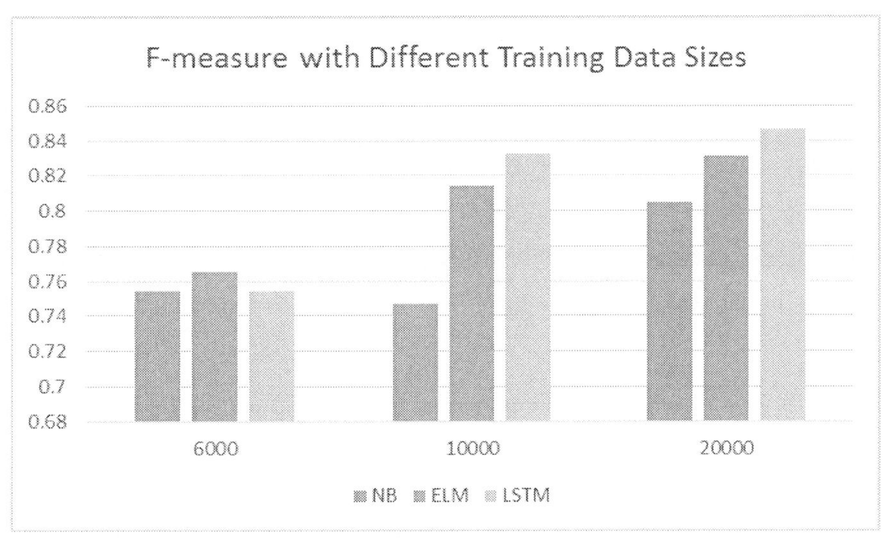


Figure 5. The effects of training data size on classification performance

As shown in Fig.5, as the training data size grows, the classification performance improves for all classifiers except for Naïve Bayes at 10,000. The best performance can be achieved for LSTM with a F-measure of 0.847 when training data size reaches 20,000. Next, the performance of three classifiers on PTT posts are shown in Fig.6.

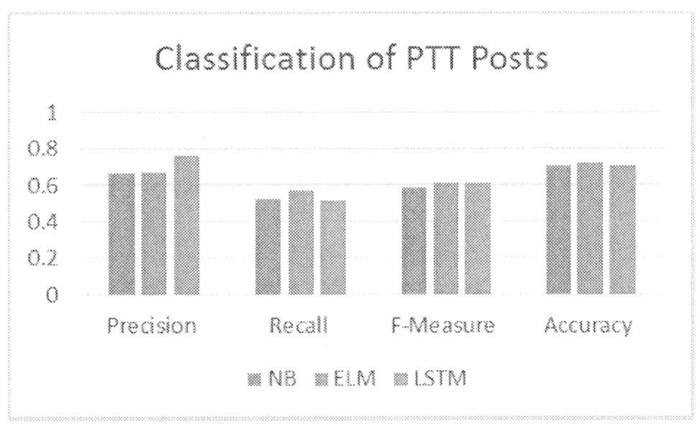


Figure 6. The performance comparison of classification for PTT posts

As shown in Fig.6, the best performance can be achieved for ELM with a F-measure of 0.615, and LSTM with a comparable F-measure of 0.613. LSTM got a higher precision but lower recall for negative posts. The reason is due to the mismatches between user ratings and the sentiment polarity of the corresponding user comments. Users often marks their ratings as "likes" for the posts they agree with, but express their strong negative opinions in their comments. This disagreement is more common in the online forum PTT due to the special characteristics in the community. The impact of this special behavior is larger for LSTM than the other two classifiers.

## 5. Discussions

From the experimental results, some observations about the proposed approach are shown as follows. First, using word embedding models, the sentiments of short texts can be effectively classified. Second, depending on different types of social media, the performance might vary. The classification performance is better for movie reviews than casual comments and posts in online forums. But the performance of LSTM is still comparable to ELM and NB. This shows the feasibility of an LSTM-based approach to short-text sentiment classification. Third, data size can also affect the classification performance. More training data can lead to better performance. Finally, special characteristics in certain online forums might lead to inferior classification performance. This behavior mismatch between user opinions in comments and user ratings reflects the sarcastic language used among the community in PTT online forum. To deal with this special characteristic, we need more training data to train "community"-specific sentiment lexicon to reflect the online behaviors of social media community.

## 6. Conclusion

In this paper, we have proposed a sentiment classification approach based on LSTM for short texts in social media. Using word embeddings such as Word2Vec model, it's feasible to train the contextual semantics of words in short texts. Also, deep learning methods such as LSTM show better performance of sentiment classification when there are more amounts of training data. For special community behaviors, further experiments using "community"-specific sentiment lexicon and larger data sizes are needed in future.

## References

[1] Y. Kim, "Convolutional Neural Networks for Sentence Classification," *Proceedings of the 2014 Conference on Empirical Methods in Natural Language Processing (EMNLP 2014)*, pp. 1746–1751, 2014.

[2] J. L. Elman, "Finding Structure in Time," *Cognitive Science*, Vol. 14, No.2, pp. 179-211, 1990.

[3] T. Mikolov, K. Chen, G. Corrado, and J. Dean, "Efficient Estimation of Word Representations in Vector Space," *Proceedings of the International Conference on Learning Representations 2013 Workshop*.

[4] S. Hochreiter and J. Schmidhuber, "Long Short-Term Memory," *Journal of Neural Computation*, Vol. 9 No. 8, pp. 1735-1780, 1997.

[5] G. B. Huang, Q. Y. Zhu, and C. K. Siew, "Extreme Learning Machine: Theory and Applications," *Neurocomputing*, 70 (1): 489–501, 2006.

[6] W. Yin, K. Kann, M. Yu, and H. Schütze, "Comparative Study of CNN and RNN for Natural Language Processing," *Computing Research Repository (CoRR)*, vol. abs/1702.01923, 2017.

[7] S. Hochreiter, Y. Bengio, P. Frasconi, and J. Schmidhuber, "Gradient Flow in Recurrent Nets: the Difficulty of Learning Long-Term Dependencies," In S. C. Kremer and J. F. Kolen, editors, *A Field Guide to Dynamical Recurrent Neural Networks*. IEEE Press, 2001.

[8] J. Pennington, R. Socher, and C. D. Manning, "GloVe: Global Vectors for Word Representation," *Proceedings of the 2014 Conference on Empirical Methods in Natural Language Processing (EMNLP 2014)*, pp. 1532–1543, 2014.

[9] A. L. Maas, R. E. Daly, P. T. Pham, D. Huang, A. Y. Ng, and C. Potts, "Learning Word Vectors for Sentiment Analysis," *Proceedings of the 49th Annual Meeting of the Association for Computational Linguistics: Human Language Technologies (HLT 2011)*, pp. 142-150, 2011.

The 2018 Conference on Computational Linguistics and Speech Processing
ROCLING 2018, pp. 224-235
©The Association for Computational Linguistics and Chinese Language Processing

# AI Clerk: 會賣東西的機器人

# AI Clerk: Shopping Assistant

張如瑩 潘桓毅 林柏霖 陳韋綸 謝佳恩 黃玟瑜 李律萱

Ru-Yng Chang, Huan-Yi Pan, Bo-Lin Lin, Wei-Lun Chen, Jia En Hsieh, Wen-Yu Huang, Lu-Hsuan Li

財團法人工業技術研究院 巨量資訊科技中心

Computational Intelligence Technology Center, Industrial Technology Research Institute

AIClerkMail@gmail.com

## 摘要

「AI Clerk」是一主動引導消費者購物的機器人，結合「口語式搜尋」、「個人化商品推薦」及「多元商品輔助資訊」特色。「AI Clerk」透過人工智慧中的自然語言處理、機器學習與自主學習，讓消費者不單能用傳統關鍵詞的方式獲知現存相關商品，譬如可限定搜尋條件〝蘋果〞其語意意指為一品牌，「AI Clerk」更能理解--描述性問句、專門術語、流行用語以及消費者感受用詞，所以能用如〝自拍好看的手機〞、〝CP 值高〞、〝ㄏ ㄒ ㄈ〞、〝泡菜牌〞等詞彙或句子段落得知相關商品，更能理解〝螢幕耐刮耐摔〞蘊含要找螢幕可能由大猩猩或藍寶石玻璃所製成。還整合各購物通路，並自動摘要各新聞、論壇、部落格等異質性輔助購物決策資訊之知識，讓消費者可迅速一覽商品關聯詞（含其正負評程度），如：小米 6 的關聯詞為〝耐刮耐摔〞、〝通話音量小〞，得知其優缺點與特性等，因此消費者不用認識大猩猩玻璃的特性，便可用〝螢幕耐刮耐摔〞找到符合該需求的小米 6，但也發現小米 6 有通話音量小之缺陷，大大減少消費者購物決策的時間，提升購物體驗便利性與滿意度。對產業而言，「AI Clerk」主動式精準行銷，可啟動另一營利模式，創造更多銷售額以及增加平台流量與點閱率。欲體驗「AI Clerk」，可前往 https://ai-clerk.com/。

AI-Clerk is a shopping assistant robot that can actively guide consumers to purchase, with the characteristics of colloquial searching, personal product recommendation, and providing diverse product-assistant information. Natural language processing, machine learning and self-learning in artificial intelligence was utilized in AI Clerk, therefore, customers can utilize natural language to get current related products. For example, consumers can set "apple" as a "brand" for searching condition. Moreover, AI-Clerk can understand descriptive statements, terminology, popular terminology and consumer experience words. Therefore, consumers can use sentences, phrases or words such as "mobile phone which can make a beautiful selfie",

"high price-performance ratio", "H ㄊㄈ, the words seem like HTC which is one of the best

electronic products in Taiwan, " and "smartphone from kimchi country" to find out the product they want. Even more, AI-Clerk understands that "a scratch-resistant and shock-resistant smartphone" means that the screen of smartphone must made by Gorilla Glass or Sapphire. In order to let consumers browse the related words of products quickly, AI-Clerk integrates many shopping channels, and summarize the information from news, social network articles and blogs actively. For instance, the related words of Xiaomi 6 are scratch-resistant, shock-resistant, communication with low volume, and so on. Therefore, consumers can search key words like "smartphone comes with scratch-resistant and shock-resistant" to easily find out Xiaomi 6 to meet the need, rather than understanding what characteristic the Gorilla Glass has. Besides, consumers get one of the disadvantages of Xiaomi 6 which is low communication volume. With AI-Clerk, consumers can obviously reduce their time on decision-making, upgrade shopping experience and satisfaction. For industry, AI-Clerk can actively precise marketing, which can start another business model to create more revenue and increase the flow of platform and click rate. If you want more information about AI-Clerk, search the website, https://ai-clerk.com.


關鍵詞：AI Clerk，商品搜尋，購物助理，語意理解

Keywords: AI Clerk, Product Search, Shopping Assistant, Semantic Understanding


一、背景動機

● 消費者購物決策過程中耗費許多時間

消費者有購物需求時，例如若需要一〝螢幕耐刮耐摔〞的手機，往往會先利用搜尋引擎進行資訊蒐集，在搜尋引擎上點開各網站——瀏覽、篩選，線上商務平台在消費者購物與決策過程中扮演的角色逐年加重，Google 2016 年的台灣數位消費者研究報告[1]

顯示，在台灣 69%人會於線上蒐集與搜尋感興趣或需求之商品進而進行線上或線下之
購物，商務平台提供消費者更多便利的購物體驗，但消費者在購物決策階段中耗費相當
多的時間在尋找適合自己或所需求的商品，例如買車前平均需花四個月做功課[2]，買一
個小小的奶瓶甚至花費三個星期[3]，調查顯示在購物前平均花費 19 個小時進行資訊蒐
集，假若到社群論壇請益，不一定能得到回應，甚至會被噓，請發問者先自行做功課，
此外，相關資訊散布在各網站，不夠集中，可能好不容易搜尋到符合條件的商品，譬如：
小米 6 這支手機具有螢幕耐刮耐摔之特性，卻在其它平台發現小米 6 竟然有通話音量小
這個個人狀況不能容許的缺點，又或者到購物網站上才發現符合條件的手機竟然已經停
售了，所以只好重新開始商品資訊蒐集的動作。此外，有 70%消費者則表示對購物搜尋
不滿意，72%消費者會因搜尋效益變好增加購物意圖[4]。

- **無法理解特殊領域商品專業術語是消費者購物決策過程中的痛**

消費者因為不曉得大猩猩或藍寶石玻璃所製成的手機螢幕變具有螢幕耐刮耐摔之
特性，因此耗費了相當多時間在搜尋和學習。大量消費者不了解的專業術語存在於許多
特殊領域的商品，如 3C 商品、汽車、美妝、保健商品等等，導致消費者無法精確描述
自己的需求，調查顯示有 85％有此困擾[5]，消費者在線上平台無法尋找符合個人需求
的商品，因此消費者在購買這類複雜商品時往往還是習慣性前往實體店面尋求協助，實
體店面需持續保有一定知識的專員花費時間了解消費者的需求，但最後消費者可能卻不
在該店面購買。

- **他山之石：KAKAKU 便利購物體驗，創造日本電子商務入口第一品牌，但仍無法
解決消費者購物決策過程的某些痛點**

在日本，五分之一日本人在購物前會至 Kakaku 價格.com[6][7]進行資訊蒐集，該
網站於 1997 年成立，2003 年上市，在 2013 年起進攻東南亞各國市場，在 2014 年創造
突破 305 億日幣營收。Kakaku 最大的吸引力在於它為了減少消費者在購物決策階段的
痛，讓商品供應商根據表單提供重要規格資訊，持續累積商品資訊豐富性，並針對每種
類商品設計回饋表單，設定口碑回饋機制，讓消費者填寫並連結常拿來比較之商品，才
得以蒐集到消費者所需的商品資訊和評論等。為達這些目的從其財報推估，Kakaku 每
個月約需花費 7410 萬日圓獎勵消費者填寫回饋資訊 [8]，但消費者仍僅能以如限定品
牌為 HTC 的檢索值進行檢索，無法以類似〝螢幕耐刮耐摔〞的方式進行檢索，消費者

還是必須花許多時間瞭解各商品不斷推陳出新的專門術語的意義（譬如：螢幕以大猩猩或藍寶石玻璃製成表示具耐刮耐摔之特性），挖掘各商品的優缺點，才能尋覓到滿足個人該此消費需求的商品。

於印尼、馬來西亞、菲律賓、新加坡、泰國、越南經營電商平台的 Lazada[9]是東南亞第一大電商平台，為讓消費者可以輸入類似搜尋條件為品牌是 HTC 的檢索值進行檢索，根據該公司新加坡 VP Engineering 透露光新加坡地區每個月就必須耗費 100 人力處理一千萬個商品資訊的雜訊，而消費者於購物決策階段的其它需求也仍未滿足。

● **現今產業聊天機器人僅能解決回答常見問題的客服人力成本，無法創造營收**

近年，許多產業為了滿足消費者商務體驗以及減少客服人力需求情形，大量引入聊天機器人，希望透過不眠不休的機器人來協助消費者解決問題，但現行的聊天機器人絕大多數為 FAQ 機器人，也就是僅能處理常見且不管任何人發問都是同樣解答的問題，如：〝送貨到台灣約需幾天？〞，但單光為達此目的，產業必須持續耗費時間以及人力成本建置知識庫才能讓機器人回答更多使用者問句，仍無法進一步協助解決消費者在購物決策中心中的疑惑，並進一步促使消費者購物成交率上升。除此之外，一般消費者的問句中常有大量的口語詞彙，如：〝CP 值高〞、〝泡菜機〞、〝拍照效果好〞，大多數的聊天機器人無法理解口語詞彙，對消費者的購物體驗是大打折扣的。

結合上述，為了解決消費者以及產業的問題，本論文提出一個能主動引導消費者購物的機器人「AI Clerk」，對消費者的亮點是「口語式搜尋」，「AI Clerk」能針對消費者各種口語問句給予個人化推薦，消費者不但無須了解專門術語，並且可以維持日常的問答方式，就可以立即推薦符合他們需求的商品和由各新聞、論壇、部落格、購物平台等異質性資料來源之相關輔助購物決策的彙整知識。對消費者而言，大大減少購物決策中資訊蒐集的時間，增加購物體驗便利性，提升其滿意度；而對於產業，「AI Clerk」有別於傳統聊天機器人，無須持續投入大量人力與時間成本建置知識庫，就能擁有超越一般聊天機器人的效果，進而達到精準行銷，提升銷售額以及增加平台流量與點閱率，且過程中累積形成「商品資訊與消費者行為之結構化歷史知識庫」還可作為資料販售或研發其它智慧應用服務的基礎，增加多項獲利來源。

## 二、相關系統

### ● 購物網站商品搜尋類

　　PChome[10]為台灣電商界龍頭，其商品搜尋模式為比對關鍵詞，意即只要商品標題或內文有出現跟消費者所下關鍵詞相同的字眼，不管其代表意義是否相同，該商品都會被推薦，也就是說當消費者輸入〝白色蘋果手機〞或〝白色　蘋果　手機〞，消費者真正的意圖最有可能是想要找到〝蘋果品牌顏色為白色的手機〞，然而輸出的結果卻很有可能會包含適用於〝蘋果手機〞的某一白色商品。此種商品搜尋模式並無法完全理解消費者下的搜尋關鍵詞的真正意義，因此更無法精準推薦消費者合適的商品。MOMO 購物網[11]為僅次於 PChome 的台灣第二大網路購物業平台。其商品搜尋模式與 PChome 的不同之處在於，MOMO 將該網站內商品標題、商品簡介及消費者所下之搜尋關鍵詞做語意理解，只有在關鍵詞及其語意都符合時，商品才會被推薦，也就是不會出現 PChome 搜尋的窘境，此搜尋模式能更精準的命中消費者心中所需，但可惜商品簡介裡充斥的專門術語且搜索範圍鎖定在該網站中商品簡介所呈現的文字。TAOBAO 淘寶[12]為一面向台灣、中國大陸、香港、澳門等大中華地區與馬來西亞的購物網站，其商品搜尋模式為根據消費者所下關鍵詞與近期累積之消費者行為分析，推薦符合該消費者所下關鍵詞的商品，然而因同性質的商品數量龐大，消費者仍需耗費相當多時間進行篩選。

### ● 購物助理類

　　世界知名購物網 eBay 為了增加購物體驗與促進購物成交率，推出 eBay ShopBot[13]，讓消費者透過 Facebook Messenger 使用 eBay ShopBot，可輸入商品品項名中的特定字串，便會出現該商品，eBay ShopBot 訴求強項在於透過消費者多次輸入和購買習慣可得知消費者慣用尺寸等，顯示符合消費者個人偏好尺寸之該商品，但它僅接受商品品項名稱之字串搜尋。

　　國內購物助理，如：瑞艾科技 Bella 虛擬機器人[14]、宇匯知識科技[15]、網際智慧[16]、優拓資訊[17]、竹間智能[18]等，目前停留在常見問題之處理。

### ● 現今產業遭遇的技術問題：缺乏領域知識庫，需持續耗費大量人力與時間成本。

　　產業為了滿足消費者之需求，如：以口語化方式詢問、不用瞭解專門術語等，會遭遇的技術問題包含缺乏專門領域知識庫，尤其隨著商品不斷推陳出新會有更多新穎的專門術語和屬性，商品也會隨時退場，知識庫必須持續不斷更新，這必須藉由大量專業人力持續介入，針對個別商品和領域資料建立與維護知識庫，且不同領域商品屬性和知識範疇落差過大，更必須針對不同領域知識建立不同知識結構，預估所付出的成本勢必非常龐大。

## 三、AI Clerk

「AI Clerk」是主動式引導消費者購物的人工智慧機器人，消費者可以透過打字或是語音輸入他們習慣的詞彙或問句，就可以立即推薦興趣商品，進而提供多元化的彙整資料，輔助他們的購物決策，使消費者可以方便的在機器人上購物，總結來說「AI Clerk」主要有以下三大功能特色：

● **個人化商品推薦**

「AI Clerk」是進階的人工智慧機器人，有別於傳統的聊天機器人只能透過知識庫建構一對一或多對一問答，「AI Clerk」可給予個人化的回覆，可以應用於常見的客服機器人，提升諮詢的能力之外，更可以發展如購物諮詢等進階應用，「AI Clerk」就像真正的售貨員，能即時有效率的推薦顧客興趣商品，引導他們購物。

● **語意聯想**

「AI Clerk」不單能理解商品名稱、規格、成分、屬性、功能、特性，「AI Clerk」利用自然語言處理的「語意理解」技術，更可以理解使用者的口語式問句，像與真實的人進行應答，例如〝適合玩遊戲〞、〝續航力佳〞、〝CP 值高〞，「AI Clerk」可以自動進行語意理解了解使用者的真正需求，準確地推薦正確商品。

除此之外，「AI Clerk」也透過「大數據分析」學習商品之關聯資訊，能理解網路上的流行用語的含義，例如〝子龍機〞代表 Asus、〝泡菜牌〞代表韓國品牌、〝ZF2D〞是 ZenFone 2 Deluxe 的縮寫等等，或是聯想專業術語的對應功能，〝螢幕耐刮耐摔的手機〞蘊含消費者可能需要由大猩猩玻璃或是藍寶石玻璃所製成的手機，有效得提升語意聯想的能力，「AI Clerk」可以準確得解決各種使用者的購物問題。

表 一彙整「AI Clerk」所支援之語意聯想功能類別與其例句。

表 一、「AI Clerk」所支援之語意聯想功能類別與其例句

| 語意聯想功能 | 例句 |
| --- | --- |
| 商品關鍵詞 | HTC |
| 描述性問句 | 續航力佳、平價、拍照好的大螢幕手機、適合玩遊戲、長輩用手機 |
| 消費者感受用詞 | 通話音量小、CP 值高 |
| 專門術語理解 | ZF2D＝ZenFone 2 Deluxe<br><br>螢幕耐刮耐摔＝大猩猩玻璃、藍寶石玻璃 |
| 流行用語理解 | ㄏㄊㄈ、泡菜牌、子龍機 |
| 設定排除條件 | 不要大陸牌、不考慮ㄏㄊㄈ |

圖 一、「AI Clerk」釋例一

- **多元輔助資訊彙整**

「AI Clerk」背後的演算法可以整理出最豐富且最相關的資訊，提供給使用者輔助購物決策，從基本的各類購物來源的商品資訊比較、相關論壇輔助文章及新聞，到商品在社群中的正負評論、商品關聯詞彙等等，讓使用者發現需要商品之外，也讓使用者了解商品的所有必要資訊，如商品特點、優缺點等，有效降低大量的購物搜尋以及決策時間。

圖 一和圖 二 顯示諮詢「AI Clerk」結果，與進一步點入看詳細商品資訊的畫面。

圖 二、「AI Clerk」釋例二

## 四、AI Clerk 技術解決方案之特色

「AI Clerk」從結構化與非結構化資料來源中，以深度學習(Deep Learning)不斷辨識與推論出與商品相關的詞彙，以結構化方式儲存著與商品和使用者行為的資訊，逐漸累積形成「商品資訊與消費者行為之結構化歷史知識庫」，而且透過自主學習技術，學習更新知識庫，使其蘊含最新資訊，節省大量人力成本，也避免商品淘汰卻出現的窘狀。

傳統相關技術研發過程多經三階段(1)人工標記與建置知識庫(2)模組建立(3)錯誤分

析。藉由錯誤分析結果，不斷回饋與進行模組修正，而人工標記與建置知識庫佔了技術研發過程幾乎 95%以上的時間與人力。「AI Clerk」所採用的技術只需人工建置小量知識庫，進行自動擴充。以 3C 類商品進行實驗評估，發現可減少 99.5%以上人工蒐集和建置知識庫的時間，假設原本每個月需要聘僱 100 個人力（每月需聘僱 100 人力的參考依據為 Lazada 新加坡地區 每月花 100 人力處理 1000 萬個商品資訊的雜訊，僅可達到類似限定搜尋條件為品牌是 HTC 之檢索效益。），以基本薪資 2 萬 2 千計算，等於至少節省 218.9 萬元成本（99.5*22,000 元），便可達到與完全以人工建置知識庫為基底所建立之模組相抗衡的結果；實驗比對，加上自動擴充知識庫所運行之模組，其效能甚至可能超越僅以純人工知識庫所建立之模組。

累積形成「商品資訊與消費者行為之結構化歷史知識庫」該知識庫蘊含彙整後的商品相關知識，並逐漸累積使用者行為，以及使用者和商品之間的關聯行為資訊，可藉由知識庫的販售增加獲利模式。除此之外，該知識庫將促使「AI Clerk」越加升級，提供更符合消費者個人特質與偏好的商品推薦。該知識庫，也可成為進一步研發出其它智慧應用服務的基礎，研發出更多智慧型應用服務。

## 五、AI Clerk 之產業效益

針對產業，「AI Clerk」就像是多了全方面且 24 小時工作的購物專員，隨時協助消費者尋找商品以及引導購物，而且建置成本相對低廉，「AI Clerk」主要有以下三大效益：

- **增加產品銷售**

我們的機器人可以進行購物諮詢，直接媒合給使用者興趣商品達到精準行銷的同時，也引導了使用者消費，替產業增加更多銷售的機會，這也是我們與市面上的聊天機器人最大的不同之處。

- **不需持續大量人力建立知識庫**

傳統聊天機器人需要產業提供大量知識庫，而我們透過大數據分析，學習最新商品關聯資訊以及使用者口語問句，讓產業不需要持續投入大量人力建置知識庫，減少了企業的成本。

- **更少成本更多智慧服務**

「AI Clerk」會逐漸形成「商品資訊與消費者行為之結構化歷史知識庫」，讓產業可以了解消費者需求，除了達到精準行銷、研發或庫存成本降低，更可進一步衍生出其它智慧型應用服務。

● **Mobile01「小惡魔市集」實際市場驗證**

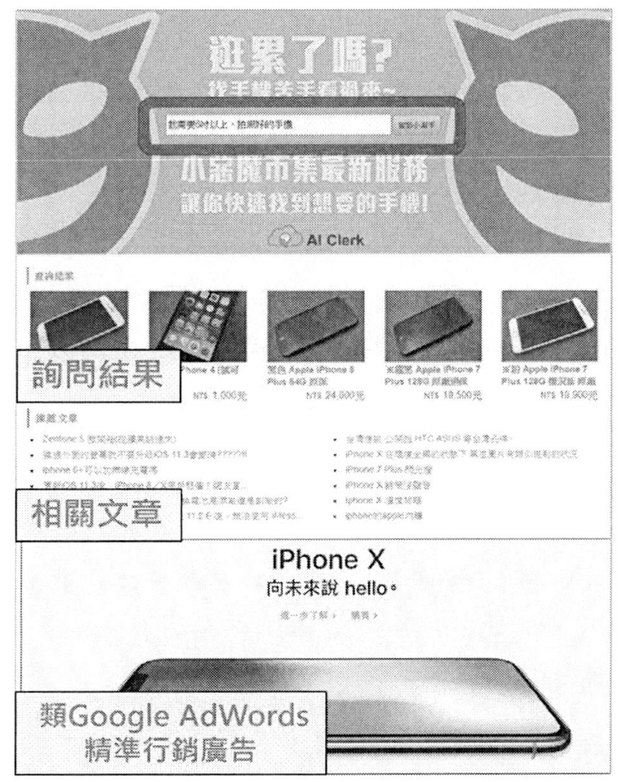


圖 三、Mobile01 小惡魔市集與「AI Clerk」的結合

目前「AI Clerk」部分概念已於全球華人最注目的 3C 社群網站 Mobile01[19]上線，在其二手交易市集「小惡魔市集」（https://www.mobile01.com/ ）[20]以手機類商品進行初步實際市場驗證。

消費者只要在 Mobile01 小惡魔市集輸入所要的手機條件，就會出現該市集上符合條件的拍賣商品，且系統將會進一步找出 Mobile01 社群討論區和小惡魔新聞中最符合該諮詢條件的商品其品牌或型號的的相關文章。未來將讓廣告主投播各商品的廣告，當消費輸入所需商品之條件後，系統還會將符合條件且已經下廣告的商品呈現出，也就是 Mobile01 因此多了類似 Google AdWords 的獲利模式。圖 三 顯示 Mobile01 小惡魔市集目前系統畫面結合未來廣告獲利模式之示意圖。

原本消費者習慣在購物前經過搜尋引擎，導引到 Mobile01 做購物前的資料蒐集，但消費者最可能的行為是繼續透過搜尋引擎找其它相關文章，所以消費者很可能不會繼續瀏覽 Mobile01 上的文章，現在透過 Mobile01 與「AI Clerk」的結合，消費者在小惡魔市集進行購物搜尋時，除了搜尋時系統已經協助其找出符合條件的商品，還可繼續瀏覽系統已協助篩選的相關文章，消費前購物決策體驗大大提升便利感。對 Mobile01 而言，透過更多的消費者網站黏著度與瀏覽量，進而增進其廣告收益，且多了類似 Google AdWords 的獲利模式。

六、結論

本論文提出一結合「口語式搜尋」、「個人化商品推薦」及「多元商品輔助資訊」特色主動引導消費者購物的機器人「AI Clerk」。有別於現存之購物助理或購物搜尋引擎，「AI Clerk」是以自然語言處理、機器學習與自主學習技術，讓消費者不單能用傳統關鍵詞的方式獲知現存相關商品，更能理解詞彙或句子段落形式的描述性問句、專門術語、流行用語和消費者感受用詞，所以能理解如〝自拍好看的手機〞、〝CP 值高〞、〝Ｈ ㄒㄈ〞、〝泡菜牌〞等語意顯示相關商品，更能理解〝螢幕耐刮耐摔〞意指要找螢幕由大猩猩或藍寶石玻璃所製成。並且自動學習摘要各異質性輔助購物決策資訊之知識，讓消費者可迅速一覽商品關聯詞（含其正負評程度），因此消費者不用認識商品的專門術語，便可用自然語彙找到符合需求之相關商品，甚至發覺可所需商品，以及各商品之特色與優缺點，可大幅減少消費者購物決策的時間，提升購物體驗滿意度。「AI Clerk」主動式精準行銷，也可啟動另一營利模式，創造更多銷售額以及增加平台流量與點閱率。


## 參考文獻


[1] Google，2016，台灣數位消費者研究報告。

[2] 買車前花 4 個月做功課？J.D. Power 說現代人愈來愈喜歡用網路找新車資訊，
https://goo.gl/uX2fYt

[3] [專訪]MamiBuy 媽咪拜創辦人兼執行長雍承書，
https://innoservice.org/9633/%E5%B0%88%E8%A8%AAmamibuy%E5%AA%BD%E5%92%AA%E6%8B%9C%E5%89%B5%E8%BE%A6%E4%BA%BA%E5%85%BC%E5%9F%B7%E8%A1%8C%E9%95%B7%E9%9B%8D%E6%89%BF%E6%9B%B8/

[4] 陳豫德，2010，台灣搜尋平台市場分析研究報告。

[5] Michael Mokhberi, 2011, Intelligent Search, https://prezi.com/7i_ui216bubd/intelligent-search/

[6] 五分之一的日本人買東西前都會先上的日本最大比價勸敗網站：Kakaku.com，https://www.inside.com.tw/2011/08/08/kakaku-com-introduction

[7] Kakaku 價格.com，http://kakaku.com/

[8] KAKAKU.COM Financial data, http://corporate.kakaku.com/ir/financial.html?lang=en

[9] Lazada, https://www.lazada.com/

[10] PChome 線上購物，https://shopping.pchome.com.tw/

[11] MOMO 購物網，https://www.momoshop.com.tw/

[12] TAOBAO 淘寶，https://world.taobao.com/

[13] eBay's ShopBot: Your new personal shopper, https://shopbot.ebay.com/

[14] 瑞艾科技 Bella 虛擬機器人，http://rai.dscloud.me/

[15] 宇匯知識科技，http://www.bridgewell.com.tw/

[16] 網際智慧，https://global.iq-t.com/

[17] 優拓資訊，https://www.yoctol.com/

[18] 竹間智能，http://www.emotibot.com/

[19] Mobile01，https://www.mobile01.com/

[20] Mobile01 小惡魔市集，https://www.mobile01.com/mpindex.php

The 2018 Conference on Computational Linguistics and Speech Processing
ROCLING 2018, pp. 236-245
©The Association for Computational Linguistics and Chinese Language Processing

# 結合卷積神經網路與遞迴神經網路於推文極性分類

# Combining Convolutional Neural Network and Recurrent Neural Network for Tweet Polarity Classification

葉致廷　Chih-Ting Yeh
國立中山大學資訊工程學系
Department of Computer Science and Information Engineering
National Sun Yat-sen University
M063040008@student.nsysu.edu.tw


陳嘉平　Chia-Ping Chen
國立中山大學資訊工程學系
Department of Computer Science and Information Engineering
National Sun Yat-sen University
cpchen@mail.cse.nsysu.edu.tw

## 摘要

隨著網路日漸發達，不分男女老少均常常使用社群網站來分享生活瑣事或是評論時事，每天產生的訊息量十分可觀，若我們去分析這些資訊得到社會大眾對事件的好惡，便可以更容易地去做較佳的決策。本文以 Twitter 做為研究對象，針對英語推文進行情緒分析，我們使用 Tweepy 從 Twitter 上收集推文，並用於訓練詞向量（Word Vector），然後使用卷積神經網路（Convolutional Neural Network，CNN）對訓練好的詞向量進行微調，使其帶有情緒特徵，之後再用於遞迴神經網路（Recurrent Neural Network，RNN）進行訓練，得出最後極性分類的結果，我們的系統使用 SemEval-2018 Task1: Affect in Tweets 子任務 V-oc 的資料集進行訓練，且與競賽結果做比較，落在大約第五名的成績。

## Abstract

With the development of the Internet, male and female, old and young, often use social network to share the trivia of everyday things and comment on current affairs. The amount of information generated every day is very considerable. If we analyze those data to get the impressions from society, we can easier to make better decisions. This paper chooses Twitter as the research subject and conduct sentiment analysis on English tweets. We use Tweepy to collect tweets on Twitter and use them to train word vector. After that, the trained word vector is fine-tuned to have emotional features by Convolutional Neural Network (CNN) . Then, the fine-tuned vector is used for training in the Recurrent Neural Network (RNN) to get the final polarity classification results. Our system uses the dataset of the subtask V-oc of SemEval-2018 Task1: Affect in Tweets for training. Compared to the results of competition, we are in the fifth place.

關鍵詞：情緒分析，極性分類，詞向量

Keywords: Sentiment Analysis, Polarity Classification, Word Vector.


一、緒論

近年來機器學習蓬勃發展，在文字的極性分類上也有相當的貢獻。在文字方面的任務中，為了讓電腦能理解人類的文字，我們需要將每個詞轉換成詞向量，若兩個詞的詞向量距離愈近則表示兩個詞的意義相近，愈遠則表示意思相差愈遠，Word2vec [1]、GloVe [2]、fastText [3]都是常見訓練詞向量的方法，而訓練出來詞向量的優劣會大大的影響極性分類的結果。在分類模型方面，無論是 CNN 模型 [4]、RNN 模型 [5]，均取得比傳統基於統計的方法更好的成果。在 CNN 模型中，使用不同大小的卷積核（Kernel）代表一次讓神經網路看多少個詞並取出它們的情緒特徵，若卷積核大小為 1 則代表一次看一個詞，若為 2 則一次看兩個詞，並透過最大池化找出對情緒影響最大的詞或詞組，最後得出分類結果。而在 RNN 模型中，則常使用長短期記憶（Long Short-Term Memory，LSTM）[6]來處理，整合整句句子的涵義然後做出判斷。兩種模型架構所注重的重點不同，CNN 偏向找出影響最大的詞或詞組，而 RNN 則是針對整句句子得出結果。
在我們的模型系統中，我們結合 CNN 與 RNN 的優點，利用 CNN 偏重於「詞」的特性，在訓練情緒分析的神經網路時允許反向傳播（Back Propagation）至嵌入層的詞向量，使詞向量帶有情緒特徵[7]，來解決詞向量可能正負面情緒詞之間距離過於接近，而使神經網路無法得知該詞為正面情感或負面情感的問題。接著我們使用調整後的詞向量於偏重「句子」的 RNN 模型中訓練。在 RNN 模型中，由於在我們主要做為評估標準的 SemEval-2018 Task1: Affect in Tweets 子任務 V-oc 為七類 +3 到 -3 的情緒分類問題 [8]，+3 表示最正面的情緒、-3 表示最負面的情緒、0 則是中性情緒，而 SemEval-2017 與之前的資料皆為三類情緒分別為 -1、0、+1 的資料，+1 為正面情緒、-1 為負面情緒、

0 為中性情緒，資料分布情形如表一。為了擴展訓練資料，我們先利用 SemEval-2017 [9]
的三類資料訓練三類模型，得到能抓到「句子」的三類情緒特徵 RNN 權重，並將這個
權重做為接下來訓練的七類模型的初始權重，使七類模型能先抓出三類的特徵再進而分
成七類，以提升準確率，最終我們以七類模型的分類結果為最後的分類結果[10]。
本文主要分為四個部分：第一部分為緒論；第二部分為研究方法，介紹資料的使用方式
與實驗流程；第三部分為實驗結果，介紹實驗的設定與結果；第四部分為結論。

表一、使用資料分布情形

| 名稱 | 正向 | | | 中性 | 負面 | | |
|---|---|---|---|---|---|---|---|
| | 1 | | | 0 | -1 | | |
| | 3 | 2 | 1 | 0 | -1 | -2 | -3 |
| SemEval-2017-ALL | 9434 | | | 16279 | 7203 | | |
| SemEval-2018 訓練集 | 125 | 92 | 167 | 341 | 78 | 249 | 129 |
| SemEval-2018 驗證集 | 53 | 35 | 58 | 105 | 34 | 95 | 69 |
| SemEval-2018 測試集 | 137 | 91 | 107 | 262 | 80 | 167 | 93 |

## 二、研究方法

### （一）、預訓練詞向量

Twitter 上的推文不僅有字數的限制，推文通常都是短短的句子，句子內容包含各種 emoji
與表情符號，文法也不如其他語料庫拘謹，甚至常會有各式英文縮寫出現，如：OMG
（Oh My God）等。因此，若是使用一般語料庫訓練詞向量會有大量的表情符號或網路
上流行的縮寫無法包含其中，而這些部分往往都是情緒最強烈的地方，所以我們採用自
行從 Twitter 收集推文的方式，藉由 Twitter 官方提供的 Tweepy 這項工具來取得推文，
收集期間為 2/27 至 4/13，推文數約 22,000,000 則，詞彙量約 192,000 個詞，表二為英文
維基百科語料庫與自行收集之推文資料集在 SemEval-2018 訓練集上是否找到對應詞彙
的狀況，可以發現到自行收集的推文資料集在 Twitter 這個文法不拘謹且有非常多新創
詞的領域上，表現優於詞彙量為十倍的英文維基語料庫，有更好的對應關係。

表二、英文維基百科與自行收集推文詞彙對應狀況之比較

| 名稱 | 詞彙量 | 未對應詞彙量 |
| --- | --- | --- |
| 英文維基百科語料庫 | 2,287,131 | 322 / 4419 |
| Tweepy 自行收集推文 | 192,307 | 163 / 4419 |

同時，我們也對收集的推文前處理[5]，包含全部轉為小寫、標記全大寫強調的詞或 hash tag 的詞、將使用者名稱、網址統一標記為<USER>與<URL>，以減低詞彙的複雜度，之後在訓練情緒分析模型的資料也經一致的前處理，以達到最好的效果。

在訓練詞向量的方式上，我們使用 Word2vec 中的 Skip-gram [11]模型來進行詞向量的訓練，如圖一，假設有個句子：You look good in that dress，Skip-gram 會選句子中的一個詞的詞向量為目標詞做為輸入，輸出為整個詞彙表的 softmax 機率，目標詞左右窗口內的詞機率愈大愈好。若目標詞為 good，窗口大小為 c = 2，則希望輸出 You、look、in、that 的機率愈高愈好，並由此來更新詞向量。但這類訓練詞向量的方式常因正負面情緒詞出現在句子中的位置相近，容易將正反義詞誤認為相似的詞而使兩者之間詞向量的距離十分接近，如有另一個句子：You look bad in that dress，這也是一個合理也常見但意義卻完全相反的句子，在選擇 bad 做為目標詞時，左右窗口的詞一樣，也皆希望輸出 You、look、in、that 的機率愈高愈好，使 good 與 bad 的詞向量會十分的接近，這點不利於情緒分析的任務，在下一小節中，我們將會減緩這個問題。

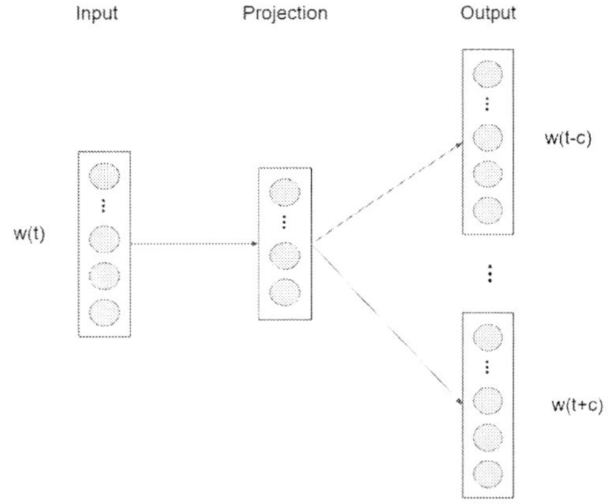


圖一、Skip-gram 模型架構

（二）、七類推文極性分類系統

我們分類七類情緒共使用三個模型，分別是 CNN 七類模型、RNN 三類模型以及 RNN
七類模型，整體模型架構圖如圖二。

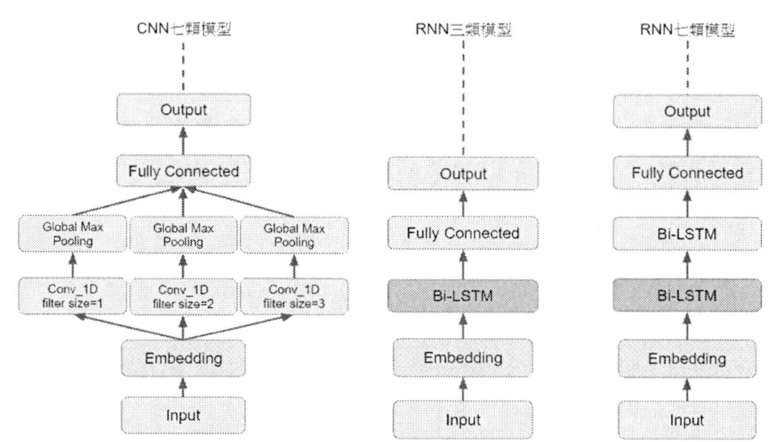


圖二、推文極性分類整體架構圖

CNN 七類模型如圖三所示，在這個模型中，我們使用 SemEval-2018 Task1: Affect in
Tweets 子任務 V-oc 之七類訓練資料，但這個模型並非得到最終分類結果的模型，而是
藉由此模型來對嵌入層（Embedding Layer）中的詞向量進行微調，用反向傳播至嵌入
層的方式，使正面情緒與負面情緒的詞向量不再那麼接近，並將這份調整過的詞向量用
於接下來 RNN 模型的嵌入層上，如圖二中黃色部分所示，以幫助我們在之後的訓練過
程中，更好的進行情緒的分類。

在此模型，在詞嵌入後經過大小分別為 1、2、3 的卷積核，相當於以一元語法（Unigram）、
二元語法（Bigram）、三元語法（Trigram）的角度來看推文，並各自取 Global max pooling
找出影響最大的 n-gram 並串接在一起，最後得出分類結果，且允許反向傳播至嵌入層，
調整詞向量，並將這份調整過後的詞向量給後續的模型使用。

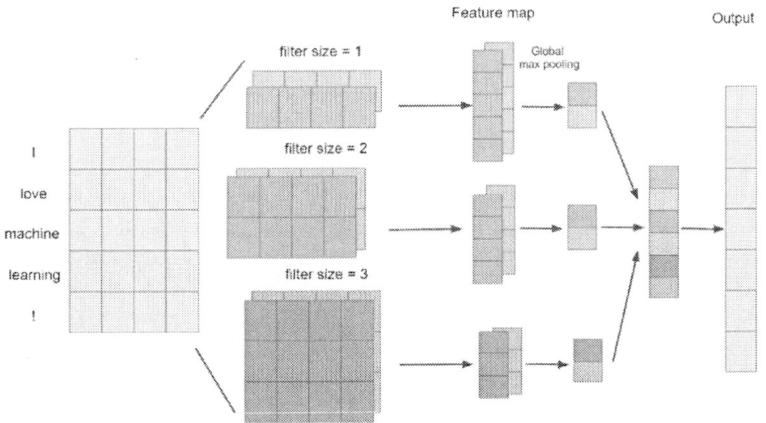

圖三、CNN 七類模型

RNN 三類模型如圖四所示，所使用的資料為 SemEval-2017 的三類資料，此模型由一層的雙向長短期記憶（Bidirectional LSTM，Bi-LSTM）構成，主要的目的為取出 Bi-LSTM 的權重，並用於最後 RNN 七類模型中初始化第一層 Bi-LSTM 的權重，如圖二綠色部分所示，使七類模型能先將推文句子中找出三類的特徵，再藉由第二層的 Bi-LSTM 進一步分成七類的情緒。

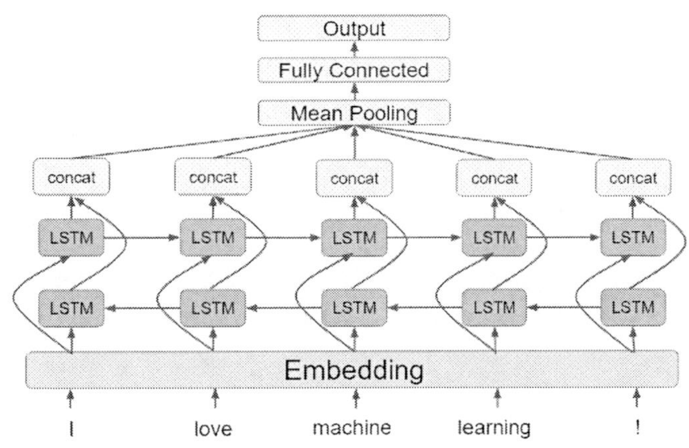

圖四、RNN 三類模型

RNN 七類模型如圖五所示，使用資料為 SemEval-2018 的七類資料，也是得出最後極性分類結果的模型，由兩層的 Bi-LSTM 所組成，第一層 Bi-LSTM 由 RNN 三類模型訓練得出的權重初始化，且採用注意力機制（Attention）[12]，使句子中重要的地方有著較高影響最後極性分類的能力，公式如下：

$$M = tanh(W_{att}X + b_{att})  \tag{1}$$

$$\alpha = softmax(\omega^T M)  \tag{2}$$

$$r = X\alpha^T  \tag{3}$$

假設輸入長度為 $N$，$d$ 為第二層 Bi-LSTM 輸出的維度、$X \in \mathbb{R}^{d \times N}$ 為第二層 Bi-LSTM 各時間的輸出 $[x_1, ..., x_N]$ 所組成的矩陣、$M \in \mathbb{R}^{d \times N}$、$W_{att} \in \mathbb{R}^{d \times d}$、$\omega \in \mathbb{R}^d$、$\alpha \in \mathbb{R}^N$、$r \in \mathbb{R}^d$。$X$ 先經過一層的全連接層轉換，且為了保留負值選擇 tanh 為激活函數，接著再乘以 $\omega^T$ 後做 softmax，得出句子中各位置的權重，句子中較重要能分辨情緒的地方會有較高的權重，最後將 $X$ 乘以注意力權重，即可得到句子經注意力機制整合後的輸出 $r$。

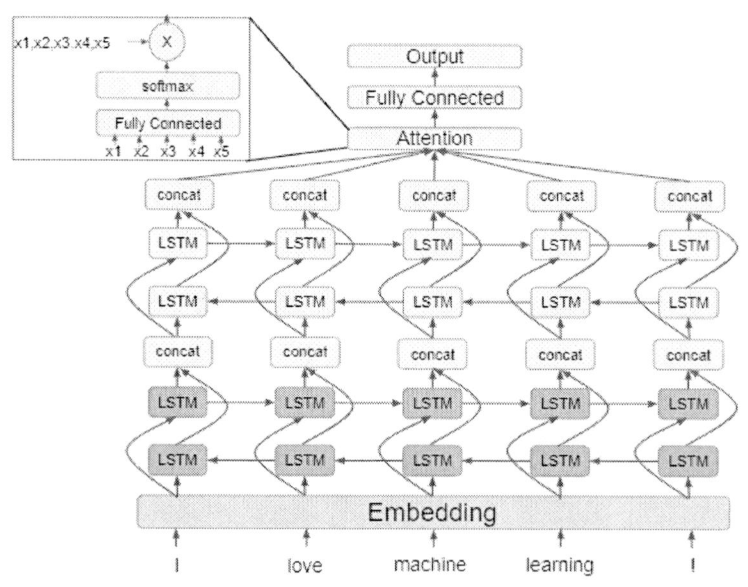


圖五、RNN 七類模型

## 三、實驗結果

本文實驗所使用資料如表一，可以發現 SemEval-2018 的訓練資料相較之下十分稀少，這也是我們需要 RNN 三類模型訓練出來的權重先幫忙做初步分成三類的主要原因，而自行收集的推文數量雖多，但未標記情緒，所以僅用來訓練詞向量。

表三、實驗資料使用狀況

| 訓練資料 | 推文數 | 使用時機 |
| --- | --- | --- |
| 自行收集之推文 | 22,000,000 | 預訓練詞向量 |
| SemEval-2017 | 32,916 | RNN 三類模型 |
| SemEval-2018 | 1,181 | CNN 七類模型、RNN 七類模型 |

在 CNN 七類模型中，共有三個不同大小的卷積核，大小分別為 1、2、3，卷積核的數目均為 200。RNN 三類模型與 RNN 七類模型使用的 Bi-LSTM 正向與反向的維度均為 200 維，雙向合計共 400 維。

在訓練過程中，學習率設為 0.001，且採用 Early stopping 的機制，若連續 10 個 epochs 驗證集的損失沒有下降，則判斷為已收斂並停止訓練，防止過度擬合於訓練資料。三個模型所使用的損失函數皆為交叉熵（Cross Entropy）。

最後所得到的實驗結果如表二，在 SemEval-2018 競賽中使用皮爾森相關係數（Pearson Correlation Coefficient，PCC.）來進行評估，公式如下：

$$\rho_{y_{true}, y_{pred}} = \frac{cov(y_{true}, y_{pred})}{\sigma_{y_{true}} \sigma_{y_{pred}}} \tag{4}$$

分子部分為推文的真實類別與神經網路預測的類別之共變異數（Covariance），標示兩者的相關性，當真實類別為 +3 最強烈正面情緒時，模型預測的類別愈正向則相關性愈高，同樣當真實類別為 -3 時，也同樣模型預測類別愈負面則相關性愈高，分母部分為真實類別的標準差（Standard Deviation）與預測類別的標準差相乘，將共變異數正規化至 +1 到 -1 之間。由實驗結果可以發現，在我們三模型的系統中若少掉任一模型 PCC. 均有下降，若少掉 RNN 三類模型，則七類模型第一層 Bi-LSTM 採用隨機初始化，需從頭訓練無法先抓出三類的特徵；若少掉 CNN 七類模型，則詞向量未經過微調，情緒極性分類的效果下降。在我們的三模型架構下，最終得到 0.800 的 PCC.，對比 SemEval-2018 Task1: Affect in Tweets 子任務 V-oc 的競賽結果，大約落在第五名的成績。

表四、實驗結果與比較

| 實驗方法 | Acc. | PCC. |
|---|---|---|
| RNN 七類模型 | 0.350 | 0.743 |
| CNN 七類模型 ＋RNN 七類模型 | 0.367 | 0.759 |
| RNN 三類模型 ＋RNN 七類模型 | 0.371 | 0.783 |
| CNN 七類模型 ＋RNN 三類模型 ＋RNN 七類模型 | **0.414** | **0.800** |

## 四、結論

我們使用 CNN 模型來微調詞向量，並使用 RNN 模型先擷取三類句子的情緒特徵，之後藉由七類模型得到最後推文極性分類的結果，結合了 CNN 與 RNN 的特性，PCC.也來到了 0.800。但我們雖然用了 CNN 來舒緩詞向量正負情緒詞可能會過於相似的問題，不過這個問題仍未完全的解決，除了對訓練完的詞向量微調的方法之外，也許可以直接從詞向量的訓練著手，更能根本的解決問題，這也是未來值得研究的課題。

在極性分類的模型方面，文字這類連續的資料非常適合強化學習（Reinforcement learning），且強化學習在其他領域如圍棋的 AlphaGo 等，皆有十分出色的表現，若我們能藉由強化學習找出句子或文字的特徵，相信準確率也會有所提升。

## 參考文獻


[1]  T. Mikolov, K. Chen, G. Corrado, and J. Dean, "Efficient estimation of word representations in vector space," arXiv preprint arXiv1301.3781, 2013.

[2]  J. Pennington, R. Socher, and C. Manning. "Glove: Global vectors for word representation," Proceedings of the 2014 conference on empirical methods in natural language processing (EMNLP), 2014.

[3]  A. Joulin, E. Grave, P. Bojanowski, and T. Mikolov, "Bag of tricks for efficient text classification," arXiv preprint arXiv:1607.01759, 2016

[4]  H. Hamden, "Senti17 at SemEval-2017 Task 4: Ten Convolutional Neural Network

Voters for Tweet Polarity Classification," arXiv preprint arXiv:1705.02023, 2017.

[5] C. Baziotis, N. Pelekis, and C. Doulkeridis. "Datastories at semeval-2017 task 4: Deep lstm with attention for message-level and topic-based sentiment analysis," In: Proceedings of the 11th International Workshop on Semantic Evaluation (SemEval-2017), pp. 747-754, 2017.

[6] F.A. Gers, J. Schmidhuber, and F. Cummins," Learning to forget: Continual prediction with LSTM", 1999.

[7] M. Cliché, "BB_twtr at SemEval-2017 Task 4: Twitter Sentiment Analysis with CNNs and LSTMs," arXiv preprint arXiv:1704.06125, 2017.

[8] S. Mohammad, F. Bravo-Marquez, and M. Salameh, "Semeval-2018 task 1: Affect in tweets," In: Proceedings of The 12th International Workshop on Semantic Evaluation, pp. 1-17, 2018.

[9] S. Rosenthal, N. Farra, and P. Nakov. "SemEval-2017 task 4: Sentiment analysis in Twitter," In: Proceedings of the 11th International Workshop on Semantic Evaluation (SemEval-2017), pp. 502-518, 2017.

[10] Z.Y. Gao, and C.P. Chen, "deepSA2018 at SemEval-2018 Task 1: Multi-task Learning of Different Label for Affect in Tweets," In: Proceedings of The 12th International Workshop on Semantic Evaluation, pp. 226-230, 2018.

[11] T. Mikolov, I. Sutskever, K. Chen, and G.S. Corrado, "Distributed representations of words and phrases and their compositionality," In: Advances in neural information processing systems, pp. 3111-3119, 2013.

[12] Y. Wang, M. Huang, and L. Zhao," Attention-based lstm for aspect-level sentiment classification," In: Proceedings of the 2016 conference on empirical methods in natural language processing, pp. 606-615, 2016.

The 2018 Conference on Computational Linguistics and Speech Processing
ROCLING 2018, pp. 246-255
©The Association for Computational Linguistics and Chinese Language Processing

# The Platform providing NLP System Deep Comparative Evaluation and Auxiliary Information for Hybrid NLP System Building ： Trial on Dependency Parser Evaluation

# 輔助建立混合性系統之自然語言處理系統深度評估平台 — 以評估依存關係分析器為例

王億祥 Yi-siang Wang

國立政治大學資訊科學系

Department of Computer Science

National Chengchi University

103305079@nccu.edu.tw

## Abstract

This platform includes two main concepts. One, provide multifaceted and deep evaluation for users of Natural Language Processing (NLP) System (such as Syntaxnet or CoreNLP), to help them choose the best one for their needs. Two, independently evaluate single NLP stage of a NLP system (such as pos tagging or dependency parsing), to provide needed auxiliary information for building up a hybrid NLP system (NLP system which composes multiple NLP system for different NLP stages) which is better than a normal NLP system. This paper will be explanation and demonstration centered on these two goals.

## 摘要

本平台包含兩大概念。 一, 提供自然語言處理(NLP)系統(如Syntaxnet或CoreNLP)的多面向且深度的衡量, 以期協助系統使用者挑選適合其需求的最佳系統。 二, 獨立地評量單一NLP階段(如詞性標注或依存關係分析), 以提供在組建比一般的系統表現更好的混合型NLP系統(不同的階段使用不同的NLP系統)時, 所需的輔助資訊。 本論文將圍繞此兩個目標展開說明和展示。

Keywords: Evaluation of NLP systems, Evaluation of NLP tools, compare NLP systems, compare NLP tools

關鍵詞： 評估自然語言處理系統, 評估自然語言處理工具, 自然語言處理系統比較, 自然語言處理工具比較

# 1. Introduction

Most NLP projects are based on NLP systems, so the performance of them will deeply affects the result of the projects. But there are so many choices and NLP technology is constantly evolving, which makes normal user hard to get the best NLP system fits their needs.

In the previous researches, some didn't reflect sentence segmentation on their evaluation[1], some evaluate on only one language[2], some evaluate only under special cases[3], and some only focus on LAS and its extension but ignore evaluation on other metrics and factors[4], [5], and some aren't properly updated to the latest annotation scheme[6].

Generally, most of these are lack of a multifaceted and deep evaluation, which means rich choices of evaluation measure, that fit different needs of users or provide evaluations in different perspectives of viewing. Furthermore, we need to be able to evaluate single NLP stage of NLP system, thus we can pick up the best NLP system in the scope of every NLP stage respectively, and concatenate them into hybrid NLP system, which is expected to have better performance than normal NLP system.

In this paper, we will first explain our research scope, then briefly introduce evaluation measures for deep and multifaceted evaluation, then comes setting and usage of experiment, finally we will show the evaluation results of the experiment to demonstrate deep evaluation and single NLP stage evaluation for hybrid NLP system building.

# 2. Scope of this Paper and the Research

This paper is about a tool and core concepts behind it, so trivial or detailed things such as implementation of metrics, execution process, will be omitted, because of the page limit. And other thing, like means of evaluating single stage, are omitted because it is largely related to API of the NLP system or it is as the same as other related works do.

Additionally, there are many things to discuss about metrics and factors of evaluation, such as suited situations and not suited situations of them, but these are not in our research scope, because the tool is positioned to provide rich choices  for users but not deeply research on them and we also expect it to be able to help the discussion on these measures. So in chapter 3 we will just briefly introduce metrics and factors.

# 3. Evaluation Measures

Though we won't deeply discuss about metrics and factors below, as mentioned above, we will briefly introduce every metric and factor and "one of" its significance for every unfamiliar metric and factor, to make readers have preliminary understanding about metrics and factors adopted.

## 3.1. Relevance Metrics

These three metrics matter when number of system prediction and gold differ.

Precision: number of correct prediction / number of system prediction

Recall : number of correct prediction / number of gold

F1-measure : (precision + recall) / 2

## 3.2. Metrics

Label Accuracy (LA) : The accuracy in assigning the correct dependency label.

Unlabelled Attachment Score (UAS) : The accuracy in assigning the correct dependency head.

Labelled Attachment Score (LAS) : The accuracy in assigning the correct head.

Morphology-Aware Labeled Attachment Score (MLAS) : Extend LAS with POS and morphological features. aims at comparability across typologically different languages, see CoNLL 2018 shared task for details[5].

Bi-lexical Dependency Score (BLEX) : Extend LAS with lemmatization, aims at evaluation closer to semantic content, see CoNLL 2018 shared task for details[5].

Dependency Branch Precision : The accuracy of path from root to a word in the dependency tree. To be a correct path, every word on the path should have correct label and parent. This metric aims at correctness of the main structure of a sentence.

Speed : Processed tokens or sentences per second, which is necessary to NLP projects that need immediate reaction.

## 3.3. Bases

Take "sentence-based" for example, instead of calculate one score in the scope of the whole document, first calculate scores in the scope of the same sentence respectively, and then take the average of these scores as the final score. This metric relieves the effect of extremely high or low performance in some sentences, see Table 1. Similarly we can get "POS-based", and "dependency-label-based" for the sake of the same purpose.

Table 1. Example of no base and sentence-based when calculating precision.

|  | A sentence | B sentnece |  |  | Equation |
|---|---|---|---|---|---|
| tokens correctly predicted | 10 | 25 | nobase |  | (10+25) / (50+35) = 0.41 |
| tokens predicted by system | 50 | 35 | sentence-based |  | (10/50 + 25/35) / 2 = 0.46 |

## 3.4. Factors

Dependency Distance : Absolute distance of parent and child of dependency in the sentence. This factor affects usage of memory and efficiency[7].

Dependency Direction : Direction from parent to child in the sentence. Relation to genre is one of the reasons that it is important[8].

Dependency Children Amount : How many words that depends on this word. Being the feature of classifying is one of the reasons that it matters[9].

Sentence Length: Number of non-space characters in a sentence. Performance under different sentence lengths might be meaningful for dataset with certain range of sentence length.

POS Tag: Performance under different POS tag matters when dataset has some POS tags frequent, or when being interested in some kinds of POS tag.

Dependency Label: Similar importance as mentioned in POS tag.

## 3.5. Other

Full / Main dependency label: For example, "nmod" is the main label of "nmod:tmod". Some people might only care for the function of main label.

POS / UPOS : There is also universal POS(UPOS) in universal dependency, aims at POS annotation acrosses languages.

## 4. Experiment Setting

### 4.1. Dataset

Table 2. Dataset and distribution of data of our experiments.

| UD_Chinese-GSD[1] | Tokens | Sentences |
|---|---|---|
| Training | 98,608 | 3997 |
| Developement | 12,663 | 500 |
| Test | 12,012 | 500 |

## 4.2. NLP Systems

### 4.2.1. Syntaxnet

Based on transition-based neural networks[10], and have a major update in 2017[11]. But pre-trained models didn't updated to the latest universal dependency[12], [13], so we will train our model with recommended setting according to the Syntaxnet's document[2].

### 4.2.2. UDPipe

UDPipe is trainable pipeline specialized for universal dependency[14], good at others also. We will use its 2017 CoNLL shared task model[15].

## 5. Usage of Platform

First activate environment using docker, "docker-compose up -d", then execute main program, "docker-compose exec app python experiment.py /path/to/dataset/directory/ <name of NLP system> [optional:NLP stage]", and the evaluation results will be stored in the database. For your dataset or NLP systems, user should write code to implement abstract classes, which we won't explain here because of the page limit.

---

[1] https://github.com/UniversalDependencies/UD_Chinese-GSD
[2] https://github.com/tensorflow/models/blob/master/research/syntaxnet/g3doc/syntaxnet-tutorial.md#part-of-spee ch-tagging

# 6. Experiment Results

Next, we will evaluate whole NLP task (will reflect result of preppended NLP works) for demonstration of deep evaluation, and independently evaluate single NLP stage for single NLP stage evaluation.

## 6.1. Deep Evaluation

There are 3 relevance metrics x 7 metrics x 4 base (include no-base) x 7 factors = roughly up to 588 scores, which proves multifaceted and deep evaluation we said. But due to the page limit, here only demonstrates several representative results and take Syntaxnet for example.

Table 3. Some scores with different relevance metrics on tokenization or POS tagging. we can also see that UPOS is hard to predicted than POS for Syntaxnet.

| NLP Task | Method | Metric | Base | Other | Score |
|---|---|---|---|---|---|
| Tokenization | Precision | - | Token | - | 98 |
| POS Tagging | Pecall | - | Token | POS | 92 |
| POS Tagging | Recall | - | POS | POS | 89 |
| POS Tagging | Precision | - | POS | POS | 93 |
| POS Tagging | F1 | - | POS | POS | 91 |
| POS Tagging | F1 | - | Token | UPOS | 79 |

Table 4. Scores on the same task but different bases. Scores differ obviously when different bases, even under the same other metrics.

| NLP Task | method | metric | Base | Other | Score |
|---|---|---|---|---|---|
| Dependency Parsing | F1 | LAS | Token | Full label | 74 |
| Dependency Parsing | F1 | LAS | Sentence | Full label | 75 |
| Dependency Parsing | F1 | LAS | POS | Full label | 77 |
| Dependency Parsing | Precision | LAS | UPOS | Full label | 76 |
| Dependency Parsing | Recall | LAS | UPOS | Full label | 92 |
| Dependency Parsing | Precision | LAS | Dependency Label | Full label | 76 |
| Dependency Parsing | Recall | LAS | Dependency Label | Full label | 70 |

Table 5. Results on metrics that are not LAS. Since there is no morphology feature and lemma in Chinese, MLAS and BLEX are omitted.

| NLP Task | method | metric | Base | Other | Score |
|---|---|---|---|---|---|
| Dependency Parsing | F1 | LS | Token | Full label | 82 |
| Dependency Parsing | F1 | LS | Token | Main label | 83 |
| Dependency Parsing | Precision | UAS | Token | - | 82 |

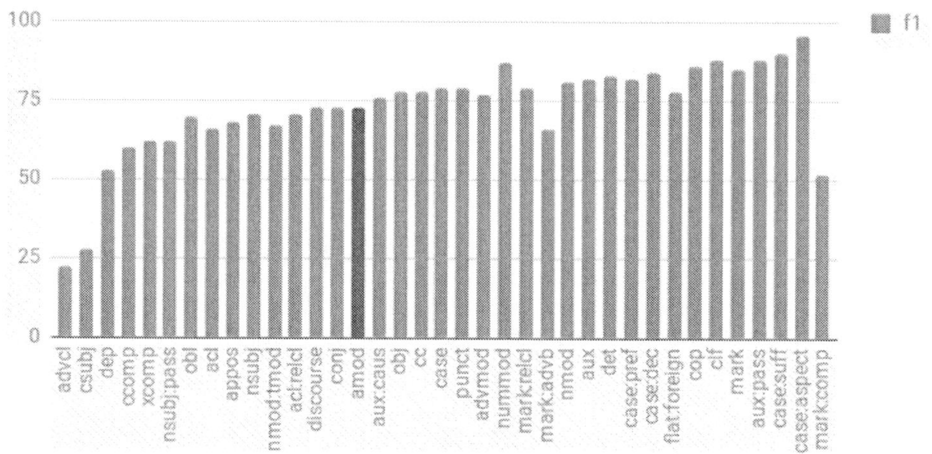

Figure 1. LAS  under different dependency labels. Scores is low under some dependency, which may be a opportunity to research the reason of it.

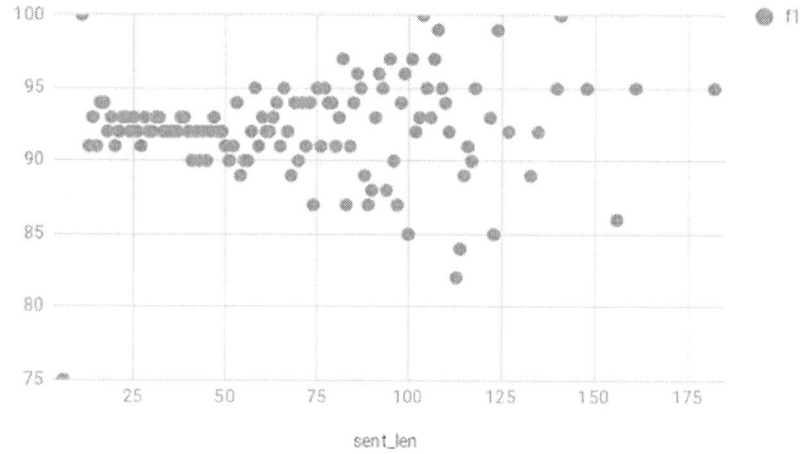

Figure 2. LAS under different sentence lengths. Performance is unstable in long sentences.

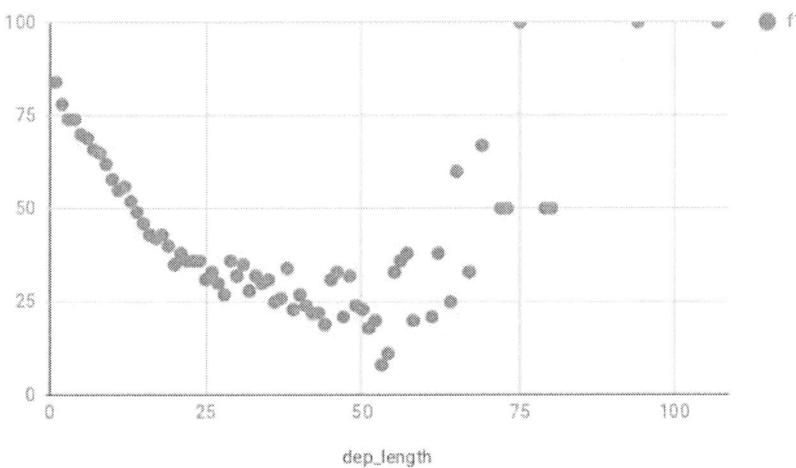


Figure 3. LAS (F1) under different dependency distances. The reason that score is low under dependency distance 50 is also worth researching.

## 6.2. Single NLP Stage Evaluation

Table 6. Independent evaluation on POS tagging for Syntaxnet and UDPipe.

| NLP Stage | POS type | Score of Syntaxnet | Score of UDPipe |
|---|---|---|---|
| POS tagging | POS | 93 | 98 |
| POS tagging | UPOS | 80 | 98 |

Table 7. Independent evaluation on dependency parsing for Syntaxnet and UDPipe

| NLP Stage | Metric | Score of Syntaxnet | Score of UDPipe |
|---|---|---|---|
| dependency parsing | LA | 88 | 89 |
| dependency parsing | UAS | 86 | 85 |
| dependency Parsing | LAS | 81 | 81 |

We can see that Syntaxnet performs better than UDPipe on head attachment, and UDpipe performs better than Syntaxnet on POS tagging. So if we can tag POS using UDPipe then parse using Syntaxnet, we should get better result on head attachment, than using just one of them to do it. Though slight difference in this case, still we showed the potential to provide auxiliary information for building hybrid NLP system (but not doing it).

# 7. Conclusions

In this paper, we first defined scope of this paper as introduction of the platform and concepts behind it, then brief introduce metrics and factors used, then came usage of the platform, and then experiment settings for technical details, finally got experiment results demonstrate the insighted multifaceted evaluation and potential to support building hybrid NLP system. So here, why we need the platform and what can the platform do is clear.

The platform is still under development, we haven't implemented speed metric, included more NLP systems and evaluated on larger corpus. But still, we have shown the main functions and potential of the platform.

Nowadays, NLP systems are more and more widely used, choosing a good NLP system contributes a lot to our projects. The platform provides rich measure for users can do some research on those then find the best evaluation for their needs. The platform also provides auxiliary information, make you possible to get better NLP system than the general one.

# References


[1] J. D. Choi, J. Tetreault, and A. Stent, "It Depends: Dependency Parser Comparison Using A Web-based Evaluation Tool," in Proceedings of the 53rd Annual Meeting of the Association for Computational Linguistics and the 7th International Joint Conference on Natural Language Processing (Volume 1: Long Papers), 2015, pp. 387–396.

[2] N. N. Alam, "The Comparative Evaluation of Dependency Parsers in Parsing Estonian," University of Tartu, 2017.

[3] M. Alabbas and A. Ramsay, "Evaluation of dependency parsers for long Arabic sentences," in 2011 International Conference on Semantic Technology and Information Retrieval, 2011.

[4] D. Z. Jan Hajič, Ed., "CoNLL-2017 Shared Task: Multilingual Parsing from Raw Text to Universal Dependencies," in Proceedings of the CoNLL 2017 Shared Task: Multilingual Parsing from Raw Text to Universal Dependencies, 2017.

[5] D. Z. Jan Hajič, Ed., "CoNLL-2018 Shared Task: Multilingual Parsing from Raw Text to Universal Dependencies," in Proceedings of the CoNLL 2018 Shared Task: Multilingual Parsing from Raw Text to Universal Dependencies, 2018.

[6] J. N. Nilsson Jens, "MaltEval: An Evaluation and Visualization Tool for Dependency Parsing," in Proceedings of the Sixth International Conference on Language Resources

and Evaluation (LREC'08), 2008.

[7]  K. Gulordava, P. Merlo, and B. Crabbé, "Dependency length minimisation effects in short spans: a large-scale analysis of adjective placement in complex noun phrases," in Proceedings of the 53rd Annual Meeting of the Association for Computational Linguistics and the 7th International Joint Conference on Natural Language Processing (Volume 2: Short Papers), 2015, pp. 477–482.

[8]  Y. Wang and H. Liu, "The effects of genre on dependency distance and dependency direction," Lang. Sci., vol. 59, pp. 135–147, 2017.

[9]  Prudhvi Kosaraju, Sruthilaya Reddy Kesidi, Vinay Bhargav Reddy Ainavolu and Puneeth Kukkadapu, "Experiments on indian language dependency parsing," in Proceedings of the ICON10 NLP Tools Contest: Indian Language Dependency Parsing, 2010, pp. 40–45.

[10] D. Andor et al., "Globally Normalized Transition-Based Neural Networks," in Proceedings of the 54th Annual Meeting of the Association for Computational Linguistics (Volume 1: Long Papers), 2016.

[11] Lingpeng Kong, Chris Alberti, Daniel Andor, Ivan Bogatyy, David Weiss, "DRAGNN: A Transition-based Framework for Dynamically Connected Neural Networks." 13-Mar-2017.

[12] Chris Alberti, Daniel Andor, Ivan Bogatyy, Michael Collins, Dan Gillick, Lingpeng Kong, Terry Koo, Ji Ma, Mark Omernick, Slav Petrov, Chayut Thanapirom, Zora Tung, David Weiss, "SyntaxNet Models for the CoNLL 2017 Shared Task," in Proceedings of the CoNLL 2017 Shared Task: Multilingual Parsing from Raw Text to Universal Dependencies, 2017.

[13] Ryan McDonald , Joakim Nivre, Yvonne Quirmbach-Brundage, Yoav Goldberg, Dipanjan Das , Kuzman Ganchev, Keith Hall, Slav Petrov, Hao Zhang, Oscar Täckström, Claudia Bedini, Núria Bertomeu Castelló, Jungmee Lee, "Universal dependency annotation for multilingual parsing," in Proceedings of the 51st Annual Meeting of the Association for Computational Linguistics, 2013, pp. 92–97.

[14] H. J. Straka Milan, "UDPipe: Trainable Pipeline for Processing CoNLL-U Files Performing Tokenization, Morphological Analysis, POS Tagging and Parsing," in the Tenth International Conference on Language Resources and Evaluation (LREC 2016), 2016.

[15] M. Straka and J. Straková, "Tokenizing, POS Tagging, Lemmatizing and Parsing UD 2.0 with UDPipe," in Proceedings of the CoNLL 2017 Shared Task: Multilingual Parsing from Raw Text to Universal Dependencies, 2017, pp. 88–99.

The 2018 Conference on Computational Linguistics and Speech Processing
ROCLING 2018, pp. 256-265
©The Association for Computational Linguistics and Chinese Language Processing

# Smart vs. Solid Solutions in Computational Linguistics

# －Machine Translation or Information Retrieval

Su-Mei Shiue
Department of Computer Science and Information Engineering
National Taipei University of Technology
t102599005@ntut.edu.tw


Lang-Jyi Huang
Department of Computer Science and Information Engineering
National Taipei University of Technology
t8599003@ntut.edu.tw


Wei-Ho Tsai
Department of Electronic Engineering
National Taipei University of Technology
whtsai@ntut.edu.tw


Yen-Lin Chen
Department of Computer Science and Information Engineering
National Taipei University of Technology
ylchen@csie.ntut.edu.tw

## Abstract

Smart solutions and solid solutions are two different approaches for computational linguistics. To receive a satisfactory result at a minimum cost, smart solutions use special properties of the on-hand application. Solid solutions, in contrast, more generally analyze the application in order that these solutions can be used for a whole class of applications. By extending a well-maintained solid solution, it may be re-used once and again, thus saving time, money, and other resources in the long run. Therefore, the research focuses on solid solutions. It To implement smart solutions, machine translation is used while information retrieval is for solid solutions.

Keywords: Smart Solutions, Solid Solutions, Computational Linguistics, Grammatical

Components, Natural Language.

# 1. Introduction

## 1.1  Destination of Computational Linguistics - Natural Transmission of Information

The goal of computational linguistics is to reproduce the natural transmission of information by modeling the speaker's production and the hearer's interpretation on a suitable type of computing machine. This amounts to the construction of autonomous cognitive machines (robots) which can freely communicate in natural language. And the development of speaking robots is a real scientific task [1].

## 1.2  Turing Test - Modeling the Mechanism of Natural Communication

The task of modeling the mechanism of natural communication on the computer was described in 1950 by [4] in the form of an 'imitation game' known today as the Turing test The computer passes the Turing test if the man or the woman replaced by the computer is simulated so well that the guesses of the human interrogator are just as often right and wrong as with the earlier natural partner. In this way Turing wanted to replace the question "Can machines think?" with the question "Are there imaginable digital computers which would do well in the imitation game?" [1, 10]

## 1.3  Eliza Program – A Prototype of Smart Solution

The Eliza program [2] simulates a psychiatrist encouraging the human interrogator, now in the role of a patient, to talk more and more about him- or herself. Eliza works with a list of words. Whenever one of these words is typed by the human interrogator/patient, Eliza inserts it into one of several prefabricated sentence templates. For example, when the word mother is used by the human, Eliza uses the template Tell me more about your ___ to generate the sentence Tell me more about your mother. Eliza program is the prototype of a smart solution in that it exploits the restrictions of a highly specialized application to achieve a maximal effect with a minimum of effort.

# 2. Smart versus Solid Solutions

For computational applications, two distinguished approaches are [1]: smart solutions and solid solutions. Smart solutions use special properties of the particular application to obtain a sufficient result at a minimum of cost. Solid solutions, on the other hand, analyze the application at a more general level such that they can be used for a whole class of applications. By maintaining and extending a solid solution, it may be re-used again and again, thus saving time and money in the long run.

## 3. Solid Solutions in Computational Applications [1]

### 3.1. Indexing and Retrieval in Textual Databases

The electronic index is built up automatically when the texts are read into the database, whereby the size of the index is roughly equal to that of the textual database itself. The use of an electronic index has the following advantages over a card index: power of search, flexibility, general specification of patterns (general specification of patterns, combination of patterns), automatic creation of the index structure, ease, speed, and reliability

The advantages of electronic search apply to both the *query* (input of the search words) and the *retrieval* (output of the corresponding texts or passages).

### 3.2 Grammatical Knowledge Improves Retrieval from Textual Databases.

### 3,2.1 Phenomena Requiring Linguistic Solutions

The reason for the surprisingly low recall of only 20 % on average is that STAIRS uses only technological, i.e., letter-based, methods [5]. Using grammatical knowledge in addition, recall could be improved considerably. Textual phenomena which resist a technological treatment, but are suitable for a linguistic solution, that is, phenomena requiring linguistic solutions, are listed below under the heading of the associated grammatical component.

(a) *Morphology:* By systematically associating each word form with its base form, all variants of a search word in the database can be found. A program of automatic word form recognition would be superior to the customary method of truncation

(b) *Lexicon:* A letter-based search does not take semantic relations between words into account. For example, the search for car would ignore relevant occurrences such as convertible, pickup truck, station wagon, and so on. A lexical structure which automatically specifies for each word the set of equivalent terms (synonyms), of the superclass (hypernyms), and of the instantiations (hyponyms) can help to overcome this weakness, especially when the domain is taken into account.

(c) *Syntax:* A letter-based search does not take syntactic structures into account. Thus, the system does not distinguish between, for example, teenagers sold used cars and teenagers were sold used cars. A possible remedy would be a syntactic parser which recognizes different grammatical relations between, for example, the subject and the object. Such a parser, which presupposes automatic word form recognition, would be superior to the currently used search for words within specified maximal distances.

(d) *Semantics:* A letter-based search does not recognize semantic relations such as negation. For example, the system would not be able to distinguish between selling cars and selling no cars. Also, equivalent descriptions of the same facts, such as A sold x to B and B bought x from A, could not be recognized. Based on a syntactic parser and a suitable lexicon, the semantic interpretation of a textual database could analyze these distinctions and relations, helping to improve recall and precision.

(e) *Pragmatics:* According to [5], a major reason for poor recall was the frequent use of context-dependent formulations such as concerning our last letter, following our recent discussion, as well as nonspecific words such as problem, situation, or occurrence. The treatment of these frequent phenomena requires a complete theoretical understanding of natural language pragmatics. For example, the system will have to be able to infer that, for example, seventeen-year-old bought battered convertible is relevant to the query used car sales to teenagers.

## 3.2.2 Linguistic Methods of Optimization

In order to improve recall and precision, linguistic knowledge may be applied in various different places in the database structure. The main alternatives (called linguistic methods of optimization), are whether improvements in the search should be based on preprocessing the query, refining the index, and/or post-processing the result. Further alternatives are an automatic or an interactive refinement of the query and/or the result.

## 4. Smart versus Solid Solutions in Computational Linguistics [1]

The different degrees of using linguistic theory for handling the retrieval from textual databases illustrate the choice between smart versus solid solutions.

## 4.1 Smart Solutions in Computational Linguistics

Smart solutions avoid difficult, costly, or theoretically unsolved aspects of natural communication, as in

(a) Weizenbaum's Eliza program [2], which appears to understand natural language,

but doesn't, as mentioned in the Introduction Section.

(b) direct and transfer approaches in machine translation, which avoid understanding

the source text (Sections. 5.1 and 5.2), and

(c) finite state technology and statistics for tagging and probabilistic parsing [3].

Initially, smart solutions seem cheaper and quicker, but they are costly to maintain and their accuracy cannot be substantially improved. The alternative is solid solutions:

## 4.2 Solid Solutions in Computational Linguistics

Solid solutions aim at a complete theoretical and practical understanding of natural language communication. Applications are based on ready-made off-the-shelf components such as

(a) online lexica,

(b) rule-based grammars for the syntactic-semantic analysis of word forms and sentences. (These methods may seem impressive because of the vast number of toys and tools assembled in the course of many decades [3]. But they do not provide an answer to the question of how natural language communication works. What is needed instead is a functional reconstruction of the engine, the transmission, the steering mechanism, and so on. That is, a solid solution.)

(c) parsers and generators for running the grammars in the analysis and production
of free text, and

(d) reference and monitor corpora for different domains, which provide a systematic, standardized account of the current state of the language.

Solid solution components are an application-independent long-term investment. Due to their systematic theoretical structure they are easy to maintain, can be improved continuously, and may be used again and again in different applications.

# 5. Smart Solutions in Computational Applications [1]

## 5.1. Beginnings of Machine Translation

The choice between a smart and a solid solution is exemplified by machine translation. Translation in general requires understanding a text or utterance in a certain language (interpretation) and reconstructing it in another language (production).

### 5.1.1 Formula to Compute the Number of Language Pairs

$n \cdot (n-1)$, where $n$ = number of different languages

For example, an EU with 23 different languages has to deal with a total of $23 \cdot 22 = 506$ language pairs.

In a language pair, the source language (SL) and the target language (TL) are distinguished. For example, 'French→Danish' and 'Danish→French' are different language pairs.

### 5.1.2 Schema of Direct Translation and Its Weakness

Each language pair requires the programming of its own direct translation system. Direct translation is based mainly on a differentiated dictionary, distinguishing many special cases for a correct assignment of word forms in the target language.

Fully Automatic High Quality Translation (FAHQT) was just around the corner, their hopes were not fulfilled. Hutchins [6] provides the following examples to illustrate the striking shortcomings of early translation systems:

### 5.1.3 Example of Automatic Mistranslations

Out of sight, out of mind. ⇒*Invisible idiot.*
The spirit is willing, but the flesh is weak. ⇒ *The whiskey is all right, but the meat is rotten.*
La Cour de Justice considère la création d'un sixième poste d'avocat général.⇒*The Court of Justice is considering the creation of a sixth avocado station.*
The first two examples are apocryphal, described as the result of an automatic translation from English into Russian and back into English. The third example is documented in Lawson [11] as output of the SYSTRAN system. An attempt to avoid the weaknesses of direct translation is the transfer approach as follows:

## 5.2. Machine Translation Today — Interlingua Approach

The importance of language *understanding* for adequate translation is illustrated by the following examples:

### 5.2.1 Syntactic Ambiguity in the Source Language

1. Julia flew and crashed the airplane.

Julia (flew and crashed the airplane)

(Julia flew) and (crashed the airplane)

2. Susanne observed the yacht with a telescope.

Susanne observed the man with a beard.

3. The mixture gives off dangerous cyanide and chlorine fumes.

(dangerous cyanide) and (chlorine fumes)

dangerous (cyanide and chlorine) fumes

The first example is ambiguous between using the verb fly transitively (someone flies an airplane) or intransitively (someone/-thing flies). The second example provides a choice between an adnominal and an adverbial interpretation. The third example exhibits a scope ambiguity regarding dangerous.

### 5.2.2 Partial Solutions for Practical Machine Translation

1. *Machine-aided translation* (MAT) supports human translators with comfortable tools such as online dictionaries, text processing, morphological analysis, etc.
2. *Rough translation* – as provided by an automatic transfer system – arguably reduces the translators' work to correcting the automatic output.
3. *Restricted language* provides a fully automatic translation, but only for texts which fulfill canonical restrictions on lexical items and syntactic structures.

The interlingua approach is based on a general, language-independent level called the interlingua. It is designed to represent contents derived from different source languages in a uniform format. From this representation, the surfaces of different target languages are generated.

### 5.2.3 Schema of the Interlingua Approach

An interlingua system handles translation in two independent steps. The first step translates the source language text into the interlingua representation (analysis). The second step maps the interlingua representation into the target language (synthesis).

It follows from the basic structure of the interlingua approach that for $n(n-1)$ language pairs only $2n$ interlingual components are needed (namely $n$ analysis and $n$ synthesis modules), in contrast to the direct and the transfer approach which require $n(n-1)$ components. Thus, as soon as more than three languages ($n > 3$) are involved, the interlingua approach has a substantial advantage over the other two.

The crucial question, however, is the exact nature of the interlingua.

# 6. Experiment

## 6.1 Music Information Retrieval (MIR) — A Solid Solution Example at Work

Purpose: To demonstrate the functionality of the Self-Organizing-Maps (SOM)-based music content representation.

Off-the-shelf tool used: MATLAB neural networks library function musicVisualizationDemoSOM.mat.

Input data: musicLargeData dataset.

Output:

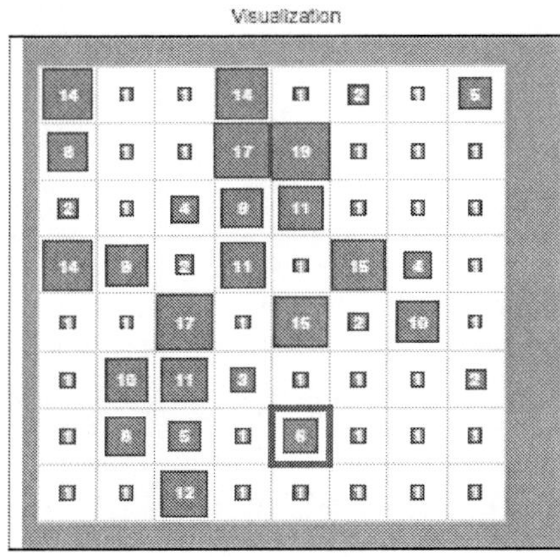


Figure 1 Visualization of selected nodes of the SOM of the data in the musicLarge Data.mat dataset.

Figure 1 presents some node visualization examples. It can be seen that in some cases, the example contains songs with female vocalists. The rest of the examples (not shown) mostly highlight songs of the same artist. In some cases, the proximity of two nodes has a physical meaning: the 3rd and the 4th examples are (practically) homogeneous with respect to the identity of the artist, and in addition, the two artists can be considered to belong to similar musical genres (Green Day and Bad Religion both fall into the punk-rock genre).

## 6.2 Talk to Eliza — A Smart Solution

Purpose: Test Eliza program
Input: Dialog in writing to Eliza on a screen

Tool used: Eliza program online [8].

Output: Eliza: Tell me more. -> Me: Of course. -> Eliza: OK… Me: -> What do me think am important now. -> Eliza: We were discussing you, not me. -> Me: O.K., I missed my mother. How do you think?. -> Eliza:

Perhaps you would like to be able to tell me more. *** Are we going to chat? I cannot help you without a dialog.    -> Me: What is the most important thing in life?    -> Eliza: Have you asked anyone else?

## 6.3 Machine Translation    － A Smart solution

Tool: Google online translation program [9].

Input in Chinese: 朝辭白帝彩雲間，千里江陵一日還，兩岸猿聲啼不住，輕舟已過萬重山

Output in English: In the remarks of the White Emperor, the Qianling River is still a day, and the two sides of   the river are screaming. The light boat has passed the Wanzhong Mountain.

Input in English: Ask not what your country can do for you. Ask what you can do for your country.

Output in Chinese: 不要問你的國家能為你做些什麼。  問你能為國家做些什麼。

Input in Japanese: どんな公園でも、両親にとって、子供たち

Output in Chinese: 適用於任何公園，父母，兒童

Output in English: For any park, parents, children

## 7. Conclusions

The main reason for the long-term superiority of solid solutions, however, is quality. This is because a 75 % smart solution is typically very difficult or even impossible to improve to 76 %. 。

The goal of computational linguistics, however, is a solid solution in science: it must (i) explain the mechanism of natural communication theoretically and (ii) verify the theory with an implementation (software machine) which may be loaded with the language-dependent lexicon and compositional operations of any natural language. The speak and the hear mode of the implementation must work in any practical application for which free natural language communication between humans and machines is desired [7, 8].

## References


[1]  Roland Hausser, *Foundations of Computational Linguistics: Human-Computer Communication in Natural Language*. 3rd ed. Springer-Verlag Berlin Heidelberg, 2014.

[2]  J. Weizenbaum, *"ELIZA – A Computer Program for the Study of Natural*

*LanguageCommunications Between Man and Machine,*" *Communications of the ACM* 9.1 (11), 1965.

[3]  D. Jurafsky, J. Martin, *"Speech and Language Processing: An Introduction to Natural Language,"Processing, Computational Linguistics, and Speech Recognition,* Upper Saddle River: Prentice Hall, 2000.

[4]   A.M. Turing, *Computing Machinery and Intelligence, Mind* 59:433–460, 1950.

[5]  D.C. Blair, and M.E. Maron, "An Evaluation of Retrieval Effectiveness for a Full-Text Document Retrieval System," *Communications of the ACM* 28.3:289–299, 1985.

[6]  W.J. Hutchins , *"Machine Translation: Past, Present, Future,"* Chichester: Ellis Horwood, 1986.

[7]  T. Giannakopoulos and A. Pikrakis, Introduction to Audio Analysis: A MATLAB Approach, Elsevier, 2014.

[8]  Eliza, Computer Therapist - CyberPsych (https://www.cyberpsych.org/eliza/)

[9]  https://translate.google.com.tw/

[10] https://en.wikipedia.org/wiki/Computing_Machinery_and_Intelligence

[11] V. Lawson, "Machine Translation," in C. Picken (ed.), 203–213, 1983.

The 2018 Conference on Computational Linguistics and Speech Processing
ROCLING 2018, pp. 266-275
©The Association for Computational Linguistics and Chinese Language Processing

# On Four Metaheuristic Applications to Speech Enhancement

# －Implementing Optimization Algorithms with MATLAB R2018a

Su-Mei Shiue
Department of Computer Science and Information Engineering
National Taipei University of Technology
t102599005@ntut.edu.tw


Lang-Jyi Huang
Department of Computer Science and Information Engineering
National Taipei University of Technology
t8599003@ntut.edu.tw


Wei-Ho Tsai
Department of Electronic Engineering
National Taipei University of Technology
whtsai@ntut.edu.tw


Yen-Lin Chen
Department of Computer Science and Information Engineering
National Taipei University of Technology
ylchen@csie.ntut.edu.tw

## Abstract

This study aims to firstly implement four well-known metaheuristic optimization algorithms which, among other things, are utilized on adaptive filter design, for dual-channel speech enhancement, with voice communication devices. The implementations are conducted in a simulation fashion using MATLAB code under its newly release version of R2018a. Lately, the study takes a closer look at these four optimization methods, based on learning from the literature of the research society, on their pros and cons while applying to speech enhancement. These four methods are, namely, (1) Accelerated Particle Swarm Optimization (APSO), (2) Gravitational Search Algorithm (GSA), (3) a hybrid algorithm of PSO (Particle Swarm Optimization) and GSA (called hybrid PSOGSA), and (4) Bat Algorithm (BA). This study performs the said implementations successfully and obtains useful experimental results which contributes to building a solid foundation for more advanced research in the near future. Besides, the implementations made by the study confirm the correctness of many a previous research works which claim that these four algorithms show better performance on improved speech quality and intelligibility as compared to that of the existing standard PSO (SPSO) based speech enhancement approach.

Keywords: Speech Enhancement, APSO, GSA, PSOGSA, BA.

## 1. Introduction

The concise characteristics and advantages of metaheuristic optimization methods as discussed in this paper for speech enhancement are listed in Table 1 below.

Table 1. Important metaheuristic optimization methods for speech enhancement

| Name | Characteristics | |
|------|-----------------|---|
| PSO | PSO does not require that the problem of optimization to be differentiated as required by classical optimization methods such as gradient descent and quasi Newton methods. Therefore, PSO can be used in optimization problems that are partly irregular, variable over time, etc. [5]. | Simple conception, quick velocit significant SNR ratio for higher ac person will percept/ recognize the v |
| GSA | An algorithm inspired by Newton"s laws of motion and gravitation force [1]. | Updating is done by considering th performance than PSO [3]. |
| PSOGSA | A hybrid algorithm of PSO and GSA [3]. | Combines the advantages of GSA a designing the adaptive filter in nois |
| APSO | Developed by Xin she Yang in 2010. APSO is simpler to implement and has faster convergence when compared to the standard PSO (SPSO) algorithm. [2] | APSO based speech enhancement i speech quality and intelligibility m |
| BA | (1) Frequency tuning: BA uses echolocation and frequency tuning to solve problems. (2) Automatic zooming: BA has a distinct advantage over other metaheuristic algorithms. of automatically zooming into a region where promising solutions have been found [4]. | BA is a bio-inspired algorithm dev diversity and provides a dynamic b search space [3]. |

## 2. Accelerated Particle Swarm Optimization (APSO) to Speech Enhancement

## 2.1 PSO: Advantages and Pseudo Code [7]

One of the most widely used swarm-intelligence-based algorithms owing to its simplicity and flexibility, particle swarm optimization, or PSO, was developed by Kennedy and Eberhart in 1995 [8]. The PSO algorithm searches the space of an objective function by adjusting the trajectories of individual agents, called *particles*, as the piecewise paths formed by positional vectors in a quasi-stochastic manner. The movement of a swarming particle is composed of two main components: a stochastic component and a deterministic component. Each particle is attracted toward the position of the current global best $g*$ and its own best location $x_i^*$ in history, while at the same time it tends to move randomly.

When a particle finds a location that is better than any previously found locations, it updates that location as the new current best for particle $i$. There is a current best for all $n$ particles at any time $t$ during iterations. The aim is to find the global best among all the current best solutions until the objective no longer improves or after a certain number of iterations. The movement of particles is schematically represented in Figure 1, where $x_i^*$ $(t)$ is the current best for particle $i$ , and $g* \approx \min\{f(x_i)\}$ for $(i = 1, 2, \ldots, n)$ is the current global best at $t$. moving toward the global best $g*$ and the current best $x_i^*$ for each particle $i$.

The essential steps of the particle swarm optimization are summarized as the pseudo code shown in Figure 2.

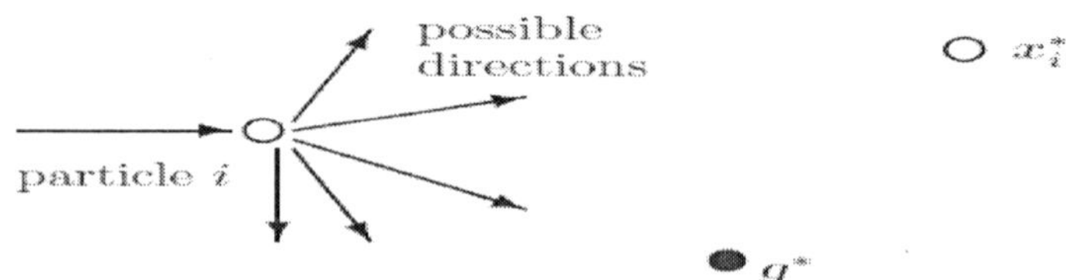


Figure 1. Schematic representation of the movement of a particle in PSO [7]

Particle Swarm Optimization

```
Objective function $f(x)$,   $x = (x_1, ..., x_d)^T$
Initialize locations $x_i$ and velocity $v_i$ of $n$ particles.
Find $g^*$ from $\min\{f(x_1), ..., f(x_n)\}$ (at $t = 0$)
while ( criterion )
    for loop over all $n$ particles and all $d$ dimensions
    Generate new velocity $v_i^{t+1}$ using equation (7.1)
    Calculate new locations $x_i^{t+1} = x_i^t + v_i^{t+1}$
    Evaluate objective functions at new locations $x_i^{t+1}$
    Find the current best for each particle $x_i^*$
    end for
    Find the current global best $g^*$
    Update $t = t + 1$ (pseudo time or iteration counter)
end while
Output the final results $x_i^*$ and $g^*$
```

Figure 2. Pseudo code of Particle Swarm Optimization [7]

## 2.2  Implement the Simulated PSO using MATLAB

The simulated PSO is implemented by MATLAB code [9] and displays the following output.

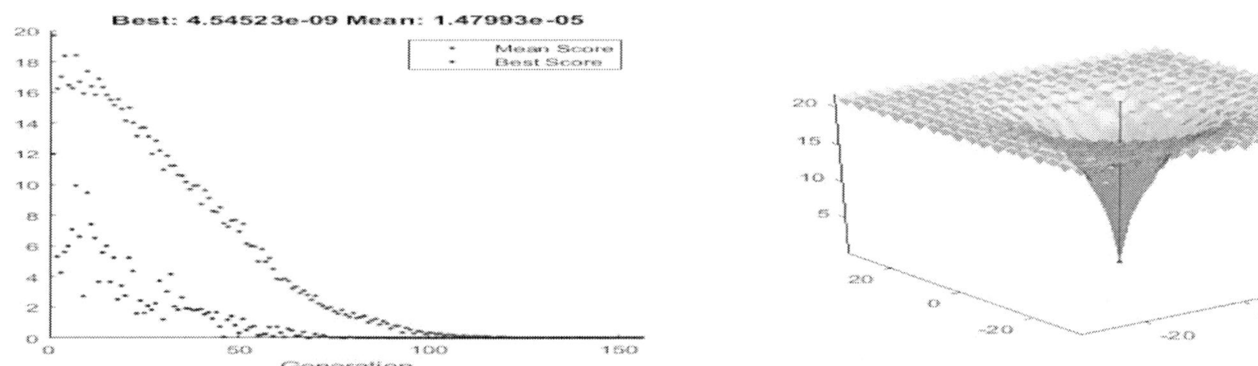


Figure 3. The PSO algorithm searches the space of the "ackleysfcn" objective function and
reaches the convergence (generation = iteration)

## 2.3  Accelerated PSO (APSO)

The standard particle swarm optimization (PSO) uses both the current global best $g*$ and the individual best $x_i^*$ (t). However, there is no compelling reason for using the individual best unless the optimization problem of interest is highly nonlinear and multimodal.

A simplified version that could accelerate the convergence of the algorithm is to use only the global best. This is the so-called *accelerated particle swarm optimization* (APSO) which was developed by Xin-She Yang in 2008 [7]. A further improvement to the accelerated PSO is to reduce the randomness as iterations proceed. That is to use a monotonically decreasing function such as

$$\alpha = \alpha_0 e^{-\gamma t},\qquad(1)$$

or

$$\alpha = \alpha_0 \gamma^t, \quad (0 < \gamma < 1),\qquad(2)$$

where $\alpha_0 = 0.5$ to 1 is the initial value of the randomness parameter. Here $t$ is the number of iterations or time steps. $0 < \gamma < 1$ is a control parameter.

## 2.4  APSO implementation

The implementation of the APSO was simulated using MATLAB code [10]. The total number of particles = 10 and that of iterations = 10. The 2D "Michalewicz" objective function is used. Two outputs are shown below.

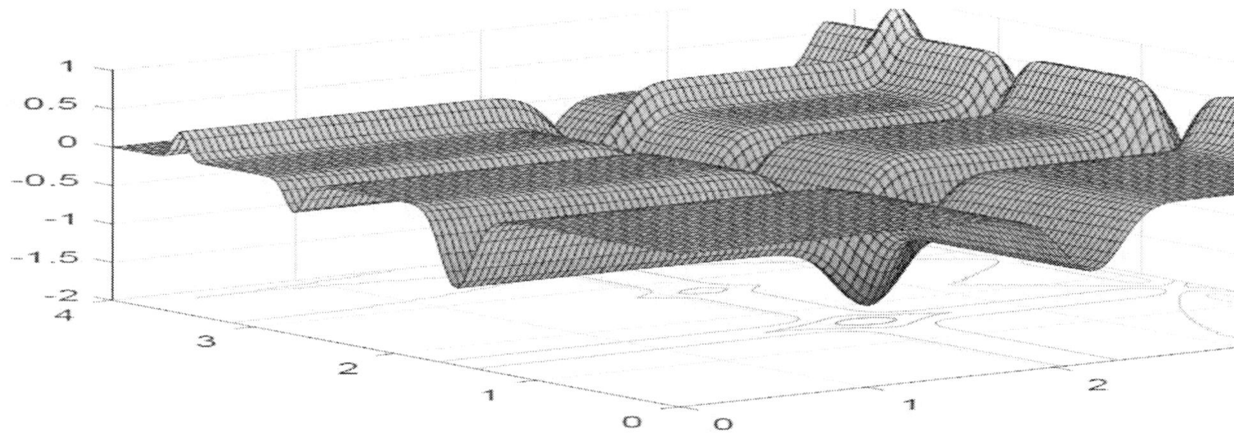

**Figure 4.** Michalewicz objective function with the global optimality at (2.20319, 1.57049).

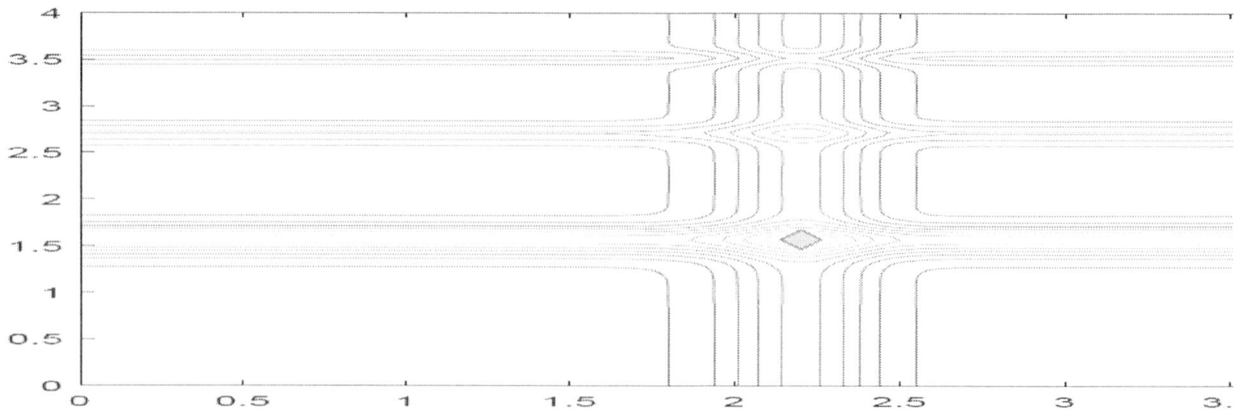

**Figure 5.** Initial and final locations of 20 particles after 10 iterations.

## 2.5  APSO implementation results for speech enhancement

The proposed algorithm does not use individual best position for updating the new locations and is capable of finding the solution in minimum number of iterations. Further, the proposed APSO algorithm is converging faster compared to SPSO algorithm [3].

# 3.  Gravitational Search Algorithm (GSA) for Speech Enhancement

## 3.1  Gravitational Search Algorithm (GSA)

Gravitational search algorithm (GSA) is an optimization algorithm based on the law of gravity and mass interactions. This algorithm is based on the Newtonian gravity: "Every particle in the universe attracts every other particle with a force that is directly proportional to the product of their masses and inversely proportional to the square of the distance between them" [11].

## 3.2  Gravitational Search Algorithm (GSA) Implementation

The implementation of the GSA was simulated using MATLAB code [11]. This experiment uses Function 1 to calculate the objective function. The output is shown below.

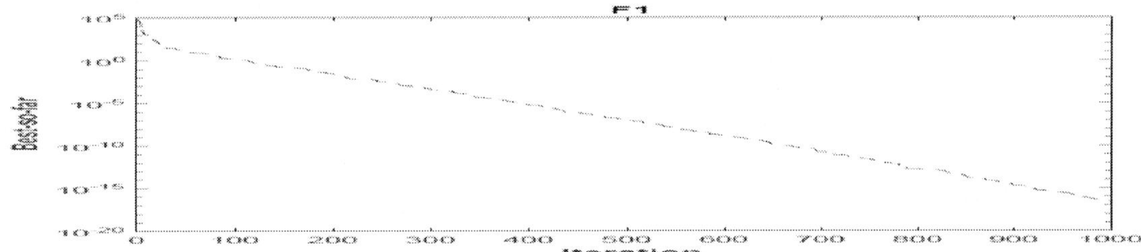

**Figure 6.** This implementation of GSA uses Function 1 to compute the value of objective function

## 3.3  GSA implementation results for speech enhancement [3]

The simulation results concluded that the performance of  GSA algorithm is better when compared to SPSO with respect to the speech  quality and intelligibility.

Table 2. Comparison of quality objective measure PESQ

| Input SNR for babble noise condition (dB) | Algorithm | PESQ scores |
| --- | --- | --- |
| 5 | SPSO | 2.0455 |
| | GSA | 2.1772 |
| 0 | SPSO | 2.2287 |
| | GSA | 2.3312 |
| −10 | SPSO | 1.6485 |
| | GSA | 1.6697 |

Table 3. Comparison of intelligibility objective measure FAI

| Input SNR for babble noise condition (dB) | Algorithm | FAI scores |
| --- | --- | --- |
| 5 | SPSO | 0.1602 |
| | GSA | 0.1735 |
| 0 | SPSO | 0.1419 |
| | GSA | 0.1545 |
| −10 dB | SPSO | 0.0689 |
| | GSA | 0.0834 |

# 4. Hybrid PSOGSA for Speech Enhancement

## 4.1 PSOGSA

The objective measures that improved SNR, PESQ, FAI and WSS have got improvement in hybrid PSOGSA algorithm when compared to the conventional GSA and standard PSO algorithms. And it can be concluded that PSOGSA can more effectively reduce the background noise of the noisy input speech [3]. The main idea of PSOGSA is to integrate the ability of exploitation in PSO with the ability of exploration in GSA to synthesize both algorithms' strength. Some benchmark test functions are used to compare the hybrid algorithm with both the standard PSO and GSA algorithms in evolving best solution [12].

## 4.2 PSOGSA Implementation

The implementation of the GSA was simulated using MATLAB code [13]. This experiment uses Function 1 to calculate the objective function. The output is shown below.

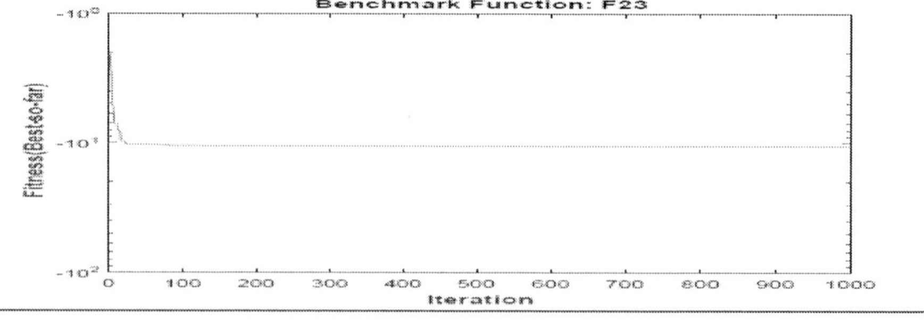


**Figure 7.** This implementation of PSOGSA uses Function 23 to compute the value of objective function

## 4.3 PSOGSA Implementation Results for Speech Enhancement

The SNR levels of the input noisy signal for babble-type noise is set at −10 ,−5, 0 and 5 dB.
Results are averaged over 10 trail runs. The performance of the algorithms
is evaluated by computing SNRI measure, and the results are tabulated. There is 10 dB
improvement in PSOGSA when compared with that of SPSO algorithm. At all other noise
input SNR levels of noisy speech (−10, 0 and 5 dB), there is almost 6 dB improvement in
SNRI with PSOGSA when compared with that of SPSO. Throughout input SNR level, there
is almost 2 dB improvement in PSOGSA when compared with that of conventional GSA.
The performance of the algorithms is also evaluated by computing intelligibility objective
measure FAI [3],

## 5.  Bat Algorithm (BA) for Speech Enhancement

## 5.1  Bat Algorithm (BA)

Bat algorithm (BA) is one of the recently proposed heuristic algorithms imitating the
echolocation behavior of bats to perform global optimization. The superior performance of
this algorithm has been proven among the other most well-known algorithms such as genetic
algorithm (GA) and particle swarm optimization (PSO) [14, 15].

## 5.2  Bat Algorithm (BA) Implementation

The original version of this algorithm is suitable for continuous problems, so it cannot be
applied to binary problems directly. Here [14, 15], a binary version of this algorithm is
available.

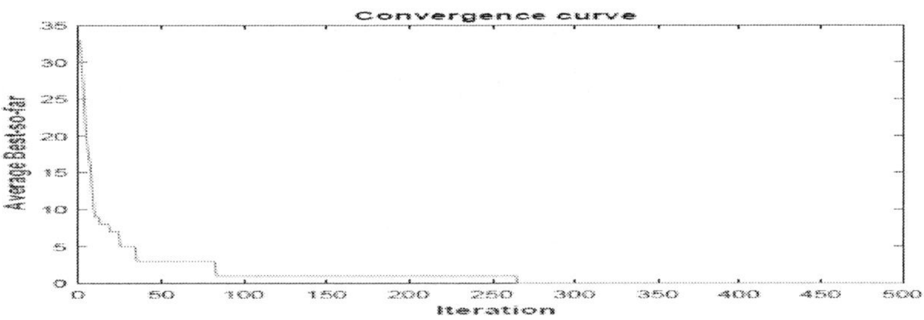


Figure 8. Implementation of the Binary version BA

## 5.3  Bat Algorithm (BA) Implementation results for speech enhancement

Other related simulation discussion on BA [3]: BA has yielded best solutions to the problem
of adaptive filtering in speech enhancement  by providing a dynamic balance between the
exploration and exploitation of search space with an automatic zooming effect. With respect
to quality and intelligibility of enhanced speech, simulation results proved that the proposed

BA-based enhancement algorithm is superior to SPSO-based enhancement algorithm and all other algorithms proposed in this research work.

Bat algorithm (BA) is one of the recently proposed heuristic algorithms imitating the echolocation behavior of bats to perform global optimization. The superior performance of this algorithm has been proven among the other most well-known algorithms such as genetic algorithm (GA) and particle swarm optimization (PSO). This version of this algorithm can be applied to binary problems directly. This study run the BA simulation successfully which was executed under MATLAB R2018a and the simulation output is displayed as follows:

## 6. Conclusions

Since the implementations of the four metaheuristic optimization algorithms (APSO, GSA, PSOGSA, and BA) are well done, which provides a good base for more advanced study in the near future, such as to create a much powerful algorithm by making a variant of a current algorithm or combining multiple algorithms' advantages.

Besides, with the work presented in [3], it is proved that the performances of the proposed algorithms are compared with the performance of the existing standard PSO based speech enhancement approach. From the results it is observed that each of the proposed algorithms achieved better performance when compared with that of standard PSO based speech enhancement approach with improved speech quality and intelligibility scores.

## References


[1]   Poonam, S. Ratnoo, Gravitational Search Algorithms in Data Mining: A Survey, IJARCCE ISSN (Online) 2278-1021 ISSN (Print) 2319 5940 International Journal of Advanced Research in Computer and Communication Engineering ISO 3297:2007 Certified Vol. 6, Issue 6, June 2017.

[2]  K. Prajna, G. S. B. Rao, K. V.V. S. Reddy, R. U. Maheswari, A New Dual Channel Speech Enhancement Approach Based on Accelerated Particle Swarm Optimization (APSO), *I.J. Intelligent Systems and Applications,* 2014, 04, 1-10 Published Online March 2014 in MECS (http://www.mecs-press.org/) DOI: 10.5815/ijisa.2014.04.01.

[3]  P. Kunche and K.V.V.S. Reddy, *Metaheuristic Applications to Speech Enhancement,* Springer Briefs in Speech Technology, Springer International Publishing AG Switzerland, 2016.

[4]  X.-S. Yang, Bat Algorithm: Literature Review and Applications, J. Bio-Inspired

Computation, Vol. 5, No. 3, pp. 141–149 (2013). DOI: 10.1504/IJBIC.2013.055093.

[5]  M. P. KUMAR, R. P. DAS, Speech Enhancement Analysis using PSO and ANFIS Methods, International Journal of Scientific Engineering and Technology Research (IJSETR), ISSN 2319-8885 Vol.05, Issue.49, December-2016, Pages:10059-10065.

[6]  S. Mirjalili, S. M. Mirjalili, X. Yang, Binary Bat Algorithm, Neural Computing and Applications, In press, 2014, Springer DOI:http://dx.doi.org/10.1007/s00521-013-1525-5

[7]  X.-S. Yang, Nature-Inspired Optimization Algorithms, Elsevier Inc., 2014.

[8]  J. Kennedy, RC Eberhart. Particle swarm optimization. In: Proceedings of the IEEE international conference on neural networks, Piscataway, NJ, USA; 1995. p. 1942–48.

[9]  A. Cirillo, https://www.mathworks.com/matlabcentral/fileexchange/30660-simple-example-of-pso-algorithm.

[10] X-S. Yang, https://www.mathworks.com/matlabcentral/fileexchange/29725-accelerated-particle-swarm-optimization.

[11] E. Rashedi, H. Nezamabadi-pour and S. Saryazdi, GSA: A Gravitational Search Algorithm, https://www.mathworks.com/matlabcentral/fileexchange/27756-gravitational-search-algorithm-gsa?focused=5194754&tab=function

[12] Paper: A New Hybrid PSOGSA Algorithm for Function Optimization, in IEEE International Conference on Computer and Information Application(ICCIA 2010), China, 2010, pp.374-377, DOI: http://dx.doi.org/10.1109/ICCIA.2010.6141614

[13] S. Mirjalili, https://www.mathworks.com/matlabcentral/fileexchange/35939-hybrid-particle-swarm-optimization-and-gravitational-search-algorithm-psogsa

[14] S. Mirjalili, https://www.mathworks.com/matlabcentral/fileexchange/35939-hybrid-particle-swarm-optimization-and-gravitational-search-algorithm-psogsa

[15] S. Mirjalili, S. M. Mirjalili, X.-S. Yang, Binary Bat Algorithm, Neural Computing and Applications, In press, 2014, Springer DOI:http://dx.doi.org/10.1007/s00521-013-1525-5

The 2018 Conference on Computational Linguistics and Speech Processing
ROCLING 2018, pp. 276-285
©The Association for Computational Linguistics and Chinese Language Processing

# 節能知識問答機器人

## Energy Saving Knowledge Chatbot

[1]陳志杰　Jhih-Jie Chen
[2]張仕穎　Shih-Ying Chang
[2]邱子晉　Tsu-Jin Chiu
[1]蔡名喬　Ming-Chiao Tsai
[1]張俊盛　Jason S. Chang

[1]國立清華大學資訊工程學系
Department of Computer Science, National Tsing Hua University

[2]工業技術研究院
Industrial Technology Research Institute

JJc@nlplab.cc, itriA00550@itri.org, ZihJin@itri.org.tw, mictsai@nlplab.cc, Jason@nlplab.cc

## 摘要

普羅大眾對於節能用電知識了解不足，使得舊家電汰換與節能方案（例：時間電價）的推動停滯不前。而近來對話機器人（chatbot）越來越流行，對話本身是極好的資訊傳遞介面，也越來越多產品知識與問答透過對話機器人來實作。本論文建立一個智慧問答機器人，提供名詞解釋、分享節電技巧、節電標章說明、家電耗電試算、試算採用時間電價的效益…等用電知識，期望能加速知識傳遞，進而推廣節能用電的實行。透過網路爬蟲收集問答資料、人工標記問題的分類、建立資訊檢索模型，並訓練支持向量機（Support Vector Machine，SVM）的分類模型，開發出節能互動問答系統，希望能增加節能知識的觸及率並提高國人的節能意識，進而提升國人節能意願。

## Abstract

The lack of understanding of energy saving knowledge leads people to be slow in replacing their old, energy-inefficient household appliances, thus impeding the energy-saving promotion by the government. Recently, chatbot becomes more and more popular since conversation is a natural and effective interface for knowledge enquiry and information sharing. In this paper, we describe the development of an intelligent chatbot, which provides terminology defintions, energy saving tips, energy saving logo explanations, calculation of power cost and so on. We hope the application will speed up the knowledge transfer and promote the energy saving in everyday life. The method involves collecting knowledge related to energy saving, labelling the collected questions into (question, answer) pairs for training and testing, and training a classifier-based chatbot using Support Vector Machine (SVM) for answering energy-saving related questions. We utilize existing chatbot development tool, Chatfuel, to develop a chatbot system. This prototype has great potential in drawing attention to energy-saving awareness and practice.

關鍵詞：問答機器人，支持向量機，網路爬蟲

Keywords: Chatbot, SVM, Web Crawler.

一、緒論

台灣用電尖峰集中在夏季，尤其夏日白天天氣炎熱，每天尖峰時刻的供電負載往往處於滿載的狀態，電力公司也面臨供電調度的挑戰。如何有效的控制、分散尖峰用電，同時減少供電調度上的危險，進而提升供電品質與穩定度，是電力公司需要面對的重要課題。

傳統節能知識的傳遞，都是以網站或是紙本的宣傳的方式，來告知節能的一些技巧，但是這種知識傳遞方式效果有限。如圖一所示，直接即時的回饋最有節能效益。本計畫選擇使用即時機器人（chatbot）的方式來建構我們的溝通互動平台，如：Facebook messenger，搭配智慧電表的即時資訊，可以在用電尖峰或是電價過高時，即時給予節能建議，這樣節能建議被採用的機率就會提升。

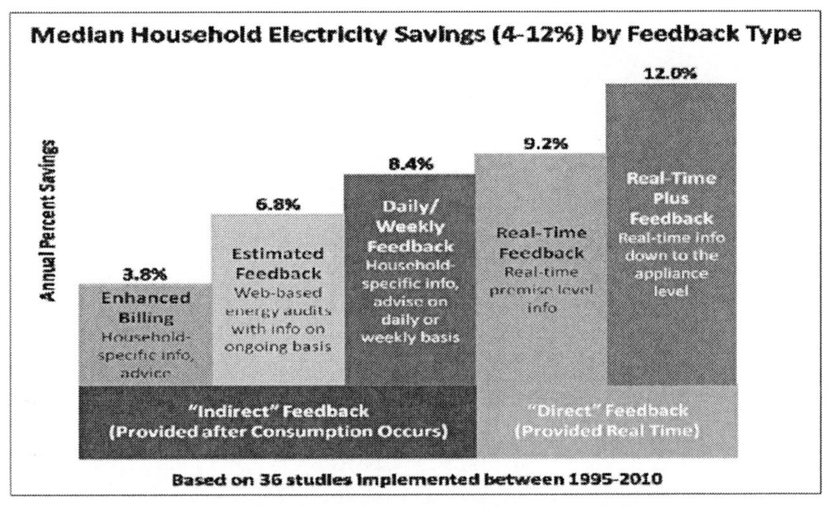


Source: Ehrhardt-Martinez et al. 2010

圖一，家庭節能回饋方式的效益比較

舉例來說，時間電價規劃，根據用電性質及需求，調整尖峰用電移轉至離峰時間使用，以達充分利用離峰電力與節省電費支出之目的。目前普羅大眾對於時間電價方案了解不足，無法明確得知參加方案會帶來什麼效益，對於日常生活又會有帶來什麼影響，時間電價方案推廣不足，民眾對於用電議題關注不夠，導致時間電價方案採用率一直處於低落，甚至是乏人問津。如何有效的推動時間電價方案，分散用電尖峰期的負載，成為現今電力公司需要重視的議題。

聊天機器人，透過對話或文字進行交談，模擬人類對話，是極佳的互動介面。而傳統問答機器人早已廣泛應用在電話客服上，透過預先設定好的指令、對話流程，即可完成簡單、例常的用戶服務，如資訊查詢，帳戶設定等。

拜近年人工智慧發展迅速所賜，近年對話機器人有了突破性的發展，自然語言處理的技術也有了長足的進步，透過擷取對話中的關鍵字，辨識使用者的目的，從資料庫中檢索相關的資訊，並回覆使用者所需要的資訊。此外，結合先進的語言生成技術，學習人類說話的行為與模式，產生接近人類對話的自然語言回覆，讓使用者感覺更加生動、親切。

相關的產品應用與開發工具也如雨後春筍般出現。**Apple** 公司應用在手機上的語音助理 **Siri**，可透過語音完成一系列日常的任務，如：設定行事曆、回覆訊息、語音導航…等，甚至可以和使用者進行聊天。**Amazon** 的智慧家庭助理 Alexa，整合各式各樣的智慧家電，可以監控家庭使用情形。此外，現有的社交平台 Facebook Messenger，也推出可客製化的對話機器人模組，結合對話管理與自然語言處理技術，幫助回答問題，並可推廣各式促銷活動。與機器對話不再是死板的過程，而是富啟發性且充滿樂趣的體驗。

本論文期望以對話機器人的技術，開發節電問答機器人。透過自然語言處理技術，達到對話的關鍵字擷取與語意理解，並結合用電、節電、政策宣導相關資訊，搭配自然語言生成技術，產生接近自然語言的回覆。也期許能提升國人對於用電相關議題的關注。

## 二、相關研究

[1]將網路論壇上的（問題，回答）的配對資料，做為 SVM 模型的訓練資料，來建立聊天機器人。[2]指出了使用網路論壇上的問答資料作為訓練資料會有的困境與挑戰，並提出了一個方法，可以在網路問答論壇有效地取得正確的問答資料。[3]則提到，可以使用一套回覆排序方法來改進回答系統的品質。[4]使用語意相似度從現有的（問題，答案）配對中找出最佳解答。

## 三、研究方法

本論文的目標為開發一個節能知識問答機器人，提供用電常識、節電秘訣與相關知識，並且可以試算用電量。研究方法我們依下列階段進行，分別為（一）節能知識整理收集，（二）問答對話流程規劃，（三）問題回答人工標注及（四）建立自動分類模型。

（一）、節能知識整理收集

取得資料是第一步，我們先整理節能相關知識的網站資料，並以具公信力的機構為主，如：能源局、台灣電力公司，透過網路爬蟲、網頁解析技術，從這些網站擷取以自然語言構成的用電知識與問答資料。此外，我們也爬取網路上與節能相關的問答資料，如：奇摩知識家，這類網站有許多自然語言描述的問題與解答，而產生這些問題的族群亦相當豐富多元，可以說是最好的問答機器人訓練資料。

1、建立關鍵字集

搜尋資料需要搜尋關鍵字，所以我們參考了能源局網頁所列的節能標章家電清單，建立了關鍵字集，搭配節能相關的字詞，並從資料中人工挑選廣告、成人內容關鍵字作為黑名單，來過濾雜訊資料。最後的家電關鍵字集有冷氣、電扇、除濕、冰箱、洗衣、燈管、烘乾、吹風機、開飲機、飲水機、燈泡、螢幕、顯示器、電熱水器、烤箱、熱水器、電鍋、電子鍋、電熱、指示燈、燈具、照明、音響、影印機、印表機、空氣清淨機、電風扇、延長線、插座。節能關鍵字集則有省電，電費，節省，環保，節能，電價，耗電。

2、搜尋引擎收集文件

我們使用爬蟲抓取 Bing 搜尋引擎的搜尋結果，並限制搜尋範圍在奇摩知識家的網域範圍（tw.answers.yahoo.com）。因奇摩知識家內建的搜尋引擎，在超過特定頁數後的結果都無法取得，我們轉而測試爬取其他搜尋引擎（Google、Bing）的搜尋結果，最後選擇可以透過爬蟲並且取得完整資料 Bing 搜尋引擎。

3、資料解析與儲存

最後，我們自 Bing 搜尋引擎取得奇摩知識家 28,533 筆問答文件，並透過網頁解析技術，將其中的網址、日期、標題、內容與最佳回答擷取出來，並依不同家電類型各自存成 json 格式的檔案，做為後續資料分析與模型訓練使用。

（二）、建立對話流程

接下來，我們利用 Chatfuel 聊天機器人平台建置我們的對話流程，Chatfuel 可以預先設定對話的內容，並且可以根據不同的回答，設計不同的對話過程，此外，也可以在對話中插入一些使用者的背景資訊，如名稱、性別、年紀……等，讓整個對話過程有更多針對不同個體有不同的變化，整體流程簡圖如圖二所示。

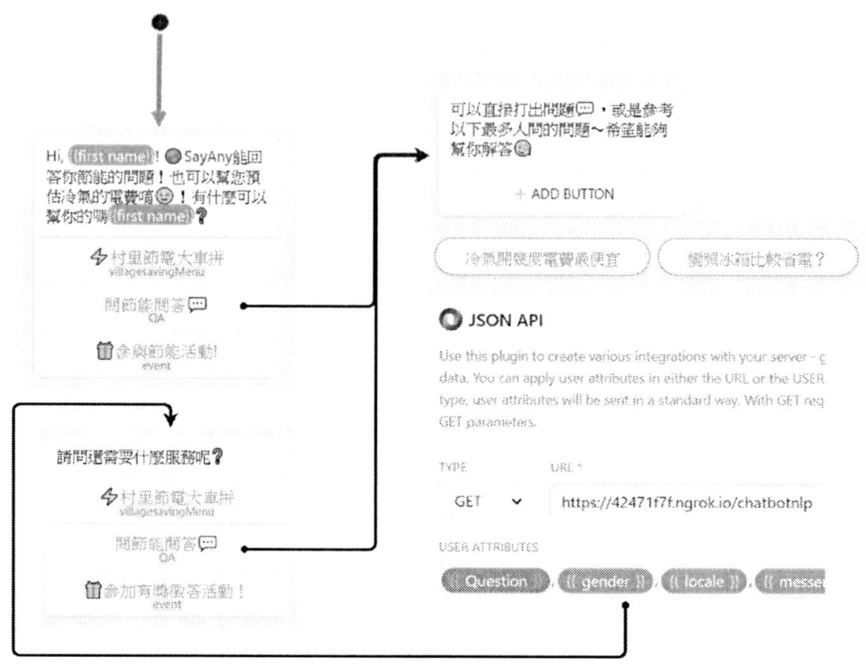

圖二、使用 Chatfuel 建構的對話流程

（三）、問題回答人工標注

為了有效地確保答案的品質與可靠度，我們預先設定好的回答的集合，並將每個問題分類到這些設定好的回答集合。接下來，我們逐項檢視問題並人工產生答案分類或歸類到現有分類，直到有一定數量的標記資料後，我們將已標注的資料匯入自動分類模型，這個分類模型可以學習標記資料中的分類模式，並自動分類剩餘的未分類資料，輔助並加速後續的人工標記過程，最後，搭配開發好的標記系統，人工進行最終的問題分類確認。

1、人工建立預設回答集

根據不同關鍵字組合的搜尋結果，我們先將問題分成了 16 個大類，接下來，便人工搜索並參考相關的節能知識與家電採購技巧，為各類型的家電問題建立回答內容（以冷氣為例，有 23 項預設的回答）。

2、自動分類模型輔助預標

人工標記是非常耗時、人力密集的工作，為了加速整體標記過程，當每個家電分類有一定數量的標記資料後，我們便使用已標記的資料訓練自動分類模型（第四小節），並使用訓練好的模型預測未標記的資料，作為該問題的預設分類。

3、人工確認預標資料

每個問題有了預設的標記後，就再也不需要將每個問題去對應十幾、二十幾個回答分類。取而代之的是，只需確認這個問題是否符合其預標，如不符合，這個問題就標示為未標記，自動分類模型可以選擇其他更符合的選項作為預標，然後重複確認的過程，或者標記者可以人工新增答案分類。如此一來，人工標記的過程就會加速許多。（如圖三）

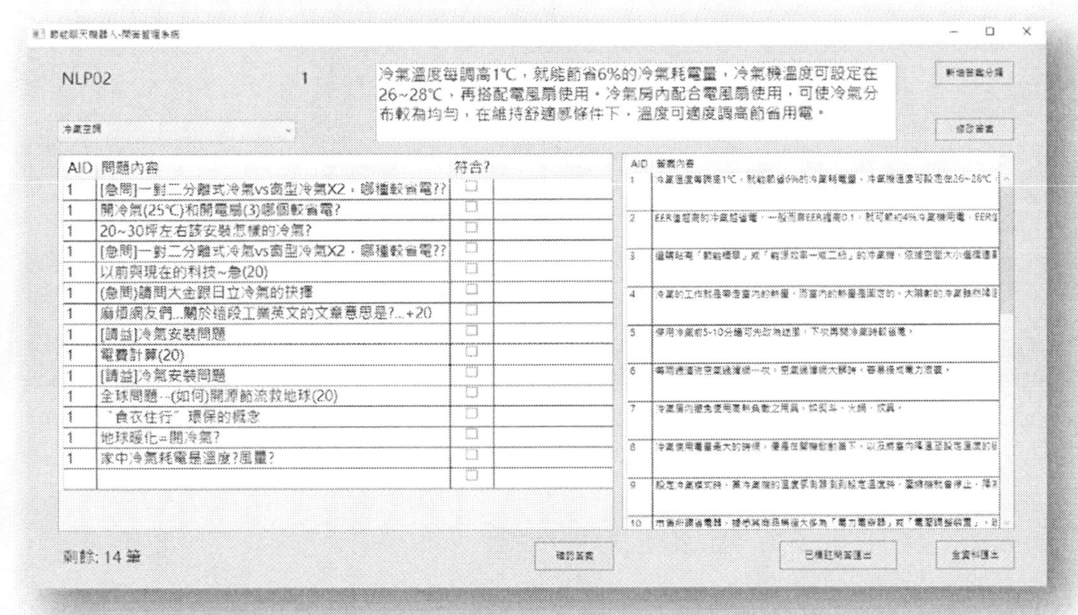

圖三、進行問題分類標記的問答管理系統

（四）、建立自動分類模型

1、資訊檢索模型

我們以 TF-IDF 模型（一種詞袋模型）為基礎，將問題的文字轉換為一固定長度的向量，藉由計算向量之間的相似度（Cosine Similarity），可以得到問題與問題之間的相似度。我們在已標注的問題資料集上建立 TF-IDF 模型後，當使用者詢問一個新的問題，我們便可以從現有資料集中找出最相似的問題，並以該問題所標註的標準回答，作為使用者問題的回答。這樣的方法不僅直覺且容易實作，分類的效果也相當不錯。此外，透過設定相似度的門檻值，我們可以自動把相似度過低的問題歸類為待處理，再進行後續的人工標注。

然而，比較相似度的步驟需要比較標注資料集中的每一個問題，一旦標注資料集數量增加，分類的速度就會呈線性的下降，這樣的模型在可擴展性（scalability）上和效率上，都有所限制。

## 2、SVM 分類模型

在向量空間找出最佳切割分類的超平面（hyperplane），相較上述的資訊檢索模型需要將輸入向量與訓練資料每個向量比較。此外，使用 SVM 分類模型並不會因為訓練資料集的大量增加而明顯影響分類速度，使得藉由增加訓練資料來改進系統效能更加可行。

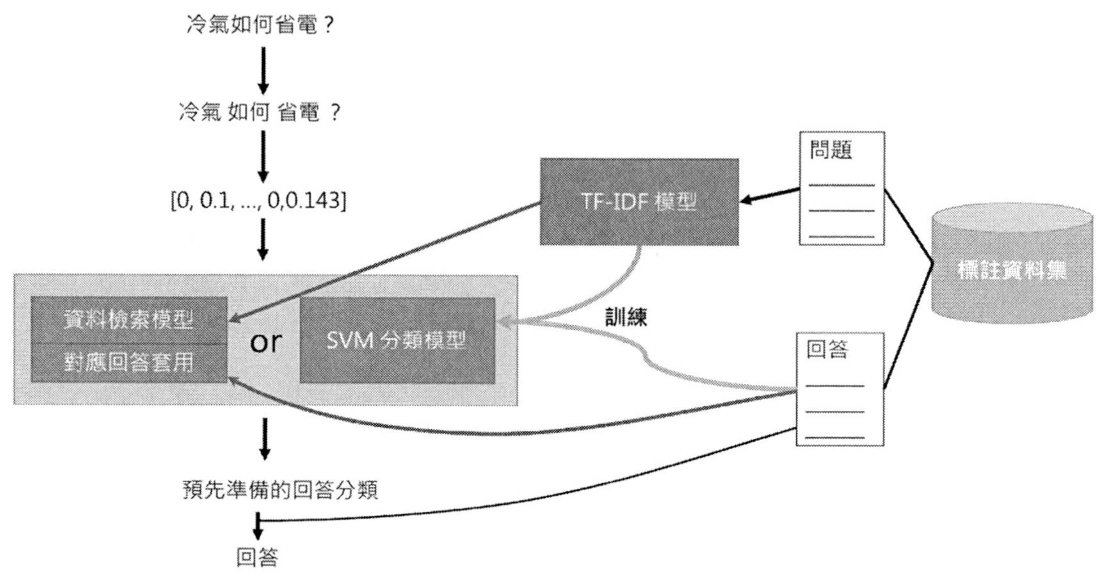


圖四、分類系統架構圖

我們的問答系統整體架構如圖五所示，透過爬蟲程式定期收集奇摩知識家的問答資料，作為我們的節能知識庫的基礎，而我們的標註系統讓標註者可以對節能知識庫的問題進行回答標記，並作為訓練自動分類模型的資料，最後，串接對話管理平台與即時通訊平台，來與使用者進行節能知識問答與傳遞。

## 3、二階分類

不同家電會有類似的問題，開發分類器的過程中我們發現，分類器有時成功辨認問題的意圖（購買家電、家電比較、名詞釋義...等），但家電的類型卻錯誤了。為了解決這個問題，我們特別設計了兩階段分類，先分類家電，再分類問題的類別，進而選出相對應的回答。問題分類針對不同家電分別訓練，共有 16 個問題語意分類器。

家電分類的模型同樣採用了上述的資料檢索模型與 SVM 分類模型，並使用 TFIDF 作為每個問題的特徵值，分類共有 16 類家電。分完家電後，再根據不同類別選用不同的問題分類器，如此一來，分類模型的類別數量可以大幅減少，初步實驗（第四節）結果也顯示二階段分類的做法能夠有效的提升回答的準確度。

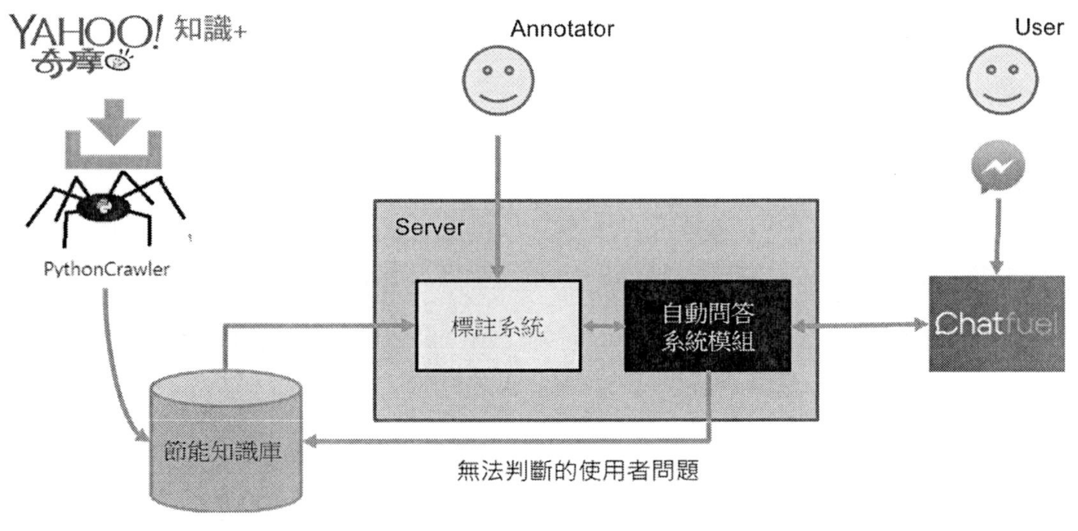


圖五、問答系統架構

## 四、實驗

（一）、資料集

透過網路爬蟲收集到的資料，完成人工標記的有 3,477 筆，每個問題都有兩個標記，一個是家電分類，另一個則是對應的回答。我們將這份資料切成訓練、測試集，比例為四比一，我們使用這 3,477 筆資料進行不同模型的實驗與評估。

（二）、實驗模型與結果

1、家電分類

分類問題所屬的家電類別，我們使用關鍵字模型作為基線（baseline），來比較我們的 SVM 分類模型。關鍵字模型將 16 類家電名稱作為關鍵字，以問題文字中最常見的關鍵字作為分類。從表一中，我們可以看到關鍵字模型有 72.1% 的準確率，而我們的 SVM 模型則有 92% 的準確度，顯著優於關鍵字模型。

表一、家電分類準確度

| 模型 | 家電分類準確度 |
|---|---|
| 關鍵字模型 | 72.1% |
| SVM 模型 | 92% |

2、問題分類

問題分類，我們比較資訊檢索模型（3.4.1）與 SVM 分類模型（3.4.2）。資訊檢索模型是將每個問題轉成 TFIDF 的向量，從訓練集中找出最相似的向量，並以這個最相似問題的回答作為回答。SVM 分類模型也使用 TFIDF 向量作為特徵值，並經過網格搜尋（Grid Searching）和交叉驗證（Cross Validation）進行參數調整（Hyperparameter Tuning）訓練出最佳的模型來進行比較。

從表中二，我們可以看到資料檢索模型在測試資料集有 66.5% 的準確度，而 SVM 分類模型則有 74% 的準確度，我們可以看到 SVM 分類模型顯著優於資料檢索模型。而針對標記資料較完整的冷氣分類進行實驗，共 1287 題、23 類，結果有 80% 的準確率。

表二、各模型問題測試集上的分類準確度

| 資料<br><br>模型 | 所有問題（3,477）<br>訓練: 2,782, 測試: 695 | 冷氣（1,287）<br>訓練: 1,030, 測試: 257 |
|---|---|---|
| 資訊檢索模型 | 66.5% | 64.2% |
| SVM (預設參數) | 73.1% | 78.3% |
| SVM (參數調整後) | 74% | 80.7% |

## 五、結論

本篇論文建立了一個問答機器人框架實踐，從資料收集、人工標記、建立對話流程、訓練自動回答分類模型，並提出一個自動分類模型輔助人工標記的循環。實驗結果顯示我們的系統有不錯的準確度，另外，我們邀請節能專家來試用，並對問答機器人有正面的評價，即使偶有回答無法完整回應問題的情形，但還是能達到相關節能知識傳遞的作用。

未來，我們將會持續收集與標記資料，並完善更多家電的問題標記。初步邀請實驗顯示，整體回答的滿意度很高，但許多情況是使用者不知道該問什麼問題，或是如何去問問題。我們也將會進行使用者研究，主動觸及使用者，而非被動的接受問題，也探討大眾對於節能所關注的議題，進行推薦問題系統的建置，進一步改善聊天過程。

參考文獻

[1]  Huang, Jizhou, Ming Zhou, and Dan Yang. "Extracting Chatbot Knowledge from Online Discussion Forums." IJCAI. Vol. 7. 2007.

[2]  Cong, Gao, et al. "Finding question-answer pairs from online forums." Proceedings of the 31st annual international ACM SIGIR conference on Research and development in information retrieval. ACM, 2008.

[3]  Hong, Liangjie, and Brian D. Davison. "A classification-based approach to question answering in discussion boards." Proceedings of the 32nd international ACM SIGIR conference on Research and development in information retrieval. ACM, 2009.

[4]  Wang, Baoxun, et al. "Modeling semantic relevance for question-answer pairs in web social communities." Proceedings of the 48th Annual Meeting of the Association for Computational Linguistics. Association for Computational Linguistics, 2010.

**Association for Computational Linguistics**
209 N. Eighth Street
Stroudsburg, Pennsylvania 18360

ISBN 978-1-5108-7751-1